Mosdos Press Literature

RUBY

Mosdos Press
CLEVELAND, OHIO

Educators transmitting appropriate values and academic excellence

Mosdos Press

Mosdos
Press

Educators transmitting appropriate values and academic excellence

Copyright © 2009 by Mosdos Press.

All rights reserved. Printed in Israel. Fifth Printing.

No part of this publication may be reproduced or distributed in any
form or by any means, or stored in a database or retrieval system,
without prior permission in writing from Mosdos Press, 1508
Warrensville Center Road, Cleveland Heights, Ohio 44121.

ISBN # 0-9801670-1-9
ISBN # 978-0-9801670-1-6 Student Edition

Mosdos Press Literature

EDITOR-IN-CHIEF
Judith Factor

CREATIVE/ART DIRECTOR
Carla Martin

SENIOR EDITOR
Abigail Rozen

COPY EDITOR
Laya Dewick

CURRICULUM WRITER
Rifky Amsel

JILL'S JOURNALS
Jill Brotman

LESSONS IN LITERATURE
Jim Garrett

TEXT AND CURRICULUM ADVISOR
Rabbi Ahron Dovid Goldberg

MOSDOS PRESS
Literature

ANTHOLOGY SERIES

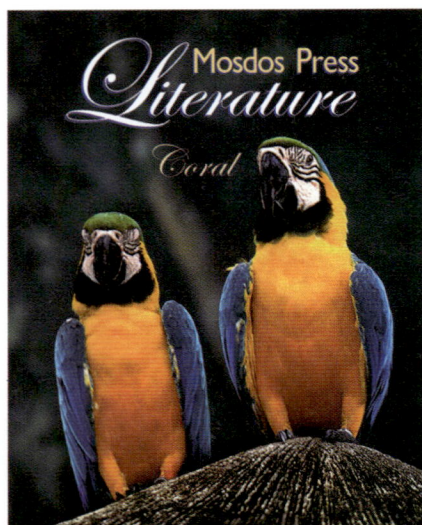

OPAL

RUBY

CORAL

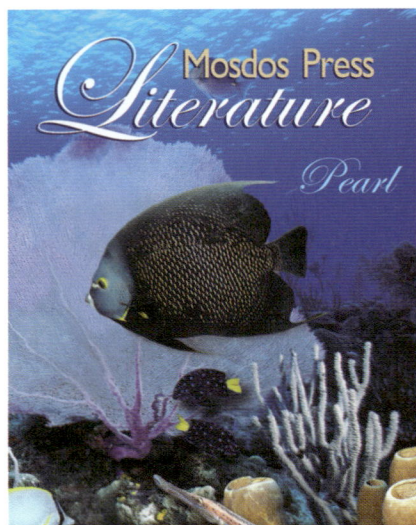

PEARL

JADE

GOLD

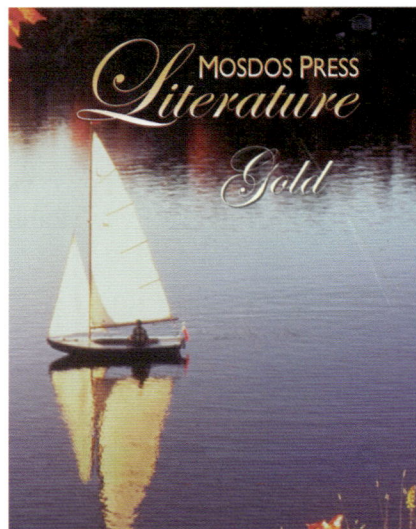

unit 1

THE THINGS THAT MATTER

unit 2

CLARITY

unit 3

HEAD, HANDS, HEART

poetry

unit 4

CARING

unit 5

DETERMINATION

unit 6

THE GRAND FINALÉ

unit 1

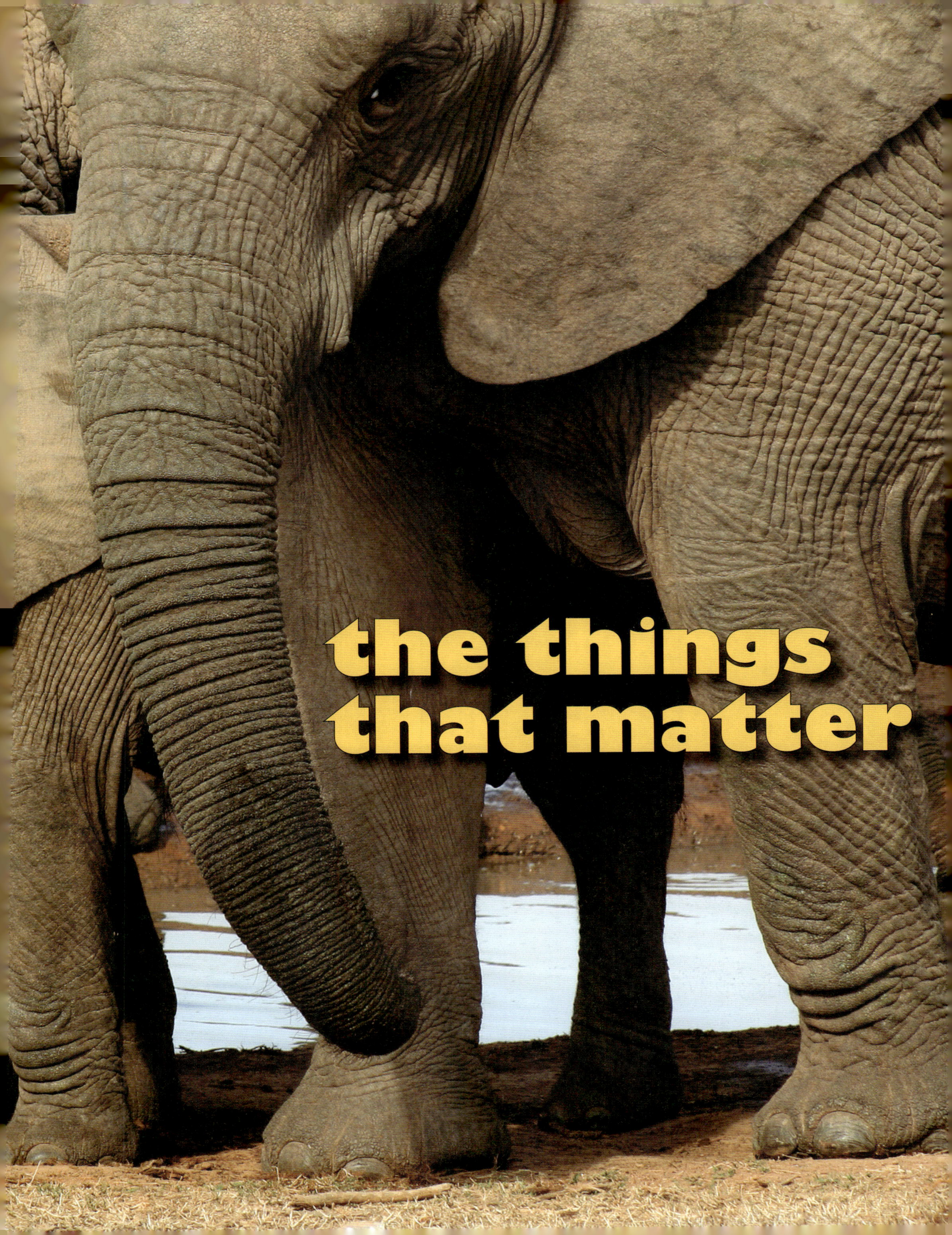

the things that matter

Lesson in Literature ...
SARAH'S ROOM

WHAT IS A STORY?

- A story has a beginning, a middle, and an end. Something in the story must change before the story is over.
- *What happens* in the story is called the **plot**.
- The *people* or animals in the story are called the **characters**.
- The *time* and *place* in which the events happen are called the **setting**.

THINK ABOUT IT!

1. In the middle of the story, something changes in Sarah's life. What is it?
2. Who are the six characters in the story?
3. Describe the setting of the second half of the story.

Sarah didn't like being the youngest in the family. With an older brother and two older sisters, Sarah always had to wait for them to do things first. On the playground or in the backyard, she had to wait. "Wait your turn!" her sister Emily said when Sarah wanted to go first. When her parents gave her brother permission to ride his bicycle to the park, Sarah asked, "Can I go too?"

"Sarah," her mother said, "you're too young. You have to wait until you're old enough."

"But when will I be old enough?" Sarah asked.

"Soon," her mother said.

Sarah thought about it. When she was younger, she had to wait to go to school. She had to wait to learn to read. She had to wait to ride a bicycle. She had to wait to swim in the pool. Now at twelve she still had to wait. She had to wait to sit at the adults' table for dinner. She had to wait for her older sisters to grow out of their clothes, and she was still waiting for her own room. Sarah didn't want to share a bedroom with her sister Emily anymore. When she asked her father about a room of her own, all he said was, "Sarah, you just have to wait."

So when her family moved into a new house, her father surprised them all when he said, "Sarah has waited long enough. In this house she gets her own room." He smiled at her. "Sarah, you get first choice. What room do you want?"

Her whole face smiled back at her father, but she didn't feel happy. She felt the eyes of her brother and her sisters staring at her. She didn't have to wait anymore, but now they had to wait.

"I like the downstairs room," she said. It was the best room in the house. It had a big window that opened to a field of tall grass behind the house. It had a big closet, too. It was also the only bedroom on the first floor.

Once the movers left, everyone in the family helped with the unpacking, carrying boxes upstairs to the other bedrooms or to the rear of the house to Sarah's bedroom. After a while Sarah noticed that her sister Anne took a long time climbing the stairs with her boxes. Ever since her hip surgery Anne used a cane. She walked slowly and couldn't carry very much, and Sarah's heart jumped when she saw Anne almost fall coming down the stairs.

Sarah liked the downstairs room. She liked the sunlight from the window and the view of the field. She even liked the big closet. But she especially liked first choice. So when her father walked past with a box, she stopped him. "I can't wait to tell you," she said. "I changed my mind. My first choice is to share a bedroom upstairs with Emily. I want Anne to have the downstairs room."

When he heard her new choice, Sarah's father immediately held out his arms to hug his youngest daughter. "You didn't wait to do the right thing," he said. Sarah didn't wait to be hugged, either. She ran into her father's outstretched arms, happy she didn't have to wait for a hug.

Blueprint for Reading

INTO . . . *Leah's Pony*

After many years of comfortable farm life, Leah's family falls upon hard times. People react in different ways when faced with a challenge. One person may react with anger. Another person may react with determination. As you read, think about the way Leah, her family, and her neighbors deal with the difficulties that come their way. Leah has no concern for herself, as she inspires others to behave with kindness and generosity.

EYES ON *Narrative Elements*

Why do we tell stories? There are many reasons. A story can have important messages, help us remember something, or create an imaginary world. In order for a story to work properly, a number of **elements**, or parts, must be present. You will learn about these elements, such as plot and setting, in the coming pages. As you read *Leah's Pony*, think about what makes the story interesting. Does anything in the story surprise you?

LEAH'S PONY

Elizabeth Friedrich

The year the corn grew tall and straight, Leah's papa bought her a pony. The pony was strong and swift and sturdy, with just a snip of white at the end of his soft black nose. Papa taught Leah to place her new saddle right in the middle of his back and tighten the girth[1] around his belly, just so.

---

1. A *girth* is a band that passes underneath a horse or other animal to hold a saddle in place.

That whole summer, Leah and her pony crossed through cloud-capped cornfields and chased cattle through the pasture.

Leah scratched that special spot under her pony's mane and brushed him till his coat glistened like satin.

Each day Leah loved to ride her pony into town just to hear Mr. B. shout from the door of his grocery store, "That's the finest pony in the whole county."

The year the corn grew no taller than a man's thumb, Leah's house became very quiet.

Sometimes on those hot, dry nights, Leah heard Papa and Mama's hushed voices whispering in the kitchen. She couldn't understand the words but knew their sad sound.

Some days the wind blew so hard it turned the sky black with dust. It was hard for Leah to keep her pony's coat shining. It was hard for Mama to keep the house clean. It was hard for Papa to carry buckets of water for the sow and her piglets.

Soon Papa sold the pigs and even some of the cattle. "These are hard times," he told Leah with a puzzled look. "That's what these days are, all right, hard times."

Mama used flour sacks to make underwear for Leah. Mama threw dishwater on her drooping petunias to keep them growing. And, no matter what else happened, Mama always woke Leah on Saturday with the smell of fresh, hot coffee cake baking.

One hot, dry, dusty day grasshoppers turned the day to night. They ate the trees bare and left only twigs behind.

The next day the neighbors filled their truck with all they owned and stopped to say good-bye. "We're off to Oregon," they said. "It must be better there." Papa, Mama, and Leah waved as their neighbors wobbled down the road in an old truck overflowing with chairs and bedsprings and wire.

WORD BANK
sow (rhymes with now) *n.*: an adult, female pig

The hot, dry, dusty days kept coming. On a day you could almost taste the earth in the air, Papa said, "I have something to tell you, Leah, and I want you to be brave. I borrowed money from the bank. I bought seeds, but the seeds dried up and blew away. Nothing grew. I don't have any corn to sell. Now I can't pay back the bank," Papa paused. "They're going to have an auction, Leah. They're going to sell the cattle and the chickens and the pickup truck."

Leah stared at Papa. His voice grew husky and soft. "Worst of all, they're going to sell my tractor. I'll never be able to

plant corn when she's gone. Without my tractor, we might even have to leave the farm. I told you, Leah, these are hard times."

Leah knew what an auction meant. She knew eager faces with strange voices would come to their farm. They would stand outside and offer money for Papa's best bull and Mama's prize rooster and Leah's favorite calf.

All week long Leah worried and waited and wondered what to do. One morning she watched as a man in a big hat hammered a sign into the ground in front of her house.

Leah wanted to run away. She raced her pony past empty fields lined with dry gullies. She galloped past a house with rags stuffed in broken windowpanes. She sped right past Mr. B. sweeping the steps outside his store.

At last Leah knew what she had to do. She turned her pony around and rode back into town. She stopped in front of Mr. B.'s store. "You can buy my pony," she said.

Mr. B. stopped sweeping and stared at her. "Why would you want to sell him?" he asked. "That's the finest pony in the county."

Leah swallowed hard. "I've grown a lot this summer," she said. "I'm getting too big for him."

Sunburned soil crunched under Leah's feet as she walked home alone. The auction had begun. Neighbors, friends, strangers—everyone clustered around the man in the big hat. "How much for this wagon?" boomed the man. "Five dollars. Ten dollars. Sold for fifteen dollars to the man in the green shirt."

Papa's best bull.

Sold.

Mama's prize rooster.

Sold.

Leah's favorite calf.

Sold.

The sign on the illustration reads:

AUCTION
FARM EQUIPMENT SALE

Leah clutched her money in her hand. "It has to be enough," she whispered to herself. "It just has to be."

"Here's one of the best items in this entire auction," yelled the man in the big hat. "Who'll start the bidding at five hundred dollars for this practically new, all-purpose Farmall tractor? It'll plow, plant, fertilize, and even cultivate for you."

It was time. Leah's voice shook. "One dollar."

The man in the big hat laughed. "That's a low starting bid if I ever heard one," he said. "Now let's hear some serious bids."

No one moved. No one said a word. No one even seemed to breathe.

"Ladies and gentlemen, this tractor is a beauty! I have a bid of only one dollar for it. One dollar for this practically new Farmall tractor! Do I hear any other bids?"

Again no one moved. No one said a word. No one even seemed to breathe.

"This is ridiculous!" the man's voice boomed out from under his hat into the silence. "Sold to the young lady for one dollar."

The crowd cheered. Papa's mouth hung open. Mama cried. Leah proudly walked up and handed one dollar to the auctioneer in the big hat.

WORD BANK

clutched (KLUCHD)
v.: held onto tightly
cultivate (KUL tih vayt)
v.: to help the plants grow by tending to the soil around them

"That young lady bought one fine tractor for one very low price," the man continued. "Now how much am I bid for this flock of healthy young chickens?"

"I'll give you ten cents," offered a farmer who lived down the road.

"Ten cents! Ten cents is mighty cheap for a whole flock of chickens," the man said. His face looked angry.

Again no one moved. No one said a word. No one even seemed to breathe.

"Sold for ten cents!"

The farmer picked up the cage filled with chickens and walked over to Mama. "These chickens are yours," he said.

The man pushed his big hat back on his head. "How much for this good Ford pickup truck?" he asked.

"Twenty-five cents," yelled a neighbor from town.

Again no one moved. No one said a word. No one even seemed to breathe.

"Sold for twenty-five cents!" The man in the big hat shook his head. "This isn't supposed to be a penny auction!" he shouted.

The neighbor paid his twenty-five cents and took the keys to the pickup truck. "I think these will start your truck," he whispered as he dropped the keys into Papa's shirt pocket.

Leah watched as friends and neighbors bid a penny for a chicken or a nickel for a cow or a quarter for a plow. One by one, they gave everything back to Mama and Papa.

The crowds left. The sign disappeared. Chickens scratched in their coop, and cattle called for their corn. The farm was quiet. Too quiet. No familiar whinny greeted Leah when she entered the barn. Leah swallowed hard and straightened her back.

That night in Leah's hushed house, no sad voices whispered in the kitchen. Only Leah lay awake, listening to the clock chime nine and even ten times. Leah's heart seemed to copy its slow, sad beat.

The next morning Leah forced open the heavy barn doors to start her chores. A loud whinny greeted her. Leah ran and hugged the familiar furry neck and kissed the white snip of a nose. "You're back!" she cried. "How did you get here?"

Then Leah saw the note with her name written in big letters:

Dear Leah,
This is the finest pony in the county. But he's a little bit small for me and a little bit big for my grandson.

He fits you much better.

Your friend,
Mr. B.

P.S. I heard how you saved your family's farm. These hard times won't last forever.

And they didn't.

ABOUT THE AUTHOR

As a child, **Elizabeth Friedrich** loved to visit her aunt and uncle's farm. There, she was allowed to ride horses and help care for some of the farm animals. Young Elizabeth thought of the farm as "a magical place." As an adult, Ms. Friedrich was able to fulfill her dream of living on a farm. She, her husband, and their two children live on a New Hampshire farm, where they are raising a small flock of sheep. In addition to writing, Ms. Friedrich enjoys traveling and collecting antiques.

The Way

Nancy Springer

The way you sway
rocked in a cradle
as the horse walks

The way the sun
5   rides warm on your shoulders
as they sway

The way the horse
talks back with its ears
to everything you say

10   The way the sound
of hooves on clay
sets you dreaming

People say, "You're back.
So what did you see
15   on the trail today?"

You say, "Nothing much."
It's not what you see
it's the way. It's the way.

Poetry shows us the way

Studying the Selection

QUICK REVIEW

1. Describe Papa's precious gift to Leah.

2. What type of weather conditions brought on the 'hard times' experienced by Leah's family?

3. How did Mama recycle things to save money?

4. Who changed the direction of the auction with a very low bid?

FOCUS

5. Leah's father told her to be brave, and Leah obeyed. What are two examples of Leah's bravery?

6. We know that a good story has a beginning, middle, and an end. Reread the story and write down one important event from the beginning of the story, the middle of the story, and the end of the story.

CREATING AND WRITING

7. Leah acted unselfishly to help her family. Do you think the townspeople would have reacted differently if an adult, rather than a child, had done what Leah did?

8. Leah was selfless during very difficult times. Think of someone you know who gave up something important to help another person. Write a paragraph describing the situation and selfless deed.

9. Create a poster for a "One Kindness a Day" campaign. Encourage people, young and old alike, to do something for others with the understanding that small acts can make a big difference. Be sure that your poster is attractive and explains the purpose of the project.

Jill's Journal:
On Assignment from the Dirty Thirties

You will never guess where I am, or what it is like here.

What if it were daytime, but when you looked out your window you couldn't see anything? Wouldn't you think it was scary, if you couldn't see anything but dust so thick you just saw blackness? Well, that is what it is like here.

It is Sunday, April 14, 1935. I am in Dodge City, Kansas. I wanted to go to a town somewhere in the Great Plains. Then I would be able to see for myself what happened on Black Sunday. That's what people called it later on. On Black Sunday, some people thought the world was coming to an end.

I am staying with the Kaufmans, a farm family. They are pretty sure that the black blizzards have come because people have plowed too much. The grass is gone. The roots of the grass used to grip the soil and keep it moist. Also, cattle

Courtesy of Library of Congress Prints and Photographs Collection.

have been grazing the land for years. They've eaten what was left of the grass.

Mr. Kaufman also told me that the farmers on the prairie have been planting the same crop—wheat—year after year after year, on millions of acres of earth. He says that planting just one crop takes all of the good nutrients out of the soil.

Then the long and terrible drought started in 1930. There has been almost no rain for five years, so the land has turned to dust.

Mr. and Mrs. Kaufman work so hard. They have been farming this land for eleven years. In fact, five of their six children were born right in this cabin! Each of the children helps (of course, not the baby). Meg is 12, Tim is 10, Robert is 8, Zack is 6, Elizabeth is 4, and little Ruthie is 18 months. I will tell you now that the baby is sick. Her mom is holding a wet cloth over her face so she won't breathe in so much dust. Meg says they are worried that Ruthie has dust pneumonia.

Well, no wonder. The cabin is always filled with grit and dust, no matter how hard everyone works to keep it clean. Tim and Zack are taking wet gunnysacks and waving them through the air. They call that sweeping the air. The gunnysacks turn black with dirt.

Any little holes or cracks in the walls or doors or windows are plugged up with newspapers and rags. But the house is not sealed tight the way our houses are. Dust still gets inside. Meg and Robert are nailing sheets over the windows now and putting blankets over the doors. But it

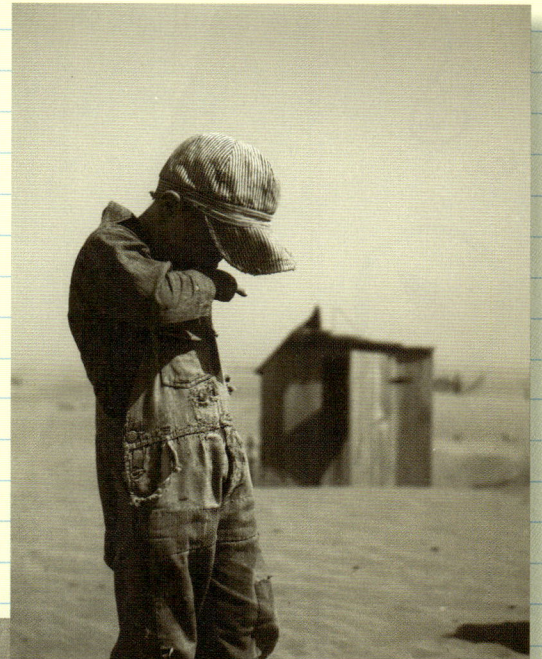

hardly seems to help. I have only been here a few days, but sometimes it feels like I could choke. The cabin is hot and very stuffy.

You should see the lot of us. Have you ever seen cowboys with kerchiefs tied over their noses and mouths? The cowboy robbers did that so no one could identify them. That's how the Kaufmans and I look. And when we go outside, if we dare, we put on these funny old goggles to protect our eyes. It is dangerous to go out, because you cannot see your hands in front of your eyes. You can get lost only a few feet from the house.

I am helping Mrs. Kaufman do laundry. We wash everything by hand in a large metal tub. Of course, the clothes are gray when we pull them from the soapy

Courtesy of Library of Congress Prints and Photographs Collection.

water. Mr. and Mrs. Kaufman carry the heavy tub outdoors together to empty it. Someone has to go to the well to bring in more water. Then it's heated in the big black iron kettle. This takes so long. I can hear grit rattling in the bottom of the kettle as it heats. Even the food we eat has grit in it.

What will happen to the Kaufmans?

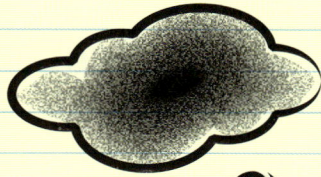

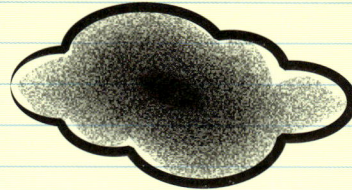

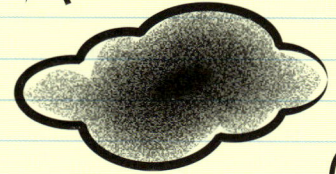

POWER SKILL:
Don't Get Lost! Learn to Read a Map.

It is important to be able to read a map. Maps tell us where we are. They tell us what is around us. A map adds to the information you may have about a place. Maps make it much easier for us to understand events in history.

If you live in the United States, do you know where your state is on the map?

If you live outside the U.S., do you know where your country is on the globe?

Many maps show directions with a compass rose, a circular figure that shows the directions north, south, east, and west. Some maps also have a scale bar to show the true size of the area on the map. These days, we go by airplane to travel long distances. Travel by plane doesn't give us the sense of distance we have when we go by car, train, bus, or on foot. So we *do* need maps.

Exercises

1. Your teacher will give you an outlined, blank map of the United States.
2. Now you are going to put in the Dust Bowl states on your map. Use a large labeled U.S. map to help you. Start at the bottom with Texas. Then add New Mexico and Oklahoma. Now add Kansas and Colorado.
3. Now write in the names of the following states: Nebraska, South Dakota, and North Dakota.
4. Finally, using a U.S. map for reference again, write in the names of other states that were affected by the Dust Bowl: Wyoming, Montana, New Mexico, Iowa, and Minnesota.
5. Now, on your maps, color in the Dust Bowl area. That was the region most badly affected during the Dust Bowl years.

Lesson in Literature ...

WHAT IS PLOT?

- In the first part of the plot we are introduced to the characters and setting.
- A problem or conflict occurs near the beginning of the story.
- At the middle or near the end of the story, something will change and there will be a turning point.
- As the story reaches its conclusion, the problems presented in the plot are solved.

THINK ABOUT IT!

1. What problem is presented at the beginning of the story?
2. What happens to change the way Katie feels about Jigsaw?
3. How has Katie changed by the end of the story?

Katie was afraid of dogs. Once when she was little, she put out a hand to pet a cute brown-and-white dog, but the dog snarled and bit her hand. Last summer she was playing outside when a large black dog came into her backyard, growling and barking. She ran inside, terrified.

Her mother tried to comfort her. "Katie, some dogs are mean but some dogs are nice. You just have to be cautious around unfamiliar dogs."

Katie didn't think she would ever like any dog. On her way to school, she always walked fast in front of a white house with a big loud dog that barked at her from behind a wire fence. She didn't like it when a neighbor from down the street walked by her house with a little white dog sniffing and pulling on a leash. She was riding her bicycle one day when she and the neighbor with the dog came to the corner of the street at the same time. The little dog jumped at her and almost knocked her off.

So when her father brought home a fluffy brown puppy, Katie was afraid and ran to her bedroom. "Katie," he called up the stairs, "come down and meet Jigsaw."

She refused to budge even when her father came into her room to talk to her. "Katie," he said, "Jigsaw is just a puppy who wants someone to love him."

Katie shook her head and crawled under the bedcovers. "I don't like any dogs. They're scary and mean."

Her mother came in and sat on the edge of the bed. "Not all dogs are mean, Katie. Do you remember what I said about strange dogs and familiar dogs? Once you meet Jigsaw and spend some time with him, you'll see. Once you're familiar with him and he's

JIGSAW

familiar with you, you'll become friends."

After her parents left her alone, Katie wondered why anyone liked dogs. She opened a book to read, thinking she would spend the rest of her life alone in her room.

Just then, the light from outside her door came on. She sat up in bed as a fluffy ball of fur leaped on her. "Oh!" Katie cried as Jigsaw pressed his nose against her hands and licked her face. "Oh!" Katie cried again, but this time she sounded as if she had just jumped into a swimming pool on a hot summer day.

When Katie put out her hand to pet Jigsaw, he just wagged his tail. As her hand stroked his ears and neck, Jigsaw curled up in Katie's arms, and she knew that Jigsaw was not like the mean dogs she knew. He was cute and friendly, and he belonged to her.

Katie's father stood in the doorway. "I'm sorry. He just got away," he said. "But by looking at you two now, I'm glad he did."

The next day when Katie saw the neighbor with the mean dog, she didn't think that all dogs were mean. She thought that she just hadn't met the little white dog yet. On her way to school, she didn't rush past the house with the dog behind the fence. She hoped the dog's owners took him for walks or let him run in the park.

Walking home from school, she couldn't wait to see Jigsaw again. As she opened the kitchen door, Jigsaw ran to her, and the two spent the afternoon getting to know each other better. Soon they became more than familiar; they became friends. Although she always remained cautious around unfamiliar dogs, Katie loved getting to know Jigsaw, a puzzle she loved solving.

Blueprint for Reading

INTO . . . *Supergrandpa*

Gustaf Håkansson does not start out as a Supergrandpa. At first, people judge him by the way he looks. They think that he is too old to do anything interesting or important. Unfortunately, some people make quick judgments based only on what they see. More thoughtful people wait before drawing conclusions. As you read, think about which characters make quick judgments and which characters judge on more than looks alone.

EYES ON *Plot*

A **plot** is what happens in a story. Before authors write a story, they must have a story plan for the plot. The story plan has many parts. The author will check the plan and ask: Does the story have a beginning, middle, and end? Is there an exciting part or turning point? Can the reader find solutions to the problems presented in the story? Do the events appear in the proper order? Does everything make sense? If the answer to all these questions is "yes," the author is ready to write the story!

Supergrandpa

David M. Schwartz

Illustrated by
Bert Dodson

Gustaf Håkansson was sixty-six years old. His hair was snow white. His beard was a white bush. His face rippled with wrinkles whenever he smiled. Gustaf Håkansson looked like an old man, but he didn't feel old, and he certainly didn't act old.

Everyone for miles around knew Gustaf. People saw him on his bicycle, rain or shine, riding through the crooked streets of Grantofta—past the baker's and the butcher's and the wooden-toy maker's, over the stone bridge leading out of town, up steep hills scattered with farms, down narrow lanes bordered by stones, then home again to his morning paper and a bowl of sour milk and lingonberries.[1]

One morning Gustaf read something very interesting in the paper. There was going to be a bicycle race called the Tour of Sweden. It would be more than one thousand miles long, and it would last many days.

---

1. *Lingonberries* are a type of berry that grow in the Scandinavian countries; they are also called mountain cranberries or cowberries.

"This Tour of Sweden is for me!" exclaimed Gustaf.

"But you're too old for a bicycle race," said Gustaf's wife.

"You'll keel over," said his son. "It would be the end of you."

Even his grandchildren laughed at the idea. "You can't ride your bike a thousand miles, Grandpa," they scoffed.

"*Struntprat*!" Gustaf answered. "Silly talk!" And he hopped onto his bike and rode off to see the judges of the race. He would tell them that he planned to enter the Tour of Sweden.

WORD BANK

scoffed (SKOFT) *v.*: mocked; ridiculed

"But this race is for young people," said the first judge. "You're too old, Gustaf."

"You would never make it to the finish," said the second judge.

"We can only admit racers who are strong and fit," said the third judge. "What if you collapsed in the middle of the race?"

"*Struntprat*!" protested Gustaf. "I have no intention of collapsing, because I *am* strong and fit!"

But the judges were not to be moved. "We're sorry, Gustaf," they grumbled. "Go home. Go home to your rocking chair."

Gustaf went home, but he did not go to his rocking chair. "They can keep me out of the race," he muttered, "but they can't keep me off the road."

The next morning, Gustaf began to prepare for the long ride ahead. He arose with the sun, packed some fruit and rye bread, and cycled far out of town—over rolling hills dotted with ancient castles, across valleys dimpled with lakes, through forests thick with birches and pines. It was midafternoon before he returned. The next day he biked even farther. Each day he added more miles to his ride.

A few days before the race, all the young cyclists boarded a special train to Haparanda, in the far north of Sweden, where the race was to begin. But Gustaf was not an official racer. He had no train ticket.

There was only one way for Gustaf to ride in the Tour of Sweden. He would have to pedal six hundred miles to the starting line!

It took him several days to bike there. He arrived just as the Tour of Sweden was about to begin.

All the racers wore numbers, but of course there was no number for Gustaf. So he found a bright red scrap of fabric and made his own.

What number should he be? He had an idea. He wasn't supposed to be in the race at all, so he would be Number Zero!

He chuckled as he cut out a big red zero and pinned it to his shirt. Then he wheeled his bicycle to the starting line.

The starting gun went off and all the young cyclists took off in a spurt. Their legs pumped furiously and their bikes sprinted ahead. They soon left Gustaf far behind.

That night, the racers stopped at an inn. They were treated to dinner and a bed.

Hours later, Gustaf reached the inn too. But there was no bed for him, so he just kept riding. While the others snoozed the night away, Gustaf pedaled into the dawn.

Early the next day, the other cyclists passed Gustaf. But he kept up his steady pace, and late that evening he again overtook the young racers as they rested. In the middle of the night, he napped for three hours on a park bench.

On the third morning, Gustaf was the first to arrive in the little town of Lulea. A small crowd of people waited, hoping to catch a glimpse of the racers zooming by. Instead they saw Gustaf. His white beard fluttered in the breeze. His red cheeks were puffed out with breath. "Look!" cried a little girl. "Look! There goes Supergrandpa!"

"Supergrandpa?" Everyone craned to see.

"Yes, yes, he does look like a Supergrandpa!"

A few clapped. Others shouted friendly greetings. Some of the children held out their hands and Gustaf brushed their palms as he rode by. "Thank you, Supergrandpa! Good luck to you."

A photographer snapped Gustaf's picture. It appeared the next day in the newspaper. The headline read:

SUPERGRANDPA TAKES A RIDE.

Now all of Sweden knew about Supergrandpa Gustaf Håkansson.

When he got hungry or thirsty, people gave him sour milk with lingonberries, tea and cake, fruit juice, rye bread, or any other snack he wanted.

Newspaper reporters rushed up to talk with him. Radio interviewers broadcast every word he spoke. Everyone wanted to know how he felt.

"I have never felt better in my whole life," he told them.

"But aren't you tired?" they asked.

"How can I be tired when I am surrounded by so much kindness?" And with a push on the pedal and a wave of his hand, Gustaf was rolling down the road again.

Once again Gustaf rode through the night, passing the other racers while they slept. When his muscles felt stiff, he remembered his cheering fans. He pedaled harder.

And so it went, day after night, night after day. By the light of the moon, Gustaf quietly passed the young racers in their beds, then slept outside, but only for a few hours. Under the long rays of the morning sun, they overtook him and left him struggling to keep up his spirits and his pace. But each day it took them a little longer to catch up with Gustaf.

On the sixth morning of the race, thousands lined the road. As Gustaf rode by, their joyful cheers traveled with him like a wave through the crowd.

"You're almost there, Supergrandpa!"

"A few more miles!"

"Don't look back."

"You're going to win!"

Win? Gustaf hadn't thought about winning. He had simply wanted to ride in the Tour of Sweden and reach the finish line. But win?

"You're out in front, Supergrandpa."

"A few more miles, Supergrandpa, and you'll be the winner!"

The winner? Gustaf glanced over his shoulder. The pack of racers was catching up. Their heads and shoulders were hunched low over their handlebars. Their backs were raised high above their seats.

Gustaf decided not to think about them. Instead he thought about his many fans. He thought about how they wanted him to win. And suddenly, he wanted to win too!

Gustaf looked ahead. In the distance he could see a bright banner stretched all the way across the road. The finish line!

Gustaf lowered his head. He raised his back. He whipped his legs around with all their might and all their motion.

The next time he looked up he was bursting through the banner and rolling over the finish line—just before another racer thundered past.

The crowd roared. People lifted Gustaf onto their shoulders. They showered him with flowers. They sang victory songs. The police band played patriotic marches.

The three judges, however, said that Gustaf could not be the winner, because he was never actually in the race. Besides, it was against the rules to ride at night. No, the big gold trophy would go to another racer, not to Gustaf.

But no one seemed to care what the judges said. Even the king stepped up to hug Gustaf and invite him to the palace. And to nearly everyone in Sweden, Gustaf Håkansson—sixty-six years old, his hair as white as snow, his beard a great white bush, his smiling face an orb of wrinkles— to them, Supergrandpa Gustaf Håkansson had won the Tour of Sweden.

ABOUT THE AUTHOR

David Martin Schwartz was born in New York, New York in 1951. After graduating from Cornell University in upstate New York, he took a job as an elementary school teacher. After a short while, he tried a variety of other jobs, such as lumberjack, veterinary assistant, and freelance writer. Mr. Schwartz has written stories and books on many different topics. He has written about restaurant food, animal life, and even about the people of the Amazon. He hopes to always write on new and unusual subjects that interest him.

If You Think You Are Beaten

Anonymous

If you think you are beaten, you are;
If you think that you dare not, you don't;
If you'd like to win, but you think you can't,
It's almost a cinch that you won't.

5   If you think you'll lose, you've lost;
For out in the world you'll find
Success begins with a person's will,
It's all in the state of mind.

     Full many a race is lost
10 Ere even a step is run,
And many a coward falls
Ere even his work's begun.

Poetry encourages us

Studying the Selection

FIRST IMPRESSIONS
Do you think that, at the end of the race, any of the judges felt bad about having misjudged Gustaf?

QUICK REVIEW

1. What was everyone's reaction to Gustaf's announcement that he wanted to participate in the Tour of Sweden?

2. How did all of Sweden find out about Supergrandpa Gustaf Hakånsson?

3. What did Gustaf do each day in order to keep up with the young bicyclists?

4. What kept Gustaf's spirits up when it became tough to continue riding?

FOCUS

5. Explain why the people felt that Gustaf had earned the title "Supergrandpa."

6. In this story, there are people who do not agree. They have different ideas about whether or not Gustaf should ride in the Tour of Sweden. Who is the disagreement between? Is it ever settled? How is it settled?

CREATING AND WRITING

7. Do you agree with the judges' decision? Why or why not? Support your answer.

8. Think of a situation where you were not judged favorably. Perhaps someone jumped to conclusions about you. They may have thought you were at fault when you were not, or thought you were a certain type of person because of the way you dressed. Write a paragraph about what took place and how you felt at the time.

9. Write a cheer for Supergrandpa that people could shout as he bicycled through your town.

Lesson in Literature . . .

CHARACTERS

- The characters are all the people in the story.
- The characters who are the most important are called the **main** characters.
- In some stories, the characters remain the same from beginning to end.
- In other stories, the characters change because of something that happens during the story.

Nana, Jennifer, and little Johnny took long walks on the beach. "North or south today?" Nana asked her grandchildren each time they climbed over the dune. Jennifer liked to go north. That beach was long and smooth with white sand, and they always walked for a mile. Johnny liked to go south. Whenever they went south, they didn't go far. Instead, they hunted for seashells in the sand. Johnny liked to see how many he could hold in his hands.

Today was a beautiful day with a soft, warm breeze. Jennifer said, "I don't care which way." They started south, and Johnny ran ahead, looking for seashells, but he ran only a little ways before he noticed something amazing. There were starfish everywhere in the sand.

"Look!" he cried, holding up a starfish. "Where did they come from?"

"They must have washed up after the rain last night," his grandmother said.

"Throw them back," Jennifer said. "They're dead."

Johnny didn't listen. He gathered as many as he could in his hands, enough that the starfish gave his cupped hands many more fingers.

Hands full, he looked up, but Nana and Jennifer had walked ahead. Down the beach they had stopped,

STARFISH

THINK ABOUT IT!

1. Who are the three characters in *Starfish*?

2. Two of the characters remain the same throughout the story. Which two?

3. The third character learns a few lessons near the end of the story. What is one of those lessons?

and Jennifer knelt in the sand. As he ran up to them, he saw what his sister had found. A live baby turtle squirmed tangled in a clump of seaweed.

"I want it," Johnny said.

"No," Jennifer said, "it's alive." She freed the baby turtle from the seaweed and held it up between her fingers while it swam the air and then gently put it down in the sand. "Okay," she said to the turtle as if it were her favorite pet, "the ocean is straight ahead. Go to the water."

"Nana," Johnny said, "tell her she has to pick up the turtle. I want it."

Nana had been standing nearby watching her grandchildren. "Pick it up yourself, Johnny," she said.

"I can't," he said. He looked at his hands, full of starfish, and looked at the turtle inching toward the water.

"Yes, you can. You have to choose."

Nana and Jennifer stood together and watched as Johnny made up his mind.

Hands full, he squatted and opened his fingers, the starfish falling like shooting stars onto the sand. Then he picked up the baby turtle, letting it swim on the palm of his hand, walked to the ocean, and let it go in the surf.

He didn't go back for the starfish.

Blueprint for Reading

INTO . . . *Two Big Bears*

Security is the feeling that we are cared for and safe. Generally, it is our parents who give us that wonderful feeling of security, but anyone can fill that role. Perhaps you are very close to your grandmother, a neighbor, or a special teacher. There may be a place—your house, a secret place you visit, a friend's home— where you feel safe and relaxed. What gives you that warm, comfortable feeling inside? As you read *Two Big Bears*, think about what makes Laura feel secure within her family.

EYES ON *Character*

Characters are all of the people found in a story. Some characters are only slightly important and are described briefly. Other characters play a very important role in the story. For these **main** characters, more details are added. Words like *shy*, *tall*, or *brave* are examples of details an author might include. This helps the reader better understand both the character and the plot. As you read *Two Big Bears*, see what you can learn about each of the main characters.

Two BIG Bears

An excerpt from Little House in the Big Woods

Laura Ingalls Wilder

One day Pa said that spring was coming.

In the Big Woods the snow was beginning to thaw. Bits of it dropped from the branches of the trees and made little holes in the softening snowbanks below. At noon all the big icicles along the eaves of the little house quivered and sparkled in the sunshine, and drops of water hung trembling at their tips.

Pa said he must go to town to trade the furs of the wild animals he had been trapping all winter. So one evening he made a big bundle of them. There were so many furs that when they were packed tightly and tied together they made a bundle almost as big as Pa.

Very early one morning Pa strapped the bundle of furs on his shoulders, and started to walk to town. There were so many furs to carry that he could not take his gun.

Ma was worried, but Pa said that by starting before sun-up and walking very fast all day he could get home again before dark.

The nearest town was far away. Laura and Mary had never seen a town. They had never seen a store. They had never seen even two houses standing together. But they knew that in a town there were many houses, and a store full of candy and calico and other wonderful things—powder, and shot, and salt, and store sugar.

They knew that Pa would trade his furs to the storekeeper for beautiful things from town, and all day they were expecting the presents he would bring them. When the sun sank low above the treetops and no more drops fell from the tips of the icicles they began to watch eagerly for Pa.

The sun sank out of sight, the woods grew dark, and he did not come. Ma started supper and set the table, but he did not come. It was time to do the chores, and still he had not come.

Ma said that Laura might come with her while she milked the cow. Laura could carry the lantern.

So Laura put on her coat and Ma buttoned it up. And Laura put her hands into her red mittens that hung by a red yarn string around her neck, while Ma lighted the candle in the lantern.

Laura was proud to be helping Ma with the milking, and she

WORD BANK

thaw *v.*: melt
eaves (EEVZ) *n.*: the overhanging lower edges of a roof
quivered (KWIV erd) *v.*: shook slightly
calico (KAL ih ko) *n.*: a plain cotton fabric printed on one side
chores (TSHORZ) *n.*: the everyday work around a house or farm; a small job that must be done regularly

carried the lantern very carefully. Its sides were of tin, with places cut in them for the candle-light to shine through.

When Laura walked behind Ma on the path to the barn, the little bits of candle-light from the lantern leaped all around her on the snow. The night was not yet quite dark. The woods were dark, but there was a gray light on the snowy path, and in the sky there were a few faint stars. The stars did not look as warm and bright as the little lights that came from the lantern.

Laura was surprised to see the dark shape of Sukey, the brown cow, standing at the barnyard gate. Ma was surprised, too.

It was too early in the spring for Sukey to be let out in the Big Woods to eat grass. She lived in the barn. But sometimes on warm days Pa left the door of her stall open so she could come into the barnyard. Now Ma and Laura saw her behind the bars, waiting for them.

Ma went up to the gate, and pushed against it to open it. But it did not open very far, because there was Sukey, standing against it. Ma said,

"Sukey, get over!" She reached across the gate and slapped Sukey's shoulder.

Just then one of the dancing little bits of light from the lantern jumped between the bars of the gate, and Laura saw long, shaggy, black fur and two little, glittering eyes.

Sukey had thin, short, brown fur. Sukey had large, gentle eyes.

Ma said, "Laura, walk back to the house."

So Laura turned around and began to walk toward the house. Ma came behind her. When they had gone part way, Ma snatched her up, lantern and all, and ran. Ma ran with her into the house, and slammed the door.

Then Laura said, "Ma, was it a bear?"

"Yes, Laura," Ma said. "It was a bear."

Laura began to cry. She hung on to Ma and sobbed, "Oh, will he eat Sukey?"

"No," Ma said, hugging her. "Sukey is safe in the barn. Think, Laura—all those big, heavy logs in the barn walls. And the door is heavy and solid, made to keep bears out. No, the bear cannot get in and eat Sukey."

Laura felt better then. "But he could have hurt us, couldn't he?" she asked.

"He didn't hurt us," Ma said. "You were a good girl, Laura, to do exactly as I told you, and to do it quickly, without asking why."

Ma was trembling, and she began to laugh a little. "To think," she said, "I've slapped a bear!"

Then she put supper on the table for Laura and Mary. Pa had not come home yet. He didn't come. Laura and Mary changed into nightgowns, and they said their prayers and snuggled into the trundle bed.[1]

Ma sat by the lamp, mending one of Pa's shirts. The house seemed cold and still and strange, without Pa.

Laura listened to the wind in the Big Woods. All around the house the wind went crying as though it were lost in the dark and the cold. The wind sounded frightened.

Ma finished mending the shirt. Laura saw her fold it slowly and carefully. She smoothed it with her hand. Then she did a thing she had never done before. She went to the door and pulled the leather latch-string through its hole in the door, so that nobody could get in from outside unless she lifted the latch. She came and took Carrie, all limp and sleeping, out of the big bed.

She saw that Laura and Mary were still awake, and she said to them: "Go to sleep, girls. Everything is all right. Pa will be here in the morning."

Then she went back to her rocking chair and sat there rocking gently and holding Baby Carrie in her arms.

She was sitting up late, waiting for Pa, and Laura and Mary meant to stay awake, too, till he came. But at last they went to sleep.

In the morning Pa was there. He had brought candy for Laura and Mary, and two pieces of pretty calico to make them each a dress. Mary's was a china-blue pattern on a white ground, and

WORD BANK

trembling (TREMB ling)
v.: shaking slightly from fear, cold, or excitement

_____

1. A *trundle bed* is a low bed on wheels, usually pushed under another bed when not in use.

Laura's was dark red with little golden-brown dots on it. Ma had calico for a dress, too; it was brown, with a big, feathery white pattern all over it.

They were all happy because Pa had got such good prices for his furs that he could afford to get them such beautiful presents.

The tracks of the big bear were all around the barn and there were marks of his claws on the walls. But Sukey and the horses were safe inside.

All that day the sun shone, the snow melted, and little streams of water ran from the icicles, which all the time grew thinner. Before the sun set that night, the bear tracks were only shapeless marks in the wet, soft snow.

After supper Pa took Laura and Mary on his knees and said he had a new story to tell them.

The Story of Pa and the Bear in the Way

"When I went to town yesterday with the furs I found it hard walking in the soft snow. It took me a long time to get to town, and other men with furs had come in earlier to do their trading. The storekeeper was busy, and I had to wait until he could look at my furs.

"Then we had to bargain about the price of each one, and then I had to pick out the things I wanted to take in trade.

"So it was nearly sundown before I could start home.

"I tried to hurry, but the walking was hard and I was tired, so I had not gone far before night came. And I was alone in the Big Woods without my gun.

"There were still six miles to walk, and I came along as fast as I could. The night grew darker and darker, and I wished for my gun, because I knew that some of the bears had come out of their winter dens. I had seen their tracks when I went to town in the morning.

"Bears are hungry and cross at this time of year; you know they have been sleeping in their dens all winter long with nothing to eat, and that makes them thin and angry when they wake up. I did not want to meet one.

"I hurried along as quick as I could in the dark. By and by the stars gave a little light. It was still black as pitch where the woods were thick, but in the open places I could see, dimly. I could see the snowy road

WORD BANK

pitch *n.*: a black, sticky tar

ahead a little way, and I could see the dark woods standing all around me. I was glad when I came into an open place where the stars gave me this faint light.

"All the time I was watching, as well as I could, for bears. I was listening for the sounds they make when they go carelessly through the bushes.

"Then I came again into an open place, and there, right in the middle of my road, I saw a big black bear.

"He was standing up on his hind legs, looking at me. I could see his eyes shine. I could see his pig-snout. I could even see one of his claws, in the starlight.

"My scalp prickled, and my hair stood straight up. I stopped in my tracks, and stood still. The bear did not move. There he stood, looking at me.

"I knew it would do no good to try to go around him. He would follow me into the dark woods, where he could see better than I could. I did not want to fight a winter-starved bear in the dark. Oh, how I wished for my gun!

"I had to pass that bear, to get home. I thought that if I could scare him, he might get out of the road and let me go by. So I took a deep breath, and suddenly I shouted with all my might and ran at him, waving my arms.

"He didn't move.

"I did not run very far toward him, I tell you! I stopped and looked at him, and he stood looking at me. Then I shouted again. There he stood. I kept on shouting and waving my arms, but he did not budge.

"Well, it would do me no good to run away. There were other bears in the woods. I might meet one any time. I might as well deal with this one as with another. Besides, I was coming home to Ma and you girls. I would never get here, if I ran away from everything in the woods that scared me.

"So at last I looked around, and I got a good big club, a solid, heavy branch that had been broken from a tree by the weight of snow in the winter.

WORD BANK

budge (BUHJ) *v.*: move even slightly
club (KLUB) *n.*: a heavy stick

"I lifted it up in my hands, and I ran straight at that bear. I swung my club as hard as I could and brought it down, bang! on his head.

And there he still stood, for he was nothing but a big, black, burned stump!

"I had passed it on my way to town that morning. It wasn't a bear at all. I only thought it was a bear, because I had been thinking all the time about bears and being afraid I'd meet one."

"It really wasn't a bear at all?" Mary asked.

"No, Mary, it wasn't a bear at all. There I had been yelling, and dancing, and waving my arms, all by myself in the Big Woods, trying to scare a stump!"

Laura said: "Ours was really a bear. But we were not scared, because we thought it was Sukey."

Pa did not say anything, but he hugged her tighter.

"Oo-oo! That bear might have eaten Ma and me all up!" Laura said, snuggling closer to him. "But Ma walked right up to him and slapped him, and he didn't do anything at all. Why didn't he do anything?"

"I guess he was too surprised to do anything, Laura," Pa said. "I guess he was afraid, when the lantern shone in his eyes. And when Ma walked up to him and slapped him, he knew *she* wasn't afraid."

"Well, you were brave, too," Laura said. "Even if it was only a stump, you thought it was a bear. You'd have hit him on the head with a club, if he *had* been a bear, wouldn't you, Pa?"

"Yes," said Pa, "I would. You see, I had to."

Then Ma said it was bedtime. She helped Laura and Mary button up their red flannel nightgowns. They knelt down by the trundle bed and said their prayers.

"Now I lay me down to sleep,
I pray the L-rd my soul to keep.
If I should die before I wake,
I pray the L-rd my soul to take."

Ma kissed them both, and tucked the covers in around them. They lay there awhile, looking at Ma's smooth, parted hair and her hands busy with sewing in the lamplight. Her needle made little clicking sounds against her thimble and then the thread went softly, swish! through the pretty calico that Pa had traded furs for.

Laura looked at Pa, who was greasing his boots. His mustaches and his hair and his long brown beard were silky in the lamplight, and the colors of his plaid jacket were gay. He whistled and sang cheerfully while he worked.

It was a warm night. The fire had gone to coals on the hearth, and Pa did not build it up. All around the little house, in the Big Woods, there were little sounds of falling snow, and from the eaves there was the drip, drip of the melting icicles.

In just a little while the trees would be putting out their baby leaves, all rosy and yellow and pale green, and there would be wild flowers and birds in the woods.

Then there would be no more stories by the fire at night, but all day long Laura and Mary would run and play among the trees, for it would be spring.

WORD BANK

hearth (HARTH) *n.*: the floor of a fireplace

ABOUT THE AUTHOR

Laura Ingalls Wilder was born in 1867 in a place in Wisconsin known as the "Big Woods." The Ingalls family later settled in the Dakota Territory, where Laura attended school and made many friends. Laura married Almanzo Wilder in 1885. The young couple struggled through illness and failure, determined to farm the land. It was not until later, when their daughter, Rose, became a writer, that Laura tried her hand at writing books. Rose encouraged her mother and, in 1931, *Little House in the Big Woods*, the first of Laura's many beloved books, was published.

March Bear

Marilyn Singer

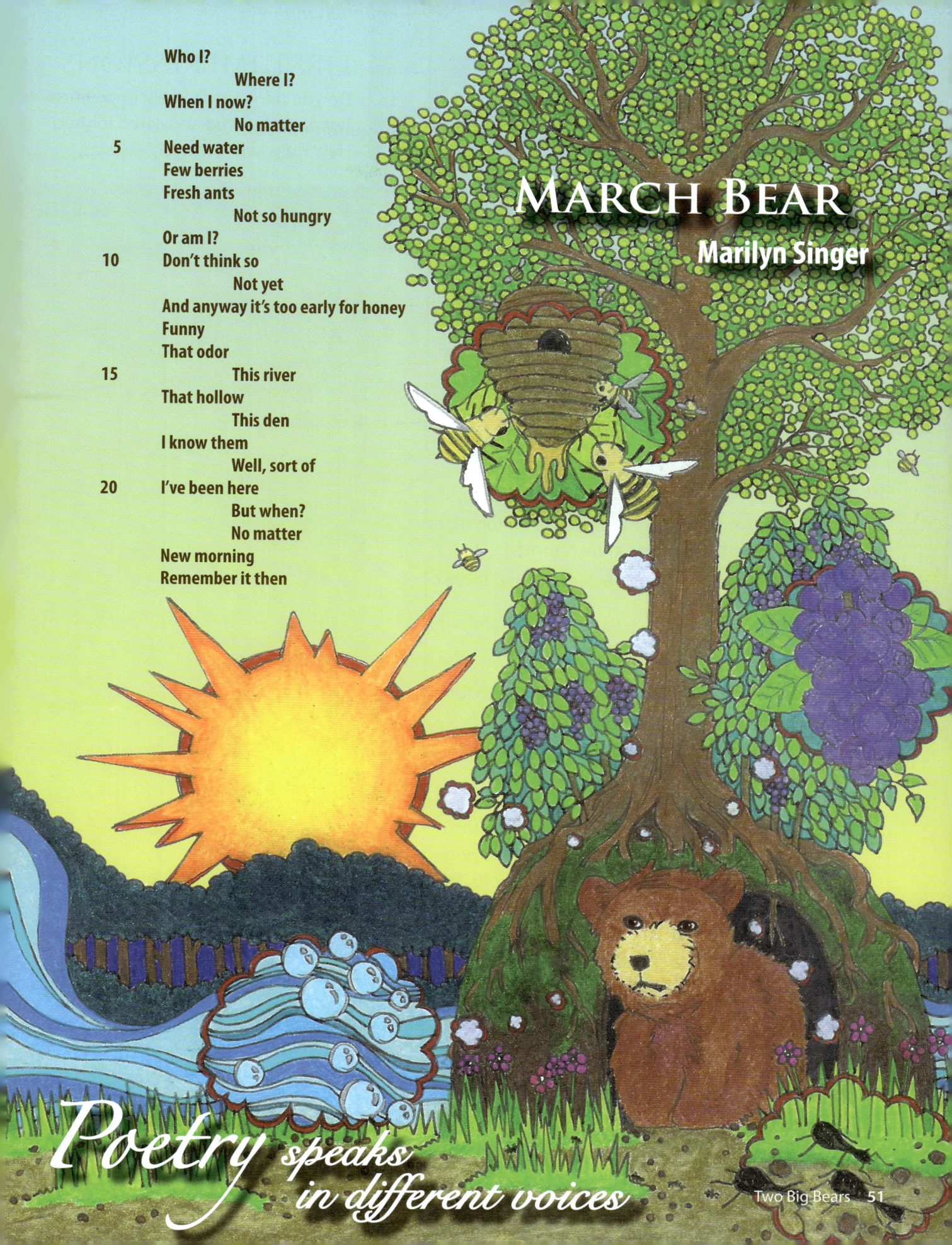

Who I?
        Where I?
When I now?
        No matter
5   Need water
Few berries
Fresh ants
        Not so hungry
Or am I?
10   Don't think so
        Not yet
And anyway it's too early for honey
Funny
That odor
15   This river
That hollow
        This den
I know them
        Well, sort of
20   I've been here
        But when?
        No matter
New morning
Remember it then

Poetry speaks in different voices

Studying the Selection

FIRST IMPRESSIONS

Do you think Laura knew how much her parents loved and cared for her? How do you know this?

QUICK REVIEW

1. Why was Pa going to town?

2. Why were Ma and Laura surprised to find Sukey out of the barn?

3. Why couldn't the girls fall asleep and what did Ma say to reassure them?

4. What did Pa have to leave at home that he wished for later?

FOCUS

5. Compare the atmosphere in the house on the night Pa was away to the night after he returned.

6. List at least three of Ma's characteristics and three of Laura's.

CREATING AND WRITING

7. Write about why it was important for Laura to follow her mother's instructions without question.

8. When a writer describes something that is not human as though it were a person, the writer is using *personification* (pur SAH nih fih KAY shun). The author uses personification when describing the wind: "All around the house the wind went crying as though it were lost in the dark and the cold. The wind sounded frightened." Imagine that the books and supplies in your desk could think, talk, and move around. Write a paragraph in which you give human traits to something in your desk.

9. Laura will surely want to share stories with her children just as Pa shared stories with her. Make a storybook with illustrations describing Laura and Ma's encounter with the bear.

Jill's Journal:
On Assignment in China

In China and Tibet and Vietnam, there is a bear called the Asiatic Black Bear. This bear has a beautiful yellow crescent on its chest, and so it is called the Moon Bear. For a long time, moon bears have been hunted and trapped.

People want to get something called *bile* from their bodies. The bile is used for medicine. But these days, the same medicine can be manufactured from herbs—the bears aren't needed for it.

I had heard about moon bears and about Mrs. Jill Robinson who is helping them. I decided to go see her. So here I am, in Chengdu. In the last twenty-four hours, I have flown on a plane for 17 hours to Hong Kong. Then I took another plane from Hong Kong. It took two more hours to get to Chengdu, which is the capital of Sichuan Province in China. (A province is a bit like a state in the United States.)

Chengdu is a very modern big city with fancy hotels, large businesses, and many cars. There are even some signs in English along the highway. I was very tired when I arrived, but I was also very excited to almost be at my destination. It took another hour to get to the Rescue Center by car.

Mrs. Robinson was waiting. She told me the following story. In 1993, she visited a place where they kept moon bears. It is called a bear farm, and the bears are kept in small cages.

Moon Bear

"I still remember thinking that these bears need to be free. They need to eat berries and nuts. They need to climb in trees to play." Then, she said, she felt a gentle paw touch her shoulder. "I turned around and one little girl bear stared up at me. I knew it could be dangerous, but I reached out and held this little bear's paw. I made a promise to myself and to the little bear that I would help create a safe place for these bears to roam free."

Seven years later, Mrs. Robinson and Animals Asia signed an agreement with the Chinese government. The government said they could rescue 500 farmed bears in Sichuan Province and start a special rescue place for the bears. The first bear, Andrew, came in October 2000. Now there are 235 bears here.

Wait a minute! I'm going to see the bears! Wow! They're so cute. A staff member is telling me who they are. There's Andrew. He is standing on tiptoe, squeezing his eyes shut and eating raisins. The next one is Bottom. She is eating cake that has been stuffed into holes in a big tree branch. Now my guide is pointing out Freedom. The guide tells me that it took a very long time for Freedom to trust humans, but now she is happy—and free. The others who are coming out are Crystal and Banjo. Now Crystal is lying in the grass, gazing into the distance. The guide is talking to me but I can't hear her words. I need a tissue. I feel so happy to be here and meet the bears.

POWER SKILL:
Speaking Slowly, Clearly, Loudly, and with Expression

Have you ever watched a play? You probably have. It can be difficult to watch a play if you can't understand what the actors are saying.

How do you feel about speaking in front of a group? You could be presenting a report, reciting a poem, or performing in a play. Doing these things well is very pleasing. You have shown that you can be grown up, and that you are not feeling embarrassed. You have given clear information to your friends and your teacher. You have entertained your audience.

The same skills are what you need to participate in helping projects. If you want to read to the blind, you have to read clearly and with expression. The same is true for talking with an elderly person whose hearing may be impaired. If you rush through your words, your words won't be understood. This will be hard on you and on the person with whom you are speaking.

Taking your words, and how you speak them, seriously, will make you feel more confident and more sure of yourself. Then you will be able to handle yourself well when you meet a new person or when you greet guests in your home.

Have you ever been in a situation in which you are with people you know but who do not know each other? You have the power to make people feel comfortable, relaxed, and happier, if you can perform the simple task of introducing them to each other.

Exercises

1. Below are five Chinese characters and their meanings. The characters are not simply letters, but stand for words. Your task is to create a picture of a moon bear who has been freed. You are going to draw her. Then you will add the Chinese characters instead of the actual sun, moon, mountains, rain, and trees. Put them where they belong in the picture. Then you can add a river, fallen logs, a bamboo forest, and so forth.
Chinese Characters:

日	月	山	雨	木
Sun	Moon	Mountain	Rain	Tree

2. Your teacher will hand out the script of a play and assign parts. Have fun!

Lesson in Literature . . .

WHAT IS SETTING?

- Setting includes the **time** and **location** in which the story takes place.

- *Time* refers to the year, season, and time of day in which the story takes place.

- The *location* may be a very specific place, for example, "Macy's Department Store in Manhattan." Or, the location may be typical of a large group of places, for example, "a school building" or "a park."

- In a play, costumes, lighting, and sound effects all help create the setting.

One sunny day a large heron flew over a small pond. Looking down, he wondered, "Is that a good pond?" and swooped down to find out.

At the edge of the pond, he stood on his long, thin legs and looked around. It looked like a perfect pond. Fish swam in cool blue water. A turtle basked on a log. A frog croaked on a lily pad. A duck waddled along the shore. A robin sang in a nearby tree. A rabbit hopped in the grass.

"Is this a good pond?" Heron called out.

Fish swam by, nodding yes.

Turtle stirred. "This log is perfect for me."

Frog croaked, "It's good. It's good."

Rabbit twitched his whiskers. "It's home."

But Duck paddled up to Heron. "There is no place for you here. This pond is ours. No vultures allowed."

"No vultures allowed?" Heron repeated, surprised. He was not a vulture; he was a Great Blue Heron. He flapped his large wings, ready to fly off for another pond where he might be welcomed.

But just then drops of rain began to fall. "That's just rain," Duck said, circling around Heron. "You have to leave this pond. No vultures allowed."

The rain fell softly at first but soon big, fat raindrops fell everywhere. The sky became dark. A loud crack of lightning lit the sky and a rumble of thunder shook the earth.

"What's that?" Duck asked.

"It's a bad storm," Heron said. He spread his two large wings. They looked like two huge umbrellas. "Hide under here."

Duck eyed the outstretched wings. "I will never take help from a vulture," Duck said. He paddled to the other side of the pond as rain fell harder.

Heron called out to the others, "Hide under my big wings!"

Fish swam away.

Turtle shifted on his log. "I can take care of myself, Vulture," he said.

THE POND

THINK ABOUT IT!

1. In the first two paragraphs of the story, the author gives five details to help us picture the setting. The first is "cool blue water." What are two more?

2. One part of setting can be the weather in which the events happen. In the story, "big fat raindrops" fall everywhere. What are two other phrases that tell us about the weather in the pond?

3. What time of day is part of the setting for this story?

Just then the lily pad under Frog sank to the bottom of the pond. Frog swam over to Heron. "Are you a vulture?"

"No, I'm a heron, Frog," Heron said.

"Why didn't you say so?" Frog said and ducked under one of Heron's wings.

Robin flew from her tree and huddled with Frog. "I don't care if you're a vulture or a heron," she said to Heron. "Thank you for sharing your wings."

Rabbit hopped over. "Thanks for the help, Mr. Heron," he said. Before he joined the others under Heron's wing, Rabbit shouted across the pond at Duck. "This is your last chance, Duck!"

But Duck refused to join the others.

After the storm ended, Turtle basked on his log. Frog found a lily pad. Robin flew back to the tree. Rabbit sniffed the wet grass. Fish swam around, and Heron stood in shallow water watching the sun come out.

Duck was last seen waddling away, alone.

Blueprint for Reading

INTO . . . *Mom's Best Friend*

Mom's best friend in this story may not be the kind of friend you were expecting to read about. You will see that Mom is devoted to her new friend no matter what comes her way. Mom displays a lot of *perseverance* (PUR suh VEER uns) throughout the story. To *persevere* is to work steadily at something even when problems come up. One who perseveres handles difficulties calmly. Patience is an important part of perseverance. As you read, you will see some of the challenges that Mom faces and the way she perseveres.

EYES ON *Setting*

Whether it is a snowy mountaintop, an African jungle, or a city street, every story has a **setting**. The setting describes the background of the story. It may include where the story takes place, when it takes place, or even what the weather is like. The mood is part of the setting. Does the author describe a tense and exciting scene, or a calm and lazy one? In *Two Big Bears*, the main setting is a farmhouse on the plains of the United States in the late 1800s. The mood is warm and friendly, but it does get frightening during the bear tales.

Notice what is included in the setting as you read *Mom's Best Friend*. Keep in mind that a story may have more than one setting.

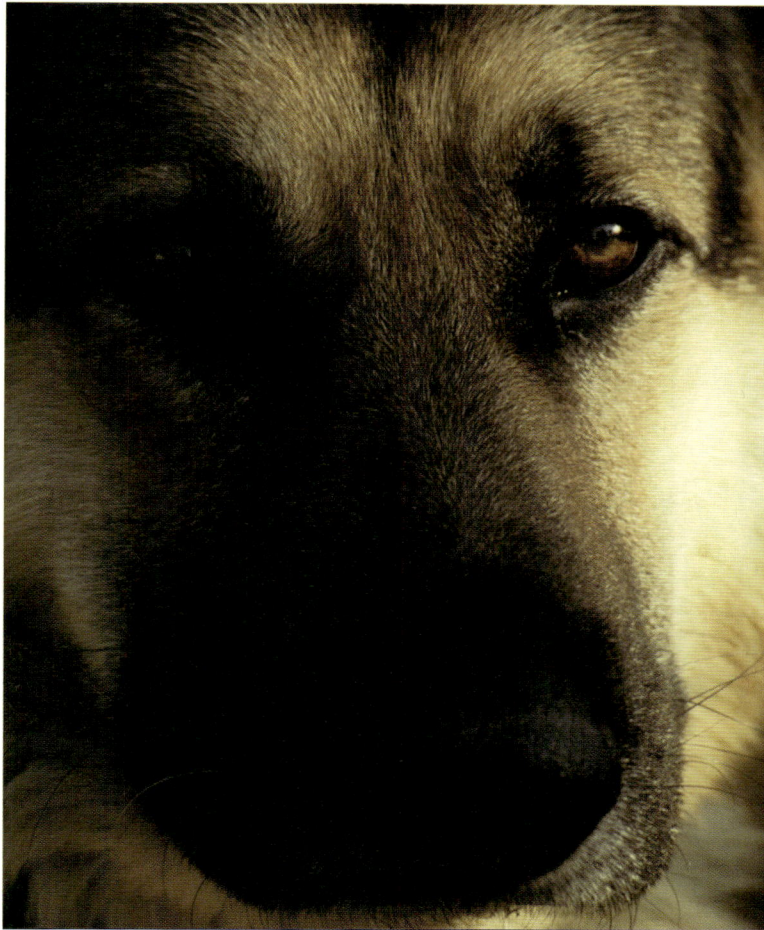

MOM'S BEST FRIEND

Sally Hobart Alexander

The best thing about having a mom who's blind is getting a special dog like Marit, Mom's dog guide. At least that's what my brother, Joel, and I used to think. Then, four months ago, Marit died. And it became the worst thing.

Marit had been with us since before I was born. Her death left a big hole in our family. I kept thinking I heard her whimpering for a game of catch. Any time I left pizza on the counter, I would race back to the rescue. But there was no sneaky dog about to steal it.

For my birthday Joel gave me a rabbit that I named Methuselah.[1] Although it helped to have a soft bunny, I still wanted Marit.

1. *Methuselah* (muh THOO zuh luh)

Mom missed her even more. She didn't lose just a sweet, furry pet. She lost her favorite way of traveling, too. She had to use her cane again, and crept along the sidewalk like a snail. Once, when she crossed the street, she missed the opposite curb and kept walking toward the traffic. I had to holler to get her onto the sidewalk.

After that, I worried about her running errands by herself. I asked her to "go sighted guide," holding Dad's, Joel's, or my arm. Sometimes she did. But mostly she used the cane. She didn't want to depend on us—or on anybody.

A lot of blind people do fine with a cane. It's like a real long arm to help them feel what's around: walkways, hedges, mailboxes.

With a dog guide, blind people use their hearing more than touch. Mom has trained her ears. It's amazing: she can tell when something, like a movie marquee, is above her head, and when she passes a lamppost. She knows from the change in the sound of her footsteps.

In spite of Mom's special hearing, I worried. I was relieved when she decided to go back to The Seeing Eye for a new dog guide.

Before Mom left, I told her I wouldn't be able to love the new dog as much as Marit. Mom hugged me and said, "The night before you were born, I wondered how I could love a second child as much as your brother. Then you came, and like magic, I was just as crazy about you."

The Seeing Eye, in Morristown, New Jersey, was the first dog guide school in the United States. (Now there are nine others.) It trains German shepherds and Labrador and golden retrievers for three months. Then, for about a month, it teaches blind people to use the dogs.

When Mom arrived at The Seeing Eye, she was met by her instructor, Pete Jackson.

I missed Mom as much as I missed Marit, but at least Mom called every night. She also wrote letters and sent pictures.

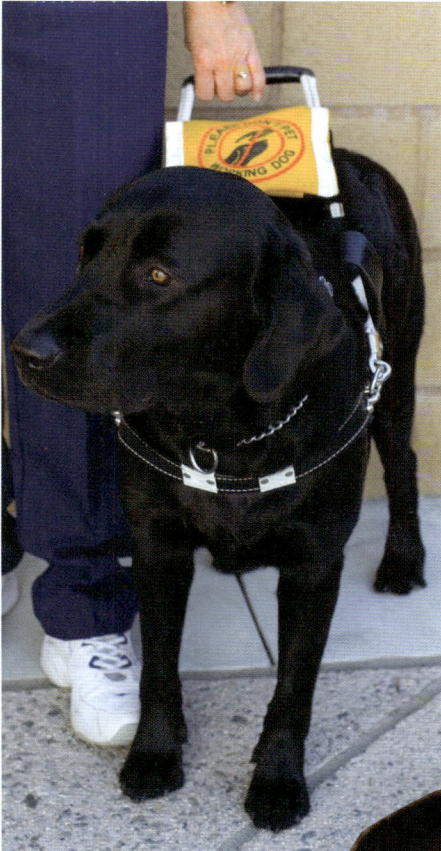

Mom's first day was a cinch. She'd gone to Seeing Eye twelve years before to get Marit, and still remembered her way around. Usually when she's in a new place she has to move from room to room with her cane, memorizing the layout.

In the morning Mom walked with Pete Jackson so that he could check her pace. He wanted to choose the dog that would suit her best. Then she was free to play the piano, exercise…and worry. Would she get along with the new dog? Would they work well together?

The next day she got Ursula. What a strange name! The staff at Seeing Eye's breeding station had named Ursula when she was born. (Ursula's brothers and sisters were also given names starting with *U*.) Dog guides need a name right away so that Seeing Eye can keep track of the four hundred or so pups born each year. At two months of age, the pups go to Seeing Eye puppy-raising families to learn how to live with people. At fifteen months, they are mature enough to return to Seeing Eye for the three-month training program.

Dad said that Ursula means "bear." But in the pictures Mom sent, Ursula looked too pipsqueaky to be called bear. Mom explained that Seeing Eye is now breeding some smaller dogs. They are easier to handle and fit better on buses and in cars.

My friends thought dog guides were little machines that zoomed blind people around. Until Mom went away, even I didn't understand all the things these dogs were taught.

But on Mom's first lesson in Morristown, Ursula seemed to forget her training. She veered on a street crossing and brushed Mom into a bush. Mom had to make her correct herself by backing up and walking around the bush. Then Mom praised her.

After ten practice runs with Pete, Mom and Ursula soloed.[2] Ursula didn't stop at a curb, so Mom had to scold her and snap

---

2. *Soloed* means they did it by themselves, without Pete's supervision.

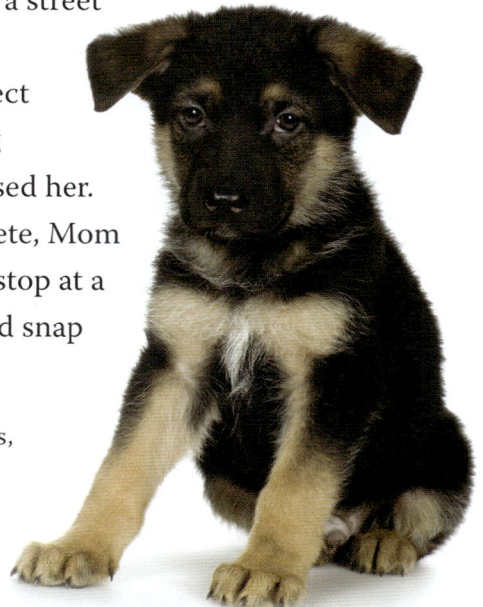

her leash, calling, "Pfui." Later Ursula crashed Mom into a low-hanging branch. "Ursula will have to start thinking tall," Mom said that night, "or I'll have to carry hedge clippers in my purse."

Even though Ursula had walked in Morristown a lot with Pete, she was nervous when Mom's hand was on the harness. Mom talked and walked differently. And Mom was nervous, too. Ursula moved so much faster than old Marit had, and Mom didn't trust her.

Every day Mom and Ursula made two trips. Every week they mastered new routes. Each route got longer and more complicated, and Mom had less time to learn it. Every night Mom gave Ursula obedience training: "Come. Sit down. Rest. Fetch." I thought she should try obedience training on Joel.

While Mom worked hard, Dad, Joel, and I went on with our normal lives—school, homework, soccer, piano, spending time with friends. We divided Mom's chores: Dad did the cooking, Joel, the vacuuming and laundry, and I did the dishes, dusting, weeding. The first two weeks were easy.

In a phone call Mom said that things were getting easier for her, too. "Remember how tough curb ramps have been for me?" she asked. "They feel like any other slope in the sidewalk, so I can't always tell that I've reached the street. Well, Ursula stopped perfectly at every ramp. And she guided me around, not under, a ladder and right past a huge parking lot without angling into it. But best of all, she actually saved my life. A jackhammer was making so much noise that I couldn't hear whether the light was green or red. When I told Ursula, 'Forward!' she refused to move and kept me from stepping in front of a car. (Of course, Pete would have saved me if Ursula hadn't.)"

Mom barely asked about us. It was all Ursula, Ursula, Ursula! She seemed to be forgetting Marit, too. When a letter came a few days later, I was sure she didn't miss anyone.

Dear Bob, Joel, and Leslie,

Today Ursula and I faced several disasters! She tried hard to ignore a boxer dog who wanted to play. A few minutes later, a Great Dane lunged out from nowhere, jumped all over her, and loped off. Ursula's instinct is to chase dogs, but she didn't move a paw after that one. As if the dogs weren't enough trouble, fire engine sirens went off. Ursula just strolled down the sidewalk.

Mostly, life is smooth here. Seeing Eye is a vacation—no cooking, no cleaning, lots of time to talk to new friends, like Dr. Holle, the veterinarian. And since I don't have many blind friends, it's a treat to be with my roommate and the twenty other students. We laugh about the same things, like the great enemy of the blind—trash collection day! Every twenty feet there's a garbage can reeking

of pizza, hoagies, old cheese. Usually Ursula snakes me around these smelly obstacles. But sometimes the temptation to her nose wins out, and I have to correct her, all the while holding my own nose.

Some trainees really inspire me, like Julie Hensley, who became blind from diabetes at twenty-two. Even though she's been blind for twelve years, she still teaches horses to do stunts. She judges her location from a radio playing music in the center of the pen, and gallops around as fast as she ever did when she could see.

Bob Pacheco used to race motorcycles and hunt. Then, two years ago, when he was twenty-nine, he developed optic atrophy and became blind two months later. He took up fishing, swimming, even trapping. But something was missing. He couldn't get around quickly enough. After the first trip with his dog guide, he was overjoyed. "Sally!" He was so excited. "I don't feel blind any more."

The dogs are wonderful, and the people here are very special. So are you.

Love, Mom

Well, life at home wasn't very wonderful or special. Dad ran out of the casseroles Mom had frozen ahead of time, and although his meals were okay, I missed Mom's cooking. Worse, the dishes kept piling up. I never knew Joel ate so much.

Then things got really bad. While Dad was teaching his American literature night class, Joel and I faced a disaster Mom and Ursula couldn't have dreamed of: the toilet bowl overflowed! We wiped the floor with towels. As Joel took the towels down to the washing machine, he found water dripping through the ceiling—all over the dining room table, all over the carpet. He ran for more towels, and I ran for the furniture polish and rug shampoo. When Dad got home, everything looked perfect. But I wrote a braille letter.

Dear Mom,
Come home soon. The house misses you.
Love,
Exhausted in Pittsburgh

Mom wrote back.

Dear Exhausted,
Hang on. We'll be home to "hound" you Thursday. Be prepared. When you see me, I will have grown four more feet.

Mom

I couldn't laugh. I was too tired and worried. What if I couldn't love Ursula? Marit was the best dog ever.

Soon they arrived. Ursula yanked at her leash and sprang up on me. She pawed my shoulders, stomach, and arms just the way Marit used to, nearly knocking me over. She leaped onto Joel, licking him all over. As she bounded up onto me again, I realized Mom was right. Like magic, I was crazy about this shrimpy new dog.

But by the end of the day, I had a new worry. Was *Ursula* going to love *me*? She seemed friendly enough, but keyed up, even lost in our house.

Mom explained that Ursula had already given her heart away three times: first to her mother, then to the Seeing Eye puppy-raising family, and finally to Pete. Mom said we had to be patient.

"Remember how Marit loved you, Leslie? When you were little, she let you stand on her back to see out the window. Ursula will be just as nuts about you. Love is the whole reason this dog guide business works."

So I tried to be patient and watched Mom work hard. First she showed one route in our neighborhood to Ursula and walked it over and over. Then she taught her a new route, repeated that, and reviewed the old one. Every day she took Ursula on two trips, walking two or three miles. She fed her, groomed her, gave her obedience training. Twice a week Mom cleaned Ursula's ears and brushed her teeth.

"I'm as busy as I was when you and Joel were little!" she said.

Mom and Ursula played for forty-five minutes each day. Joel, Dad, and I were only allowed to watch. Ursula needed to form her biggest attachment to Mom.

Mom made Ursula her shadow. When she showered or slept, Ursula was right there.

Still, Ursula didn't eat well—only half the amount she'd been eating at Seeing Eye. And she tested Mom, pulling her into branches, stepping off curbs. Once she tried to take a shortcut home. Another time, because she was nervous, she crossed a new street diagonally.

Crossing streets is tricky. Ursula doesn't know when the light is green. Mom knows. If she hears the cars moving beside her in the direction in which she's walking, the light is green. If they're moving right and left in front of her, it's red.

I worried about Ursula's mistakes, but Mom said they were normal. She kept in touch with her classmates and knew that their dog guides were goofing, too. One kept eating grass, grazing like a cow. Another chased squirrels, pigeons, and cats. Still another always stopped in the middle of the street, ten feet from the curb.

Once in a while her friends got lost, just like Mom, and had to ask for help.

Mom said it takes four to six months for the dogs to settle down. But no matter how long she and Ursula are teamed up together, Ursula will need some correcting. For instance, Ursula might act so cute that a passerby will reach out to pet her. Then Mom will have to scold Ursula and ask the person not to pet a dog guide. If people give Ursula attention while she's working, she forgets to do her job.

After a month at home, Ursula emptied her food bowl every time. She knew all the routes, and Mom could zip around as easily as she had with Marit.

"Now it's time to start the loneliness training," Mom said. She left Ursula alone in the house, at first for a short time while she went jogging with Dad. Ursula will never be able to take Mom jogging because she can't guide at high speeds.

Each week Mom increased the amount of time Ursula was alone. I felt sorry for our pooch, but she did well: no barking, no chewing on furniture.

Then Mom said Joel and I could introduce Ursula to our friends, one at a time. They could pet her when she was out of harness.

Every morning Ursula woke Joel and me. Every night she sneaked into my bed for a snooze.

Finally Mom allowed Joel and me to play with Ursula, and I knew: shrimpy little Ursula had fallen for us, and we were even crazier about her.

But we haven't forgotten Marit. Joel says that Ursula is the best dog alive. And I always say she's the best dog in this world.

ABOUT THE AUTHOR

Sally Hobart Alexander had a wonderful childhood growing up in the Pennsylvania countryside. As a girl, she liked to write and tell stories. In her twenties, she contracted a rare disease, which caused her to lose her eyesight. She completed a training program for the blind, then earned a degree in social work, and married. Today, she and her husband have two grown children, a son and a daughter. Mrs. Alexander's goal is to live an ordinary life despite her disability. "I write about disabled people trying to do the same thing," she says.

Studying the Selection

QUICK REVIEW

1. Who is Mom's best friend?

2. Why does Leslie's Mom need a dog guide?

3. Why was Leslie so worried about Mom getting a new dog guide?

4. List at least three types of behavior that are included in training a dog at The Seeing Eye.

FOCUS

5. Leslie was very concerned about the new dog at the beginning of the story. How did she feel about Marit and Ursula at the end of the story?

6. Explain why the two main settings in this story are both very important to Mom.

CREATING AND WRITING

7. Write about someone you know who doesn't give up despite a disability or some other challenge.

8. We know what Leslie thought about Ursula. Now, tell us what Ursula thought about Leslie, her Mom, and the whole business of being trained as a dog guide! Write a paragraph—it may be humorous or serious—in which Ursula describes her feelings.

9. Mom's hearing is exceptional. She pays attention to sounds that we take for granted. At home, sit quietly for five minutes with your eyes closed and listen carefully to all the sounds that surround you. You will notice things you may not have noticed before. You may hear the sound of your mother's shoes, the squeak of a floorboard, the grating of the cabinet door that needs to be oiled, or the ticking of a clock. Write a list of six to eight sounds that you hear now, that you ordinarily don't notice at all.

Lesson in Literature ...

When my teacher invited an ornithologist to talk to our class about birds, I wasn't excited at all. Birds? I thought. I don't care about birds. Why do I need to learn about birds?

The next day I wasn't paying attention when he stood in front of the class, but I looked up when he made a loud noise like a high-pitched bugle call. "That," he said, "is the call of the Puerto Rican parrot."

The ornithologist switched off the classroom lights and said, "Let's look at the first slide." There on the slide was a small, funny-looking green bird with a red forehead and white around its eyes. "The Puerto Rican parrot," the ornithologist said, "is an endangered species. Only thirty-five of these birds are alive in the world today."

That's when I sat up. Only thirty-five of them are alive in the world today? I felt my hand rising. "Why?" I asked.

"Good question," the ornithologist said. "When I started my work, the Puerto Rican parrot was nearly extinct." He explained that he and other ornithologists helped to save these parrots by studying their habitat, raising some of them in captivity, and later releasing them into new habitats in the wild.

I wasn't excited about birds before, but now I was. Finding out about the Puerto Rican parrot interested me.

I was excited about birds until the ornithologist showed the next slide.

"Here's the next slide," he said. I couldn't believe it. On the slide was the ugliest bird I had ever seen. It was very large and very black and had a long, hooked beak and an ugly red bald head. I couldn't stop looking at it.

The ornithologist told us that the California condor was almost extinct. I wondered why anyone wanted to save such an ugly bird. The California condor looked ugly and mean. He switched to a slide of two climbers on the side of a mountain. One of the climbers was the ornithologist!

The next slide was of four big black birds flying high in the sky. "When I took this picture," he said, "those four condors were half of the entire population of California condors."

FOR THE BIRDS

THINK ABOUT IT!

1. What change takes place in the student's attitude by the time the story has finished?

2. What, in your opinion, would the author like to change in your attitude to birds?

3. In your opinion, what does the ornithologist mean when he says, "we too can make a difference"?

The next slide showed a steep perch where he found a condor's nest. The next slide was a close-up of a full-sized condor. While he talked about the condor's egg, I looked closely at the bird. It did look ugly and mean at first, but the more I looked at it, the more I saw it wasn't ugly or mean at all.

When he finished his talk about birds, the ornithologist told us that we too can make a difference in the world. I decided I wanted to find out more about the colorful parrot and even the ugly condor. These and all endangered birds needed more people to know about them. I wondered if I could do anything to help.

Blueprint for Reading

INTO . . . *The Tiger, the Persimmon and the Rabbit's Tail*

What are you afraid of? Snakes? Spiders? Being laughed at? Everyone is afraid of something. The question is: How do we handle our fears? The worst thing people can do is to allow their imaginations to run wild. Then their fears grow and grow until, what once frightened them, now terrifies them. The best solution to being afraid is to look directly at the thing you fear, and then face it, find out more about it, and make a plan to deal with it.

In the funny story that follows, the once brave tiger grows more and more frightened. Why? Can you explain why the tiger was so frightened? What could he have done differently?

EYES ON *Theme*

Every story has a theme. The **theme** is the main idea of the story. Sometimes the theme is very clear and obvious. The author might even start the story by telling the reader what the main idea is. Other times, the author hides the theme and makes the reader work at figuring out what the story's message, or theme, is. *The Tiger, the Persimmon and the Rabbit's Tail* is a story whose theme is hidden below the surface. You will have fun reading this humorous tale. When you have read and enjoyed it, ask yourself: Is there a serious message underneath the light words? What is the story's theme?

The Tiger, the Persimmon and the Rabbit's Tail

RETOLD BY
SUZANNE CROWDER HAN

A long, long time ago, a
huge tiger lived deep in the
mountains. His roar was so loud
that all the other animals would hide when
they heard him coming. He was so confident of
himself that as he roamed through the forest he would
roar out a challenge for any creature to match his strength.

Then one cold winter day, hunger forced him to leave the snow-covered forest in search of food. Stealthily he crept into the yard of a house at the edge of a village and looked around.

He saw a large fat ox in a stall near the gate. The sleeping animal made his mouth water. He crept closer to the stall. Then, just as he was ready to pounce, he heard a baby crying.

"Human babies certainly have an odd way of crying," said the tiger and, being very curious, he crept closer to the house. "He's really loud. How can his mother stand the noise?" he wondered.

"Stop crying! Do you want the tiger to get you?" shouted the mother.

"How did that woman know I was here?" the tiger asked himself and he crept closer to the house.

"Hush! If you don't stop crying, the tiger will get you," said the mother.

But the baby cried even louder, which angered the proud tiger. "That baby isn't afraid of me? I'll show him!" said the tiger, creeping closer to the room.

WORD BANK

stealthily (STELL thih lee) *adv.*: softly and secretly

"Oh! Here's a dried persimmon!" said the mother and the baby stopped crying at once.

"What in the world is a dried persimmon? That bratty baby stopped crying immediately. A dried persimmon must be really scary and strong. Even stronger than me," said the tiger and a chill ran up and down his spine. "I better forget the baby and go eat that ox before that dried persimmon gets me. I should have known better than to come to a house on a day like this. I surely don't want to run into that dried persimmon."

The tiger slinked into the stall and, since he was shaking all over, sat down to calm his nerves. At that moment, however, something touched his back and felt up and down his spine. "Oh, no!" he said to himself. "It's the dried persimmon. It's got me. I'm going to die for sure."

"What a nice, thick coat. And so soft," said the man who had sneaked into the stall to steal the ox. "I'll get a lot of money for this calf!" The thief put a rope around the tiger's neck and led him out of the stall.

WORD BANK

persimmon (pur SIH mun) *n.*: a large, plumlike orange fruit that is sweet when very ripe

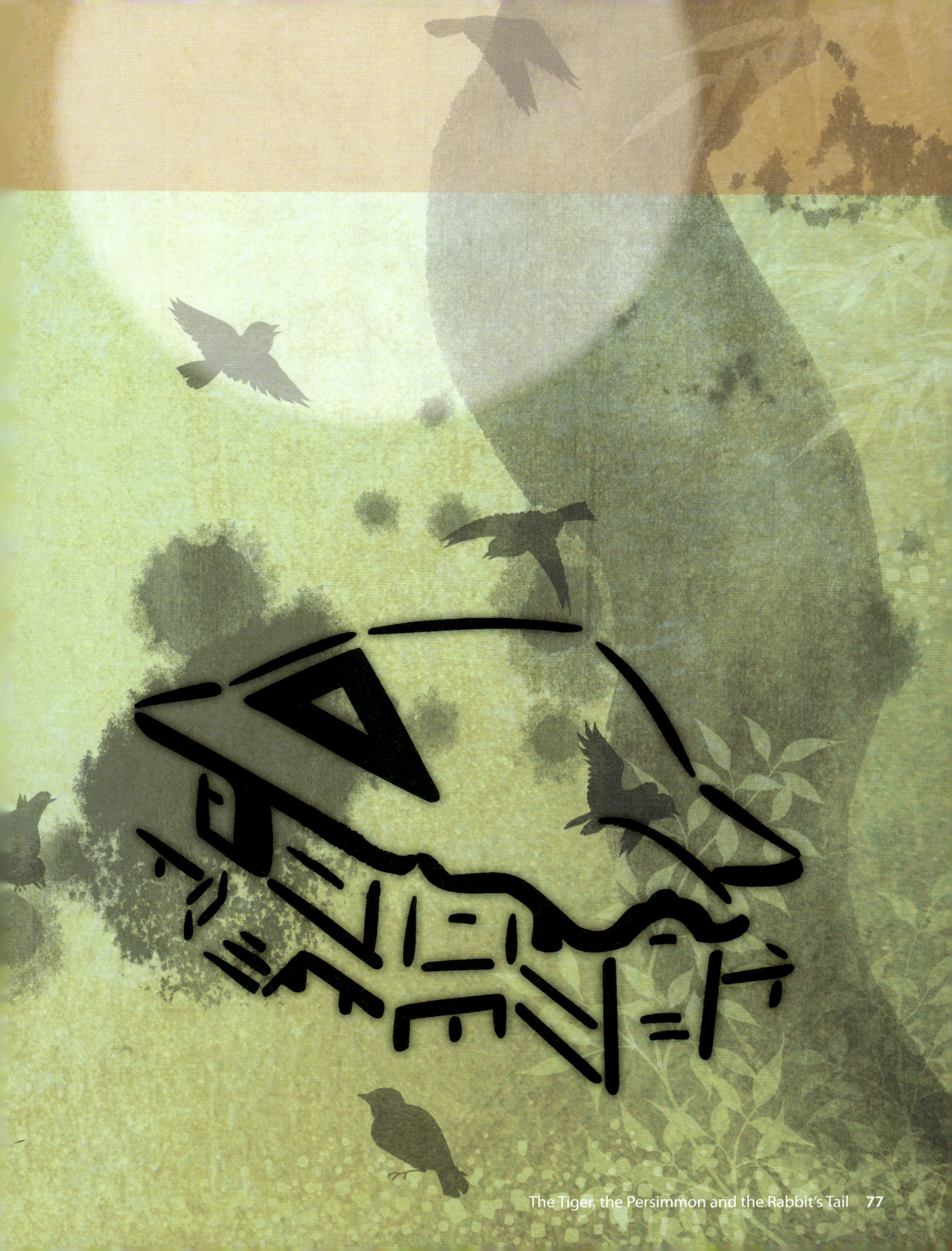

"Oh my. What can I do? This is without a doubt that dried persimmon," moaned the tiger to himself. "Oh what can I do? I can't roar. I can't run. I can only follow it. Oh this is the end of me."

The thief was very happy to have in tow what he thought was a very fine calf that he could sell for a lot of money. Thinking he should get away from the area as fast as possible, he decided to ride the calf and thus jumped onto the tiger's back.

"That's strange," said the thief, "this doesn't feel like any calf I've been on before." He began to feel the tiger's body with his hands. "Oh my. This isn't a calf. It's a huge tiger," he cried. "What can I do? What can I do?"

The thief was so frightened to discover he was riding a tiger, he nearly fell off. "Oh, I have to hold on," he said, grasping the tiger tighter. "If I fall off, that will be the end of me for sure. He'll gobble

me up before I even hit the ground," he said, squeezing the tiger with his legs. "Just calm down," he told himself, "and try to think of how to get away."

"I'm going to die. I'm going to die," moaned the tiger as the thief tightened his hold on him. "What rotten luck to die at the hands of a dried persimmon! I must try to get him off my back. That's the only thing I can do," he said and he began to shake his body. Then he tried jumping and bucking. Over and over he shook and jumped and bucked as he ran but the thief held on tight.

After a while they came to a grove of trees. When the tiger ran under a large one, the thief grabbed hold of a branch, letting the tiger run out from under him, and quickly climbed through a hole in the tree trunk and hid inside.

The tiger knew immediately that the dried persimmon was off his back but he didn't even think about trying to eat it. He just kept running as fast as he could deeper into the mountain. Finally he stopped and let out a sigh of relief. "Oh, I can't believe I'm alive. I just knew that dried persimmon was going to kill me." He was so happy to be alive, he rolled over and over on the ground, smiling all the while.

"Oh Mr. Tiger," called a rabbit who had been awakened by the tiger rolling around on the ground, "why are you so happy? How can you be so happy in the middle of the night?"

"I almost died today," replied the tiger, "so I'm happy to be alive."

"What's that?" asked the rabbit, hopping closer to the tiger. "You almost died?"

"That's right," explained the tiger. "A horrible dried persimmon caught me. I've just this moment escaped from it."

"What in the world is a dried persimmon?" asked the rabbit.

"You fool! You don't know what a dried persimmon is?" laughed the tiger. "Why it is the scariest, strongest thing in the world. Just thinking about it gives me chills."

"Well what in the world does it look like?" asked the rabbit.

"I don't know," said the tiger, "I was so scared I really didn't get a good look at it."

"Well where is it now?" asked the rabbit.

"I think it must be up in a tree," said the tiger.

"Where is the tree?" asked the rabbit. "I think I'll go have a look at that dried persimmon."

"What? Are you crazy? As weak as you are, it will devour you right away," said the tiger.

"If it looks like it is going to grab me, I'll run away. After all, there's no one faster than me," laughed the rabbit.

WORD BANK

devour (dih VOW ehr) *v.*: to swallow hungrily

The tiger told the rabbit the directions to the tree. "I'm warning you," he said as the rabbit hopped away, "that dried persimmon is a scary, horrible thing. Be careful."

At last the rabbit came to the tree. He looked all around the tree and up in the branches but he did not see any thing that looked scary. He looked again. Then he looked in the hole in the trunk and saw a man who was pale and shaking all over.

The rabbit laughed all the way back to where the tiger was waiting. He explained what he found, but the tiger wouldn't believe him.

"I'll go back to the tree and prevent him from leaving and you come see for yourself," said the rabbit and he left.

The rabbit went back to the tree and stuck his rump in the hole in the tree trunk to wait for the tiger to come.

"Come on, Tiger," called the rabbit when he saw the tiger slowly approaching. "There's nothing to worry about. I have the hole plugged up."

When he heard this, the thief decided he must do something to keep the tiger from coming in the hole. He took some strong string from his pocket and tied it to the rabbit's tail. Then he pulled it hard to keep the rabbit from running away.

The rabbit shrieked because of the pain and the tiger took off running. "See I told you not to mess with that dried persimmon. Now the horrible thing has you," yelled the tiger.

The rabbit struggled with all his strength to get away. The harder he tried to run, the harder the thief pulled on the string. The rabbit finally got away but not with his tail—that was left dangling from the thief's string.

ABOUT THE AUTHOR

As a girl growing up in South Carolina, **Suzanne Crowder Han** loved to read biographies and animal stories. Upon graduating from college, Suzanne joined the Peace Corps. She was sent to Korea in 1977, where she worked as a health care volunteer. When her two years in the Peace Corps were over, she decided to stay in Korea. There, she married, and worked as a writer and editor. The author's first book, a collection of Korean folktales, was followed by many more children's books. Suzanne tests her books on her daughter, Minsu, who, like children around the world, enjoys her mother's stories.

Here She Is

Mary Britton Miller

Jungle necklaces are hung
Around her tiger throat
And on her tiger arms are slung
Bracelets black and brown;
5   She shows off when she lies down
All her tiger strength and grace,
You can see her tiger blaze
In her tiger eyes, her tiger face.

Studying the Selection

What if the tiger had known what a dried persimmon really is? Would the story be very different?

QUICK REVIEW

1. What caused the tiger to lose confidence and become frightened?

2. Did the tiger know what a dried persimmon looked like?

3. What was the thief thinking after he stole the animal? What was the tiger thinking?

4. What happened to the rabbit at the end of the story?

FOCUS

5. Do you think that the tiger and the rabbit were good friends? What about after the persimmon incident?

6. What, in your opinion, is the story's message?

CREATING AND WRITING

7. Who do you think was more frightened, the tiger or the man? Explain your answer.

8. Choose two animals other than a tiger and a rabbit. Write a story involving these animals and something they are afraid of. You may add a line to give the moral or message of the story.

9. What did the scary dried persimmon look like? Draw a picture of what you think the tiger imagined.

ACTIVITY ONE

Don't Forget Your Jacket!

1. Every book has a jacket, or book cover. Your job is to create a jacket for one of the stories you've read in Unit One. Choose one of the following stories to use for your project: *Leah's Pony*, *Supergrandpa*, *Mom's Best Friend*, *Two Big Bears*, or *The Tiger, the Persimmon and the Rabbit's Tail*.

2. Your teacher will distribute paper and explain how to fold it in order to make a book jacket.

3. Draw an interesting front cover for your story. Include a picture that is important to the story. The title and author should be written on this side as well.

4. The *spine* of the book is the thin side that one sees when the book is upright on the shelf. The title and author are printed there.

5. Have you ever stopped to read the back of a book jacket? If you have, you know that two things are usually put there. The first is a paragraph that summarizes the story without revealing the end of the book. The publishers don't want to ruin the excitement for the reader! For the back of your book jacket, write a summary of the story in about five sentences.

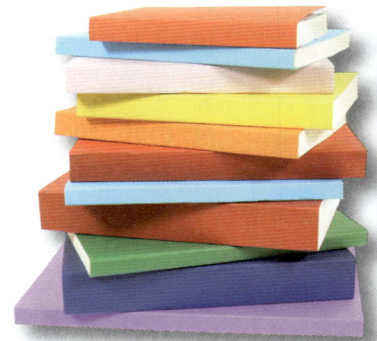

Leah's Pony

Two Big Bears

Supergrandpa

Mom's Best Friend

The Tiger, the Persimmon and the Rabbit's Tail

6. Below the summary found on the back of many books, the publishers often place one or two short *reviews* of the book. A review is comments about the book. Your second job is to write a brief review of the story. Include your opinion of the story along with the reason you have that opinion. You may include an example from the story to support your opinion.

7. Display your projects in a classroom 'library' for all to see.

ACTIVITY TWO

Ladies And Gentlemen.....

1. You have been chosen to present an award to one of the characters in this unit.

2. Think about the different lessons or themes found in each story. Then, think about positive character traits that are described in each story. Making a list or chart may help you organize the information.

3. Choose one character that you believe deserves an award for a positive act and can serve as a role model for others.

4. Write a speech that explains the purpose of the award and why this character deserves to win it. Do not write your explanation in one sentence. Saying that a character is devoted or honest is not enough. Be sure to support your decision with information from the story, and give your award a title!

5. After writing the first draft of your speech, look it over and make any corrections that are necessary. Then practice it aloud, either in front of a family member or the mirror, to prepare for the classroom presentation.

ACTIVITY THREE
Animal Talk

1. Your teacher will divide students into groups of three or four.

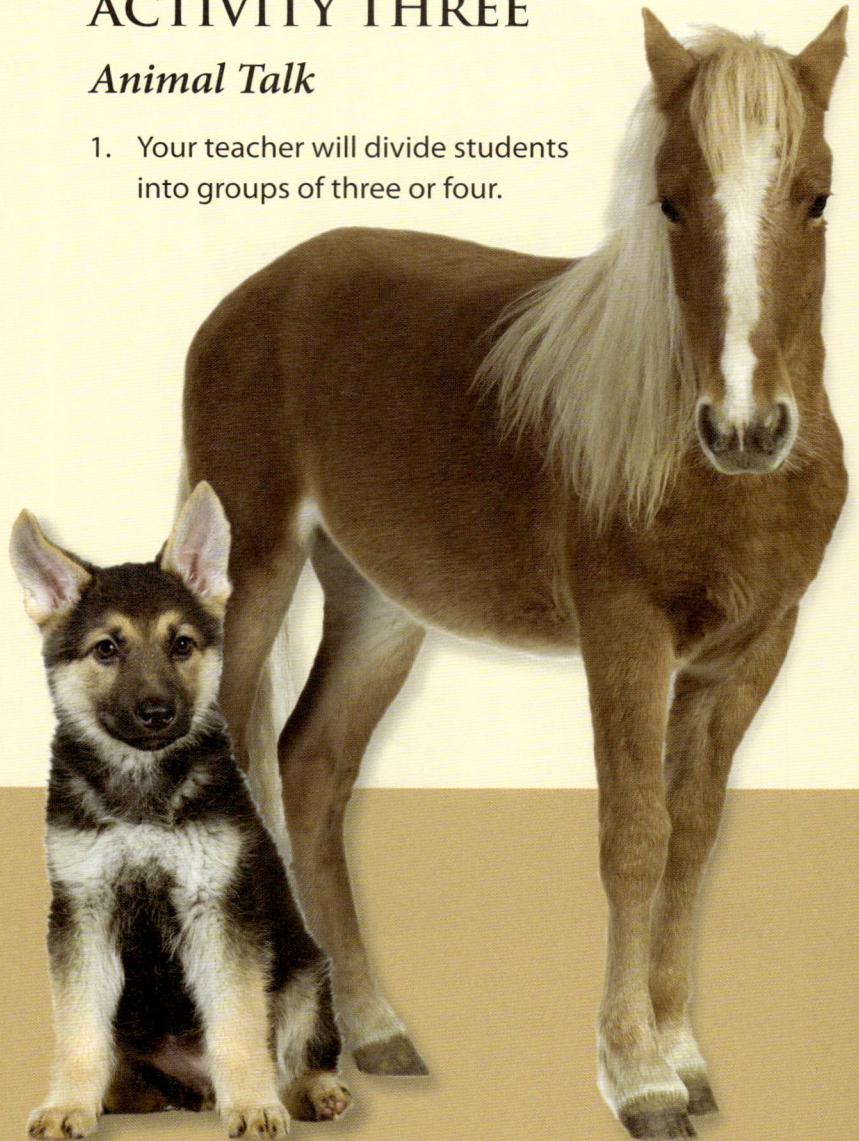

2. Each member of your group should pick an animal character from one of the stories in Unit One *(Leah's pony, Marit, Ursula, Sukey, Ma's bear, Pa's bear, the tiger, the rabbit)*. Each person will act the part of one animal.

3. Imagine that all these animals met. Assume that they are all familiar with all of the stories. What would they say to one another? Would they have some good advice for each other? Would they laugh at or make fun of one another? Would they defend something they had done in the story to the others?

4. Write down the dialogue that would take place and then share it with your class. Be sure to make it interesting and creative.

ACTIVITY FOUR
We All Make Mistakes

1. Many characters in Unit One took risks or made mistakes. To take a risk is to take a chance with the possibility of causing damage to oneself or to others. For example, Leah took a risk by selling her pony and bidding for the tractor. She wasn't sure if her plan would work or if her parents would approve of it. The tiger made several mistakes, while the rabbit took a risk.

2. Think about a time that you took a risk or made a mistake. Write about what happened and what you learned from the experience.

unit 2

clarity

Lesson in Literature

WHAT IS INTERNAL CONFLICT?

- **Internal** means inside. **Conflict** means struggle, or battle.
- An **internal conflict** is a *struggle* that takes place inside a person's mind.

- A story about internal conflict is about someone who must make a choice.
- The choice will usually be between two moral values, such as right and wrong, truth and falsehood, or kindness and cruelty.

THINK ABOUT IT!

1. In the middle of the story, Cynthia asks herself, "Why had she ever thought it was okay to pluck flowers from Mrs. Hudson's garden?" Can you answer this question?

2. What helped Cynthia see that it was wrong to take flowers from Mrs. Hudson's garden?

3. What extra step did Cynthia take to make up for what she had done wrong?

THE FLOWER GARDEN

Cynthia loved flowers. Whenever she walked to the playground, she admired a neighbor's beautiful flower garden of white tulips and yellow daffodils. She liked to stop and smell the flowers, even touch their delicate petals. One day, though, she stopped, looked over both shoulders, and plucked a tulip for herself.

When she met her friends at the playground, they all said something nice to her about her flower. "It is so beautiful," her friend Katie said.

"I love it!" her friend Rachel said.

The next day Cynthia plucked another flower, a bright daffodil and the next day, another. After a few days she told her friends about the flower garden. "It's not far," she said. "There are flowers for all of us."

It was a warm afternoon in early summer when Cynthia and her friends circled around the garden, choosing flowers for themselves. "This one?" Cynthia asked as she plucked tulips and daffodils for her friends.

All the girls were smiling at their flowers when Cynthia saw a car pull into the driveway of the house beside the garden and an old woman in a kerchief open the car's trunk and remove gardening tools. Cynthia was sure the woman didn't see the three girls with flowers in their hands circled around her garden.

"Let's go," Cynthia said quietly. All that afternoon, at the playground and later up in her room at home, she thought about the woman in the kerchief. Her mother once told her that the woman who owned that house, a Mrs. Hudson, kept to herself and lived all alone because her husband died years ago and her grown children lived far away. That night Cynthia thought to herself, Why had she ever thought it was okay to pluck flowers from Mrs. Hudson's garden?

The next day, on her way to the playground, Cynthia walked around Mrs. Hudson's house, not past her garden, and she didn't have a flower to show off to her friends. She did the same thing the next day and the next day. "We miss your flowers," her friend Rachel said.

Cynthia knew she had been wrong to pluck even one flower from someone else's garden. Even though it was beautiful, it belonged to someone. The flower garden on the way to the playground was hers only to admire. But Cynthia still felt bad, because not plucking any more flowers from Mrs. Hudson's garden just wasn't enough. What else could she do?

It was a sunny morning in July when Cynthia, in a kerchief and garden gloves, knocked on Mrs. Hudson's front door. "I'm Cynthia. Do you need some help in your garden, Mrs. Hudson?" she asked.

"I sure do. That garden's been giving me some trouble," Mrs. Hudson replied, with a twinkle in her eye.

"I think I know what you mean," Cynthia said, a shy smile inching across her face.

Blueprint for Reading

INTO . . . *Sato and the Elephants*

We all make mistakes. Some, like dialing a wrong number or making errors in addition, are easy to recognize and correct. Others, such as embarrassing someone or blurting out a secret, are more difficult to repair. We do not always realize at first that we have made a mistake. However, when the moment comes, we feel like a light bulb has gone on. We know what we have done wrong and often know what behavior we must change. Will we have the strength and courage to make the change? As you read *Sato and the Elephants*, see if you can find the moment that Sato understood his mistake. Does Sato change his behavior? Is Sato someone you could admire?

EYES ON *Internal Conflict*

Have you ever had difficulty deciding whether or not to tell a "little white lie"? Did you ever have trouble deciding whether or not to reveal something that was told to you as a secret? If so, you've had an internal conflict. A **conflict** is a struggle or an argument. An **internal conflict** is a struggle that takes place *internally*, within our own selves, when we are trying to make a decision. As you read the following story, see if you can identify Sato's internal conflict.

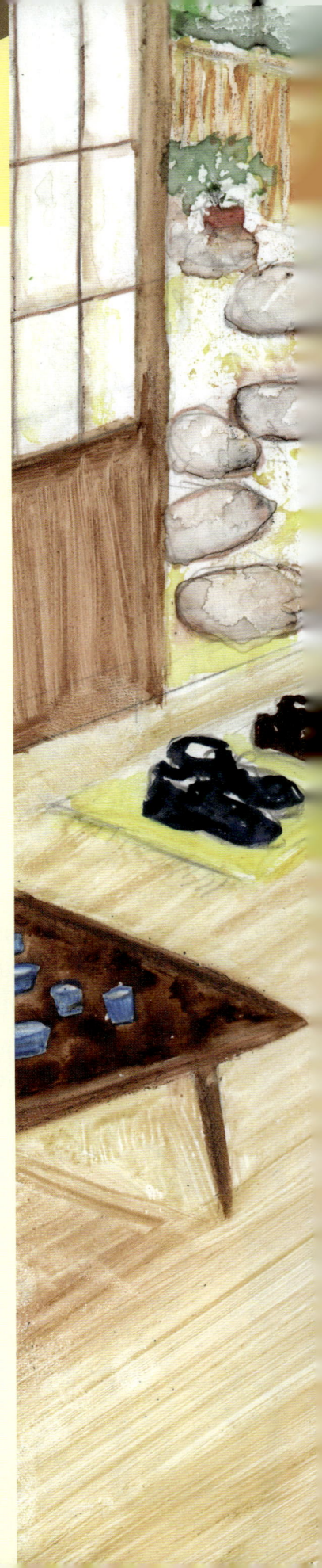

Sato and the Elephants

Juanita Havill

Sato[1] was a happy man. From morning to night he did what he wanted to do. He carved figures from creamy white pieces of ivory. Rabbits and monkeys. Turtles and fish. Dragons with smooth, delicate scales, and birds that looked as if they would fly right out of his hands.

As a boy, Sato had watched his father work. A master carver of netsuke[2] and okimono,[3] he was famous for the

---

1. The name *Sato* (SAH toh) means *to come to understand.* As the story progresses, you will see why the author named this character Sato.
2. A *netsuke* (net SOO kee) is a miniature carving attached to the end of a cord hanging from a pouch.
3. An *okimono* (oh kee MOH noh) is an ornament.

beauty and precision of his ivory figures. One day he carved a netsuke and gave the figure to Sato. Sato was so pleased that he hung the figure on a cord and wore it always around his neck. Whenever he touched the smooth, polished figure, he told his father, "Someday I will be a great ivory carver like you."

Sato learned much from his father about the secrets of ivory. He learned that the best ivory was hard and dense and fine-grained. He learned how to saw and file the ivory, and to shave and pare it with knives. He learned how to sand, then polish a figure until it shone.

But he was young when his father died. It would take many more years of hard work before Sato could carve with his father's skill. Someday, he promised himself, he *would* be a master ivory carver.

Whenever Sato finished a carving, he took it to Akira, the dealer. Akira admired Sato's work and always sold the figures for a good price. With the money Sato was able to buy more ivory from Akira.

WORD BANK

precision (prih SIZH un) *n.*: being exact about every detail
dense (DENSS) *adj.*: thick and tightly packed together
pare (PAIR) *v.*: to cut off the outer layer

One Saturday after Akira paid him, Sato asked, "What piece do you have for me to carve?"

Akira shook his head. "I don't have anything today, Sato. Ivory is becoming harder to find. I guess there aren't as many elephants. Maybe next week."

Sato walked home slowly, sadly. He would have nothing to carve now. He thought about Akira's words. Then he thought about the elephants. Ivory came from their long tusks, he knew. But whenever he held and carved a piece, he couldn't believe it came from an elephant. Ivory was as hard and heavy as rock. As plentiful as rocks, too, Sato had always thought.

The next Saturday Sato went back to Akira's shop. Again there was no ivory on display. But the dealer, seeing Sato, pulled a parcel from a drawer, unwrapped it, and set it on the table.

"Oh," Sato gasped. It was a beautiful piece, the size of his two fists, and creamy as foam on the sea. His hands shook as he picked it up and felt its strength and firmness. From this ivory he hoped to carve a masterwork.

"This is the piece I have been waiting for!" he shouted.

The price was high. "It's very rare," said Akira.

"I will take it," Sato said, though he knew it would cost almost all of his savings.

When he got home, Sato sat on his mat before his workbench. He turned the block over and over in his hands, eager to shape and smooth it. What should he carve? This piece was too large to become a netsuke strung on a cord. He didn't want to waste any of it. He studied the ivory. It would speak to him. It would tell him what to carve.

For a long time Sato stared. Then suddenly a vision appeared to him, as clear as if magic had already carved the figure: a big head, wide ears, powerful legs.

Sato's heart thumped wildly. He closed his eyes and breathed deeply to control his excitement. He must plan and carve carefully.

First he made a small clay model of the figure he would carve. Then he began to pencil light marks on the ivory to guide his hands. But the image was so distinct that he soon dropped his pencil and picked up a small saw.

He cut away the edges and corners and chiseled a rough shape. With a knife he grated the ivory, making a rhythmic, scritching sound. Then he smoothed the ivory and began to carve again. From time to time, he lay down his knife to flex his hand. But when he turned back, the image still shone in the ivory like a beacon.

Sato forgot about everything but the figure. He ate only handfuls of rice, drank tepid green tea, and slept hardly at all. Week after week he worked, often past midnight, stopping only when he could no longer make his hands obey his mind.

Then late one night, his knife slipped and cut a thin streak across his finger.

"Ai!" Sato cried out.

WORD BANK

chiseled (TCHIH zuld) *v.*: carved with a *chisel*, a tool with a cutting edge designed to carve a hard material
beacon (BEE kun) *n.*: a light used as a warning signal
tepid (TEP id) *adj.*: lukewarm

Only a small cut, he thought. I'm tired. I should rest before I make some horrible mistake.

But as he got up, he noticed something dark within the ivory. What was it? Only a shadow, Sato was certain. But he sat back down to look more closely. The shadow remained. A flaw? In this perfect piece? Sato's body felt weak, his chest so heavy he could hardly breathe. How could he carve a masterwork from a flawed piece of ivory? Hope drained from his heart.

In shock Sato began to cut tiny chips from around the flaw. He had never before seen anything so strange. Why, the flaw wasn't even part of the ivory. It was something else. Hard. Corroded. Metallic.

Suddenly Sato realized what it was: a bullet. A cry filled his mind, eerie and strange, like the trumpeting of elephants mourning their dead. Elephants who had died so that Sato might have ivory to carve.

Sato set his tools down. He bent his head before the unfinished figure, covered his face with his hands, and wept.

After a while he began to carve again. As if in a trance, he carved all night. By morning he was covered with a fine, white dust. He wiped the figure with a soft cloth and cleaned and polished the "flaw." Then he set it on the low table beside his futon and lay down to rest. The figure glowed as if sunlight shone within it. It was just as he had imagined, except for one thing. A dark, shiny bullet was buried in its forehead like a jewel.

Exhausted, Sato gazed at the figure. Its white sides seemed to breathe, and with each breath the elephant grew. Its trunk swayed, and its huge ears spread like sails.

Sato rubbed his eyes. He raised himself on his elbow, then rose to his knees. The elephant towered above him. Slowly it bowed, and Sato understood that he was to climb onto its back. As the elephant stood, Sato felt his stomach lurch. He was afraid to look down.

"Where are you taking me?" he cried out.

The elephant trudged on in silence. Sato felt the wind in his face, first cool, then warm, then hot. The sun drummed down upon him.

Across the African savannah,[4] he saw a herd of elephants. The largest raised its trunk and trumpeted. The white elephant kneeled, and Sato slid off its back. Then it became small and hard, an ivory figure again. Sato picked it up and put it inside his shirt, next to his skin.

Sato walked toward the herd. As he drew near, the elephants parted, forming a clear path to their leader. Sato trembled, but he had no choice. He had to follow the path. How small and helpless he felt, and how ashamed and sorrowful!

When he looked up at last, he was staring at the giant elephant's tusks, as smooth and graceful as stony carvings. He looked into its small eyes. Then he reached inside his shirt for the ivory statue. He held it up for the elephant to see.

The elephant closed its eyes and nodded. Then it raised its front legs. Sato covered his face with his arms, terrified that the elephant would crush him.

---

4. A *savannah* is a large area of flat land near the tropics that has coarse grass and a few, scattered trees.

WORD BANK

trudged (TRUJD) *v.*: walked slowly and heavily

Instead, it backed away to join the others, who now encircled Sato. Their huge bodies swayed from side to side, and their trumpeting echoed as they marched around him, slowly at first, then faster and faster. Dust rose in clouds as their massive feet pounded the earth. Sato felt the ground shake, and he shuddered with fear.

When the dust settled, Sato awoke in his room. He lay on his futon, gripping the ivory elephant in his hands, thinking one thought. He could never become a master ivory carver.

The next day Sato bought new tools. Then he purchased an inexpensive piece of stone. Someday, perhaps, he would carve a masterwork from marble. But for now he had much to learn about the secrets of stone.

Sato never sold the ivory elephant. He kept it on the table by his futon so that he would see it each day when he awoke and each night before he went to sleep.

ABOUT THE AUTHOR

Juanita Havill grew up in Mount Carmel, Illinois. She has lived in France, Illinois, and Minnesota, and now lives in Arizona with her husband and children. As a girl, she would make up poems and recite them to her mother. Fearing she could not earn very much money writing poems, her mother encouraged her to be a teacher. She followed her mother's advice, but also continued to write. To date, she has published fifteen children's books, and teaches at the college level. For Ms. Havill, writing is a way of discovering what one really feels about the important things in life.

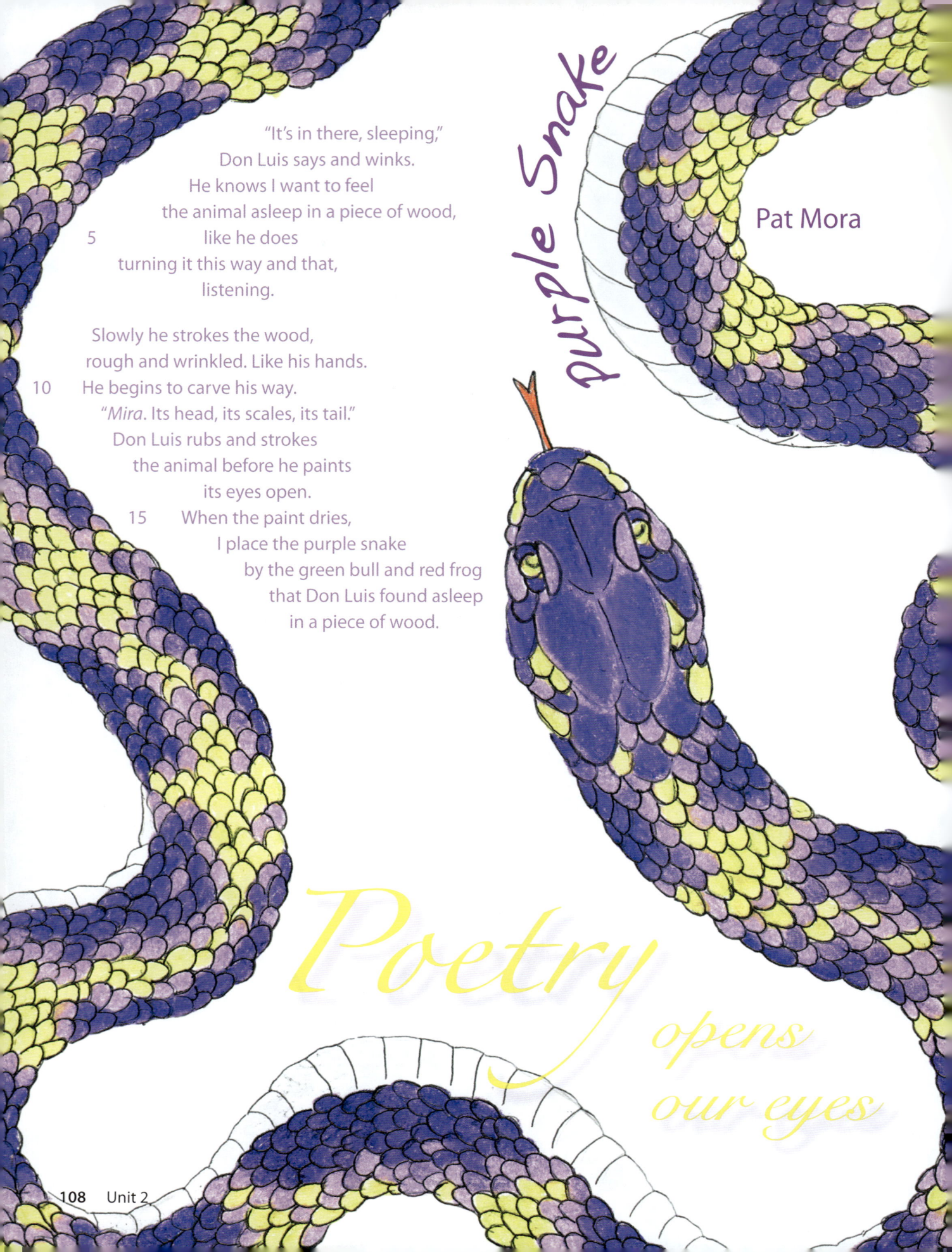

purple snake

Pat Mora

"It's in there, sleeping,"
Don Luis says and winks.
He knows I want to feel
the animal asleep in a piece of wood,
5   like he does
turning it this way and that,
listening.

Slowly he strokes the wood,
rough and wrinkled. Like his hands.
10   He begins to carve his way.
"*Mira*. Its head, its scales, its tail."
Don Luis rubs and strokes
the animal before he paints
its eyes open.
15   When the paint dries,
I place the purple snake
by the green bull and red frog
that Don Luis found asleep
in a piece of wood.

Poetry

opens

our eyes

Studying the Selection

QUICK REVIEW

1. What type of work did Sato do? Who did he learn the craft from?

2. What was Sato's dream at the beginning of the story?

3. What was Sato's reaction when Akira brought out a special piece of ivory for him?

4. What "flaw" did Sato find in his new piece of ivory?

FOCUS

5. Do you think Sato should have stopped carving ivory? Why or why not?

6. What was Sato's internal conflict?

CREATING AND WRITING

7. Why did Sato decide to carve stone instead of ivory? Write a paragraph that answers this question.

8. Write about someone who had a dream and then made a change to make the dream come true.

9. Sato carved ivory and then stone. He made a clay figure before he began the actual carving. Use the clay that your teacher gives out to create an animal model.

Lesson in Literature...

WHAT IS EXTERNAL CONFLICT?

- **External** means outside. **Conflict** means struggle, or battle.

- An **external conflict** is a *struggle* with something *outside* of oneself.

- A story about external conflict tells of the struggle of a person or a group against something or someone.

- An external conflict is not always between right and wrong. It can be a struggle between two people or a person and a force of nature, like a blizzard or hurricane.

Marcy loved her house and her neighborhood. She loved her cozy bedroom and the big fireplace in the living room. She loved the backyard and the swing beneath the oak tree. She loved her friends, and she loved Mrs. Watson, the kind old lady who lived next door. So when her father told her they had to move to an apartment, Marcy was upset. She went upstairs and peered out her bedroom window at the lonely swing swaying in the wind. She went outside and sat quietly in the grass under the big oak tree. She even went over to Mrs. Watson's house.

"We have to move!" she complained.

"I know," Mrs. Watson said softly. "But you'll come and visit, won't you?"

"Of course, I will," Marcy said.

But after she moved away, Marcy missed her old house and neighborhood so much she didn't want to go back to visit. When she walked to the park, she took a different street. When she rode her bicycle, she went the other way. When she rode in the car with her parents, she asked, "Can't we go another way?"

"You can't just avoid the old house and the old neighborhood forever, Marcy," her father told her.

She didn't visit Mrs. Watson, either.

But a few weeks later, Marcy's mother brought her bad news. "Mrs. Watson's in the hospital," she explained. "She needs surgery, and she needs someone to collect her mail

NEIGHBORS

THINK ABOUT IT!

1. How did Marcy react to the move her family was forced to make?

2. What event caused Marcy to change her behavior?

3. What would you say is the difference between "a neighbor" and "a good neighbor"?

and water her plants while she's gone. I promised her you'd go over there tomorrow."

"I don't want to go," Marcy said.

Her mother's eyes softened. "I know you miss the old house," she said, "but Mrs. Watson needs your help."

The next morning a thick blanket of snow covered the ground. School was closed. Snowplows moved slowly up and down the streets. It took Marcy's father two hours to shovel out the driveway. Marcy's mother told her, "The snow's too deep. Mrs. Watson will understand if you don't go today."

"No," Marcy said. "I'll go."

"Here's the key," Marcy's mother said, smiling gently.

Bundled up, Marcy walked all the way from the apartment to her old street, her footprints the only trail in the deep snow. She almost turned back because of the cold, but when she made it to her old street, the houses looked so beautiful under the covering of fresh snow that she was suddenly glad she decided to help Mrs. Watson.

After unlocking the front door, she emptied the mailbox and watered the flowers and plants that seemed to be everywhere. She even shoveled the walkway up to Mrs. Watson's front door. Before she left, she discovered a handwritten note pinned to the back door. "Thank you, Marcy. You're such a good neighbor."

After that, Marcy went back every day while Mrs. Watson was in the hospital, because she finally realized what it means to be someone's neighbor.

Blueprint for Reading

INTO . . . *Amelia's Road*

Have you ever worked on one of those puzzles where you have to find the person or object that doesn't belong? In real life, no one wants to be the person who doesn't fit in. We all want to feel that we belong to some group. This group may be our family, our neighbors, our class, or our friends. No one wants to feel awkward or excluded. Pay close attention to how Amelia feels about belonging and how that changes by the end of the story.

EYES ON *External Conflict*

Every story has a conflict—that's what makes you want to find out what happens in the end! Conflict is a struggle between two forces. When the struggle takes place inside a person's mind, as it does in *Sato and the Elephants*, it is called **internal conflict**. When a struggle takes place between two forces that are not in a person's mind, but are part of the outside world, the struggle is called **external conflict**. A captain, struggling to keep his ship from sinking in a raging storm, is part of an external conflict; he and his ship are on one side of the conflict, the wind and water are on the other side. As you read *Amelia's Road*, think about the story's external conflict.

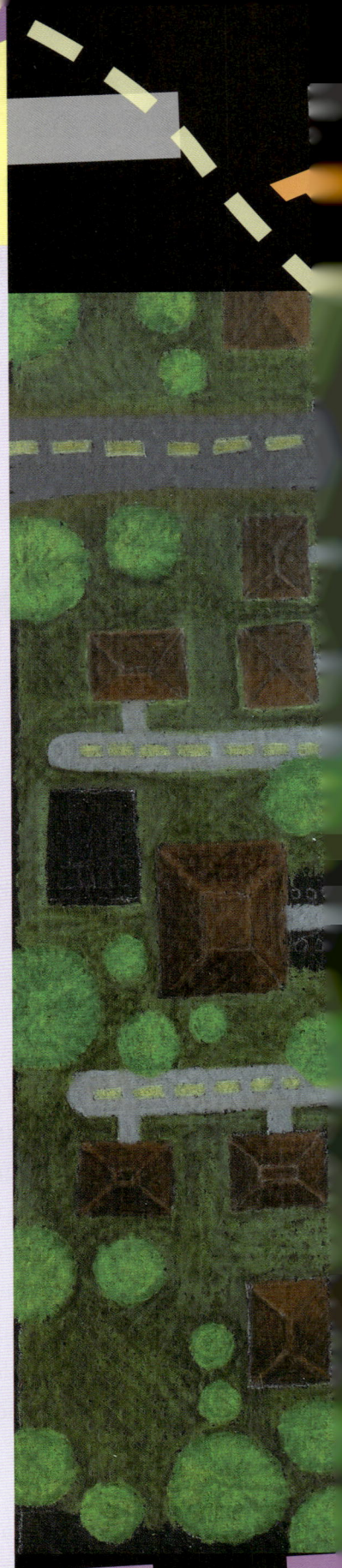

Amelia's Road

Linda Jacobs Altman

Amelia Luisa Martinez hated roads. Straight roads. Curved roads. Dirt roads. Paved roads. Roads leading to all manner of strange places, and roads leading to nowhere at all. Amelia hated roads so much that she cried every time her father took out the map.

The roads Amelia knew went to farms where workers labored in sunstruck fields and lived in grim, gray shanties. *Los caminos*, the roads, were long and cheerless. They never went where you wanted them to go.

Amelia wanted to go someplace where people didn't have to work so hard, or move around so much, or live in labor camps.

Her house would be white and tidy, with blue shutters at the windows and a fine old shade tree growing in the yard. She would live there forever and never worry about *los caminos* again.

WORD BANK

grim *adj.*: serious and unpleasant
shanties (SHAN teez) *n.*: cabins or houses that are roughly built and in a state of disrepair

It was almost dark when their rusty old car pulled to a stop in front of cabin number twelve at the labor camp.

"Is this the same cabin we had last year?" Amelia asked, but nobody remembered. It didn't seem to matter to the rest of the family.

It mattered a lot to Amelia. From one year to the next, there was nothing to show Amelia had lived here, gone to school in this town, and worked in these fields. Amelia wanted to settle down, to belong.

"Maybe someday," said her mother, but that wonderful someday never seemed to come.

"Mama," Amelia asked, "where was I born?"

Mrs. Martinez paused for a moment and smiled. "Where? Let me see. Must have been in Yuba City. Because I remember we were picking peaches at the time."

"That's right. Peaches," said Mr. Martinez, "which means you were born in June."

Amelia sighed. Other fathers remembered days and dates. Hers remembered crops. Mr. Martinez marked all the important occasions of life by the never-ending rhythms of harvest.

The next day, everybody got up at dawn. From five to almost eight in the morning, Amelia and her family picked apples. Even though she still felt sleepy, Amelia had to be extra careful so she wouldn't bruise the fruit.

By the time she had finished her morning's work, Amelia's hands stung and her shoulders ached. She grabbed an apple and hurried off to school.

Last year, Amelia spent six weeks at Fillmore Elementary School, and not even the teacher had bothered to learn her name.

This year, the teacher bothered. She welcomed all the new children to her classroom and gave them name tags to wear. She wore a name tag herself. It said MRS. RAMOS.

Later, Mrs. Ramos asked the class to draw their dearest wishes. "Share with us something that's really special to you."

Amelia knew exactly what that would be. She drew a pretty white house with a great big tree in the front yard. When Amelia finished, Mrs. Ramos showed her picture to the whole class. Then she pasted a bright red star on the top.

By the end of the day, everybody in class had learned Amelia's name. Finally, here was a place where she wanted to stay.

Amelia couldn't wait to tell her mother about this wonderful day. Feeling as bright as the sky, she decided to look for a shortcut back to camp. That's when she found it.

The accidental road.

Amelia called it the accidental road because it was narrow and rocky, more like a footpath that happened by accident than a road somebody built on purpose.

She followed it over a grassy meadow, through a clump of bushes, and down a gentle hill. There, where the accidental road ended, stood a most wondrous tree. It was old beyond knowing, and quite the sturdiest, most permanent thing Amelia had ever seen. When she closed her eyes, she could even picture it in front of her tidy white house.

Amelia danced for joy, her black hair flying as she twirled around and around the silent meadow.

Almost every day, when work and school were over, Amelia would sit beneath the tree and pretend she had come home.

More than anywhere in the world, she wanted to belong to this place and know that it belonged to her.

But the harvest was almost over, and Amelia didn't know what she'd do when the time came for leaving.

She asked everyone for advice—her sister Rosa, her parents, her brother Hector, her neighbors at camp, and Mrs. Ramos at school, but nobody could tell her what to do.

The answer, when it came, was nearly as accidental as the road.

Amelia found an old metal box that somebody had tossed into the trash. It was dented and rusty, but Amelia didn't care. That box was the answer to her problem.

She set to work at once, filling it with "Amelia-things." First she put in the hair ribbon her mother had made for her one holiday; next came the name tag Mrs. Ramos had given

her; then a photograph of her whole family taken at her last birthday; and after that the picture she'd drawn in class with the bright red star on it.

Finally, she took out a sheet of paper and drew a map of the accidental road, from the highway to the very old tree. In her best lettering, she wrote *Amelia Road* on the path. Then she folded the map and put it into her box.

When all the apples were finally picked, Amelia's family and the other workers had to get ready to move again. Amelia made one more trip down the accidental road, this time with her treasure box.

She dug a hole near the old tree, and gently placed the box inside and covered it over with dirt. Then she set a rock on top, so nobody would notice the freshly turned ground.

When Amelia finished, she took a step back and looked at the tree. Finally, here was a place where she belonged, a place where she could come back to.

"I'll be back," she whispered, and then she turned away.

Amelia skipped through the meadow, laughed at the sky, even turned cartwheels right in the middle of the accidental road.

When she got back to the camp, the rest of the family had already started packing the car. Amelia watched them for a moment, then took a deep breath and joined in to help.

For the first time in her life, she didn't cry when her father took out the road map.

ABOUT THE AUTHOR

Linda Jacobs Altman loves to write. A list of her publications is more than five pages long! Ms. Altman has written on a variety of subjects, including the Holocaust, Alzheimer's disease, and the California Gold Rush. She also writes under a variety of names. Linda Jacobs, Linda Jacobs Altman, and Claire Blackburn are all one and the same person! When an author writes under a name that is not his or her real name, the author is using a *pseudonym,* sometimes called "a pen name."

Poetry is about feelings

Since Hanna Moved Away

Judith Viorst

The tires on my bike are flat.
The sky is grouchy gray.
At least it sure feels like that
Since Hanna moved away.

5   Chocolate ice cream tastes like prunes.
December's come to stay.
They've taken back the Mays and Junes
Since Hanna moved away.

Flowers smell like halibut.
10 Velvet feels like hay.
Every handsome dog's a mutt
Since Hanna moved away.

Nothing's fun to laugh about.
Nothing's fun to play.
15 They call me, but I won't come out
Since Hanna moved away.

Studying the Selection

FIRST IMPRESSIONS

Do you think Amelia's accidental road and metal box will help her adjust to the next move?

QUICK REVIEW

1. Why did Amelia hate roads and maps?

2. What work did Amelia's family do that required they move from place to place?

3. How did Amelia's family mark and remember important dates?

4. What did Amelia do that made her feel as though she truly belonged in this place?

FOCUS

5. More than anything, Amelia wanted to feel like she belonged. Why is that feeling so important?

6. Amelia feels that Mrs. Ramos is different from other teachers she has had. What might have caused difficulties with other teachers?

CREATING AND WRITING

7. Where do you feel a real sense of belonging? Write a few paragraphs that answer this question.

8. Write about someone who, purely by chance, finds something that changes his or her life. Your story may be either true or fictional.

9. Amelia filled a box with "Amelia-things." Find a container that you like and fill it with items that are meaningful to *you*. You may create replicas of precious objects with craft materials, or make photocopies of documents or drawings instead of using the originals. Add a little note to each item explaining why you chose to include it.

Jill's Journal:

On Assignment in the Supermarket and the Field

So what is *your* favorite fruit? Apples? Strawberries? Blueberries? Watermelon? Bananas?

Maybe it depends upon the season. Apples are best in the fall. That is the time that apples become ripe and are picked. An apple in the autumn is more delicious than summer fruits like nectarines and raspberries.

Lots of us live in cities, where fruits and vegetables from other parts of the country, or even other countries, are sold at the supermarket during *any* season. Still, fruits and vegetables are tastiest when they are grown close to where we live, in the *right* season.

What's your favorite vegetable? Maybe you don't like vegetables. But what about a ripe, red, juicy tomato? Oh, wait a minute! I forgot that tomatoes are really fruits. But corn on the cob is delicious. That's sort of a vegetable, even though it is not green. Nothing is better than corn on the cob at the end of the summer, with butter and salt. Yummmm!

How did I start talking about fruits and vegetables? Well, I was walking down the aisles of the supermarket and came to the produce section. This is the section of a supermarket that sells fruits and vegetables.

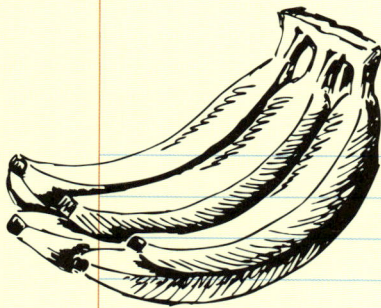

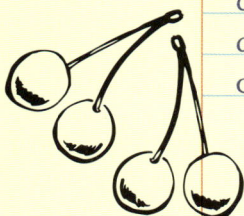

Okay. Where do these crops come from? We know that farmers and their families are supposed to plant the crops and harvest them. When we are little kids, lots of us see books about farms—at least farms the way they used to be a long time ago.

I decided then and there I wanted to go someplace where crops are being picked. I wanted to see who does it and what it is like.

Well, here I am in California and I am standing right now in a field where everyone is picking, picking, picking. It is only 4:00 A.M. I am yawning. How can anyone work at 4:00 A.M.? But even young people are out here working until they have to go to school.

The people who do it are trying to get ahead in life. So they work hard to save money for a house and maybe, one day, a farm of their own. The crops can't wait for the people. They have to be picked at the right time, no matter what the weather is. That is another reason why the people have to work such long hours. When the kids come home from school, they have to start working all over again. They give almost all the money they earn to their parents.

This is hard work! I have to keep stooping and my back hurts. All around me, people have to climb to get high up, then they climb down, then they climb up. And they carry such heavy loads. A ten-year-old girl named Iselda tells me I must wear gloves. Otherwise I could get sick, because the plants are treated with poisons to kill insects. She says she is allergic to the chemicals that are sprayed on tobacco and strawberries. Touching the leaves gives her a bad reaction.

"Actually," she says, "this is not a bad place. There are clean bathrooms and places to wash our hands. We don't have to go down to a brook to wash and to try to clean our clothes. There is pollution from the plants and soil in the water, and my Mama says we can't go near the water."

"Iselda, is there anything good about being a farmworker who moves from place to place?" Iselda thinks for a moment. "Well, I do like meeting lots of different people. I like seeing different places. And, I know one thing about myself: I can stick to a job and work hard. That makes me pretty grown up, doesn't it?" She leans her head close to me. "I will tell you a secret." She smiles a little smile. "I have always dreamed of becoming a teacher. Do you think I could?"

POWER SKILL:

What Is Fiction? What Is Nonfiction?

Fiction and nonfiction are words you will hear a lot in your literature or English classes. Maybe you know what these words mean already. But here goes:

Fiction   Fiction is a story or book in which the plot and the characters are created by the author. Short stories, novels, plays, and even some poetry are fiction. Fiction is not true, but it *seems* true because it makes sense. It may not have *actually* happened, but it *could* have happened.

Nonfiction   Nonfiction is an essay, an article, or a book in which the people and events that are described are actually real. The people are alive or have lived in the past. The events the author writes about have actually occurred. Nonfiction includes biographies, autobiographies, stories about historical events, newspaper articles, science and mathematics literature, and what we just call "true stories."

Amelia's Road is fiction, but migrant farmworkers are real. The story probably makes sense to you, because you are able to understand Amelia's feelings.

Exercise

Create a collage about migrant farmworkers. This must be real. In your collage you will include pictures of the many different crops that the farmworkers pick. Remember, every fruit and vegetable you eat may be picked by farmworkers. Also include pictures that show some of the difficult parts of the lives of farmworkers: They don't have enough money, they live in shacks when they are moving around, they don't get to stay in school long, they are always saying goodbye to friends. Add anything else you can think of.

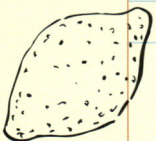

Lesson in Literature...
THE TREE HOUSE

WHAT IS SEQUENCE?

- **Sequence** means order. The numbers 1, 2, 3, 4, 5 are listed here in sequence. The numbers 3, 5, 1, 4, 2 are listed out of sequence.

- When the events of a story are given in sequence, the story is clear and easy to follow.

- When a story is disorganized and events are described out of order, the reader or listener will have difficulty following the story.

- Sequence is especially important in instructions, recipes, and eyewitness reporting.

THINK ABOUT IT!

1. Which is harder: making rules or enforcing them?

2. In your own words, explain what the purpose of most of the rules in Tommy's tree house was.

3. Put the following events in their proper sequence. Rewrite the following five events in their correct order.

   - Tommy asks his mother how she came up with the family rules.
   - Tommy thinks of many possible rules for his tree house.
   - Tommy announces there will be rules for his tree house.
   - Tommy makes a sign welcoming all to his tree house.
   - Tommy writes down the house rules.

After his father hammered the last nail into the wood frame of the tree house in the backyard, Tommy announced to his family, "There will be rules in my tree house."

"Rules?" His mother laughed. "What rules?"

"Rules that everyone has to follow," Tommy said proudly.

Tommy's mother smiled at her ten-year-old son. "We have rules in our house, Tommy. The trick is to get people to follow them. How will you do that?"

Tommy knew what his mother was talking about. He followed his parents' rules, most of them, anyway. He cleared the table after dinner. He did his homework at night. He brushed his teeth before bed. He took out the garbage at night. He made his bed—well, sometimes he made his bed and sometimes he didn't.

Sometimes he forgot.

"If someone around this house made his bed every morning…," his mother said.

"He tries," his father added.

"He could try harder," his mother said, "and he could put his clothes away in his drawers or in the hamper."

Suddenly, Tommy had an idea. "I'll write them down!"

"That's a wonderful idea!" his mother said.

That night Tommy wrote and wrote. He made a list of rules, but the list grew and grew. How many rules should he have? He wrote out twenty rules, but some rules sounded like other rules. Then he thought of exceptions to rules. After a while he wasn't sure which rules ought to be rules and which ought to be dropped. Who knew rules for a tree house could be so complicated? Were parents allowed in the tree house? Were friends and neighbors? Were eating and drinking allowed in the tree house? Was homework allowed in the tree house? Was anyone not allowed to enter? Should there be a rule for anyone who entered? A secret handshake? A special knock? What about cleaning up the tree house? What rules should he write down for that?

Finally, he went to his mother. "I'm stuck," he said. "How did you come up with the rules of our house?"

"Well," she said. She sat softly on the sofa and patted a spot beside her for him to sit. "Well," she said again. "We have rules so we can work together and get along as a family, Tommy. We have rules so we all take responsibility by taking care of ourselves and each other." She ran her fingers through his hair and smiled. "So that's why you have to make your bed in the morning."

The next morning Tommy was up early. He made his bed. At breakfast he handed his mother a sheet of paper. It read:

Tree House Rules

All are welcome in this tree house. The only rule of this tree house is to take good care of the tree house and anyone who is in the tree house.

"That's the best set of rules I ever read," Tommy's mother said.

Blueprint for Reading

INTO . . . *The Hatmaker's Sign*

It is usually free. People love to give it but don't want to receive it. It can be terribly confusing or very clear. It can be very good or extremely bad. Some people ask for it and then throw it away. What is it? *Advice!*

Have you ever worked long and hard at a job and been very satisfied with the results? Then, just as you were congratulating yourself on a job well done, along came the critics. "It needs a little more color"; "Maybe you should move that to the right"; "It's good, but you made it too small." If you were so polite that you followed every suggestion, what would happen is—well, read *The Hatmaker's Sign*, and you'll find out!

EYES ON *Sequence*

"Whip six egg whites. Remove cake from oven. Sift two cups of flour. Allow cake to cool. Add one teaspoon of vanilla. Set oven at 350°. Put the icing on. Mix two cups of sugar with the flour and baking powder." What's wrong with these instructions? It's obvious! *They are not in any order!* Without an order, instructions are impossible to follow.

Just as instructions must be given in order, a story's events must also have some **sequence**, or order. We usually tell a story in the order that the events happened. Sometimes, though, the story is told as a *flashback*, a memory of something that happened in the past. As you read *The Hatmaker's Sign,* notice the sequence of events and how the author organized the story.

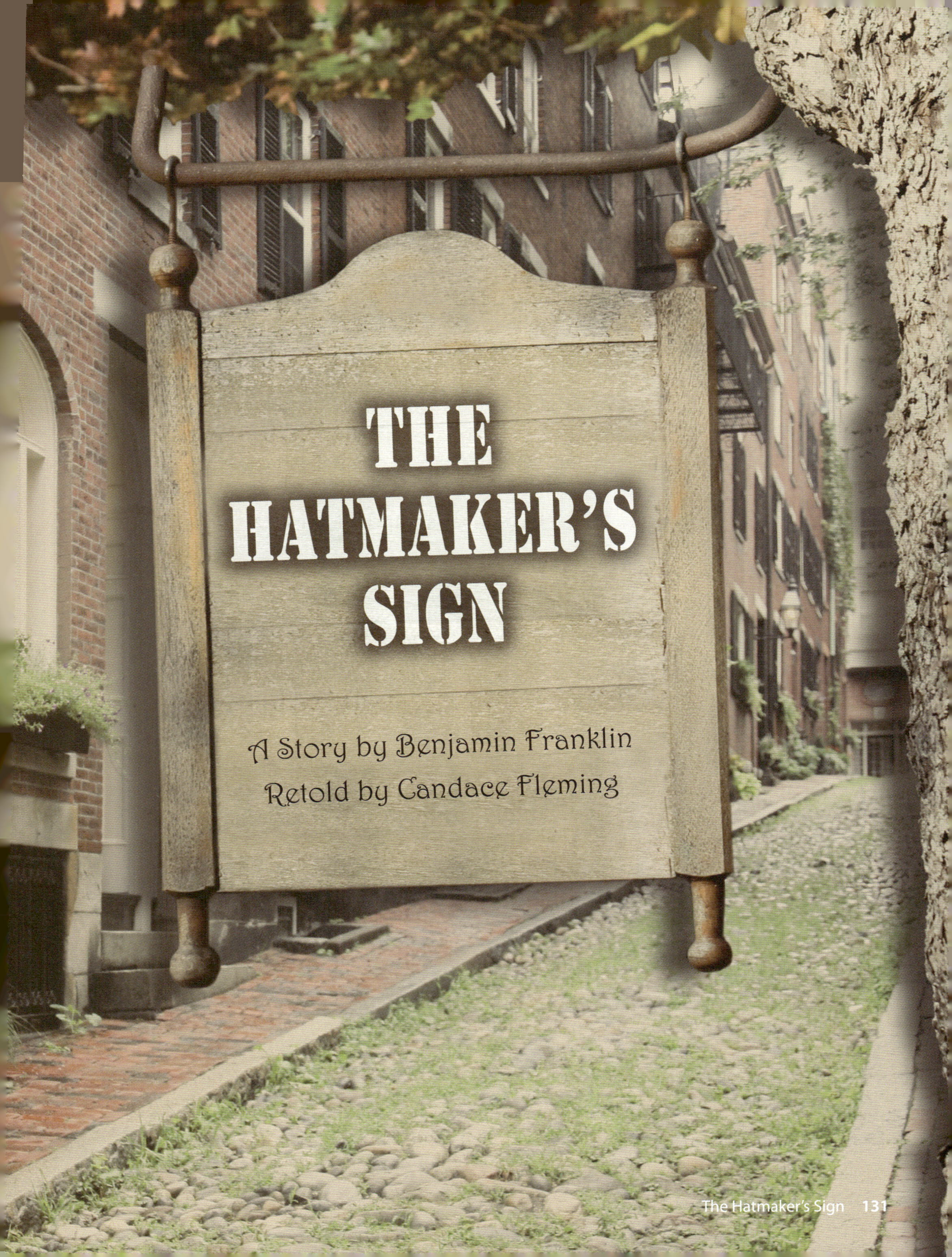

THE HATMAKER'S SIGN

A Story by Benjamin Franklin

Retold by Candace Fleming

At last!

After endless hours of scribbling and struggling, Thomas Jefferson had written it. And it was perfect. Every word rang. Every sentence sang. Every paragraph flowed with truth.

"It is exactly right," Jefferson exclaimed. "The Continental Congress[1] will surely love it."

But the next morning, after Jefferson's wonderful words had been read aloud, the Congress broke into a noisy debate.

"I do not like this word," quibbled one delegate. "Let's replace it."

"And this sentence," argued another. "I think we should cut it."

"What about this paragraph?" shouted still another. "It must be removed!"

While the Congress argued around him, Thomas Jefferson slumped into his chair. His face flushed red with anger and embarrassment.

"I thought my words were perfect just the way they were," he muttered to himself.

Just then he felt a consoling pat on his shoulder. He looked up and into the sympathetic eyes of Benjamin Franklin.

"Tom," Benjamin Franklin said, smiling, "this puts me in mind of a story."

WORD BANK

quibbled (KWIH buld) *v.*: argued about some small, unimportant detail
delegate (DELL uh gut) *n.*: one person sent by a group of people to represent them at a convention
sympathetic (SIM puh THET ik) *adj.*: understanding and supportive

1. The *Continental Congress* was a group of American leaders who met in 1774, 1775, and 1776 to declare independence from England and establish the United States of America.

In the city of Boston, on a cobblestoned street, a new hat shop was opening for business.

All stood ready. Comfortable chairs had been placed before polished mirrors. Wooden hatboxes were stacked against one wall. And the front window was filled with tricorns[2] and top hats, coonskins, and wool caps.

There was only one thing the hat shop did not have—a sign.

But the hatmaker, John Thompson, was working on it.

Knee-deep in used parchment and broken quill[3] pens, John struggled to create a sign for his shop. And at long last, he wrote one. It read:

JOHN THOMPSON, HATMAKER
FASHIONABLE HATS SOLD
INSIDE FOR READY MONEY

2. *Tricorns* (TRY kornz) are three-cornered hats that were fashionable in the days of the American Revolution.
3. Before fountain pens were invented, people wrote by dipping the feather, or *quill*, of a bird into ink, and writing.

WORD BANK

cobblestone (KOB ul stone) *n.*: a small, naturally rounded stone, used in paving roads
parchment (PARCH ment) *n.*: a stiff, heavy, ivory-colored paper made from the skins of sheep or goats

Beneath the words, John drew a picture of a hat.

"It is exactly right," John exclaimed. "Customers will surely love it."

But before hurrying to the sign maker's shop, where his words and picture would be painted onto board, John showed his parchment to his wife, Hannah.

"Oh John," Hannah giggled after reading what John had written. "Why bother with the words 'for ready money'? You're not going to sell hats for anything else, are you? Remove those words and your sign will be perfect."

"You're probably right," sighed John.

So John rewrote his sign. Now it read:

JOHN THOMPSON. HATMAKER. FASHIONABLE HATS SOLD INSIDE

Beneath the words he drew a picture of a hat.

Parchment in hand, John headed for the sign maker's shop.

He had gone as far as the Old North Church when he met Reverend Brimstone.

"Where are you strolling on such a fine morning?" asked the reverend.

"To the sign maker's shop," replied John. He held out his parchment.

Reverend Brimstone read it.

"May I make a suggestion?" he asked. "Why don't you take out the words 'John Thompson, Hatmaker'? After all, customers won't care who made the hats as long as they are good ones."

"You're probably right," sighed John.

And after tipping his tricorn to the reverend, John hurried back to his hat shop and rewrote his sign. Now it read:

FASHIONABLE HATS

SOLD

INSIDE

Beneath the words he drew a picture of a hat.

Parchment in hand, John headed for the sign maker's shop.

He had gone as far as Beacon Hill when Lady Manderly stepped from her carriage and into his path.

"What have you there?" asked the haughty lady. She plucked the parchment from John's hand and read it.

WORD BANK

haughty (HAW tee)
adj.: snobbish; arrogant

"Absurd!" she snorted. "Why bother with the word 'fashionable'? Do you intend to sell unfashionable hats?"

"Absolutely not!" cried John.

"Then strike that word out," replied Lady Manderly. "Without it, your sign will be perfect."

"You are probably right," sighed John.

And after bidding the lady farewell, John hurried back to his hat shop and rewrote his sign. Now it read:

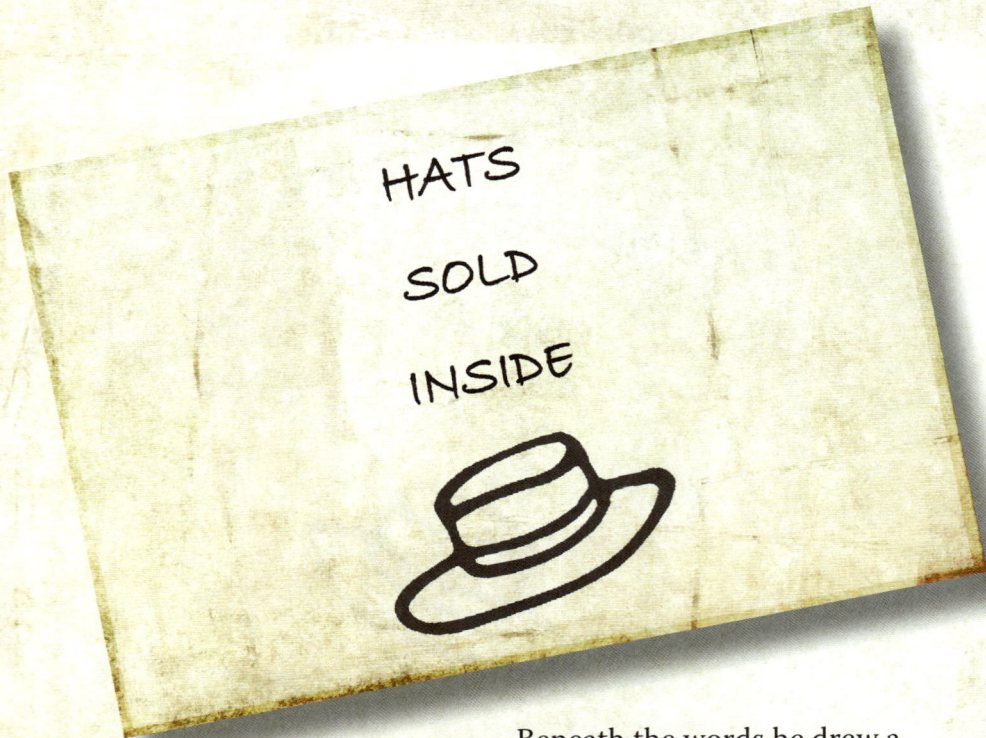

HATS

SOLD

INSIDE

Beneath the words he drew a picture of a hat.

Parchment in hand, John headed for the sign maker's shop.

He had gone as far as Boston Common when he met a British magistrate.

The magistrate, always on the lookout for unlawful behavior, eyed John's parchment.

Word Bank

absurd (ub ZURD)
adj.: ridiculous
magistrate (MADJ iss trayt)
n.: a government worker who enforces the law

"Hand it over or face the stockades!"[4] demanded the magistrate.

John did. He gulped nervously as the magistrate read it.

"Tell me hatter," bullied the magistrate. "Why do you write 'sold inside'? Are you planning on selling your hats from the street? That is against the law, you know. I say delete those words if you want to stay out of jail. And if you want your sign to be perfect."

"Yes, sir. No, sir. I mean I will, sir," stammered John.

And after hastily bowing to the magistrate, John hurried back to his hat shop and rewrote his sign.

Now it read:

HATS

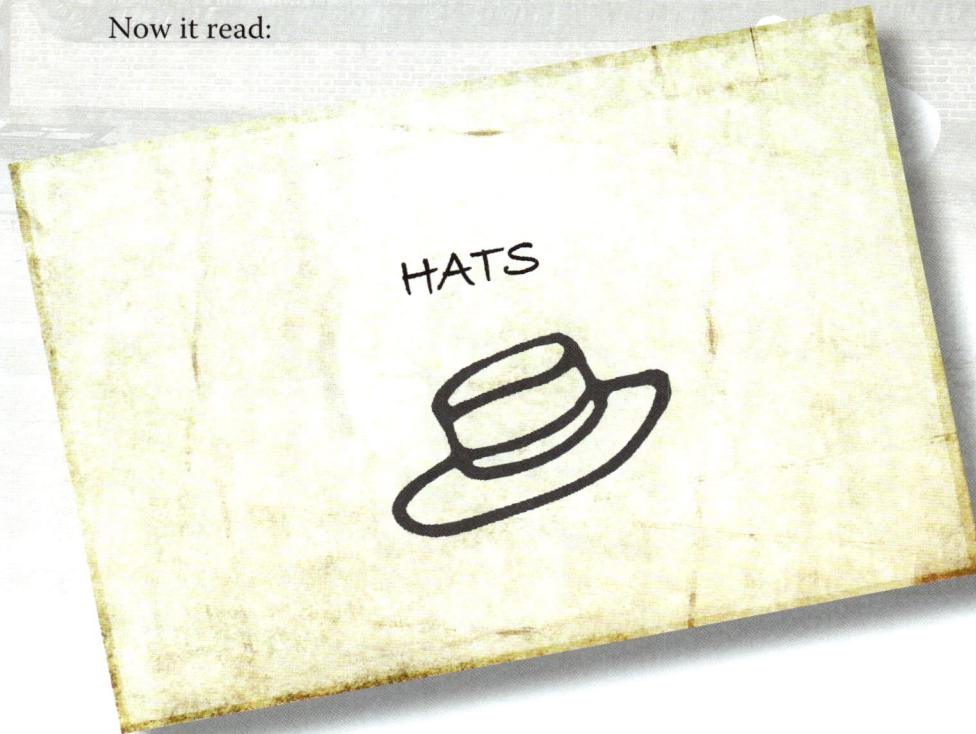

Beneath the word he drew a picture of a hat.

Parchment in hand, John headed for the sign maker's shop.

He had gone as far as the Charles River when a brisk breeze

---

4. A *stockade* is an enclosed area where prisoners are kept.

snatched the parchment from his hand and dropped it at the feet of two young apprentices sitting on a crate of tea.

The first apprentice picked up the parchment and read it.

"Hey, mister," he said. "Why do you write 'hats' when you already have a picture of one?"

"Yes, why?" asked the second apprentice.

"It would be a much better sign without that word," suggested the first apprentice.

"It would be perfect," added the second apprentice.

"You are probably right," sighed John.

And after tossing each boy a halfpenny, John hurried back to his hat shop and rewrote his sign. Now it read:

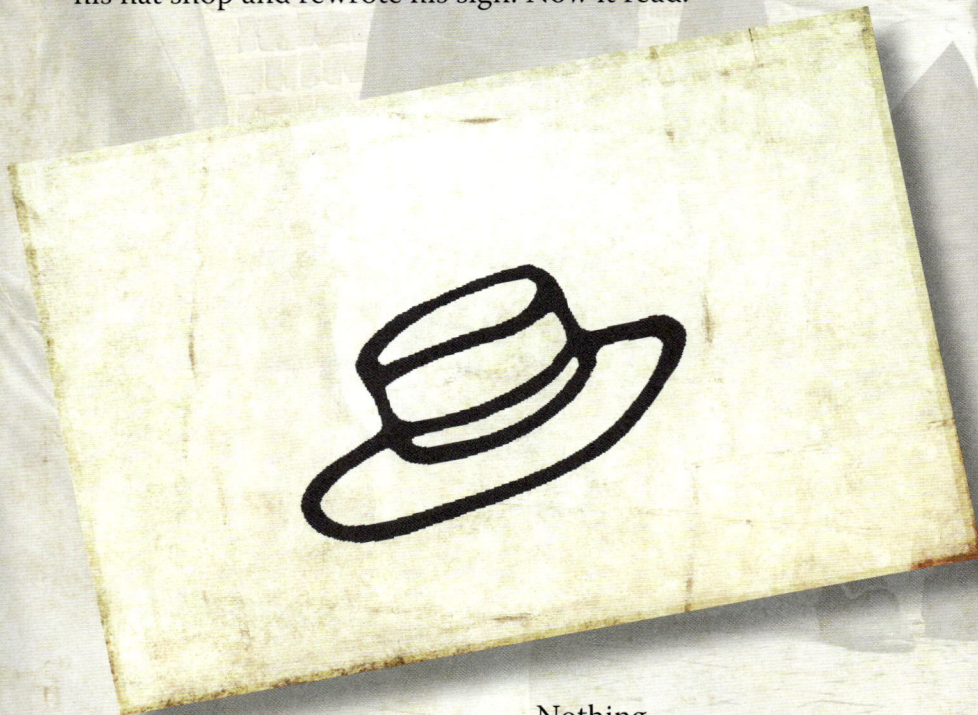

Nothing.

He drew a picture of a hat.

Parchment in hand, John headed for the sign maker's shop.

He had gone as far as Harvard College when he met Professor Wordsworth.

WORD BANK

apprentice (uh PREN tiss) *n*.: a person who works for another in order to learn a trade

John shoved his parchment under the professor's nose. "Please, sir," he said. "Would you tell me what you think of my sign?"

The surprised professor straightened his spectacles and peered at the picture.

"Since you ask my opinion, I shall give it," said Professor Wordsworth. "However, I must ask you a question first. Are you displaying your hats in your shop's front window?"

John nodded.

"Then this picture is useless," declared the professor. "Everyone will know you sell hats simply by looking in your window. Eliminate the picture and your sign will be perfect."

"You are probably right," sighed John.

And after pumping the professor's hand in thanks, John hurried back to his hat shop and rewrote his sign.

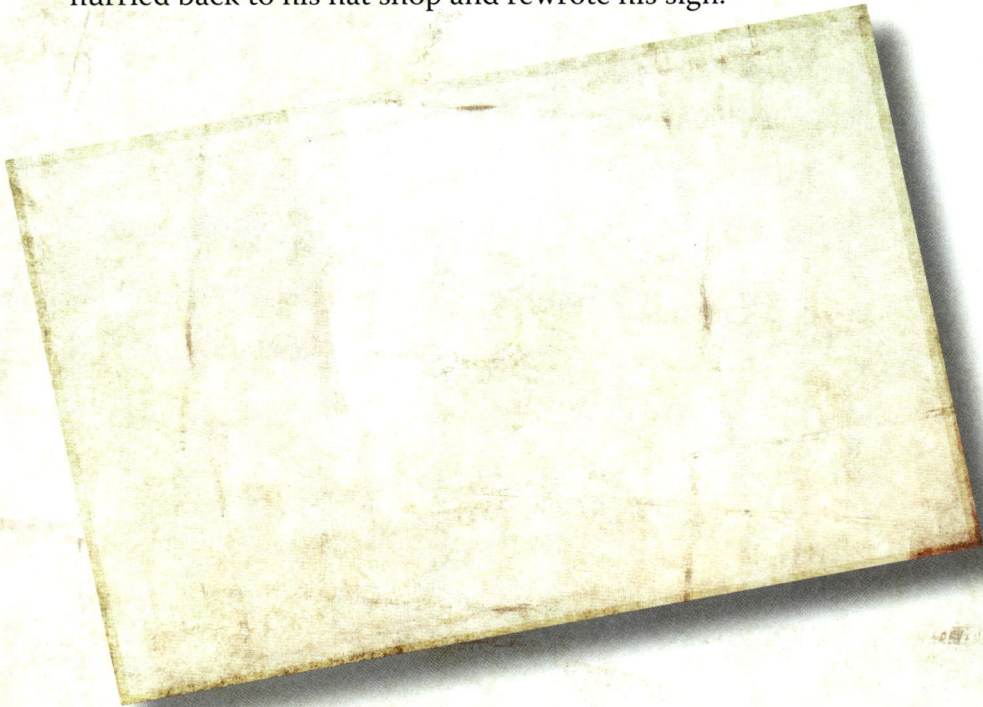

Now it read nothing.

It showed nothing.

It was wordless and pictureless and entirely blank.

Parchment in hand, John headed to the sign maker's shop.

Past the Old North Church and Beacon Hill. Past Boston Common and the wharf and Harvard College.

At long last, John arrived at the sign maker's shop. Exhausted, he handed over his parchment.

"I do not understand," said the puzzled sign maker as he stared at the empty parchment. "What does this mean? What are you trying to say?"

John shrugged. "I do not know anymore," he admitted. And he told the sign maker about his new hat shop, and his sign, and how no one had thought it was perfect enough.

When he had finished, the sign maker said, "May I make a suggestion? How about:

'John Thompson, Hatmaker
Fashionable Hats Sold Inside for Ready Money.'

"Beneath the words I will draw a picture of a hat."

"Yes!" exclaimed John. "How clever of you to think of it. That is exactly right! Indeed, it's perfect!"

JOHN THOMPSON, HATMAKER
FASHIONABLE HATS SOLD
INSIDE FOR READY MONEY

"So you see, Tom," concluded Benjamin Franklin. "No matter what you write, or how well you write it, if the public is going to read it, you can be sure they will want to change it."

For several moments, Thomas Jefferson pondered Franklin's story. Then sighing with acceptance, he listened as the Congress argued over the words that rang, the sentences that sang, and the paragraphs that flowed with truth.

And surprisingly, when the debate was done, and the changes were made, most believed Thomas Jefferson's Declaration of Independence was exactly right. Indeed, they thought, it was perfect!

ABOUT THE AUTHOR

Almost from the time she could talk, **Candace Fleming** told stories. She was so good at it, that people believed her imaginary tales were true. Her parents encouraged her to put her stories in writing, and soon, she had notebooks full of stories and poems. She loved words, especially long, musical words like her favorite one, cornucopia! When she had children of her own, she fell in love with children's stories all over again. She decided to write about some of her favorite American heroes. One of those favorites was Benjamin Franklin, who appears in The Hatmaker's Sign.

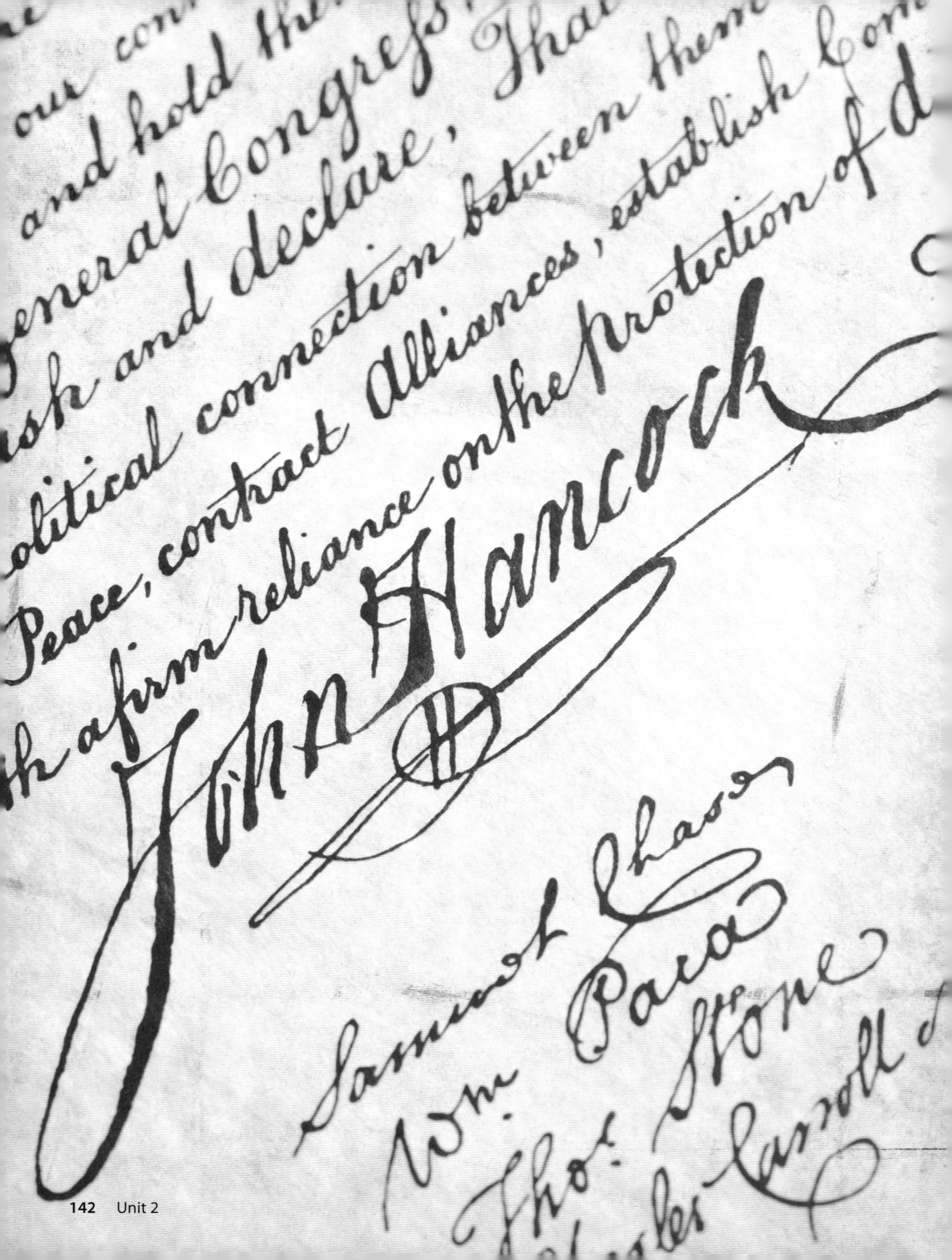

our con...
and hold th...
eneral Congress...
ish and declare, That...
olitical connection between the...
Peace, contract Alliances, establish Co...
th a firm reliance on the Protection of d...

John Hancock

Samuel Chase

Wm. Para

Tho? Stone

Carroll

Studying the Selection

QUICK REVIEW

1. As the story opens, what had Thomas Jefferson just completed?

2. In Ben Franklin's story, what had John Thompson prepared for the opening of his new store?

3. What was the only thing left on John's sign after he spoke with the apprentices?

4. Who finally suggested that John use the same words and picture that he had planned to use in the first place?

FOCUS

5. Why was John exhausted by the time he reached the sign maker's shop?

6. Write down one thing you noticed about the sequence of the story that made it organized and easy to read.

CREATING AND WRITING

7. Did John want everyone's advice to help him decide what the sign should say? Write a few sentences describing John's feelings.

8. Write a short fictional story about a child who worked hard on something and was disappointed later on when others did not like it or take it seriously.

9. Make a creative sign for a new store or business that you would like to open.

Lesson in Literature...

WHAT IS FORESHADOWING?

- **Foreshadowing** is found in many stories. It is a term for the clues the author places in the first part of a story that hint at what will happen later in the story.

- Foreshadowing takes many forms. It can be part of the story's setting—for example, *a dark, rainy day*. It can be a few words spoken by a character. In a play, it can be background music.

- Foreshadowing keeps the reader guessing. Will something happen, or won't it? Were these words a clue, or weren't they?

The day his father told him the story of Jackie Robinson, Michael started his baseball card collection. Before long he had enough cards to fill two shoeboxes he kept beneath his bed. Each night before he fell asleep, he flipped through his cards, studying the players' biographies and statistics and looking into each player's eyes. He asked, "Are you as good as Jackie Robinson was? Are you as courageous as Jackie Robinson was?" He remembered what his father told him: "Jackie Robinson was not only a talented baseball player; he was a courageous man."

When his grandmother visited, Michael told her about Jackie Robinson and his baseball card collection. She smiled and said, "I have a surprise for you." The next weekend when he visited her house, she took an old hat box out of a closet. Inside were baseball cards. "You can have any of them, Michael," she said. That afternoon he studied them one by one. When he came to an old, faded card at the bottom, a wide smile grew across his face. It was the one card he hoped for. It was a Jackie Robinson card.

At home that night he showed the Jackie Robinson card to his father. "Grandma said I could keep it," he said.

"She did?" his father said, and looked at him just as closely as he looked at the worn edges of the old Jackie Robinson card. Because of that look, Michael thought his father was angry.

But it was Michael's mother who knocked on his bedroom door that night. He was under the covers, the hat box of cards opened on his lap. She sat on the edge of his bed. "What did your father tell you about Jackie Robinson?" she asked.

Michael repeated the story of Jackie Robinson, a second baseman for the old Brooklyn Dodgers of the 1940s and 1950s and the first African-American player in major league baseball. Jackie Robinson, Michael told his mother, was a courageous man because he didn't fight back when angry fans taunted him because they wanted only white players in the major leagues. "Mom, I love all my baseball cards," he said. "But I

A BASEBALL CARD

- Foreshadowing can be found not only in mysteries, but also in comedies, sad stories, happy stories, and even poetry.

THINK ABOUT IT!

1. In the first paragraph, Michael remembers his father saying, "Jackie Robinson was not only a talented baseball player; he was a courageous man." Which words in this line hint at the story's theme?

2. What hint does the reader get that the baseball cards have a special meaning to Michael's father?

3. Were you able to predict what Michael would do before you came to the end of the story?

love this Jackie Robinson card the best."

"Michael," his mother said softly, "those cards belonged to your uncle, the one who died before you were born."

"Uncle Harry?"

"Yes. Grandma kept them all these years in memory of Harry. Grandma loves those cards."

The next weekend when Michael visited his grandmother he brought the hat box of cards with him and sat next to her on the couch as she flipped through all the cards. Dabbing tears from her eyes with a tissue, she told him the story of his Uncle Harry, a courageous young man who didn't complain during a long, painful illness. Uncle Harry, Michael realized, was a courageous man, too.

When his father came to bring him home, Michael left the hat box full of baseball cards, his Grandma's baseball cards, on a table beside the couch so she could look through them every day. He left the Jackie Robinson card on top.

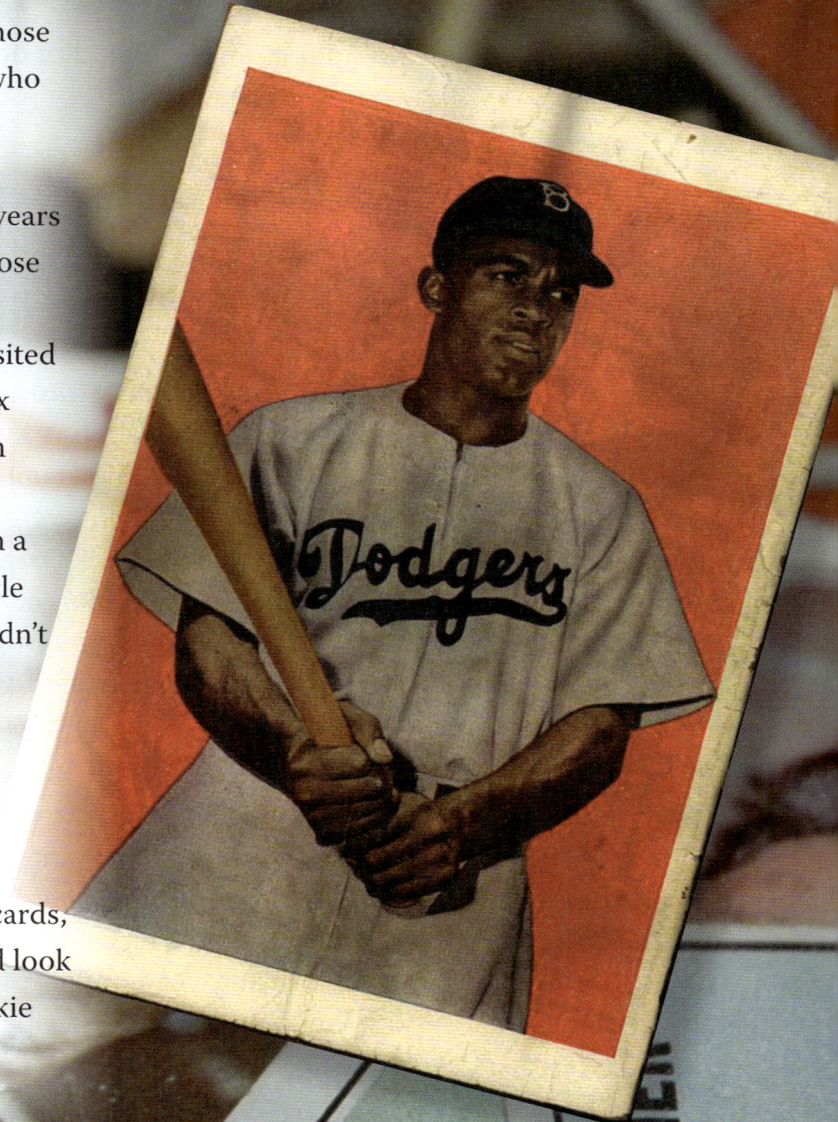

Blueprint for Reading

INTO . . . *Dad, Jackie, and Me*

What would it feel like if people did not want to talk or play with you? What if you were told that you were not smart enough or strong enough to join a group? Have you had an experience where you were not given a fair chance? As we learned in *Supergrandpa,* people make unfair judgments at times. When we develop an unfavorable opinion about someone or something without having a lot of information, it is called *prejudice*. Prejudice comes with a lot of unpleasant "partners," such as meanness, intolerance, and selfishness. As you read *Dad, Jackie, and Me,* identify the characters who suffer from the prejudice of others.

EYES ON *Predicting Outcome*

There are people who would love to see into the future. While this is not possible, we often get hints about a future event. The trouble is, we usually don't really notice these hints until after the event takes place! For example, if your friends were planning a surprise party for you, even if they tried their best to keep everything a secret, clues and hints would probably come out. You might notice that something was different, but you wouldn't think about it much. Later on, though, when you were at the surprise party, you would remember the hints and clues and say, "Oh! So that's why you did that…"

In a short story or book, an author will often plant information near the beginning of the story that hints at what is going to happen later on. The hints and clues are called **foreshadowing**. For the reader, deciding which parts of the story are foreshadowing is like working out a puzzle. Using the clues to guess what will happen at the end is like trying to solve a mystery. As you read *Dad, Jackie, and Me,* see if you can identify the foreshadowing and predict what will happen later.

Dad, Jackie, and Me

Myron Uhlberg

My ear was glued to the radio, like every other ear in Brooklyn.

It was Opening Day, 1947. And every kid in Brooklyn knew this was our year. The Dodgers were going to go all the way!

We had Jackie Robinson, the first Negro player in major league baseball.

As I listened to the game, the minutes melted into hours; the innings folded one into another. I could see it all in my mind's eye: pitch after pitch, swing after swing. I dreamed of the day I could see it all for myself.

Our neighborhood was only a short subway ride from Ebbets Field, home of the Dodgers and their new first baseman.

I loved baseball. I loved the Brooklyn Dodgers. I hated the New York Giants, and they hated Jackie Robinson.

One day, my father came home early from work. He walked into my bedroom and announced, "We're going to Ebbets Field."

He didn't say it out loud. My father was deaf, so he signed the words with his hands. I couldn't believe it. Dad had never seemed to care much about baseball.

"I want to meet Jackie Robinson," Dad signed.

I was finally going to see a real game. Today the Dodgers were playing the Giants. And we were going to cream 'em.

I got my glove and ball, Dodgers cap, and scorecard. I stuck my lucky pencil behind my ear. As we went down the steps, I tossed the ball to Dad. But he'd never played baseball like me. He dropped it.

I couldn't wait to get to the ballpark. But the whole ride I kept thinking, There's no way Dad can meet Jackie Robinson. Besides, Jackie doesn't know sign language.

How would they talk to each other?

The line to get in to Ebbets Field snaked around Sullivan Place and up to Bedford Avenue. My dad let me hold my ticket. I clutched it for dear life.

Finally, we were through the turnstile. My dad held my hand as we moved with the rest of the crowd through the gloomy underbelly of the stadium, up the dark ramp. Then we tumbled into bright sunlight.

I shut my eyes against the glare. When I opened them again, my breath caught in my throat. I had never seen anything so perfect as the inside of Ebbets Field.

There, laid out at my feet, was the emerald green field, each blade of grass reflecting the light from the afternoon sun.

The angles of the field were sharply marked in two lines of white chalk.

The dirt base paths formed a perfect diamond carpet dotted with fat canvas bags at each base and a black rubber plate at home.

I knew if I lived to be a hundred, I would never again see a sight so beautiful.

"Hey, peanuts! Hey, hot dogs! Get 'em while they're hot!"

Dad and I sat on the right field line, right behind first base, Jackie's position.

The Dodgers Sym-Phony was marching up and down the aisles playing "The Worms Crawl In, the Worms Crawl Out." The music was earsplitting. Dad couldn't hear it, but he laughed along with everyone else at the sight of the raggedy band's tattered clothes, cowbells, and whistles.

When the game started and Jackie ran out on the field, Dad yelled real loud, "Jackiee, Jackiee, Jackiee!" Only it didn't come out that way. It sounded like, "AH-GHEE, AH-GHEE, AH-GHEE!" Since my dad couldn't hear, he had no way of knowing what the words should sound like.

Everyone looked at my dad.

I looked at my shoes.

As Jackie stood at first base, the Giants began hooting and hollering. They called Jackie names. Horrible names. "What are they saying?" Dad asked.

"Bad things," I said.

"Tell me." Some of those words I had to finger spell. I knew no sign for them. Dad listened with a sad little smile on his face.

In the ninth inning, Jackie bunted, and beat the throw to first. Then he stole second.

On the next Dodgers hit, he moved to third. The score was tied at four-all.

The Giants pitcher took a long windup, and Jackie dashed for home. We all jumped to our feet yelling, "Jackiee, Jackiee, Jackiee!"

"AH-GHEE, AH-GHEE, AH-GHEE!" Dad screamed.

This time, nobody seemed to notice.

Forget about the Giants. They were nothing! We had Jackie Robinson.

Every day when Dad came home from work, he started asking me questions. Not about school. About baseball. He wanted to know everything I knew. Especially about Jackie Robinson.

"What's Jackie's batting average?"

".247," I said.

"How's that figured?"

I explained.

"What's an RBI?" he asked.

"Runs batted in."

"Fielding average. What's that mean?"

I told him.

"You teach me baseball," he signed.

"Okay," I said.

One night, Dad came home with a baseball glove.

"Let's have a catch," he signed.

We tossed the ball back and forth until Mom called us for supper. Dad missed the ball every time. The only way he could hold it was by trapping the ball against his chest with both hands. That had to hurt, but Dad just smiled.

"Jackie never drops the ball," he signed. "He catches it with one hand. Not like me."

All that week we practiced. Dad dropped the ball most every time. Even when I threw it underhand.

"Throw it regular," Dad said.

Dad and I kept going to games whenever we could. Every time Jackie came out to his position, Dad chanted right along with the crowd. AH-GHEE, AH-GHEE, AH-GHEE.

Jackie never looked over at us. He just stared down the line at the next hitter.

One Sunday, the Dodgers were playing the St. Louis Cardinals. What a game! Our pitcher had a no-hitter going.

And then it happened. On a simple grounder that he knew he couldn't beat, a Cardinal player crossed first base and spiked Jackie—on purpose! Fifty-two thousand eyes popped. Twenty-six thousand jaws dropped. Twenty-six thousand tongues were stilled.

Then, in that awful silence, my father jumped to his feet.

"NOOOO!" he screamed. "NOT FAIR! AH-GHEE, AH-GHEE, AH-GHEE!"

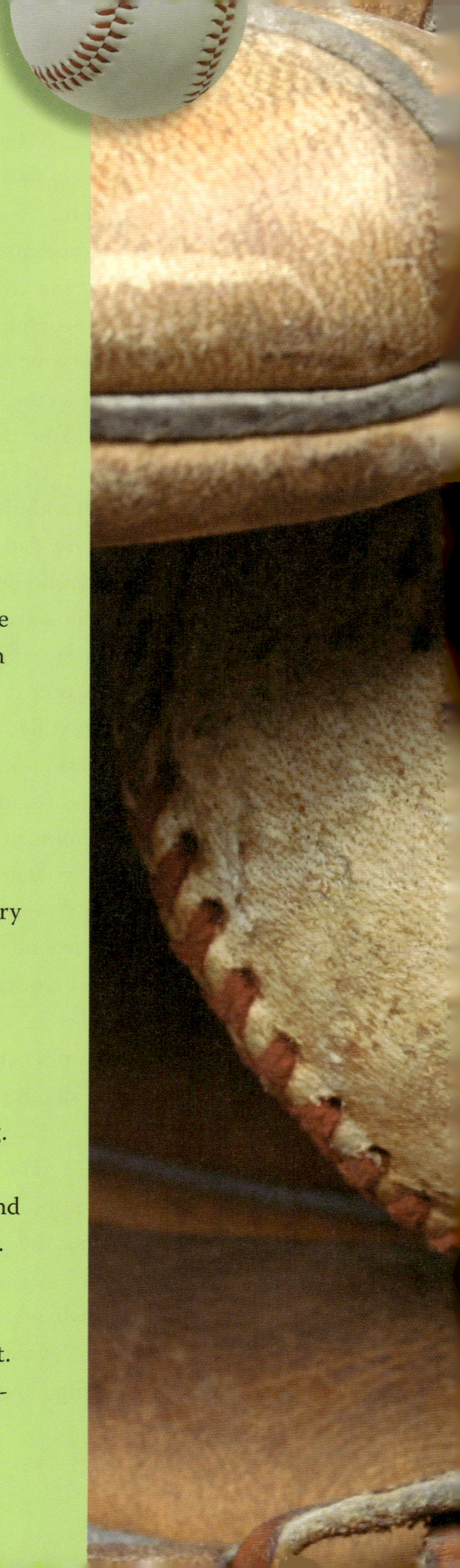

The Brooklyn crowd went nuts. They leapt to their feet and joined my father. "JACK-IE, JACK-IE, JACK-IE!"

The name bounced off the brick walls, climbed the iron girders, and rattled around under the wooden roof.

But Jackie just stood at first base, his face a blank mask, blood streaming down his leg. It was almost as if he didn't hear the crowd.

All that month, Dad and I followed everything Jackie did. We read and reread every report of every game that was printed in *The New York Daily News*.

Dad started a scrapbook. If there was any mention of Jackie Robinson, he cut out the article and pasted it in his scrapbook.

The scrapbook got thicker.

The Dodgers kept winning.

And the opposing teams kept riding Jackie Robinson.

But Jackie never reacted. He didn't even seem to notice. And he never complained.

The Dodgers clinched the pennant that season when the Cards beat the Cubs. Dad and I went downtown the next day to see the big parade to honor Jackie. And back in the neighborhood, we had a block party to celebrate.

It didn't matter whether the Dodgers won the last game of the season, since we were already over the top. But Dad and I didn't care. We went to Ebbets Field anyway. We went to see Jackie Robinson.

In the third inning, Jackie smacked the ball to deep left field for a double. Then he flew home like the wind, his feet barely touching the base path.

The Brooklyn crowd went crazy. "Go, Go, Go, Jackieeee!"

"GOO, GOO, GOO, AH-GHEEEE!" my dad screamed right along with them.

Finally, late in the day, as deep shadows stretched across the infield, Jackie caught a line drive hit down the first base line. It was the last out of the game.

As the crowd cheered, Jackie stood alone at first base, staring at the ball in his glove. Then he turned and threw it into the stands—right to my father!

That's when my dad did something he had never done before. He reached up and caught the ball in his bare hand!

I'm not sure, but I think I saw Jackie Robinson smile. My dad dropped the ball into my empty glove.

And just like that, the baseball season of 1947 was over.

Author's Note

This story is a work of fiction. Parts of it, however, are based in truth.

My father, who was deaf and spoke only with his hands, worked as a printer for *The New York Daily News*. One night in 1947, he brought home the paper—the ink not quite dry—and excitedly showed me the bold headline: BROOKLYN DODGERS SIGN JACKIE ROBINSON. Beneath it was a photo of two smiling men: the president of the Brooklyn Dodgers, Branch Rickey, and the grandson of a slave, Jackie Robinson.

"Now, at last," my father signed to me, "a Negro will play in the major leagues!"

And from the day he joined the Brooklyn Dodgers until the day he retired, Jackie Robinson was the main topic of conversation in our small Brooklyn apartment during every baseball season.

My father could not throw or catch a baseball, let alone hit one. As a boy in 1910, he attended a deaf residential school, where playing sports was not encouraged. In those days most people considered deaf children severely handicapped and thought teaching them sports a waste of time. What could my deaf father possibly have in common with this Negro baseball player, Jackie Robinson?

During Jackie's first year as a Dodger, my father took me to many games. He told me to watch carefully how the opposing team would single Jackie out for unfair treatment, how they would actively discriminate against him on the field just because his skin was brown. "Just you

watch," he said. "Jackie will show them that his skin color has nothing to do with how he plays baseball. He will show them all that he is as good as they are."

Throughout his life my father also experienced the cruelty of prejudice. "It's not fair that hearing people discriminate against me just because I am deaf," he told me. "It doesn't matter, though," he always added. "I show them every day I am as good as they are."

One summer day, late in that rookie season of 1947—during which Jackie had quietly endured racial taunts, threats on his life, numerous bean balls, and even deliberate spikings—my father told me about another hero.

"There was a deaf man born in 1862," he signed to me, "who was also a baseball player. His name was William Ellsworth Hoy, but his teammates quickly nicknamed him 'The Amazing Dummy.'

"In those days no one could imagine that a deaf man could play major league baseball. The deaf were thoughtlessly called 'deaf and dumb.' It was common for the hearing to refer to a deaf person as a 'dummy.'

"But Dummy Hoy showed them all," my father continued. "He played fourteen years in the major leagues. He was smart and fast like Jackie, and in his rookie year he stole a record eighty-two bases. One day, he threw three men out at home plate from the outfield, which had never been done before. And, most importantly, he taught umpires to use hand signals to call balls and strikes."

As he told that story, I began to understand the connection between Jackie Robinson and my deaf father. Like Dummy Hoy before them, they were both men who worked to overcome thoughtless prejudice and to prove themselves every day of their lives.

—M.U.

ABOUT THE AUTHOR

Myron Uhlberg was born in 1933 to Lou and Sarah Uhlberg, who "just happened to be deaf." Although he never thought of his parents as handicapped, he observed that some people were prejudiced against them, simply because they were deaf. In his book, *Dad, Jackie, and Me*, he explains how his father, like Jackie Robinson, was sometimes the victim of prejudice. In real life, Jackie was the main topic of conversation at the Uhlberg home. From the day he joined the Dodgers, Jackie Robinson was Lou Uhlberg's hero. For Myron, though, the real hero was his own Dad.

Poetry *is about the things we cheer*

Analysis of Baseball

May Swenson

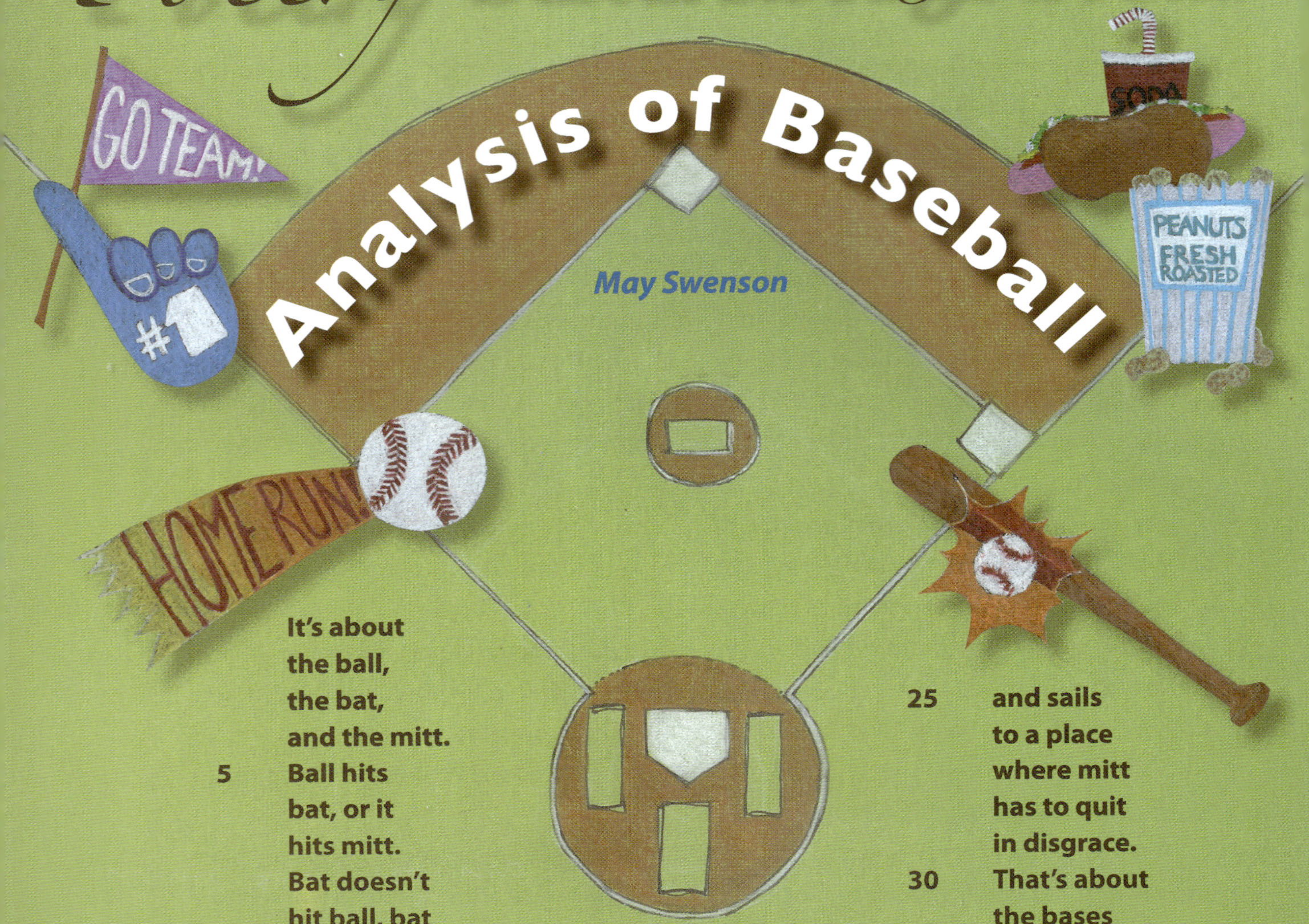

It's about
the ball,
the bat,
and the mitt.
5   Ball hits
bat, or it
hits mitt.
Bat doesn't
hit ball, bat
10 meets it.
Ball bounces
off bat, flies
air, or thuds
ground (dud)
15 or it
fits mitt.
Ball fits
mitt, but
not all
20 the time.
Sometimes
ball gets hit
(pow) when bat
meets it,

25 and sails
to a place
where mitt
has to quit
in disgrace.
30 That's about
the bases
loaded,
about 40,000
fans exploded.
35 It's about
the ball,
the bat,
the mitt,
the bases
40 and the fans.
It's done
on a diamond,
and for fun.
It's about
45 home, and it's
about run.

Studying the Selection

QUICK REVIEW

1. What team was the narrator a fan of?
2. Because he was a fan, how did he spend most of his free time?
3. What surprise did Dad have for his son?
4. What important step had the Dodgers taken by asking Jackie Robinson to join the team?

FOCUS

5. What lifelong lessons can the boy learn from his father and Jackie?
6. Did you think Dad would ever meet Jackie Robinson? What are some clues that the author places in the story that allow you to think he will?

CREATING AND WRITING

7. People were prejudiced against Jackie because of his race and against Dad because of his deafness. Sometimes people make prejudiced comments thinking that you agree with them. What would you say to someone who made a prejudiced comment about either Jackie or Dad, thinking that you felt the same way? Write two or three sentences in which you tell the person not to include you in this prejudiced way of thinking.

8. Write a short story about an athlete who joins a team but finds that the team members have made up their minds to dislike the newcomer. Plan the story in your mind so that you know what happens in the end before you start writing. Place clues in the story that help the reader predict the ending.

9. Pretend you are "the voice of the Brooklyn Dodgers" on the radio. It is the last game of the season and Jackie comes to bat. He hits a ball deep into left field and… Write four or five lines that you, the radio announcer, say on the air. You may use lots of capital letters and exclamation points to show the excitement in your voice!

Lesson in Literature . . .
TURTLE, TORTOISE, OR TERRAPIN?

WHAT IS A MAIN IDEA?

- Every literary form, whether it is a drama, a poem, a novel, a short story, or an essay, must have a **main idea**.

- In an essay, such as the one that follows, each *paragraph* also has a main idea.

- In a well-written paragraph, all the details will be closely connected to its main idea.

- As you read any written work, ask yourself, *What is the main idea here?*

THINK ABOUT IT!

1. Select one sentence from the first paragraph which clearly states the essay's main idea.

2. Which of the following topics is not covered in the second paragraph?

   a. what turtles eat
   b. where turtles live
   c. the size and weight of turtles

3. Read the third paragraph carefully. The main difference between turtles, tortoises, and terrapins is the way they move around and where they live. Describe that difference.

It's easy to recognize a turtle, right? Its hard shell, thumb-like head, and slow walk give it away. What if, though, that turtle inching along in the grass or basking on the log beside the pond is not a turtle but a tortoise or a terrapin? What makes a turtle a turtle?

Everyone believes they know a turtle when they see one, but did you know there are about 300 species of turtles? Some are aquatic, which means they live in water. Others are terrestrial, which means they live on land. Some turtles are amphibious; that is, they live both in water and on land. Some, like the giant tortoise of the Galápagos Islands, can weigh up to seven hundred pounds; others, like the Northern spider tortoise of Madagascar, can weigh less than an ounce and fit in the palm of your hand. Turtles like the red-eared slider are kept as pets in home terrariums, while others like the great leatherback sea turtle are highly endangered.

Turtles are generally divided into these three groups: sea turtles, tortoises, and terrapins. Aquatic turtles, or sea turtles, swim in warm waters throughout the world and migrate to lay their eggs on secluded beaches. A unique feature of the sea turtle is that it has flippers for swimming instead of legs. Sea turtles also have descriptive names like loggerhead, flatback, leatherback, and green and black sea turtles. Many terrestrial, or land-dwelling, turtles are known as tortoises. A very common land turtle is the North American box turtle, which is identifiable by its domed shell and thumb-like head. Its smaller cousin is the American mud turtle. Unlike a sea turtle, a tortoise has legs and is unable to swim or even float. Amphibious turtles, some of which are known as terrapins, are common in North America and have names such as the wood, painted, snapping, and spotted turtles. Unlike a sea turtle or a tortoise, a terrapin, whose habitat is both water and land, has webbed feet for swimming, usually in freshwater ponds, streams, and lakes, and in the case of the diamondback terrapin, in tidal marshes and ponds.

So you see a turtle. What is it? Is it a sea turtle, tortoise, or terrapin? If it looks like a turtle, then most likely it is a turtle. But take a closer look. How big is it? Is its habitat the ocean, the woods, or a freshwater lake? Does it have flippers, short legs, or webbed feet? A problem for turtle lovers is that there are so many species of turtles to recognize, but the joy of turtle lovers is that there are so many species of turtles to enjoy. Is it a sea turtle, tortoise, or terrapin? It doesn't matter. If it's a turtle, it's one of nature's most interesting species.

Blueprint for Reading

INTO . . . *And Now the Good News*

Have you ever visited an historical village? Have you eaten food from a package or jar that listed "preservative" as one of its ingredients? Is there a photograph or piece of china that has been saved and handed down from generation to generation in your family? In one way or another, each of these has been preserved. *Preservation* is the process of keeping something safe and in good condition. In this story, another type of preservation is discussed—the preservation of endangered animals and their habitats. As you read *And Now the Good News,* think about why this preservation is so important.

EYES ON *Main Ideas and Details*

Have you ever seen a rag doll? It just flops around. Do you know why? It has no backbone! A poorly written story can be like that. If it has no "backbone"—no one idea holding it together—it just flops around. A good story has one **main idea** that holds it together. In a nonfiction piece such as the one you are about to read, the main idea is easy to find. It is usually presented in the title or the first few paragraphs. Once the main idea is presented, the writer must show how each new idea is connected to the main idea.

And Now the Good News

from *And Then There Was One*

Margery Facklam

A "doomsday" book lists all the animals in danger of extinction. Its official name is *The Red Data Book*. It's published each year by the International Union for Conservation of Nature and Natural Resources. In a book of so much bad news, can we ever find anything good?

The good news is that some animals get off the list, when they make a comeback. The American alligator was once in danger of extinction because a lot of people thought that alligator skin looked better on shoes and luggage than on the alligator. Then a law was passed in the 1970s to protect the big reptiles from harm. Now there are so many alligators

that they are causing problems. They are turning up on golf courses and in private lakes. One huge alligator was found basking in the sun on a runway at the West Palm Beach International Airport. The alligator population is up to a million, and some way must be found for alligators and people to live side by side.

When a large predator like the alligator thrives, dozens of smaller animals thrive with it. Alligators make room for an entire community in their water holes. Fish, turtles, snakes, frogs, and snails settle in. Herons, ibis, egrets, spoonbills, and other birds stay close because they can find food, and so do raccoons, muskrats, wild pigs, and other mammals. As long as the alligator keeps the water hole weeded and open, the whole community lives well.

Protecting a large animal is a real bargain because it saves whole ecosystems.[1] When we protect one habitat, we help all the

1. All living things interact with their environments. That combination—the living thing and its environment, and the way the two interact—is called an *ecosystem.*

WORD BANK

basking (BASS king) *v.*: lying in something pleasantly warm (like the sun)
predator (PREH duh tor) *n.*: an animal that hunts other animals for food
thrives *v.*: grows and improves
habitat (HAB ih TAT) *n.*: the place where a plant or animal is naturally found

animals that live there. In order to help the African elephant, we must help all the animals of the Serengeti.[2] In that 5,000-square-mile area, there are more than 400 species of birds, 50 kinds of mammals, and tens of thousands of insects and other invertebrates.[3]

Zoos and wildlife sanctuaries are part of the good news. About 90 percent of the mammals and 75 percent of the birds in American zoos were born in captivity. No longer can an expedition go into the jungle and capture a tiger or monkeys. No one is allowed to catch a dolphin in the open ocean for a marine exhibit or research without permission from the government.

---

2. The *Serengeti* (SAIR en GET ee) is a plain in Tanzania which has a huge wildlife reserve.
3. *Invertebrates* are animals that do not have a spine.

WORD BANK

sanctuaries (SANK chew AIR eez) *n.*: a portion of land set aside by the government, where wildlife can live in safety from hunters

expedition (EX puh DISH un) *n.*: a journey or voyage made to a distant place for a certain purpose

Unfortunately, many dolphins, seals, and sea turtles are trapped illegally in fishing nets that trail for miles behind commercial fishing ships. People are trying to design safer nets that will allow turtles and sea mammals to escape if they are caught. They are also trying out different regulations that would require fishing ships to haul in nets more frequently, which could save large animals caught in them from drowning.

Zoos were once prisons of concrete cages and iron bars. Although some are still prisons, the best zoos display animals in large areas much like the animals' own habitats. Many rare animals have bred and raised their young in zoos, but it's not always easy. Panda babies are rare enough in nature and rarer still in zoos. Only 1,000 pandas live in their native China and Tibet,[4] and only 100 in zoos around the world. Three zoos outside of China—in Mexico, Madrid,[5] and Tokyo[6]—have raised panda cubs. Ling-Ling, a panda at the National Zoo in Washington, D.C., has given birth to several cubs, but none has lived more than a few hours despite careful veterinary care.

---

4. *Tibet* (tuh BET) is a region in China.
5. *Madrid* is the capital city of Spain.
6. *Tokyo* is the capital city of Japan.

WORD BANK

commercial (kuh MUR shul) *n.*: made by companies to be sold in stores; not homemade

For many wildlife experts, the big goal is to breed animals in captivity and return them to their native homes. But that's not as easy as it sounds. You might think that all you'd have to do is open a cage to let an animal know it's free, but that doesn't always work. In Indonesia, workers at one rehabilitation center try to move once-captive orangutans back into the jungle, but many of the animals won't go. The big red apes like to hang around the feeding station, where bananas and other good food are handed out. When workers take them by the hand and lead them into the forests, some orangutans drag their feet like ornery children. A few may stay alone in the forest overnight, but the next morning they are back in time for breakfast. Part of the problem is too little forest and too many captured orangutans that need homes in it.

The National Wildlife Refuge System cares for 400 habitats from the Florida Keys to Alaska. They protect green sea turtles and monk seals in Hawaii, whooping cranes in Texas, and trumpeter swans in Montana. They provide safe feeding and resting grounds for the annual migrations of thousands of ducks, geese, and other birds.

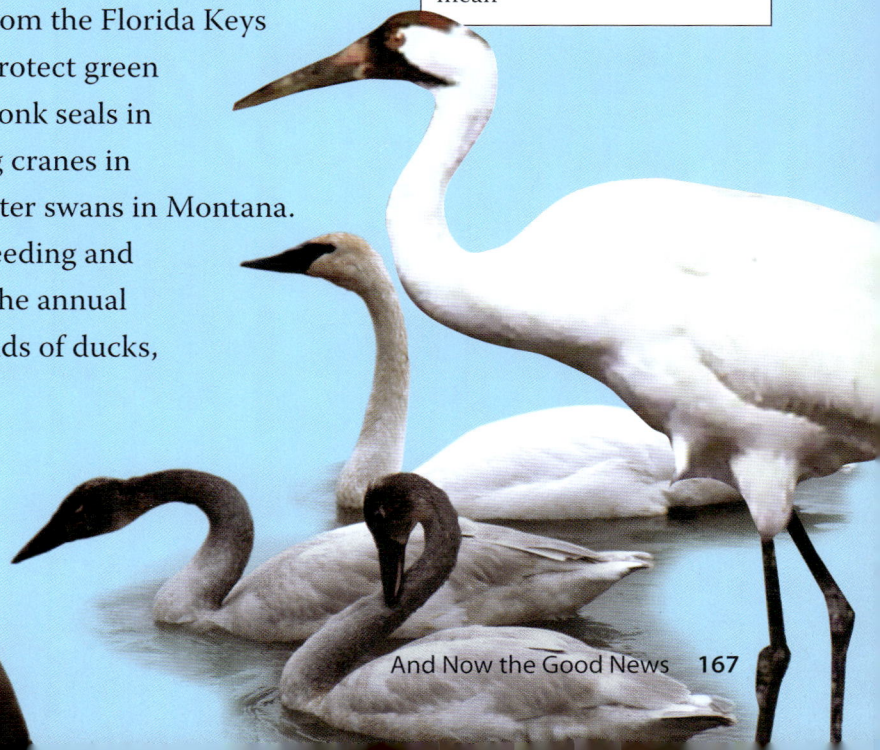

WORD BANK

rehabilitation (REE huh BIH luh TAY shun) *n.*: a returning to good health

ornery (OR nuh ree) *adj.*: mean

Bald eagles have found help in the refuge system, too. When the eagle was chosen as our national symbol in 1782, there were probably 75,000 of the big birds nesting in the U.S. territory. Today there are fewer than 3,000. It wasn't until 1940, when bald eagles were on the edge of extinction, that Congress passed a law to protect them. But even when they were safe from hunters, eagles' eggs were destroyed by DDT because the adult birds had eaten fish contaminated by the pesticide.

Now the wildlife experts take the first clutch of eggs[7] from an eagle's nest and put them in an incubator until they hatch. With her eggs gone, the eagle will lay a second clutch of eggs, which she will raise. When an eagle is found without eggs, or whose chicks have died, the scientists place three-week-old eaglets from an incubator in its nest. The foster parents usually adopt the chicks and raise them as their own.

---

7. A *clutch of eggs* is a group of eggs that are all laid at the same time.

Sometimes they use a process called *hacking*. Rangers build nests on platforms high atop towers in wilderness areas where there are no eagles. They place eight-week-old eaglets in these nests. At first, humans feed the eaglets, although they are careful to stay out of sight. They use a puppet that looks like an eagle, because they don't want the young eagles to *imprint* on humans. The first moving object a newly hatched baby bird sees is "imprinted" on its brain as its mother. Gradually, the eaglets are fed less and less to encourage them to fly off and hunt their own prey. It's a long, slow process, but it works.

The whooping crane is another success story. In 1941, there were only sixteen whooping cranes, but now there are more than 200. They are still on the endangered list, but their numbers are growing.

The Endangered Species Act became law in 1973. It makes it a crime for anyone to sell or transport an endangered species or a product made from the body of an endangered species. That means people can't sell rhinoceros horns or tiger skins. No longer can certain tropical birds be transported or sold or kept as pets. It is illegal for an endangered animal to be "killed, hunted, collected, harassed, harmed, pursued, shot, trapped, wounded, or captured." The law also sets aside some "critical" habitats for some species. That means that no federal government agency can use the habitat of an endangered species. Unfortunately, it does not protect the same area from private projects. For example, where an eagle is nesting, a federal highway or an

army base can't be built because it's paid for by our taxes. But someone might be able to build houses or a shopping mall or a factory, unless state or local governments protect the land.

The shy, bashful marine mammal called a manatee is a distant cousin to the elephant, although it looks like a cross between a seal and a baby hippo.

Some grow to be 12 feet long and weigh 3,000 pounds. They used to live a quiet life in Florida's waterways, but there are few left. Now they must compete with hundreds of thousands of small power boats. Someone has said that the manatee is going off the earth for the same reason that shows go off the air—no sponsor. Who will sponsor the gentle manatee and other animals that cannot speak for themselves?

It's easy to get people interested in saving cuddly animals such as pandas and baby seals, or elegant, dramatic animals such as tigers and snow leopards. But what about a butterfly or a tiny fish called the snail darter? Should these be saved? Does it matter that the last dusky sparrow died in 1989?

CAUTION

MANATEE AREA

We tend to forget that we are the only creatures who can make choices. Instead of adapting to an environment, we can change it. If we're cold, we can put on warm clothes and turn up the heat. Too hot? Just turn on the air conditioner. Want to fly? Just get on an airplane. Run out of food? Buy groceries from anywhere on earth at the supermarket. We can change the rules. We are the ones with imagination and power.

All creatures large and small have the right to live because they share their home planet with us. We can do nothing about the way animals adapt to the changes in the environment, but we *can* do something about how the environment changes. We can keep the earth clean. We can stop polluting and destroying the habitats of other living things. We can learn from the past and begin planning for the future.

ABOUT THE AUTHOR

As a young girl, **Margery Facklam** spent every Saturday at the Buffalo Museum of Science in Buffalo, New York. During high school, she worked in the reptile house at the Buffalo Zoo. After graduating from college, she married and raised five children. After her youngest child was grown, she went back to working with animals in a zoo. At the same time, she began to write books on scientific topics, sometimes with her husband, Howard Facklam, or her daughter, Margaret Thomas. Several of her books were illustrated by her son, Steven, making her writing career a real family affair!

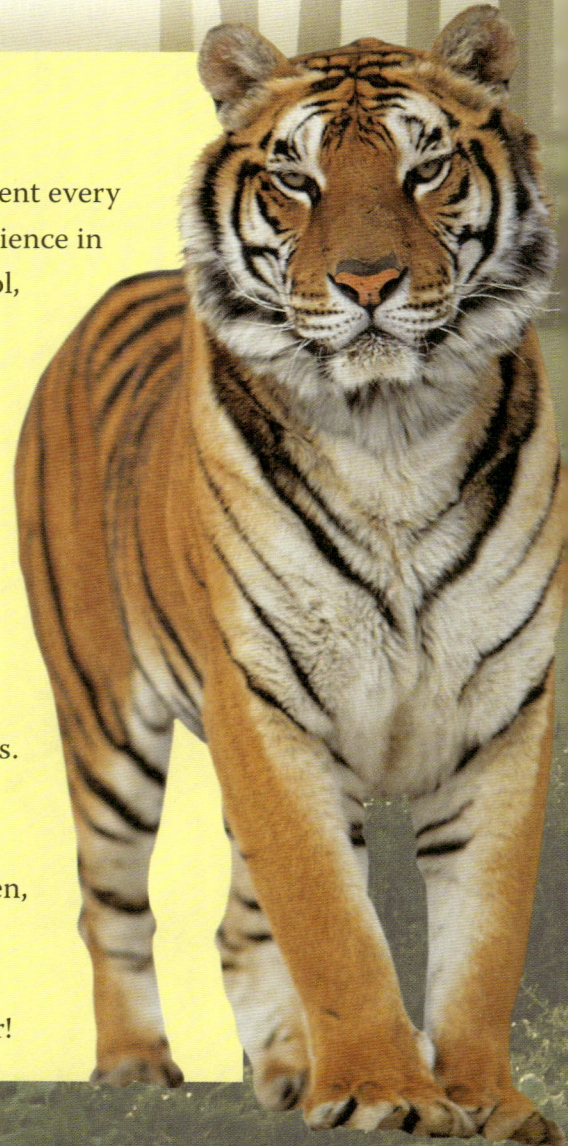

Hurt No Living Thing

Hurt no living thing;

Ladybird, nor butterfly,

Nor moth with dusty wing,

Nor cricket chirping cheerily,

5   Nor grasshopper so light of leap,

Nor dancing gnat, nor beetle fat,

Nor harmless worms that creep.

Christina Rossetti

Poetry makes us care

Studying the Selection

QUICK REVIEW

1. What is the purpose of *The Red Data Book*?
2. Why is it a "bargain" to protect a large animal?
3. List five animals that were mentioned as endangered.
4. What became illegal as a result of the Endangered Species Act of 1973?

FOCUS

5. Why do you think this selection is entitled *And Now the Good News*?
6. Look on page 170 at the paragraph that begins with the words, "The Endangered Species Act." Reread this paragraph. What is the main idea? Write it down. The topic sentence is the first sentence of the paragraph. Write three important details that connect to the topic sentence.

CREATING AND WRITING

7. Write about something other than wildlife that you feel should be preserved and protected. This can be something that is important only to you or that is important to large numbers of people.
8. Write about a group of fourth graders who can communicate with animals. What do they discuss with endangered animals?
9. Choose an endangered animal from your teacher's list. Create an ad campaign that will interest people in helping these animals. Think of a slogan and a logo as well as an ad. Remember that while you need to present true information, you must also try to touch the hearts of people.

Jill's Journal:
"They Loaded Up Their Trunks and They Moved to Tennessee"

Lottie

Billie

Tange

Flora

Shirley

Tarra

Liz

Dulary

Zula

Debbie

Bunny

Misty

Winkie

Sissy

Frieda

Minnie

Ronnie

I really do have some good news.

I've just heard about the Elephant Sanctuary in Hohenwald, Tennessee! A *sanctuary* for animals means a place where they are protected and cannot be hunted.

The Elephant Sanctuary is the largest natural refuge in the United States for endangered African and Asian elephants. The elephants live on 2,700 acres of green pastures, forests, and ponds. They have a heated barn to sleep in on cold winter nights. You *cannot* just go there to see them. (Otherwise I would be in Tennessee right now!) They are *not* on display. The Elephant Sanctuary rescues old, sick, or needy elephants so that they can live like elephants.

The Sanctuary educates people about the danger of elephants becoming extinct. Elephants are intelligent and are very social. Female elephants must live in groups. If an elephant is not with other elephants she becomes very depressed. Elephants talk with each other by trumpeting and stomping their feet.

If a female elephant meets an elephant that she knew, let's say twenty years ago, she makes a joyful noise. Then they hug each other tightly with their trunks. Elephants cry tears. When one of the elephants at the Sanctuary died, her two closest elephant friends stood and slept by her body until the humans took the body away the next morning. The two friends searched for her with trumpeting cries. When they found where she had been buried, they stayed at her grave for many days.

I can tell you the names of all of the elephants at the Sanctuary: Tarra, Shirley, Bunny, Sissy, Winkie, Dulary, Tange, Zula, Flora, Misty, Billie, Debbie, Frieda, Liz, Lottie, Minnie, and Ronnie. All of them are girls. These elephants have had hard and lonely lives in circuses and carnivals. Now they spend their days eating, playing with toys (such as old tires), wallowing in the mudhole, hanging out with their friends, spending time in the pond, exploring the land, and sleeping.

POWER SKILL:
Making a Table, or in This Case, an Elechart!

A table, which looks like a group of boxes in rows and columns, is different from a table you eat on. The kind of table we are talking about is a handy way of making information easier to see and easier to understand. Tables also help us make comparisons. For example, look at what each of seventeen elephants at the Elephant Sanctuary eats each day:

Tarra Eats Each Day...
130 lbs. hay and/or vegetation
1 lb. hand-mixed whole grains (oats, barley, wheat)
2 lbs. soaked wheat bran
10–20 lbs. fruits and vegetables   **Favorite: watermelon**

Shirley Eats Each Day...
150 lbs. hay and/or vegetation
20 lbs. hand-mixed whole grains (oats, barley, wheat)
20 lbs. fruits and vegetables   **Favorite: apples**

Bunny Eats Each Day...
130 lbs. hay and/or vegetation
20 lbs. hand-mixed whole grains (oats, barley, wheat)
10 lbs. soaked wheat bran
2 lbs. ground corn
10–20 lbs. fruits and vegetables   **Favorite: oranges**

Sissy Eats Each Day...
100 lbs. shredded hay (50% alfalfa and 50% Timothy) and/or vegetation
30 lbs. hand-mixed soaked whole grains (oats, barley, wheat, cracked corn)
20 lbs. fruits and vegetables   **Favorite: carrots**

Winkie Eats Each Day...
130 lbs. hay and/or vegetation
20 lbs. hand-mixed whole grains (oats, barley, wheat)
2 lbs. ground corn
2 lbs. soaked wheat bran
10–20 lbs. fruits and vegetables   **Favorite: potatoes**

Dulary Eats Each Day...

120 lbs. hay and/or vegetation

10 lbs. hand-mixed whole grains (oats, barley, wheat bran)

15 lbs. fruits and vegetables

Favorite: sugar cane

Tange Eats Each Day...

130 lbs. hay and/or vegetation

5 lbs. hand-mixed grains (oats, barley)

1 lb. soaked wheat bran with blackstrap molasses

10–20 lbs. fruits and vegetables   **Favorite: watermelon**

Zula Eats Each Day...

130 lbs. hay and/or vegetation

7 lbs. hand-mixed grains (oats, barley, wheat bran with blackstrap molasses)

3 lbs. soaked wheat bran with blackstrap molasses

10–20 lbs. fruits and vegetables   **Favorite: watermelon**

Flora Eats Each Day...

130 lbs. hay and/or vegetation

7 lbs. hand-mixed grains (oats, barley, rice bran with blackstrap molasses)

10–20 lbs. fruits and vegetables   **Favorite: bananas**

Misty Eats Each Day...

120 lbs. hay and/or vegetation

10 lbs. hand-mixed whole grains (oats, barley, wheat)

10 lbs. fruits and vegetables   **Favorite: bananas**

Billie Eats Each Day...

120 lbs. hay and/or vegetation

10 lbs. hand-mixed whole grains (oats, barley, wheat bran)

17 lbs. fruits and vegetables   **Favorite: hickory tree branches**

Debbie Eats Each Day...

120 lbs. hay and/or vegetation

10 lbs. hand-mixed whole grains (oats, barley, wheat bran)

15 lbs. fruits and vegetables   **Favorite: bamboo**

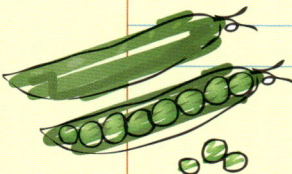

Frieda Eats Each Day...

130 lbs. hay and/or vegetation

20 lbs. hand-mixed whole grains (oats, barley, wheat bran)

30 lbs. fruits and vegetables **Favorite: broccoli**

Liz Eats Each Day...

130 lbs. hay and/or vegetation

20 lbs. hand-mixed whole grains (oats, barley, wheat bran)

30 lbs. fruits and vegetables **Favorite: broccoli**

Lottie Eats Each Day...

120 lbs. hay and/or vegetation

12 lbs. hand-mixed whole grains (oats, barley, wheat bran)

15 lbs. fruits and vegetables **Favorite: bamboo**

Minnie Eats Each Day...

120 lbs. hay and/or vegetation

10 lbs. hand-mixed whole grains (oats, barley, wheat bran)

15 lbs. fruits and vegetables **Favorite: bamboo**

Ronnie Eats Each Day...

120 lbs. hay and/or vegetation

10 lbs. hand-mixed whole grains (oats, barley, wheat bran)

15 lbs. fruits and vegetables **Favorite: bamboo**

Is there a better way to list all of this information? Of course there is—in a table! Follow the instructions in the Exercises below.

Exercises

1. A table has rows and columns for its categories. Your table is an Elechart that is going to include ten elephants. So you will need ten rows plus the rows you use for your headings. You pick which ten elephants you want to use, out of the seventeen described above. Don't use the two we have given in the example.

   Your columns will be: Elephant's Name, Hay & Vegetation, Whole Grains (Lbs., Type), Other, Fruits & Vegetables, Favorite. So your table will have seven columns. Notice that Whole Grains is a major category and Lbs. and Type are subcategories. Remember to leave lots of space if you draw your lines before you put in the information.

Look at the last row in the model. The word Lbs. appears in columns 2, 3, and 6. You can see that a table makes it possible to add quantities. To get you started, here is your model table:

My Elechart

Column 1	2	3	4	5	6	7
Elephant's Name	**Hay & Vegetation**	**Whole Grains**		**Other**	**Fruits & Vegetables**	**Favorite**
		Lbs.	**Type**			
Zula	130 lbs.	7 lbs.	Oats, barley, wheat bran with blackstrap molasses	3 lbs. soaked wheat bran with black-strap molasses	10-20 lbs.	watermelon
Flora	130 lbs.	7 lbs.	Oats, barley, rice bran with blackstrap molasses		10-20 lbs.	bananas
Total	Lbs.	Lbs.			Lbs.	

2. How many pounds of hay and vegetation do all of your ten elephants eat each day?

3. How many pounds of fruits and vegetables do your ten elephants eat each day?

ACTIVITY ONE
Greetings!

1. You have seen aisles of greeting cards in many stores. Now you have a chance to create your own greeting card for a character in one of the stories in Unit Two.

2. Choose from the following list of characters. One of them will receive your greeting card.

   Sato
   Amelia
   The Hatmaker
   Dad (in *Dad, Jackie, and Me*)
   Son (in *Dad, Jackie, and Me*)
   Jackie Robinson

3. Think of a message that you would like to send to this character. For example, you may write a good-bye card to Amelia or a card congratulating Jackie Robinson on winning the World Series.

Sato and the Elephants

Amelia's Road

The Hatmaker's Sign

JOHN THOMPSON, HATMAKER
FASHIONABLE HATS SOLD
INSIDE FOR READY MONEY

Dad, Jackie, and Me

And Now the Good News

4. Using craft materials, make a greeting card and write your message inside. Be creative!

Thank you!

5. Post the cards for all to see.

ACTIVITY TWO

Story Cinquains

1. A **cinquain** (sing KAYN) is a particular type of poem that has five lines.

   Line 1: one word—the topic (noun)

   Line 2: two words that describe the topic (adjectives)

   Line 3: three words that describe what the topic does (verbs)

   Line 4: four words that describe your feelings about the topic (can be a complete sentence)

   Line 5: a synonym for the topic or one word that sums it up

2. Choose one character or theme from Unit Two. Some themes of the stories in this unit are: making mistakes and learning from them, the sense of belonging, accepting criticism, prejudice, and preservation.

3. Write a cinquain about the character or theme you have chosen. Follow the line pattern above. There are very few words in this poem so choose your words carefully. Try to use specific and lively words and to avoid overused words.

4. Samples:

one word	*Fear*
two words	*Strong emotion*
three words	*Makes one shiver*
four words	*Control, challenge, confront, overcome*
a synonym	*Fright*

Supergrandpa
Energetic senior
Enjoys bicycle riding
Caring, motivated, modest, inspirational
Winner!

5. Share your cinquain aloud with your class. Compare your poem to those that are written on the same topic.

ACTIVITY THREE
Review Board

1. Your teacher will divide your class into groups.

2. Each group represents a committee that writes reviews to be included in a monthly literature magazine. A review is a paragraph telling a bit about the book without revealing the most important parts or the ending. It gives the reader an idea of why they might want to read this book. A review can include positive and negative ideas about the story.

3. Discuss the stories included in Unit Two—*Sato and the Elephants, Amelia's Road, The Hatmaker's Sign, Dad, Jackie, and Me,* and *And Now the Good News*. Choose

three stories for which you would like to write reviews.

4. Together, write three reviews, each one about a different selection. Be sure to edit and proofread your work.

5. When you are done, write the reviews neatly so that they can be included in a class review binder.

6. As the year goes on, students may add reviews of any book they have read, not just stories in this textbook.

ACTIVITY FOUR   *Moment of Clarity*

1. Imagine looking outside through a foggy window. You wipe away the moisture and, suddenly, the view is crystal clear. Sometimes our thoughts, like the foggy window, are unclear. An experience, a comment, even some idea that enters our mind, can make things clear. When we come to understand something that we did not really understand before, we have *clarity*.

2. In this unit, many characters achieve clarity towards the end of the story. It is like an 'aha!' moment.

   For example:

   Sato had, until now, carved ivory without thinking too much about where the ivory came from. Sato faces the fact that the beautiful ivory he wishes to carve can be had only if someone kills an elephant. Once he makes this connection, he has clarity. It is clear to him he can no longer use ivory for his carvings.

   The hatmaker (and Thomas Jefferson) realize that, in spite of what all the critics have to say, their work is nearly perfect—just as they thought.

3. Write an essay about a personal situation where you reached a 'moment of clarity.' Perhaps you discovered a new solution to an old problem. You may have learned something new about a person that changed your feeling about that individual. You might have conquered some fear by looking inside yourself and uncovering strength you didn't know you had. Describe the problem you started with and then explain what it took for you to see the situation clearly.

unit 3

head,
hands,
heart

Lesson in Literature...
HUTCHMAN'S HEROES

CHARACTERS

- A character can be a person, an animal, or some imaginary creature.

- We watch how each character behaves.

- Some characters are described in a simple way, and we see only one or two personality traits. For example, the girl is mischievous and bright, or the boy is serious and shy.

- Other characters are more complicated. We see many sides of their personality and character.

THINK ABOUT IT!

1. What is the problem that the children face?

2. Why did the children love Mrs. Hutchman?

3. List three of the characters in the story and describe each one with a single adjective. For example: *Mary. Kindhearted.*

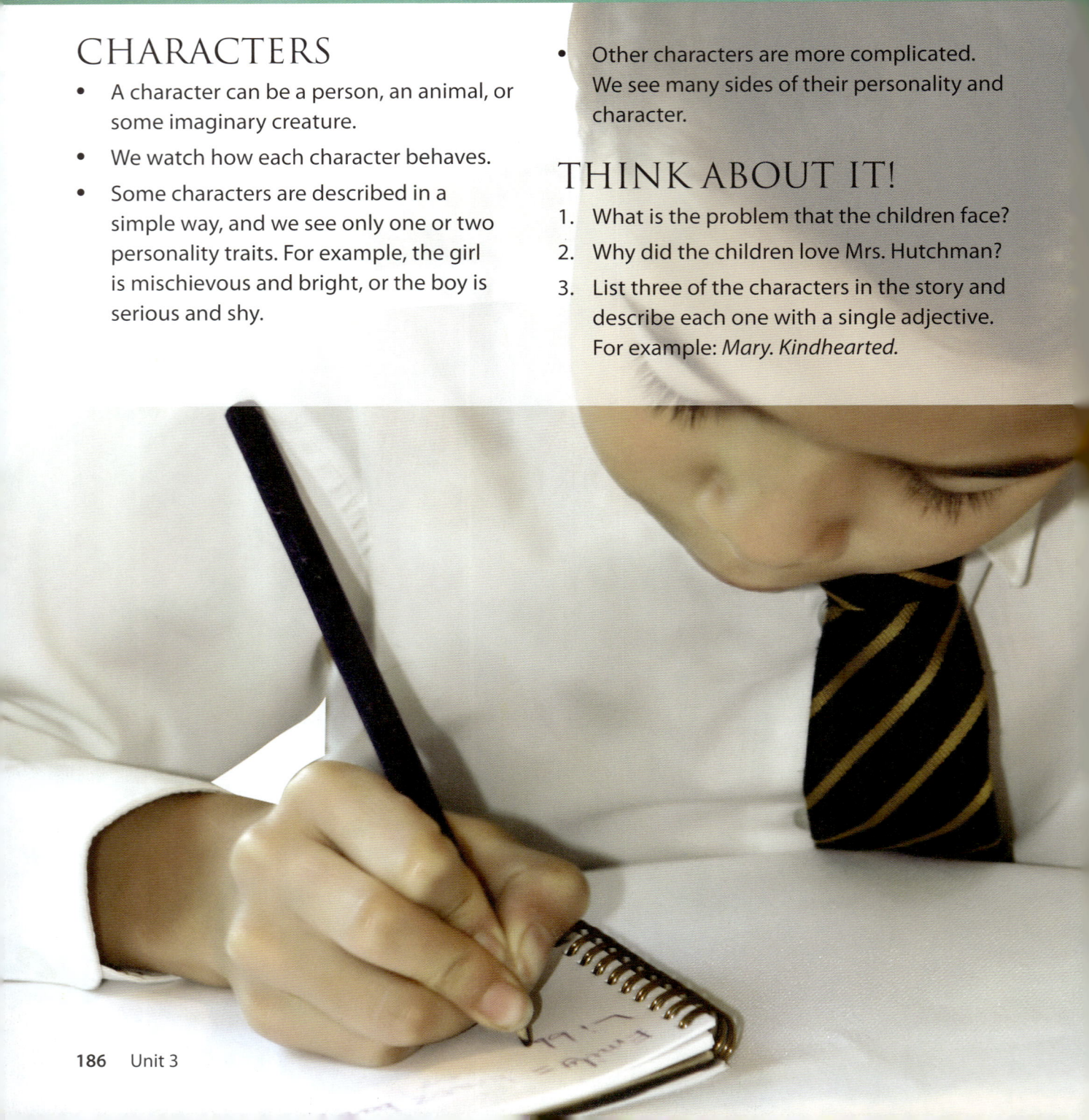

It was the worst thing that could happen to the fourth grade at Sandy Hook Elementary School. When Michael found out, he couldn't believe it and walked off by himself. When Bobby saw his friend alone, he joined him. When Ruth found out, she felt like crying. She ran over to Eileen and told her the bad news. As soon as Eileen heard, tears came to her eyes, and she told Susan. But it was Margaret who finally asked, "What's wrong? Why is everyone so sad?"

The rumor was true. Their teacher, Mrs. Hutchman, was leaving Sandy Hook before the end of the school year. Everyone loved Mrs. Hutchman. In the mornings she smiled when she greeted them, and in the afternoons she smiled when she said good-bye. But during lessons Mrs. Hutchman expected a lot of them. Behind her long dark hair and black-framed glasses, she asked them challenging questions. When they answered, she studied their faces as if her look could draw knowledge out of them.

She called a class meeting. "I have an announcement," she said, looking from child to child, "but many of you know it already."

"Why are you leaving us?" asked Margaret, who was usually very quiet. "Don't you want to teach us anymore?"

Mrs. Hutchman smiled. "Margaret," she said, "I love teaching you, but my husband's job transferred him to Florida. We have to move out of town."

The next day the entire class sat in a circle at recess.

Ruth took charge. "We need a plan."

"Let's convince her to stay," Eileen said optimistically.

"Let's misbehave for the rest of the year," said Bobby who liked to misbehave.

Susan stood up. "Let's buy her a present."

"No," Margaret said, her eyes shining. "Let's *be* her present."

Michael turned to look at Margaret. "How can we be a present?"

"We can make a present of our best work for Mrs. Hutchman and give it to her on her last day," she said proudly.

"I like that idea," Michael said.

He and Ruth divided their classmates into groups. The children who liked writing decided to write a story for Mrs. Hutchman. Those who liked geography planned a map of the route to Florida. The children who liked stories selected one of Mrs. Hutchman's favorite children's books to give to her as a gift. The children who liked science decided to write a report for her on dangerous animals of the Everglades.

On Mrs. Hutchman's last day the class threw her a good-bye party. For gifts, she received wonderful samples of all her students' best work. "You are my heroes," she said. "These gifts will always remind me of you. But tomorrow I expect you to get right down to work for Miss Washington, your new teacher."

That was Mrs. Hutchman. They were going to miss her a lot.

Blueprint for Reading

INTO . . . *Eddie, Incorporated*

Anyone who has been involved in sports knows that no one person can make the team win. There must be a team effort. Imagine a basketball game in which all the players want to shoot baskets. No one is willing to pass the ball. No one is willing to guard. Everyone wants to be a star. The team may win once or twice, but they will never be a championship team. The world of sports is not the only area where people need to be team players. We are often in situations where we must work with others. Starting and running a business is one of those situations. As you read the next story, think about how the friends work together to build *Eddie, Incorporated*.

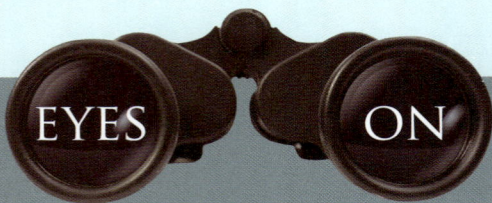

EYES ON *Character*

Almost everyone is fascinated by other people. Most books, stories, plays, songs, and articles are written about people! There are many ways to find out what a person is really like. Can you think of a few?

When we meet a new person, there is no narrator to say, "Tim is ten years old and was born in Ohio. He is shy but a loyal friend." We learn about people in different ways. When we read about a person, the writer uses many methods to tell us about them. Often, the writer will place clues here and there so that the character's personality slowly unfolds before us. Read the following paragraph:

Pat prepared to study for her American history test with Anna, the new girl in her class. She had already started studying but there was a lot of material to review. Textbook and notes were on her desk and a pencil was in her blonde hair. The red, white, and blue cookies were just the right snack. Even though most people did not want to study with Anna, Pat did not mind. She just wanted to do well on the test.

What do you know about Pat from this paragraph? Look carefully for clues. We can learn about characters from their language, actions, thoughts, and feelings.

Eddie,
Incorporated

Phyllis Reynolds Naylor

The South End Middle School was composed of sixth, seventh, and eighth graders instead of the usual junior high arrangement. Every noon, the students had an hour off for something called activity period. During this time they ate their lunch and afterwards they could walk around, talk with teachers, use the library, and go outside and throw Frisbees.

Eddie called a business conference during activity period. While their other sixth-grade friends were shooting baskets over on the concrete, Eddie, Dink, and Elizabeth sat on the wall at the driveway entrance and had a meeting.

It was understood from the beginning that they were partners. They would all three be bosses, so nobody could tell them what to do.

Anselmino's Aluminur

"We've got to have advertising," said Eddie.

Elizabeth lifted her face toward the warm May sun and closed her eyes for a moment. She wore huge, round, blue-tinted glasses, and her hair was pulled up in a large topknot.

"What we need," she said, "is to rent a plane that would fly all over Detroit trailing a banner that said, 'Anselmino's Aluminum Recycling Now Open for Business.' "

She even looked like an executive.

"Elizabeth can do advertising," said Eddie, and knew she'd think of

> ## WORD BANK
>
> **executive** (egg ZEK yoo tiv) *n.*: a person who has a position of leadership in a business or company

something, even without the plane. "We also need someone in charge of supply—to find out where the cans are and go after them."

"I could use Dad's garbage can carrier and go around collecting," Dink said. He was wearing a tee-shirt with Godzilla[1] on the front. He didn't look like an executive, but he did look as though he could walk over half of Detroit pushing a one-hundred pound load.

"You've got it," said Eddie. "Vice-president in charge of supply."

"Hey, Eddie," Billy Watson called. "Let's shoot a few baskets."

"Not now," said Eddie. "We've got business."

---

1. *Godzilla* (gud ZILL uh)

Eddie himself was in charge of the factory, which was half the Anselminos' basement. He set up a card table with a clock and a pen and a notebook on it. He propped up a long piece of rain gutter under the basement window as a chute, a packing box to catch the cans, a tub to rinse them in, a hair dryer to dry them, a sledge hammer to flatten them, and a box of leaf bags to bind them up in five-pound bundles.

All week long Elizabeth went about the neighborhood tacking handmade posters on telephone poles. The announcement read:

Tired of litter? Sick of Junk?

ANSELMINO'S ALUMINUM RECYCLING COMPANY

needs your old cans

And then it listed Eddie's address and phone number.

Dink had painted a big OPEN sign on the back of a dart board to set up outside the house. The Anselmino Aluminum Recycling Company would begin its first day of business on Saturday, May 17, at nine o'clock.

"I'll be here at eight-thirty, in case there's a line," Elizabeth said to Eddie on Friday.

"And we ought to put in a night deposit box so people will have some place to put their cans after we're closed," Dink suggested. He said he would make one and bring it with him on Saturday.

Even Eddie's brother Joseph was interested in the company.

"How much can you get for aluminum cans, Eddie?" he asked at dinner.

"Seventeen cents a pound."

Joseph figured it out on the calculator he had wedged between his leg and the seat of his chair. "Only five hundred and eighty-eight pounds and

Profits

you'll have a hundred dollars," he said, and went on to figure the interest.

"What are you going to do with the profits?" Eddie's other brother, Roger, asked Eddie. "Have you thought of investing it somewhere? The bank gives five and one half percent."

Actually, Eddie had been thinking of putting it in the back of his top dresser drawer under the extra shoelaces, but he said he'd consider investing.

"And what about Dink and Elizabeth?" Mr. Anselmino asked. "Are you putting them on salary, or do they share the profits?"

Eddie wasn't sure.

"If they're on salary," his father said, "that means you pay them a certain amount each week regardless of how much the company takes in. If the company loses money, you'll have to pay them out of your allowance or something. But if the company makes money, they still get only their salary and you get all the rest."

It wasn't difficult to decide that one. Eddie, Dink, and Elizabeth were a team. It would be share and share alike. Even if they made a hundred dollars the first day, they'd split it three ways.

"We're sharing the profits," he said, and realized he was beginning to sound like Roger. It was a good feeling, especially when he understood what he was talking about.

"Who's going to pay for the leaf bags you took out of the tool shed?" asked Mrs. Anselmino.

"We'll take it out of our earnings," Eddie told her. They hadn't even opened for business and already they were sixty-three cents in debt.

He woke at five the next morning and looked out the window to see if a line was forming yet. The street was still dark and empty. He knew he wouldn't sleep anymore, so he got up, dressed, and went out on the porch to wait.

The paper boy came by, followed by his dog. The mutt was holding something in his mouth that looked familiar. Eddie went down the steps and took it away from him. It was one of the advertisements for the Anselmino Aluminum Recycling Company.

"Hey, where'd he get this?" Eddie called after the boy.

The paper boy shrugged. "I don't know. It was blowing around on the street back there."

Eddie went down to the corner. The poster had been ripped off the telephone pole. There was still a piece of it left. He walked over to the next street. That poster was there, but someone had drawn two tanks on it, having a war, with smoke and bombs all over the words. At the next telephone pole, someone had crossed out Eddie's telephone number and scribbled in the number for the fire department instead.

He went back home and sat on the steps. This neighborhood didn't have too many old cans; it had too many rotten children. Anselmino's Children Recycling Company, that's what it ought to be. They ought to go around collecting bratty kids in Dink's garbage cart, weigh them in, tie them in sacks, and send them off to Siberia.

Mrs. Anselmino found Eddie still on the porch at seven o'clock and made him come in for breakfast. She put a plate of scrambled eggs before him and a sausage and an English muffin and then, on the spur of the moment, she poured him a half cup of coffee and filled the cup up with cream.

"Now," she said, "you're ready for business."

Tired of litter?
Sick of Junk?
ANSELMINO'S
ALUMINUM
RECYCLING
COMPANY
needs your
old cans
555-1212

He was beginning to feel good again.

Dink and Elizabeth arrived at eight-thirty. Dink had brought a night-deposit box made out of an ice cream container. On the curb at the end of the driveway he placed the dart board sign saying, OPEN.

At five minutes till nine, they took their places—Dink outside the basement window, Elizabeth at the bottom of the chute, and Eddie at the card table desk.

On the top of the first page of his notebook, Eddie wrote, "The Anselmino Aluminum Recycling Company" and, as an afterthought, added, "Incorporated," though he wasn't sure what it meant.

Underneath, he made six vertical columns with a ruler. At the top of the first column he wrote, "Date." At the top of the second,

WORD BANK

vertical (VUR tih kul) *adj.*: going up and down, not from side to side

he wrote "Number of cans." At the top of the third, "Number of pounds." At the fourth, "Income," the fifth, "Expenses," and at the top of the final column he wrote "Profit." Then, after a moment, he added, "...or Loss."

Nine o'clock came, nine-fifteen, and at twenty after, Dink yelled, "Somebody's coming!"

There were footsteps on the driveway outside, and the sound of the mailman's voice. He wanted to know where the aluminum deposit was, and Dink directed him to the open window.

The sleeve of a blue uniform came through the window and deposited one empty iced tea can in the rain gutter.

Clunk-ity...Clunk-ity...thunk.

WORD BANK

income (INK um) *n.*: the money an individual or business makes during a given time period

It was a very lonely sound. The iced tea can lay all by itself in the bottom of the packing box, and the blue uniform disappeared.

Elizabeth picked up the can and dropped it in the water in the wash tub, placed it under the hair dryer for a minute, and then flattened it with the sledge hammer.

"One," she said, as she set it over against the wall.

Eddie made a mark in the second column of his notebook beside May 17.

About ten o'clock, Mr. Clemmons came over with an armload of cans he had picked up in the alley. He dropped them down the chute one after another: *clunkity, clunkity, thumpity, bang, thud.* It was a beautiful noise.

"Hey, thanks a lot!" said Dink outside the window.

Now it was more like a factory. Elizabeth had barely taken all the cans out of the packing box when Dink's mother came around to the window and deposited a few cola cans and seven ginger ales. There were cans in the packing case at the bottom of the chute, cans floating about in the wash tub, cans under the hair dryer, and cans waiting to be smashed.

"This is more like it," said Eddie.

Things slowed a little over the lunch hour. Mrs. Anselmino brought down some salami sandwiches, and they took turns eating and standing out on the driveway to direct people to the deposit window.

Billy Watson and some boys from the South End Middle School rode over on their bikes, stuck their heads in the window and yelled crazy things. One of them rolled a rock down the chute. But after they went away, Elizabeth's father arrived with two grocery sacks full of cans.

"Way to go!" whooped Dink from outside as he poured the cans down the rain gutter.

Eddie and Elizabeth were working as fast as they could.

About three o'clock the hair dryer began to smell funny, and Eddie decided that maybe it needed a rest, so they finished drying the cans with a towel.

At four, old Mrs. Harris came by pulling a little wagon. It was piled high with cans, and she stooped down outside the window and began dropping them one at a time down the chute.

Eddie and Elizabeth stared. There were baked beans cans and creamed corn cans and scalloped potato cans and about twenty fruit cocktail. Only one of the cans was aluminum; the rest were tin, and the baked bean can still had a frankfurter in the bottom.

"Why didn't you stop her, Dink?" Elizabeth called up after the woman had left.

"I didn't have the heart," he said. "She pulled that wagon four blocks, so I just thanked her, and she said there were more cans where those came from."

At five o'clock, Eddie took the OPEN sign and put it behind the house. He closed the basement window and put the night deposit box in front of it. Then he and Dink and Elizabeth went back to the basement to tally up the day's profits.

There were one-hundred and thirty-six cans. Eddie brought down the bathroom scale to see how many pounds that would be. They began putting the flattened cans on the scales one at a time. The marker barely moved. Three cans…four cans…
"Maybe the scale is broken," said Elizabeth.

Around ten cans, they could tell that the marker had moved halfway between zero and one. It took twenty-one cans to make a pound.

Carefully they divided the cans into little heaps of twenty-one each. Six piles of cans with ten left over. Six pounds of cans at seventeen cents a pound.

Eddie went to his desk and figured it out. One dollar and two cents. He entered it under "income." Then he remembered the sixty-three cents they owed for the leaf bags and put that in the column marked "expenses." One dollar and two cents

minus sixty-three cents left a profit of thirty-nine cents. And thirty-nine cents divided between Eddie, Dink, and Elizabeth was thirteen cents apiece.

"At least you didn't go in the hole," Mr. Anselmino said at dinner that evening.

"And people know where to bring the cans now," said Roger.

"And he paid off his debt to me the very first day," said Mrs. Anselmino.

Joseph had not brought his pocket calculator to the table that evening, but Eddie could tell, by the way he pressed his fingers against the table top one at a time, that he was figuring something out in his head. "Thirteen cents a day, six days a week, fifty-two times a year, at five and a half percent…" he was saying to himself.

But Eddie wasn't interested in what he could make if the Anselmino Aluminum Recycling Company lasted a year. He was wondering if it would last a month. Eight hours a day for only thirteen cents was just a little more than one-and-a-half cents an hour, which meant he'd have to work a day and then some just to afford a stamp to mail his income tax. Bosses had more problems than anybody.

ABOUT THE AUTHOR

Born to write is the only way to describe **Phyllis Reynolds Naylor**! From the time her mother began reading books to her, she has made up her own stories. As a first grader, little Phyllis made up stories about the pictures in her reader and told them to her teacher! In the fifth grade, she would rush home every day to write down her latest story. Soon after she graduated from college, she began to write full-time and has so far published 115 books! Mrs. Naylor lives in Maryland with her husband. They have two grown sons, Jeff and Michael.

Studying the Selection

FIRST IMPRESSIONS
Do you think Eddie, Dink, and Elizabeth worked well together as a team?

QUICK REVIEW

1. What did Eddie and his friends agree on first, before they started to discuss the business details?

2. What job was each person given?

3. How much money could the group earn from collecting and recycling cans?

4. What made the basement feel like a factory?

FOCUS

5. Why would Eddie and his friends give up their activity period and the regular games with classmates to work on their business?

6. What character traits helped Eddie, Elizabeth, and Dink start their business?

CREATING AND WRITING

7. Write about a group of children working together on a school project. Include a problem they had and how they solved it.

8. Choose one character from the story. Develop his or her characteristics further. Let the reader get a more detailed peek into his or her life. Include more character traits, interests, talents, physical details, strengths, and weaknesses. Write one paragraph about the character. Then write one more paragraph about this character that includes something that takes place a few weeks after the story, *Eddie, Incorporated*.

9. Your teacher will divide your class into groups of three or four students. Brainstorm with your group about what rules and strategies are most important for teamwork and success. Once you have written down your ideas, find a creative way to share them with your classmates. Make an easy to remember rhyme, a pocket checklist, an attractive poster, or another method. This way, you will all remember to practice these guidelines for future projects.

Jill's Journal:
On Assignment at the Town Dump

I am standing at the top of a hill at the town dump. What do you think I see? I see an awful lot of stuff that could be recycled. Not only is this a huge waste of money but—and this is far more important—what we throw away is polluting the land, the air, and the water.

Over there—see where I am pointing?—is a computer: the whole thing—mouse, monitor, CPU, keyboard. Oh my. Look over here! A mountain of aluminum cans, bottles, and plastic bags! And the paper! And the newspaper! I read that they dug up a 35-year-old newspaper from a landfill and it could still be read. I also read that it takes 500 years for Styrofoam to decompose in the ground. I see what must be hundreds of Styrofoam cups. Would you ever have thought that a dump would be such an upsetting place?

Here's a quick quiz.

Question 1 To make paper, a lot of water is needed. How much water can be saved if recycled paper is used instead of shredded wood?

      10%   20%   40%   60%

Answer   60%

We may not have unlimited amounts of water. We need to conserve water and keep our water clean.

Question 2 Recycling the print run of a single Sunday issue of *The New York Times* would spare how many trees?

      10,000   25,000   50,000   75,000

Answer   75,000

Many people recycle, but more people don't. Some schools and businesses recycle, but many schools and businesses don't. Why doesn't everyone recycle when it is so important? Well, lots of people don't know how much it matters. In places where people are new to the country, people often don't recycle. In places where people are very poor, people often don't recycle. But for the rest of us, it may seem like just too much trouble. Also, we don't see the bad results right away. Besides, it is easy to say, "What difference will it make if I don't recycle? I am just one person."

Half of the communities in the United States have curbside recycling—the city picks up the recycling each week when it comes to get the rest of the trash and the garbage. That means that all that the household must do is have some extra

plastic trash containers and toss their recyclables in the right containers. Sometimes, of course, it also means that a container or a can needs to be washed before it is thrown away—but it doesn't have to be scrubbed!

It is understandable that people don't want extra work. But everything that matters needs care. Our world is precious, and we must take care not to spoil it. We want the water to be clean and pure. We want the air we breathe to be fresh and healthy. We want to make sure the fish can live in the oceans and that no animal is hunted to extinction.

Recycling should not be thought of as a chore. We should look at it as an opportunity to demonstrate how much we value the wonderful world we live in.

POWER SKILL:
Conduct an Experiment; Keep a Log of the Results

Do you know what a logbook is? It's the daily record or journal kept by the captain of a ship on a journey. This is your journey into recycling for two weeks. You are the captain of the ship. You will keep a log of your daily progress with your Recycling-in-Class Experiment.

This activity needs to begin with a solid plan, just as the characters in the story made a solid plan.

1. First, the teacher must appoint a student to lead a class discussion on what steps the class will take to recycle all the trash created by them in school. The project will last two weeks.
2. In your town, what does it take to recycle? Is there curbside pickup, or do you need to take your recyclables to a recycling center? Does the city provide containers, or do you need to provide your own? What types of trash is recyclable where the school is located?
3. Start by calling City or Town Hall to find out what the regulations are. Cities usually require that recyclables be put in three groups, as follows: (1) newspapers; (2) paper and cardboard boxes; (3) aluminum cans, steel cans, glass bottles and jars, plastic bags, and plastic containers. Plastic containers have numbers on the bottom. Turn over a plastic milk bottle and you will see the number 1 inside a triangle. Many towns only pick up #1 and #2 plastic. Other cities take every number plastic container.
4. When you have this information—about curbside pickup vs. recycling center; about whether the city provides containers; about what is recycled and what is not; about whether you need large blue or clear plastic recycling bags from the supermarket—tell your teacher what you have learned.
5. Your class will need to make a decision about whether they can bring in or purchase three extra plastic waste bins or whether to use doubled paper supermarket bags. You will also need to determine where these extra bins or bags will stand.

6. Line your bins with large blue or clear plastic bags to hold the recyclables, and label each bin so that the recyclables don't get mixed up.

7. Finally, the class needs a notebook in which to make daily entries. The first entry should briefly describe the first class meeting about setting up the recycling project. Each day write down the events connected with your project. How do people in your class feel about doing this? How many of each type of container is recycled each day? Enter your information clearly, so that you will be able to make a table of the daily recycling at the end of the week. The rows will be the days. The columns will be for aluminum cans, glass bottles or jars, plastic containers, paper and magazines, and newspapers.

Exercises

Your exercises will include the following:

1. Your recycling project, to be conducted for two weeks.
2. Your logbook, in which you will keep a daily record.
3. Your table, Our Two-Week Recycling-in-Class Experiment, which will look like this:

Our Two-Week Recycling-in-Class Experiment

Day	Aluminum Cans	Glass Bottles and Jars	Plastic Bottles, Containers, and Disposable Cups	Paper and Magazines	Newspapers
[starting day]					

All of your aluminum cans, other cans, glass bottles, and plastic are kept in the same container—if that is how your city collects or divides it. It is important to have a separate count of what is being thrown out.

Lesson in Literature ...

MAJOR AND MINOR CHARACTERS

- A **major** character is one of the **main** characters in a story. The action, dialogue, and narration are centered on these characters.

- The author will give the reader a lot of information about the main character.

- A **minor** character is one who does not play an important role in the story.

- The author may use minor characters to make the story more realistic, to represent one idea, or to add to the plot.

We're the Hill family. It's funny our last name is Hill because we live in a house on the top of a hill. I'm the youngest Hill. But when the biggest snowstorm in history hit last winter, I was the one who saved the day.

That morning I looked out my bedroom window. Snow was falling from the sky as if it were being dumped. The school play was that night, and I had a lead part. How would I get to the school?

SNOWSTORM!

THINK ABOUT IT!

1. What is the problem that must be solved by the characters in the story?

2. Who is the major character in the story? Name two minor characters.

3. In your opinion, what are the two most important personality traits of the major character in this story?

I ran downstairs.

My sister Meg and my brother Fred were pulling on coats, hats, boots, and gloves.

"Can I help?" I asked.

"No," they said together. "You're too young."

Mom stood in the kitchen, shouting into the phone, "The car is stuck! What do we do?"

"Can I help?" I asked her.

"No, honey," Mom said, "stay inside."

At the front door Dad and my oldest brother Sam took turns shoveling out a short path from our front door.

"Need any help?" I asked.

"No," my father said. "You're not big enough."

Snow fell and fell. That afternoon I pulled on snow boots, a heavy coat, and a hat and gloves. I was determined to help. So I climbed out of my bedroom window and stood on top of a mountain of snow almost as high as the second floor. The snow was so high I walked onto the roof of the garage!

"Be careful!" my father shouted from below.

I looked down. Dad and Sam shoveled. Meg and Fred shoveled. Mom stood in the doorway.

Seeing them, I knew it was up to me not to work but to think. How would I get down the hill and to the school play?

"Everybody!" I said loudly. "I have an idea!"

Meg and Fred stared up at me.

"I'll use the sled," I shouted.

Meg looked at Fred. Fred looked at Sam. Sam looked at Mom. Mom looked at Dad.

"You'll use the sled!" Dad repeated, shouting up to me. "I'll get Uncle Bill to meet you at the bottom of the hill and drive you to the school. Pack your things!"

"She'll use the sled!" everyone in the family said together.

Before I knew it, I was sledding down the hill. Beside me, my precious cargo was in a small basket strapped to the sled. In it was my costume for the school play. I was going to make it to opening night after all. Thanks to my family and, of course, my sled, I saved the day and the play.

Blueprint for Reading

INTO . . . *Heatwave!*

In 1904 a World's Fair was held in St. Louis. One of the most popular treats for sale was ice cream. Arnold Fornachou, an ice cream vendor, was selling bowl after bowl of it to eager customers when, suddenly, he noticed he was out of bowls! What could he do? If the ice cream melted it would be worthless. Another vendor, Ernst Hamwi, was selling *zalabia*, a crisp waffle. Seeing Arnold's panic, he grabbed a *zalabia*, rolled it into a cone shaped holder, and rushed over to the ice cream stand to show Arnold how the waffle could be used to hold ice cream. Americans have not stopped enjoying ice cream cones since that day!

When Ernst Hamwi grabbed the waffle, he was using his *ingenuity*. That means he was using his ability to think of new, creative solutions to a problem. When you use your ingenuity, you refuse to let a problem stop you; you explore every possible solution from every possible angle. As you read *Heatwave!*, notice how the main character uses ingenuity to help her family.

EYES ON *Major and Minor Characters*

As we have seen, a story has both **main**, or **major**, characters and **minor** characters. Imagine telling the story of *Goldilocks and the Three Bears* to a group of young children. Would you need to give a lengthy description of Goldilocks' parents? No, and there is a good reason for that. Goldilocks' parents are only minor characters in the tale and do not help move the story along. The main, or most important, characters are Goldilocks and the three bears. Anyone they happened to meet on their walk in the woods would be minor.

In the following story, see if you can determine which characters play a key role and are **major characters**, and which play only a small part and are **minor characters**.

Heatwave!

Helen Ketteman

My big brother, Hank, used to tease me that girls couldn't be farmers. But he sure changed his tune the day the Heat Wave hit.

I was feeding the chickens when I heard a loud roar. I looked out across the horizon and saw a big old clump of crinkled, yellow air rolling across the sky. A flock of geese flew in one side and came out the other side plucked, stuffed, and roasted.

I hollered for Ma and Pa and Hank, but before they got outside, the Heat Wave hit. The mercury blasted out of the porch thermometer like a rocket. Ma's flowers pulled themselves up by their roots and crawled under the porch looking for shade.

WORD BANK

horizon (huh RY zun) *n*.: the place in the distance where the earth and sky seem to meet

plucked (PLUKD) *v*.: pulled out, like feathers from a bird

By the time everybody
ran outside, the Heat Wave
had gotten snagged on the barn's
weather vane. It was near harvest
time, so we raced to the cornfield to
save what we could. But by the time we
got there, it was already too late. The
corn had started popping. It looked
like a blizzard had hit. One of our old
hound dogs turned blue and froze
when he saw it. I wrapped him in a
blanket, and he thawed out okay.

Then we heard a commotion in the pasture. We raced over. The cows were hopping around like rabbits. The ground had gotten too hot, so we herded them inside the barn. They still looked miserable, though. Pa figured their milk had gotten too hot, so we set to milking. As it turned out, the cows had jumped so much, they'd churned their milk to butter. It came out melted. We'd milked the last of the butter when I had an idea.

We scrubbed a couple of shovels and the beds of the pickup trucks, then I sent Pa and Hank to the field to fill the pickups with popcorn.

When they were done, they brought the trucks around, and we all pitched in and poured the butter over the popcorn. Then Hank and Ma drove the truck to the drive-in down the road. In no time at all, they sold every last bit of that popcorn, then hurried home.

We still had plenty of worries. We hurried to the field where we had oats planted. Sure enough, they had dried out. I tried wetting them down, but that didn't turn out to be such a good idea.

Soon I felt something slimy and thick rising up around my ankles. In another minute, it was waist high, and I could barely move. Turned out I'd created a whole field of oatmeal. It was lumpy, just like Ma's, and I about drowned in the stuff.

WORD BANK

commotion (kuh MO shun) *n.*: noise and disturbance
herded (HURD id) *v.*: drove or led (cows)
churned *v.*: shook and beat milk to turn it into butter

I dog-paddled to the edge and crawled out. Whoo-ee! The oatmeal was sticky! I told Pa we should bottle it, which we did later. It made fine glue.

It was then that I caught a whiff of something burning. I followed my nose to the barn and hurried inside. The cows were steaming, and their coats were starting to singe. Those poor critters were about to cook! We hosed them down and turned fans on them. It helped, but not enough. Pa always said I was the quickest thinker in the family, and I knew it was up to me to think of something else.

I figured it was time to take on the Heat Wave. I thought blowing air on it would help, but we needed the fans for the cows. Besides, we didn't have near enough fans to cool the Heat Wave down. Then I had another idea. A huge flock of crows, all beating their wings at once, might work. One thing Kansas has is plenty of crows. And I knew how to get them to come.

WORD BANK

whiff *n.*: a slight smell
singe (SINJ) *v.*: to burn slightly

We dumped several
fifty-pound bags of flour and
a bunch of yeast in the trough by
the barn, then stirred in water with
shovels. That dough rose so fast we had
to run for our lives. It rolled over several
chickens, then picked up the tractor and
Sally the mule. Ended up big as the barn.

A few minutes later, the dough started
baking in the heat. Smelled awful good,
and that's what I was counting on. Crows
can't resist the smell of baking bread,
and soon every crow in Kansas came
flocking to the farm. Their wings
made so much wind, we had to tie
ourselves around a giant tree trunk
to keep from being blown away.
It felt cooler already.

The trouble was, those
crows didn't keep flying.
They lit on the bread
and started eating. The
temperature shot right back
up, and I figured we might be
licked.

The crows pecked at the bread until
they freed Sally and the chickens. None of them
were a bit worse for wear. In fact, they were right
frisky. I figured all that yeast had caused their spirits
to rise.

WORD BANK

trough (TROFF) *n.*: a long,
boxlike container used
to hold food or water for
animals

Seeing Sally gave me one more idea. I told Pa to hitch her to the plow, and she plowed up a section of land in record time. While Pa was plowing, I found what I needed. I gave everyone lettuce seeds, and we started planting. Those seeds sprouted as soon as they hit the dirt.

The bigger the lettuce grew, the cooler the air got. That Heat Wave put up a fight, all right. It rippled and twisted and squirmed like a bucking bronco. But as the lettuce cooled the air more, the Heat Wave started shrinking, until it finally disappeared altogether.

The weather vane and the barn cooled down, and the cows stopped steaming, too. They didn't seem much affected, except the fuzz on their hides never grew back. Ma had to knit them all sweaters for the winter.

WORD BANK

affected (uh FEK tid) *v.*: influenced

So that's how
I saved the farm, by
planting lettuce. In case
you're wondering how lettuce
could cool the air, it wasn't just any
kind of lettuce, you see. It was iceberg
lettuce. I did make one mistake, though. I
miscalculated the amount of lettuce I needed
and planted too much.

Kansas had an awful early snowfall that
year, but none of us ever let on why.

WORD BANK

miscalculated (mis KAL kyuh LAY tid) *v*.: judged incorrectly

About the Author

About the Author

Helen Ketteman grew up in a quiet town
in Georgia, turning to books for the excitement
and adventure she craved. When she married, she and her
husband moved to Chicago, where their two sons were born.
The family then moved to Seattle, Washington, and Helen started
to write picture books for children ranging in age from preschool to
fifth graders. Mrs. Ketteman has published sixteen picture books so far.
She travels all over the country speaking and meeting with teachers and
librarians. Who knows? She may come to *your* city one day!

Be Glad Your Nose Is On Your Face

Be glad your nose is on your face,
not pasted on some other place,
for if it were where it is not,
you might dislike your nose a lot.

5   Imagine if your precious nose
were sandwiched in between your toes,
that clearly would not be a treat,
for you'd be forced to smell your feet.

Your nose would be a source of dread
10 were it attached atop your head,
it soon would drive you to despair,
forever tickled by your hair.

Within your ear, your nose would be
an absolute catastrophe,
15 for when you were obliged to sneeze,
your brain would rattle from the breeze.

Your nose, instead, through thick and thin,
remains between your eyes and chin,
not pasted on some other place—
20 be glad your nose is on your face!

Jack Prelutsky

Studying the Selection

QUICK REVIEW

1. In what way did Hank tease his sister?
2. What happened to the cornfield when the Heat Wave hit?
3. Was watering the oats a good idea? Why or why not?
4. What did the author use to attract the crows?

FOCUS

5. Which silly parts of the story made you laugh the most? Why is it good to read some stories that are not realistic and serious?
6. What important role did Pa and Hank play even though they were minor characters?

CREATING AND WRITING

7. The story does not mention how the family protected themselves from the heat throughout the Heat Wave. Write a paragraph about how the family protected themselves. Your ideas should be creative and funny.
8. Write a short and original fantasy involving the weather.
9. Choose three items from home or school and think of a new and unusual use for each. For example, a bottle cap could be used as a cookie cutter and an iron could be used to warm up food. Then, share your ideas with the class.

Lesson in Literature...

WHAT IS DIALOGUE?

- **Dialogue** is the conversation that takes place between the characters in a story or play.

- Quotation marks are placed around lines of dialogue.

- Dialogue tells us what the characters are thinking and doing. It may also *foreshadow* future events.

- Sometimes the conversation between two characters tells the story for the author.

THINK ABOUT IT!

1. In one word, what is the subject of the dialogue between Julie and her mother?

2. What does Julie learn about her mother as the dialogue continues?

3. What is one thing you learned about Julie from the dialogue?

How Can a Horse Run so Fast?

"How can a horse run so fast?" Julie asked her mother. Julie Walker and her mother Eileen sat together on a grassy hill overlooking a pasture. Below them two foals (young horses) galloped awkwardly around in circles.

"They're amazing, aren't they?" Eileen said to Julie with a hint of awe in her voice.

Julie looked at her mother. "They look clumsy to me," she said.

"They're clumsy now," Eileen said, smiling, "but I guess you can say that horses are built for speed. Thoroughbreds, the racing horses, have been clocked at over forty miles per hour. That's with a saddle and a rider!"

While mother and daughter had eaten a picnic lunch, they had enjoyed watching the two foals run around. Julie had named them Midnight and Sparky.

"They have funny-looking legs," Julie said.

"Their legs are just different than ours," Eileen replied. "Their legs don't have knees and ankles or muscles like ours, Julie. Their legs are only skin and hair, bone, tendons, ligaments, cartilage, and hooves."

Julie's eyes widened as she listened to her mother talk about horses. "How do you know so much about horses?"

Eileen smiled, remembering her love of horses from her childhood. "When I was your age, I loved horses. I loved to watch them run in races and jump in competitions. All I wanted to do was to learn to ride."

"Weren't you afraid?" Julie asked.

"At first I was afraid," Eileen said.

"Isn't it dangerous to ride?"

"No," Eileen said cautiously. "Horses are strong animals, Julie, but with proper riding lessons anyone can enjoy riding a horse." Eileen paused briefly to look closely at her daughter. "I know I enjoyed riding," she said.

Julie knew that as a girl her mother loved horses, but she didn't realize until just then that her mother still loved everything about horses. "Did you ever ride in competitions?" she asked her mother.

"Yes, I was an equestrian," Eileen said with a laugh. "I rode in a few show jumping competitions, but I liked all kinds of riding, because some horses walk, others trot, some lope, some jump, and others gallop. It all depends on the horse and the rider." Eileen felt like a teacher giving a lesson.

"I think I'd like to learn to ride," Julie said softly. "But not one of these foals. They're too clumsy for me."

Mother and daughter laughed together. "Of course not, Julie. Not yet. These foals are too young for riding, but just wait. In a couple of years you may be taking a riding lesson and the horse you're on will be Midnight or Sparky."

"I think I'll recognize them," Julie said.

"I bet you will," Eileen said. "I know I remember every horse I ever rode."

Julie looked at her mother's face. Now she knew why her mother loved everything about horses.

Blueprint for Reading

INTO . . . from *The Wright Brothers:*
Pioneers of American Aviation

Do you remember learning to ride a bike? When you first started, you probably didn't think you could do it and you wobbled back and forth. Then came that wonderful moment when you just *knew* you could! That *knowing*, that confidence, kept the bike straight as you pedaled. A big step toward succeeding at something is having the confidence that you can succeed. Do you think you can get a part in the school play? Do you believe that you can get a better grade next time? Would you be willing to approach an older, popular student? Do you think that you can make a difference?

As you will see, the Wright brothers could not have accomplished what they did without self-confidence. *Self-confidence* means being positive and believing in yourself and your abilities. As you read the story, think about what contributed to the boys' self-confidence.

EYES ON *Dialogue*

Dialogue helps us understand characters and makes them more believable. Read the following dialogue.

"I am going to organize the lists and call Mrs. Tanner. Tammy, you get some extra drinks and napkins. Ben, you can get some extra paper. In order for this project to work, be prepared to follow my instructions very carefully."

What do you know about the person speaking? Even though you don't know the person's name or too many details about the speaker, you have learned something about the speaker's personality. The speaker is an organized, take-charge person. As you read the following story, notice how much the dialogue reveals about the characters.

An excerpt from

The Wright Brothers
Pioneers of American Aviation

Quentin Reynolds

Susan Wright wasn't like other mothers. She was younger and more fun than most other mothers, and she liked to laugh and she liked to play games with her three youngest children; Wilbur, who was eleven; Orville, who was seven; and Katharine, who was four.

The other mothers would shake their heads and say, "Susan Wright spoils those children; lets 'em do anything they want. No good will come of it."

But Susan Wright only laughed. In the summer she'd pack a picnic lunch and she, the two boys and little Kate (no one ever called her Katharine) would go and spend a day in the woods. Mrs. Wright knew the name of every bird and she could tell a bird by his song. Wilbur and Orville learned to tell birds too.

One day they sat on the banks of a river near Dayton, where they lived. Wilbur and Orville were fishing. Everyone called Wilbur "Will," and of course Orville was "Orv." The fish weren't biting very well. Suddenly a big bird swooped down, stuck his long bill into the river, came out with a tiny fish, and then swooped right up into the sky again.

"What makes a bird fly, Mother?" Wilbur asked.

"Their wings, Will," she said. "You notice they move their wings and that makes them go faster."

"But Mother," Will said, not quite satisfied, "that bird that just swooped down didn't even move his wings. He swooped down, grabbed a fish, and then went right up again. He never moved his wings at all."

"The wind doesn't just blow *toward* you or *away* from you," she said. "It blows *up* and *down*, too. When a current of air blows up, it takes the bird up. His wings support him in the air."

"If we had wings, then we could fly too, couldn't we, Mother?" Wilbur asked.

"But G-d didn't give us wings." She laughed.

"Maybe we could make wings," Wilbur insisted.

"Maybe," his mother said thoughtfully. "But I don't know. No one ever did make wings that would allow a boy to fly."

"I will some day," Wilbur said, and Orville nodded and said, "I will, too."

"Well, when you're a little older maybe you can try," their mother said.

That was another thing about Susan Wright. Most other mothers would have said, "Oh, don't be silly, who ever heard of such nonsense!" But not Susan Wright. She knew that even an eleven-year-old boy can have ideas of his own, and just because they happened to come from an eleven-year-old head—well, that didn't make them foolish. She never treated her children as if they were babies, and perhaps that's why they liked to go fishing with her or on picnics with her. And that's why they kept asking her questions. She always gave them sensible answers.

They asked their father questions too, but he traveled for his work and was away a lot.

"It's getting chilly," Mrs. Wright said suddenly. "Look at those gray clouds, Will."

Wilbur looked up. "It's going to snow, I bet," he said happily.

"No more picnics until next Spring," his mother said. "Yes, it looks like snow. We'd better be getting home."

As they reached home, the first big white snowflakes started to fall. They kept falling all that night and all the next day. It was the first real snowstorm of the year.

In the morning the wind was blowing so fiercely that Wilbur found it hard to walk to the barn where the wood was stored. The wind was so strong it almost knocked him down. He burst through the kitchen door with an armful of wood for the stove, and he told his mother about the wind.

"The thing to do is to lean forward into the wind," she said. "Bend over, and that way you get closer to the ground and you get under the wind."

That night, when Wilbur had to make the trip for more wood, he tried his mother's idea. To his surprise it worked! When he was bent over, the wind didn't seem nearly so strong.

After a few days the wind stopped, and now the whole countryside was covered with snow. Wilbur and Orville, with little Kate trailing behind, hurried to the Big Hill not far from the house.

Orville's schoolmates were all there with their sleds. It was a good hill to coast down because no roads came anywhere near it, and even if they had, it wouldn't have mattered. This was 1878 and there were no automobiles. Horse-drawn sleighs traveled the roads in winter. The horses had bells fastened to their collars, and as they jogged along the bells rang and you could hear them a mile away.

Most of the boys had their own sleds; not the flexible fliers boys have now, but old-fashioned sleds with two wooden runners. No one ever thought of owning a "bought" sled. In those days a boy's father made a sled for him.

The boys who had sleds of their own let Wilbur and Orville ride down the hill with them. Ed Sines and Chauncey Smith and Johnny Morrow and Al Johnston all owned sleds, but they liked to race one another down the long hill. When this happened Wilbur and Orville just had to stand there and watch. Late that afternoon the boys came home, with little Kate trailing behind, and their mother noticed that they were very quiet. She was wise as well as fun, and she soon found out why they were unhappy.

"Why doesn't Father build us a sled?" Wilbur blurted out.

"But Father is away, Will," his mother said gently. "And you know how busy he is when he is at home. He has to write stories for the paper and he has to write speeches. Now suppose we build a sled together."

Wilbur laughed. "Whoever heard of anyone's mother building a sled?"

"You just wait," his mother said. "We'll build a better sled than Ed Sines has. Now get me a pencil and a piece of paper."

"You goin' to build a sled out of paper?" Orville asked in amazement.

"Just wait," she repeated.

Will and Orv brought their mother a pencil and paper, and she went to her husband's desk and found a ruler. Then she sat down at the kitchen table. "First we'll draw a picture of the sled," she said.

"What good is a picture of a sled?" Orville asked.

"Now Orville, watch Mother." She picked up the ruler in one hand and the pencil in the other.

"We want one like Ed Sines has," Orville said.

"When you go coasting, how many boys will Ed Sines's sled hold?" she asked.

"Two," Wilbur said.

"We'll make this one big enough to hold three," she said. "Maybe you can take Kate along sometimes." The outline of a sled began to appear on the paper. As she drew it she talked. "You see, Ed's sled is about four feet long. I've seen it often enough. We'll make this one five feet long. Now, Ed's sled is about a foot off the ground, isn't it?"

Orville nodded, his eyes never leaving the drawing that was taking shape. It was beginning to look like a sled now, but not like the sleds the other boys had.

"You've made it too low," Will said.

"You want a sled that's faster than Ed's sled, don't you?" His mother smiled. "Well, Ed's sled is at least a foot high. Our sled will be lower—closer to the ground. It won't meet so much wind resistance."

"Wind resistance?" It was the first time Wilbur had ever heard the expression. He looked blankly at his mother.

"Remember the blizzard last week?" she asked. "Remember when you went out to the woodshed and the wind was so strong you could hardly walk to the shed? I told you to lean over, and on the next trip to the woodshed you did. When you came back with an armful of wood you laughed and said, 'Mother, I leaned 'way forward and got under the wind.' You were closer to the ground and you were able to lessen the wind resistance. Now, the closer to the ground our sled is the less wind resistance there will be, and the faster it will go."

"Wind resistance...wind resistance," Wilbur repeated, and maybe the airplane was born in that moment. Certainly neither Will nor Orville Wright ever forgot that first lesson in speed.

"How do you know about these things, Mother?" Wilbur asked.

"You'd be surprised how much mothers know, Will." She laughed. She didn't tell the boys that when she was a little girl at school her best subject had been arithmetic. It just came naturally to her. It was the same when she went to high school. And when she went to college, algebra and geometry were her best subjects. That was why she knew all about things like "wind resistance."

Finally she finished the drawing. The boys leaned over the table to look at it. This sled was going to be longer than Ed's sled and much narrower. Ed's sled was about three feet wide. This one looked as if it would be only half that wide.

"You made it narrow," Wilbur said shrewdly, "to make it faster. The narrower it is, the less wind resistance."

"That's right." His mother nodded. "Now let's put down the exact length of the runners and the exact width of the sled."

"But that's only a paper sled," Orville protested.

"If you get it right on paper," she said calmly, "it'll be right when you build it. Always remember that."

" 'If you get it right on paper, it'll be right when you build it,' " Wilbur repeated, and his mother looked at him sharply. Sometimes Will seemed older than his eleven years. Little Orville was quick to give you an answer to anything, but as often as not he'd forget the answer right away. When Will learned something he never forgot it.

"Mother, you make all your clothes," Wilbur said thoughtfully. "You always make a drawing first."

"We call that the pattern," his mother said. "I draw and then cut out a pattern that's exactly the size of the dress I am going to make. And..."

"If the pattern is right, it'll be right when you make the dress," he finished. She nodded.

"Now you two boys get started on your sled." She smiled. "There are plenty of planks out in the barn. Find the very lightest ones. Don't use planks with knots in them. You saw the planks to the right size, Will—don't let Orville touch the saw."

"May we use Father's tools?" Wilbur asked breathlessly.

His mother nodded. "I don't think your father will mind. I know you'll be careful with them. Just follow the drawing exactly," she warned once more.

The two boys, followed by little Kate, hurried out to the barn. Both realized that this was an important occasion. Wilbur always chopped the wood for the stove when his father was away, but he had never been allowed to use the gleaming tools that lay in his father's tool chest.

Three days later their sled was finished. They pulled it out of the barn and asked their mother to inspect it. She had her tape measure with her and she measured it.

The runners were exactly the length she had put down in her drawing. In fact, the boys had followed every direction she had given them. The runners gleamed. Orville had polished them with sandpaper until they were as smooth as silk.

"We thought of one other thing, Mother," Will said. "We found some old candles in the woodshed. We rubbed the runners with the candles. See how smooth they are?"

Mrs. Wright nodded. She had forgotten to tell the boys that, but they'd thought it out for themselves. "Now try your sled," she told them.

Followed by Kate, the boys dragged their new sled to the hill only a half a mile away, where their pals were coasting. They looked at the new sled in amazement. It was long and very narrow. It looked as though it wouldn't hold anyone. The runners were thin compared to those on their own sleds.

"Who made that for you?" Ed Sines asked.

"Mother showed us how," Wilbur said proudly. Some of the boys laughed. Whoever heard of a boy's mother knowing how to make a sled?

"It looks as if it would fall apart if you sat on it," Al Johnston said, and he laughed too.

"Come on, we'll race you down the hill," another cried out.

"All right, two on each sled," Wilbur said. He wasn't a bit afraid. He was sure the drawing had been right, and because he and Orv had followed the drawing, he knew that the sled was right.

They lined the four sleds up. Will and Orv sat on their sled, but it didn't "fall apart." Suddenly Wilbur got an idea.

"Get up, Orv," he said. "Now lie down on the sled...that's it...spread your legs a bit." Will then flopped down on top of his brother. "Less wind resistance this way," he whispered.

"Give us all a push," Ed Sines yelled.

And then they were off. It was an even start. The four sleds gathered speed, for at the top the slope was steep. Will looked to the right. Then to the left. He brushed the stinging snow out of his eyes but he couldn't see the other sleds. He looked behind. They were straggling along, twenty and now thirty feet in back of him. The new sled skimmed along, the runners singing happily. Both Will and Orv felt a strange thrill of excitement. They approached the bottom of the long hill. The other sleds were far, far behind now.

Usually when the sleds reached the bottom of the hill they slowed down abruptly and stopped. But not this sled. It kept on; its momentum carried it on and on a hundred yards farther than any of the other sleds had ever reached. Finally it stopped.

Shaking with excitement, Will and Orv stood up.

"We flew down the hill, Orv," Will said breathlessly.

"We flew," Orv repeated.

Now Ed and Al and Johnnie ran up, excited at what had happened. No sled had gone so far or so fast as the one Will and Orv had built.

"You *flew* down the hill," Ed Sines gasped. "Let me try it?"

Wilbur looked at Orv, and some secret message seemed to pass between them. They had built this sled together, and it was the best sled there was. They'd always work together building things.

"Orv," Will said, "I've got an idea. This sled can do everything but steer. Maybe we can make a rudder for it. Then we can make it go to the right or to the left."

"We'll get Mother to draw one," Orv said.

"We'll draw one, you and I," Wilbur said. "We can't run to Mother every time we want to make something."

By now little Kate had come running down the hill.

"You promised," she panted. "You said you'd take me for a ride."

"Come on, Kate." Will laughed. "The three of us will coast down once. And then you can try it, Ed."

They trudged up the hill, pulling the sled. Two words kept singing in Wilbur's ears. "We flew...we flew...we flew...."

Orville and Wilbur Wright continued to plan and work together. They used the Wright Cycle Shop for many projects. They made over and improved bicycles, they built a printing press on which they printed a newspaper, and together they planned and built a glider. This was the very plane they flew at Kitty Hawk, North Carolina. They improved it and added an engine, and for the first time, on December 17, 1903, a glider flew under its own power. The glider, which Wilbur and Orville had built, was the first airplane to fly with a man on board. This invention made the Wright brothers famous all over the world.

The brothers always remembered the lesson they had learned from their mother. They always worked by a plan. "Get it right on paper, and it'll be right when you build it," Susan Wright had said. That is exactly what they did.

ABOUT THE AUTHOR

Quentin Reynolds led a very exciting life. Born in New York in 1902, he became a war correspondent (a journalist who travels with the army and reports about the war) during World War II. He reported from Europe, the Pacific, Russia, North Africa, and the Middle East. When London was being bombed, he stayed there and broadcast a weekly radio program of encouragement. During and after the war, Reynolds met the leaders of many countries. When he became ill at the end of his life, he did not complain or even tell anyone of his pain. He was 62 when he passed away in 1965.

The Inventor Thinks Up Helicopters

Patricia Hubbell

"Why not

a

vertical

whirling

winding

bug,

that hops like a cricket

crossing a rug,

that swerves like a dragonfly

testing his steering,

twisting and veering?

Fleet as a beetle.

Up

down

left

right,

jounce, bounce, day and night.

It could land in a pasture the

    size of a dot . . .

Why Not?"

Poetry teaches us to ask questions

Studying the Selection

QUICK REVIEW

1. What lesson did Wilbur learn during the snowstorm?
2. What did all the neighborhood children like to do for fun during the winter?
3. Who actually built the new sled and how long did it take?
4. What two ideas did Will and Orv come up with all on their own?

FOCUS

5. What are three lessons you can learn from this selection?
6. Choose three lines of dialogue from different parts of the story that reveal something important about a character.

CREATING AND WRITING

7. Write about something that you have always wanted to do but are afraid you will fail at. What makes you feel you will not succeed? Next to your reasons for thinking you *cannot* reach this goal, write down some plan to help you reach it.
8. Write a realistic but fictional story about how the Wright brothers—or fictional characters— try to help humans fly. The story may be serious, humorous, or a mixture of the two. Remember: It should be realistic, not a fantasy.
9. Draw a sketch of something you would like to build. Use a ruler or other drawing tools and try to be as accurate as possible.

Jill's Journal:
On Assignment in Dayton, Ohio

It is May 1877. I have been invited by Mrs. Susan Wright to take tea this afternoon at 3:00. I am so pleased. Her handwritten invitation was delivered early this morning to the boardinghouse where I am staying.

My hostess, Mrs. Granville Dooley, has said that the gardener will take me over in the buggy. How very considerate people are in these times!

The Wright family has lived in Dayton, Ohio at 7 Hawthorn Street for a little longer than six years. (I have been told that their youngest son, Orville, was born there.) The house, which is quite stately, was newly built for them when they moved here in 1871. It must be quite a change for Milton Wright, Mrs. Wright's husband. Why, he was born in a log cabin!

Well, we have arrived. I have checked my pocket watch and it is just 3:00 on the nose. The buggy ride was surprisingly smooth. No bumps. (Can you imagine? There are less than twelve miles of paved roads in Dayton until 1900!)

The Wrights have been married since 1859. I am looking forward to meeting their five children. Let me see now, there's Reuchlin, who is 16 already. Lorin—he's 13 or 14. Wilbur is 10. Orville is five and little Katharine is two.

Mrs. Wright greets me at the door. How exciting to meet a person from history! Have you ever wondered what people actually looked like long ago or what fashions were like? Did you ever wish you could go back in time?

Well, I am here to say that her clothing is very fine. She is wearing a black dress that looks like it is made of taffeta or silk—it has a grainy, shiny texture. Of course, it is long—it goes down to her laced up shoes. At the neck it has a scalloped white lace collar that closes with a white bow. The dress has those wonderful puffy sleeves, snugly fitting cuffs and shoulders, and a narrow waist. I do wish we could wear such styles today. Mrs. Wright's hair is dark brown, parted in the middle and tucked into a bun at the back.

"How kind of you to come," she says. "My husband is away on one of his journeys, but all of the children are here for you to meet." She gestures with her right hand to the house. "Please come in. We are so glad you could join us for tea."

We enter a room where the walls are lined with books. "This is the downstairs library. My husband's books are kept in the upstairs library." She

Courtesy of Special Collections and Archives, Wright State University.

7 Hawthorn Street
Dayton, Ohio

laughs gently. "He is generous with his books, as he is with all things. But he likes to know where to find them on his return home. So those books remain upstairs in his study." She pauses. "I know you are a writer, so I thought we could take tea here in the library, amongst all of the books."

A smallish oval table with carved legs and a lace tablecloth is set with china and a tea service. On a silver tray are cakes and scones. I hear laughing and shouting coming from the entryway. Four young men come in, nearly running, slowing themselves down, followed by a toddler with a red ribbon in her long hair. "Wait!" Katharine cries. She is wearing a red velvet dress with pantaloons and miniature versions of her mother's shoes in white. I hold out my hand to her and she hides behind her mother.

Each of the boys introduces himself with a little bow. They are formally dressed in suits of a sort and very gentlemanly. Katharine comes from behind

her mother to curtsy. "I am delighted to meet each of you," I say, smiling.

We are about to sit in the circle of chairs that has been set out, when Reuchlin blurts out, "Mother, I think I have fixed your sewing machine!" Mrs. Wright says, "Why Reuch, that's my boy!" She pronounces his name *Roosh*. Reuch says, "Well, Mother, I just did as you suggested." Wilbur turns to me and says proudly, "My Mother can fix or make anything." Mrs. Wright lowers her head modestly.

The children munch their cakes quietly as we talk. Mrs. Wright reminds me that the Civil War was not so long ago. "So many fine young men died. But my husband and I were very much opposed to the evils and suffering of slavery. Of course, he is still very much concerned with the problems of our countrymen."

I wish I could tell her how her sons will change the world. I wish I could tell her what a fine person Katharine will be, how she will care for and help Orville and Wilbur, and how Lorin will assist his brothers.

I remind myself that in my mind I must stay here in 1877. I should enjoy and be grateful for the opportunity to sit with this wonderful woman and her young family.

POWER SKILL:

How Does an Author Successfully Transport Us to Another Time and Place?

When a story is set in a certain time period, the author includes many details that help the reader feel right at home in that era. As you read Jill's Journal, you may not have even noticed how many small bits of the 1870s you took in as you focused on the plot and characters. However, if you had to write a piece of fiction set in a different time period, you would have to do quite a bit of research to find out what clothing your characters should wear, what their houses should look like, what kind of manners they should have, and even how their spoken English should differ from our modern English. The following exercise will help you organize what you know about life in the 1870s. Draw a simple cluster. In the center circle write "The 1870s." Into each one of the cluster circles, write one detail of setting, costume, language, manners, or anything else that helped create the 1870 atmosphere in the story.

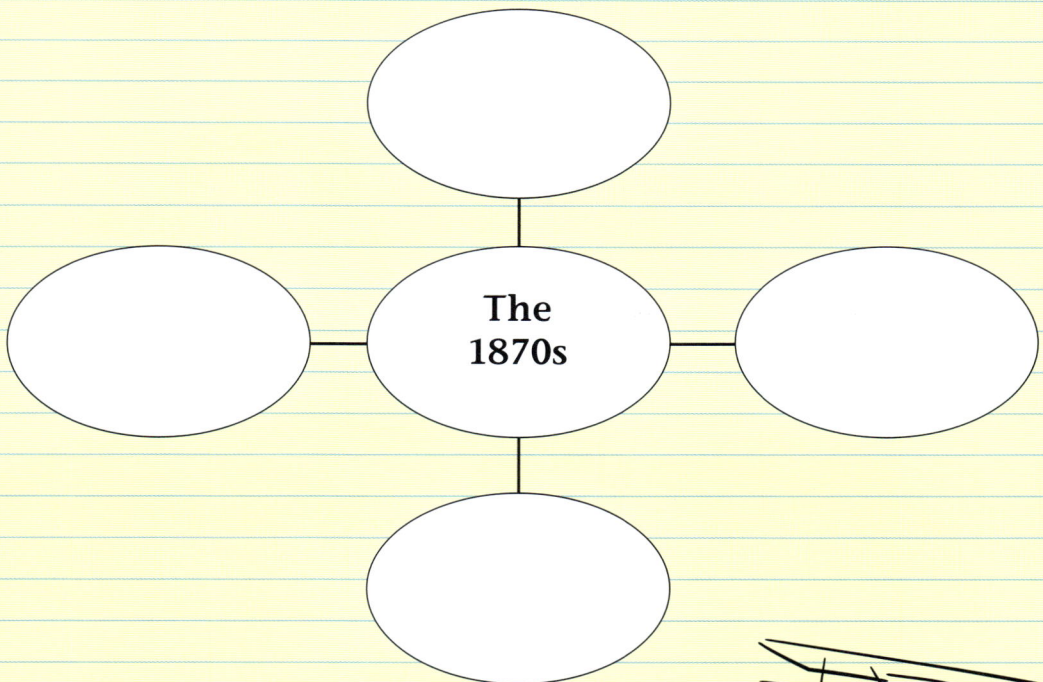

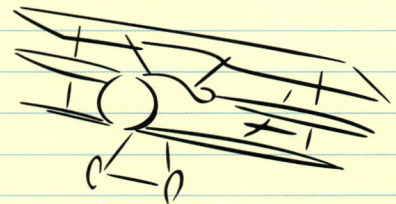

The 1870s

Lesson in Literature . . .

WHAT IS INTERNAL DIALOGUE?

- *Internal* means inside. *Dialogue* is conversation. **Internal dialogue** is a conversation that takes place inside the mind of a character.

- Internal dialogue reveals what the character is thinking, feeling, or planning to do.

- Everyone experiences internal dialogue. We call it *thinking*.

- In a story, internal dialogue is different from ordinary dialogue. It is not usually written as a conversation between two speakers. It is written as part of the narration.

THINK ABOUT IT!

1. The first paragraph describes Bobby's thoughts. These thoughts could have been divided between two different people. Imagine that, instead of *thinking* these lines, Bobby was *talking* to his friend Tom. Write a dialogue between Bobby and Tom, using quotation marks. It should start like this:

   Bobby: "
   Tom: "

2. Sometimes, we can tell what people are thinking by the looks on their faces. When Mr. Keller arrives, what is the look on his face? What is the look on Bobby's face? Make sure you base your answer on the words in the story that describe the feelings of both characters.

3. Copy one line of dialogue out of the story. Make sure you include the quotation marks. Then copy out one line of narrative that describes an internal dialogue. That line will not have quotation marks.

BICYCLE

Today was not a good day for a bicycle lesson, Bobby thought. It wasn't raining or cold, but he was sure he didn't want to learn to ride today. What's the big deal about learning to ride a bike, anyway?

He was at the park, waiting for his neighbor Mr. Keller who had volunteered to give him a few lessons. "You'll be a bicycle rider in no time!" Mr. Keller had told him.

Bobby wondered if Mr. Keller was right.

He looked across the grass and down the street. Mr. Keller must have forgotten about the lesson. He decided he'd waited long enough, but he hadn't taken ten steps for home when his stomach sank. There was Mr. Keller on a bike riding across the empty parking lot. He circled around him, whistling and smiling. "This will be you in a few minutes!"

Bobby felt panicky.

It wasn't that he didn't like bikes. He did. He loved watching bicyclists ride past his house on sleek, shiny racing bikes. He liked the excitement on the faces of boys and girls his age when they rode their bikes to school or to the park. Bobby even liked when he saw a father on a bike with a child in a seat behind him or a mother and a daughter pedaling happily on a tandem bike.

He just wasn't sure if he could do it! He couldn't imagine staying up on a bike by balancing on two wheels and knew he'd never figure out the steering or the brakes.

"Let's get started," Mr. Keller said.

Mr. Keller instructed him on climbing onto the bike, and he explained balancing, steering, and braking. "But you just have to try it, Bobby. Don't worry if you fall. It's trial and error. Everybody falls at first."

Those last words caught Bobby's attention. "Everybody falls?" he asked.

"Everybody," Mr. Keller said. "You learn by falling. Each fall brings you closer to riding."

After hearing that, Bobby inched his leg over the bar. So what if I fall a couple of times? Everybody falls. I'll be closer to riding!

Mr. Keller pushed the bike as Bobby pedaled hard. "I'm here," Mr. Keller said, running along beside him. "Hold the handle bar straight! Pedal, Bobby!" It was a few seconds before Bobby realized that Mr. Keller had stopped running. He was riding on his own! "Remember the brakes!" he heard Mr. Keller call from far behind.

He was a bicycle rider!

Later, he fell once and fell again. Of course, it took time to learn the steering and the braking. But Mr. Keller was right. Each fall brought him closer to riding. In no time he learned to ride a bicycle. It was a lesson he would never forget.

Blueprint for Reading

INTO . . . *The Imperfect/Perfect Book Report*

People are cheering! The scoreboard is flashing! Teammates are urging each other to play their best! It is a lively baseball game and only one team can win. Playing against each other with lots of energy and the belief that the best team will win is called *competition*. People are constantly competing against one another, but is it always a good thing? Read the following story and see what you think about the competition that exists between the main character and her classmates.

EYES ON *Internal Dialogue*

Do you ever wish that you had special powers and could hear what your parents or friends were thinking? While that is not likely to happen, we are given the opportunity to find out what characters in stories are thinking. **Internal dialogue** tells us about the characters' inner thoughts. *Internal* means inside, and *dialogue* is conversation. When we "overhear" internal dialogue, it is as if we are hearing the characters talking to themselves. As you read, notice how internal dialogue adds to this story.

The Imperfect/Perfect Book Report

Johanna Hurwitz

There was no doubt about it. Zoe Mitchell was just as smart as Cricket Kaufman. Everyone who had known Cricket since she had been the star of the morning kindergarten class, back when she was five years old, agreed. Finally, she had met her match.

In some ways, it made Cricket feel strange not to be the best student in the class. But at the same time, she worked harder than ever and found that she liked school better and better. She was learning so many new things. It was hard to decide if it was because now she was in fourth grade or because she was working not to let Zoe get ahead of her. Lucas Cott was smart too, but it wasn't the same thing. Maybe it was because he was the smartest boy in the class and she had been the smartest girl. Now, whenever test papers were handed back, Cricket craned her head to see what mark Zoe had gotten. Almost always, the two girls had performed equally well.

Mrs. Schraalenburgh beamed proudly at them both when they each got 100 percent on the fractions test in arithmetic. But she also congratulated Julio for improving his score. When Cricket walked to the back of the room to use the pencil sharpener, she was able to see that Julio had almost as many problems wrong as he had gotten right. Mrs. Schraalenburgh was a funny teacher. She always said she was proud of all her students and to prove it she never singled one person out above the others. Maybe that was why it wasn't quite so bad that Zoe Mitchell was such a good student. If Cricket wasn't the teacher's pet this year, neither was Zoe. No one was. With a different "personality of the day" selected each morning, and students like Julio being congratulated even when they could only answer half the questions, everyone was treated equally.

Still, when Mrs. Schraalenburgh said that once a month everyone had to write a book report, Cricket was delighted. She loved reading and a book report would be fun for her to write. She would do one that was so much better than everyone else's that Mrs. Schraalenburgh would have to admit that she was the very best student in the class. Although Cricket was pleased with the new assignment, there were loud groans from the back of the room.

"Quiet!" Mrs. Schraalenburgh scolded. "If you have something to say, raise your hands and I will call on you." She looked at Lucas, who had made the loudest groan.

"Don't you like to read, Lucas?" asked the teacher.

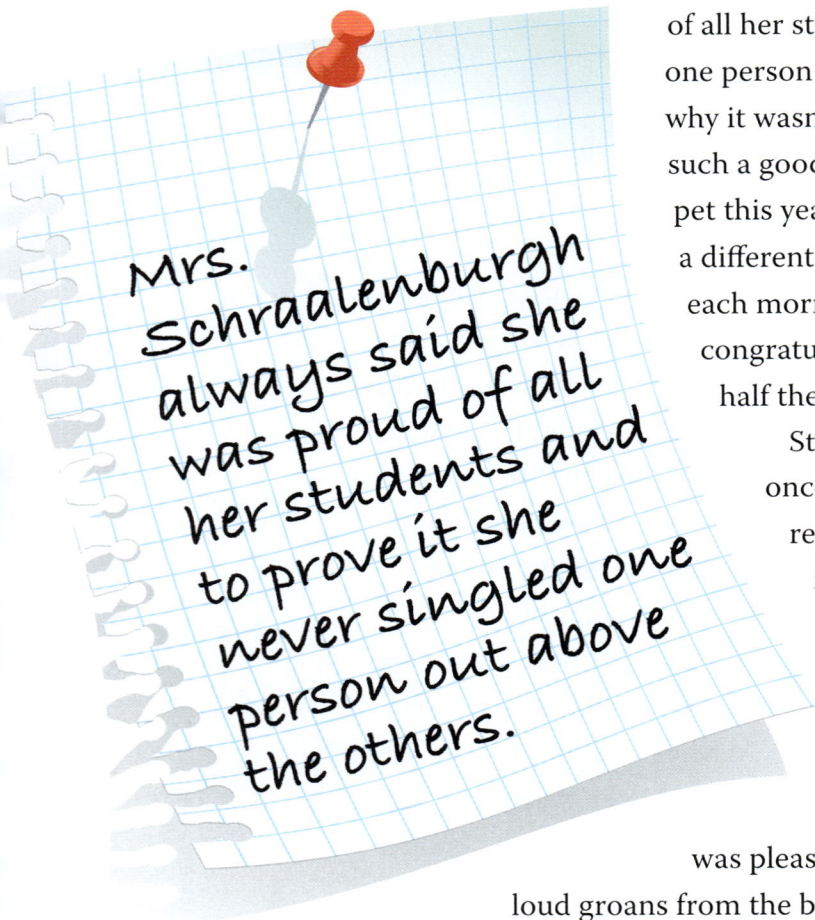

Mrs. Schraalenburgh always said she was proud of all her students and to prove it she never singled one person out above the others.

"Sure," said Lucas. "But I don't like writing book reports."

"A book report is a way of sharing something that you have enjoyed with the rest of the class," said Mrs. Schraalenburgh. "It should tell your classmates whether or not they too should read that book."

Lucas did not look convinced. Cricket knew he read a lot of books. She saw him checking them out of the school library when the class had library time. But she also knew he was lazy about doing homework. She, on the other hand, couldn't wait to begin. She would make the best book report that anyone ever did. Then, perhaps finally, Mrs. Schraalenburgh would know what a great student she was.

Cricket had read so many books since the school year had begun that at first she couldn't make up her mind which to use for her report. Finally, she decided to write her report on the book that she had given to Zoe. It was *Dear Mr. Henshaw* by Beverly Cleary. It was too bad she couldn't find a copy of it in the library. But Cricket remembered the story very well, and she thought she could write a report from her memory. Her memory was very good and it had been only a couple of weeks since she had read the book.

Cricket sat down and wrote, covering both sides of a sheet of loose-leaf paper as she told all about the book. Then, very neatly, she copied it over. She used a razor-edged marking pen that she had bought with her allowance last week. The letters came out clear and neat, but near the bottom of the page, she made a mistake. Cricket didn't want to have any crossing-out on her report. So she took a fresh piece of paper and copied her report over again, very slowly this time so that she wouldn't make

Finally, Cricket decided to write her report on the book that she had given to Zoe. It was Dear Mr. Henshaw by Beverly Cleary.

another error. When she was finished, it looked beautiful. It was the neatest piece of homework that she had ever done.

Then, to enhance the report, she decided to make a special cover for it. She took two sheets of red-colored paper. With her pencil and a ruler, she drew lines across the top of the page. She did it very, very lightly so that afterward she would be able to erase the lines. Then, using the block letters that they had been learning to do in art class, she wrote the title and the author.

Dear Mr. Henshaw
By Beverly Clearly

Book Report By
Cricket Kaufman

Underneath, she drew a picture of a boy sitting at a desk and writing. People who hadn't read the book might think it was supposed to be a picture of Cricket writing her book report, but if you read the book or at least read Cricket's report about it, you would know that it was supposed to be Leigh Botts, the main character in the story. He was always writing letters to his favorite author, who was named Mr. Henshaw. Cricket colored in the picture with her markers, and she erased the lines from the top of the paper.

Cricket had her own stapler. She used it to staple the top cover and the back cover to the page with her report. When she was finally finished, it was time for bed. She had missed her

favorite Thursday evening show. But she was so proud of her completed book report that she didn't even mind. Wait until Mrs. Schraalenburgh sees my wonderful report, she thought. She knew that the teacher would have to be very impressed with her careful work.

The next morning Cricket proudly handed in her report.

"You didn't tell us we had to make covers," said Connie Alf when she saw Cricket's masterpiece.

"We didn't have to make covers," said Julio. Cricket looked at the paper he was putting on the teacher's desk. Wait until Mrs. Schraalenburgh saw that he had written a report about *Mr. Popper's Penguins*, which she had read to them at the beginning of September. It was cheating to write a report about a book that you hadn't even read. Listening didn't count. And besides, everyone in the class already knew about the story. Julio will be in big trouble, Cricket decided.

"I wrote about the book that you gave me," Zoe whispered to Cricket as she put hers in the pile. "It was a great book and it was fun to write about it." She smiled at Cricket. But Cricket did not smile back. It hadn't occurred to her that Zoe would use the same book that she did for her report.

"How long was your report?" Cricket asked her.

"It was all one side and a little bit of the other side of the paper," said Zoe.

Cricket began to feel better. Her report was longer and her report had a fancy cover. Her report had to be a lot better than Zoe's. In fact, having another report on the same book to compare with hers would make Mrs. Schraalenburgh realize all the more how much effort Cricket had put into the assignment.

She smiled at Zoe. It was a good thing that they had both written about the same book, after all.

Mrs. Schraalenburgh took all the reports and put them inside her canvas tote bag. "I'll take these home to read over the weekend," she promised. "On Monday, I'll give them back and we'll share them together."

All weekend Cricket glowed inside as she thought about her wonderful book report. She just knew that her teacher was going to love it. She couldn't wait until they were returned on Monday. Mrs. Schraalenburgh would probably write on the report how fabulous it was.

The reports were not returned to the students until after lunch on Monday. Cricket could hardly sit still as the teacher walked about the room handing them back. She decided she would try and keep a straight face. It would be hard not to grin from ear to ear when she was reading the teacher's comments. But on the other hand, it would look as if she were showing off when other students such as Julio got bad marks on their reports. She held her breath as Mrs. Schraalenburgh stood at her desk and sorted through the remaining papers in her hand.

"Here's yours, Cricket," said the teacher. She patted Cricket on the back. "I'm sure you'll do better next time, so don't worry too much about your grade."

Cricket couldn't imagine what the teacher was referring to. There was nothing written on the red cover of her report, but when she opened it up, she saw a B– written on the top of the page. Cricket couldn't believe it. How could she possibly have gotten such a low mark? This was an A+ report. It didn't make sense. Then Cricket noticed that on the inside of the back cover, Mrs. Schraalenburgh had written a message.

Cricket's eyes blurred with tears. She couldn't believe it. Mrs. Schraalenburgh didn't like her report. So what if she had spelled the author's name wrong? What did it matter? She had never said that spelling was going to count in their book reports.

"I am going to have a few people read their reports out loud to share them with us now," said Mrs. Schraalenburgh. "Let's start with Julio," she said.

Cricket blinked back her tears. If she had gotten a B−, Julio must have gotten a D.

"I gave Julio an A for his report," the teacher said as Julio walked proudly up to the front of the room.

"Even though Julio wrote about a book that we have already read and talked about in class this year, he has captured the humor of the story and what he has to say about the book will make anyone who hasn't already read it want to read it," she said.

Julio cleared his throat and waited until he had everyone's attention. Then he read his report. It was short, Cricket noted. But he made everyone laugh when he reminded them of one of the funny scenes in the book.

"Suppose you wrote about a book you didn't like," said Connie.

"Why would you bother to do that?" asked Mrs. Schraalenburgh. "If you didn't like the book, you should have stopped reading it and looked for another one."

All the children looked at each other. They had never heard a teacher say that you should stop reading a book.

"Do you know how many books are in the school library?" Mrs. Schraalenburgh asked.

"One hundred," guessed Julio.

Cricket raised her hand. She had once asked the librarian, so she knew the correct answer.

"Many, many more than a hundred," said Mrs. Schraalenburgh.

"Two hundred," someone called out.

"No speaking out," Mrs. Schraalenburgh reminded the students. "Cricket, do you know?" asked the teacher.

"Eight thousand," she said.

There were loud gasps. Eight thousand was a big number.

"That's right," said Mrs. Schraalenburgh. "And don't you think that if there are eight thousand books right here in this school building you could find one that you would like? So why would you waste your time reading a book you don't like?"

"But if we have to make book reports every month from now on, we'll need to find more than *one* book," Lucas pointed out.

"That's right," Connie agreed.

"I suspect that if you gave it a try, you could find many, many books that you will like among the eight thousand books in the school library. And what about the public library? Do you know how many books they have there?"

"Eight thousand," someone guessed.

Mrs. Schraalenburgh shook her head. "The next time you go, ask the children's librarian how many books are in the collection there," she said.

"And next time, Julio will write about a new book. One that he hasn't read or heard read to him before," Mrs. Schraalenburgh added. "Right, Julio?"

Julio grinned at the teacher. "Right," he said. "I want to see if I can make an A every time."

"That's the spirit," said Mrs. Schraalenburgh.

Next she called on Zoe.

Zoe went to the front of the room and began reading. Cricket was surprised to hear her name in the report. Zoe said, "I picked this book because it was given to me by my friend Cricket Kaufman. At first I thought I wouldn't like it because it was all in letters. But before I knew it, I was right in the middle of the story of Leigh Botts and his problems…"

Cricket could hardly believe that Zoe considered her to be her friend. Just because she gave her that book it didn't make them friends. That hadn't been her idea. Her mother

had insisted that she bring a gift when she went to Zoe's party. And now Zoe had gotten an A writing about it when Cricket had only got a B−. It just didn't seem fair.

Zoe finished reading her report. "How many people want to read that book, now that they have heard about it?" asked Mrs. Schraalenburgh.

Every hand in the class except Cricket's went up.

"Now you know why Zoe got an A on her report. She has done an excellent job of sharing her pleasure with all of us. I notice that Cricket didn't raise her hand. But she doesn't have to read the book. She already did," said the teacher, smiling at Cricket. "And when she gave a copy of it to Zoe as a present, she was sharing her pleasure of the book in still another way."

Cricket could have said that when she bought the book for Zoe, she hadn't even read it yet. But she didn't. She liked what Mrs. Schraalenburgh said about her sharing the pleasure of the book by giving it as a present. It almost made up for the bad mark she got.

Mrs. Schraalenburgh wrote Beverly Cleary's name on the chalkboard so that everyone could copy it and said, "Now when you go to the library, you'll know who the author is." Cricket blushed to see the correct spelling on the board. It had really been foolish on her part to write a book report when she didn't have the book right in front of her to copy the author's name. She wouldn't make that mistake again.

A few other students read their book reports too. Cricket noticed that none of them had made covers for their reports. It had been silly of her to waste her time making a fancy cover if Mrs. Schraalenburgh didn't give her extra credit for it.

"There isn't time to read any more reports," said Mrs. Schraalenburgh after a while. "This was just to get us started. Next month, we will have oral book reports and everyone will have a turn. So start looking for a good book to read. Don't wait until the last minute."

The bell rang for dismissal. Zoe edged over to Cricket. "Thanks again for the book," she said.

Cricket nodded her head. She was relieved that Zoe didn't ask her what grade she had gotten on her report. If the situation had been reversed and Cricket had received an A and Zoe had not read her report aloud, Cricket knew she would have been dying to ask.

"I'll bet we have the same taste in books," said Zoe. "Maybe we could go to the library together after school sometime. You could show me the books you've read and I could show you the ones I've read."

Cricket found herself smiling at Zoe. It sounded as if it might be fun. There had never been another girl in school who liked to read as much as she did. Maybe Zoe was right. Maybe she would be a friend to her.

"Okay," she agreed. And suddenly, it didn't matter so much what grade she had gotten on her report. Next time she would get an A. And if Zoe got one too, it wouldn't be so terrible. After all, they were the two smartest girls in Mrs. Schraalenburgh's class.

About the Author

The daughter of a bookseller and a library assistant, **Johanna Hurwitz** grew up surrounded by books. From the time she was a little girl growing up in the Bronx, she knew she would be a writer. First, though, she became a librarian, got married, and had two children. Drawing on the experiences of her daughter, her son, and her own childhood, Mrs. Hurwitz has written more than 50 books for children and young adults. Although reading has taken her "all over the world," in real life she still lives in the New York area, not far from where she started out!

You and I

Mary Ann Hoberman

Only one I in the whole wide world
And millions and millions of you,
But every you is an I to itself
And I am a you to you too!

5   But if I am a you and you are an I
And the opposite also is true,
It makes us both the same somehow
Yet splits us each in two.

It's more and more mysterious,
10   The more I think it through:
Every you everywhere in the world is an I;
Every I in the world is a you!

Poetry is about you and me

Studying the Selection

FIRST IMPRESSIONS

Do you think Cricket was the only one competing, or were other students, such as Zoe or Julio, also in competition with each other?

QUICK REVIEW

1. Which two girls were the smartest in Mrs. Schraalenburgh's class?

2. How did things change for Cricket when Zoe joined her class?

3. What book did both girls use for their book report?

4. Why did Cricket receive a much lower grade than she expected?

FOCUS

5. Why, at the end of the story, did Cricket feel it didn't matter so much what grade she had gotten on her report?

6. "Wait until Mrs. Schraalenburgh sees my wonderful report, she thought." What does this line of internal dialogue tell us about Cricket? Why is it important to the story?

CREATING AND WRITING

7. Write about a time that you had a positive or negative experience competing with a classmate or a sibling.

8. Write about a child your age who moves to a new town. The child will be the main character in your story. Your main character meets a new neighbor of the same age, and immediately thinks that they cannot be friends. Later on this changes. Your story should include answers for some of the following questions:

   - Why did the main character move to a new town?
   - What was it that made the main character think that the neighbor could not be their friend?
   - What was it that made the neighbor seem unfriendly?
   - What did the neighbor think about the main character?
   - Do some of the feelings change? How and why?

   Try to use internal dialogue in your story to help answer these questions.

9. Your teacher will give you a piece of cardboard that looks like a book cover. Write the title and author of a book you would like to recommend to your classmates on your cover. Add an illustration and one or two sentences telling why you think that your classmates would like this book. Put the finished book cover on the bulletin board for everyone to enjoy.

Lesson in Literature . . . .

BEYOND THE MOUNTAINS

POINT OF VIEW

- A story's point of view depends on who is telling the story.

- Sometimes a story is told from the narrator's point of view.

- Most nonfiction works are written from the narrator's point of view.

- In works of fiction, a story may be told from a character's point of view.

THINK ABOUT IT!

1. Is this story told only through a narrator, or is dialogue used to reveal some of the plot?

2. In the second paragraph, we learn how Anthony felt about his host family. Write two sentences to describe Anthony's visit from the point of view of the host family.

3. In your opinion, do the narrator and Anthony have the same point of view? Explain your answer.

Anthony didn't know what to expect when his airplane landed in Managua, Nicaragua. He had lived his whole life in the United States, and this trip was the first time he had ever set foot in a foreign country. He was nervous. All he knew about Nicaragua was that it was a Central American country between Honduras and Costa Rica and the Pacific Ocean and the Caribbean Sea. Would he understand the people? Would the people understand him? How could he possibly understand anything about a poor country in Central America?

The first thing Anthony observed was the beauty of Nicaragua. As his group of college students traveled in the capital city of Managua, he noticed the magnificent mountains surrounding the city. In the city he saw big houses where wealthy people lived, but he also saw many shacks on the outskirts of the city where poor people lived. He saw something else, too. The Nicaraguan people, rich and poor, were just like the people he knew at home in the United States. The family that hosted him for two nights during his stay in Managua seemed a lot like his own family back home.

When Anthony and his group traveled into the country, a poor farming family hosted them for two nights. In the country Anthony met families that lived together in very small houses. He met hardworking parents, mostly mothers, who cooked, worked in the fields, and took care of their children. He met children who worked alongside their mothers and who loved to play games with visitors. Despite their circumstances, Anthony understood that these poor people were like anybody he might meet in his hometown in the United States. Although they spoke Spanish and didn't own as many possessions as most Americans, the people he met were full of love and life. He began to feel a strong attachment to the people of Nicaragua.

Anthony, though, was most impressed by something else he saw in Nicaragua. When his group visited an orphanage for handicapped children, he was surprised by the large number of children who lived there. When he realized that they had no homes and no families, he was even more surprised by their friendliness, joy, and excitement when visitors arrived. Anthony didn't think he would ever forget the little girl who took him by the hand to show him around the orphanage.

On his way to the airport, just before he left Nicaragua, Anthony caught another glimpse of the mountains. At the beginning of his trip, he thought his lasting memory of Nicaragua would be the beauty of those mountains, but at the end of his trip he knew differently. His lasting memory of Nicaragua would be the beauty of its people. He would never forget their kindness, friendliness, and hospitality. *Someday*, he thought, *I'll come back to Nicaragua. Someday, I'll come back.*

Blueprint for Reading

INTO . . . *Justin Lebo*

What does it mean to be *selfless*? The suffix *-less* means "without," or "not having." Care*less* means without care. Hope*less* means without hope. Self*less* means without self, without thinking of *yourself*. When you are selfless, you put someone or something before yourself. The *someone* may be a friend, a parent, or anyone who needs your help. The *something* may be an organization that needs your support. But being selfless does not mean that you give everything and get nothing. As you read, see if you can understand what Justin gained from being selfless and giving.

EYES ON *Point of View*

A birthday party was held at the home of four-year-old Brian Melton. When his father came home, Brian ran to the door and said, "Daddy! You missed all the fun! A bottle of red soda exploded when we opened it and got all over everything! The kids said it was the best party ever!" When Mr. Melton walked into the kitchen, Mrs. Melton said, "Jim, this was the worst birthday party I have ever given! A bottle of red soda exploded and ruined my carpet." As Mrs. Melton was sighing, Brian's older sister, Joannie, walked in looking bored. "Mom, I don't know how you put up with those little kids. All they do is eat and run around." Mr. Melton wrinkled his brow. He couldn't figure it out. It sounded as though there had been three different parties in his house: an exciting one, a terrible one, and a boring one! Which one was it?

The answer is, of course, that the party was all three—exciting, terrible, and boring—depending on your **point of view**. Your *point of view* is the way you look at a situation. As you read *Justin Lebo*, see if you can identify the point of view from which the story is being told.

JUSTIN LEBO

PHILLIP HOOSE

Something about the battered old bicycle at the garage sale caught ten-year-old Justin Lebo's eye. What a wreck! It was like looking at a few big bones in the dust and trying to figure out what kind of dinosaur they had once belonged to.

It was a BMX bike with a twenty-inch frame. Its original color was buried beneath five or six coats of gunky paint. Now it showed up as sort of a rusted red. Everything—the grips, the pedals, the brakes, the seat, the spokes—were bent or broken, twisted and rusted. Justin stood back as if he were inspecting a painting for sale at an auction. Then he made his final judgment: perfect.

Justin talked the owner down to $6.50 and asked his mother, Diane, to help him load the bike into the back of their car.

When he got it home he wheeled the junker into the garage and showed it proudly to his father. "Will you help me fix it up?" he asked. Justin's hobby was bike racing, a passion the two of them shared. Their

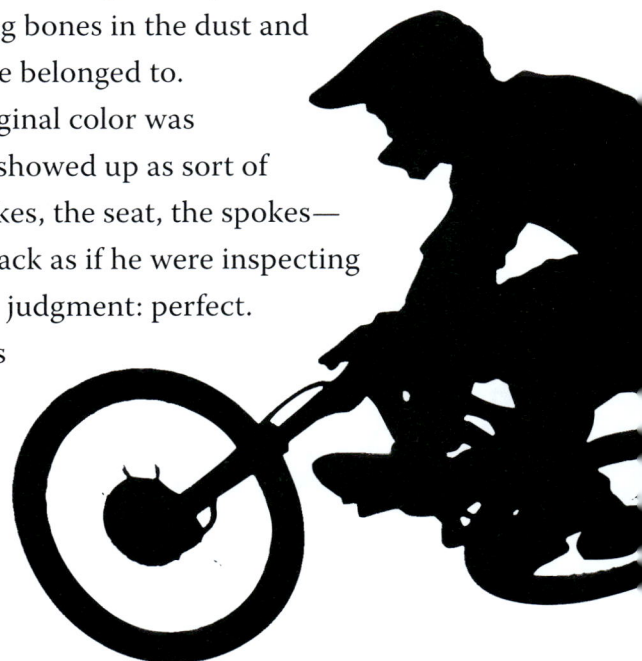

garage barely had room for the car anymore. It was more like a bike shop. Tires and frames hung from hooks on the ceiling, and bike wrenches dangled from the walls.

After every race, Justin and his father would adjust the brakes and realign the wheels of his two racing bikes. This was a lot of work, since Justin raced flat out, challenging every gear and part to perform to its fullest. He had learned to handle almost every repair his father could and maybe even a few things he couldn't. When Justin got really stuck, he went to see Mel, the owner of the best bike shop in town. Mel let him hang out and watch, and he even grunted a few syllables of advice from between the spokes of a wheel now and then.

Now Justin and his father cleared out a work space in the garage and put the old junker up on a rack. They poured alcohol on the frame and rubbed until the old paint began to yield, layer by layer. They replaced the broken pedal, tightened down a new seat, and restored the grips. In about a week, it looked brand new.

Justin wheeled it out of the garage, leapt aboard, and started off around the block. He stood up and mashed down on the pedals, straining for speed.

It was a good, steady ride, but not much of a thrill compared to his racers.

WORD BANK

realign (REE uh LYN) *v.*: to return to their proper position

Soon he forgot about the bike. But the very next week, he bought another junker at a yard sale and fixed it up, too. After a while it bothered him that he wasn't really using either bike. Then he realized that what he loved about the old bikes wasn't riding them: it was the challenge of making something new and useful out of something old and broken.

Justin wondered what he should do with them. They were just taking up space in the garage. He remembered that when he was younger, he used to live near a large brick building called the Kilbarchan Home for Boys. It was a place for boys whose parents couldn't care for them for one reason or another.

He found "Kilbarchan" in the phone book and called the director, who said the boys would be thrilled to get two bicycles. The next day when Justin and his mother unloaded the bikes at the home, two boys raced out to greet them. They leapt aboard the bikes and started tooling around the semicircular driveway, doing wheelies and pirouettes, laughing and shouting.

WORD BANK

tooling (TOOL ing) *v.*: driving or riding in a vehicle
semicircular (SEM ee SUR kyuh lur) *adj.*: shaped like half of a circle
pirouettes (PEER oo ETS) *n.*: a dance step in which the dancer whirls about on one foot

The Lebos watched them for a while, then started to climb into their car to go home. The boys cried after them, "Wait a minute! You forgot your bikes!" Justin explained that the bikes were for them to keep. "They were so happy," Justin remembers. "It was like they couldn't believe it. It made me feel good just to see them happy."

On the way home, Justin was silent. His mother assumed he was lost in a feeling of satisfaction. But he was thinking about what would happen once those bikes got wheeled inside and everyone saw them. How would all those kids decide who got the bikes? Two bikes could cause more trouble than they would solve. Actually, they hadn't been that hard to build. It was fun. Maybe he could do more…

"Mom," Justin said as they turned onto their street, "I've got an idea. I'm going to make a bike for every boy at Kilbarchan for the holidays." Diane Lebo looked at Justin out of the corner of her eye. She had rarely seen him so determined.

When they got home, Justin called Kilbarchan to find out how many boys lived there. There were twenty-one. It was already June. He had six months to make nineteen bikes. That was almost a bike a week. Justin called the home back to tell them of his plan. "I could tell they didn't think I could do it," Justin remembers. "I knew I could."

Justin knew his best chance was to build bikes almost the way GM or Ford builds cars: in an assembly line.[1] He would start with frames from three-speed, twenty-four-inch BMX bicycles. They were common bikes, and all the parts were interchangeable. If he could find enough decent frames, he could take parts off broken bikes and fasten them onto the good frames. He figured it would take three or four junkers to produce enough parts to make one good bike. That meant sixty to eighty bikes. Where would he get them?

---

1. In an *assembly line*, a product is manufactured piece by piece. As each part of the product is made, it is passed to the next worker, who adds the next piece to it, and so on, until the entire product is completed.

WORD BANK

interchangeable (IN tur CHAYNGE uh bul) *adj.*: two things that can be used in place of one another
proposal (pruh PO zul) *n.*: a suggested plan
gingerly (JIN jur lee) *adv.*: with great care

Garage sales seemed to be the only hope. It was June, and there would be garage sales all summer long. But even if he could find that many bikes, how could he ever pay for them? That was hundreds of dollars.

He went to his parents with a proposal. "When Justin was younger, say five or six," says his mother, "he used to give some of his allowance away to help others in need. His father and I would donate a dollar for every dollar Justin donated. So he asked us if it could be like the old days, if we'd match every dollar he put into buying old bikes. We said yes."

Justin and his mother spent most of June and July hunting for cheap bikes at garage sales and thrift shops. They would haul the bikes home, and Justin would start stripping them down in the yard.

But by the beginning of August, he had managed to make only ten bikes. Summer vacation was almost over, and school and homework would soon cut into his time. Garage sales would dry up when it got colder, and Justin was out of money. Still, he was determined to find a way.

At the end of August, Justin got a break. A neighbor wrote a letter to the local newspaper describing Justin's project, and an editor thought it would make a good story. One day a reporter entered the Lebo garage. Stepping gingerly through the tires and frames that covered the floor, she found a boy with cut fingers and dirty nails,

banging a seat onto a frame. His clothes were covered with grease. In her admiring article about a boy who was devoting his summer to help kids he didn't even know, she said Justin needed bikes and money, and she printed his home phone number.

Overnight, everything changed. "There must have been a hundred calls," Justin says. "People would call me up and ask me to come over and pick up their old bike. Or I'd be working in the garage, and a station wagon would pull up. The driver would leave a couple of bikes by the curb. It just snowballed."

By the start of school, the garage was overflowing with BMX frames. Pyramids of pedals and seats rose in the corners. Soon bike parts filled a toolshed in the backyard and then spilled out into the small yard itself, wearing away the lawn.

More and more writers and radio reporters called for interviews. Each time he told his story, Justin asked for bikes and money. "The first few interviews were fun," Justin says, "but it reached a point where I really didn't like doing them. The

publicity was necessary, though. I had to keep doing interviews to get the donations I needed."

By the time school opened, he was working on ten bikes at a time. There were so many calls now that he was beginning to refuse offers that weren't the exact bikes he needed.

As checks came pouring in, Justin's money problems disappeared. He set up a bank account and began to make bulk orders of common parts from Mel's bike shop. Mel seemed delighted to see him. Sometimes, if Justin brought a bike by the shop, Mel would help him fix it. When Justin tried to talk him into a lower price for big orders, Mel smiled and gave in. He respected another good businessman. They became friends.

The week before the holidays Justin delivered the last of the twenty-one bikes to Kilbarchan. Once again, the boys poured out of the home and leapt aboard the bikes, tearing around the snow.

And once again, their joy inspired Justin. They reminded him how important bikes were to him. Wheels meant freedom. He

thought how much more the freedom to ride must mean to boys like these who had so little freedom in their lives. He decided to keep on building.

"First I made eleven bikes for the children in a foster home my mother told me about. Then I made bikes for all the women in a homeless shelter. Then I made ten little bikes and tricycles for the kids in a home for sick children. Then I made twenty-three bikes for the Paterson Housing Coalition."

In the four years since he started, Justin Lebo has made between 150 and 200 bikes and given them all away. He has been careful to leave time for his homework, his friends, his coin collection, his new interest in marine biology, and of course his own bikes.

Reporters and interviewers have asked Justin Lebo the same question over and over: "Why do you do it?" The question seems to make him uncomfortable. It's as if they want him to say what a great person he is. Their stories always make him seem perfect, which he knows he isn't. "Sure it's nice of me to make the bikes," he says, "because I don't have to. But I want to. In part, I do it for myself. I don't think you can ever really do anything to help anybody else if it doesn't make you happy.

"Once I overheard a kid who got one of my bikes say, 'A bike is like a book; it opens up a whole new world.' That's how I feel, too. It made me happy to know that kid felt that way. That's why I do it."

ABOUT THE AUTHOR

Phillip Hoose writes books, essays, stories, and articles. He has written on a wide variety of subjects, including stories about endangered species, a perfect World Series game, and a championship basketball team. He wrote one of his most popular books, *Hey, Little Ant*, with his daughter Hannah, who was only nine years old at the time. Mr. Hoose works for an organization dedicated to protecting the habitats of endangered species. He lives in Portland, Maine where, in addition to writing books, he writes and performs his own songs.

HOLDING UP THE SKY

A TALE FROM CHINA

One day an elephant saw a hummingbird lying on its back with its tiny feet up in the air. "What are you doing?" asked the elephant.

The hummingbird replied,
5 "I heard that the sky might fall today,
and so I am ready to help hold it up,
should it fall."

The elephant laughed cruelly.
"Do you really think," he said,
10 "that those tiny feet could help hold up the sky?"

The hummingbird kept his feet up in the air,
intent on his purpose, as he replied,
"Not alone. But each must do what he can.
And this is what I can do."

Poetry shares big ideas

Studying the Selection

QUICK REVIEW

1. What did Justin look for at garage sales?

2. What did Justin do with the junkers he brought home?

3. How did Justin collect enough bicycles and money for this project?

4. To whom did Justin donate twenty-one bikes?

FOCUS

5. Why was freedom an important concept in this story?

6. Write at least two sentences describing some event in the story from the point of view of one of the following individuals: Mel, Mom, or the director of the Kilbarchan Home for Boys.

CREATING AND WRITING

7. Everyone has their own unique combination of talents. Write about how you can contribute to individuals and groups in your community. You may write about your past involvement in a project or an idea you have for the future.

8. Write about a group of students who raise money to help needy children attend summer camp. Include details about the campaign. Describe the feelings about the project from the point of view of the students and of the needy children.

9. Think of a creative way to make a model bicycle. You can use any material such as pipe cleaners or aluminum foil. Speak to your teacher about which materials you would like to use. When your model is complete, write a meaningful slogan on it, such as, "Giving is a cycle."

wrap-up

head, hands, heart

ACTIVITY ONE

Be a Model Character

1. Choose any *main* character from the stories in this unit.

2. Write a list of all the details in the story about the character's dress, hobbies, and personality traits.

3. Using materials provided by your teacher, design pictures or objects that represent the character you have chosen. For example, if your character has a big heart, draw and cut out a "big heart." Let us say you chose Justin Lebo; your objects might include a wrench or a toy bike. Place the four or five objects you have chosen onto an upturned shoe box or some similar platform. Attach a sign that tells which character you have chosen. Write a little explanation of each object in your display onto a piece of paper. Glue the paper to the side of the box.

*Eddie,
Incorporated*

Heatwave!

The Wright Brothers

*The Imperfect/
Perfect Book
Report*

Justin Lebo

ACTIVITY TWO

The Same Game

1. For this activity, you may choose any major or minor character from the stories in this unit.

2. Choose a character that is most like you.

3. List the ways that you are like the character. Include things like the way you look, your personality, and your favorite hobbies and sports activities. Compare the way you feel about school and the subjects you like most and least.

4. You may also list some differences.

5. Tell the class in an interesting and clear speaking voice how you are most like the character you have chosen.

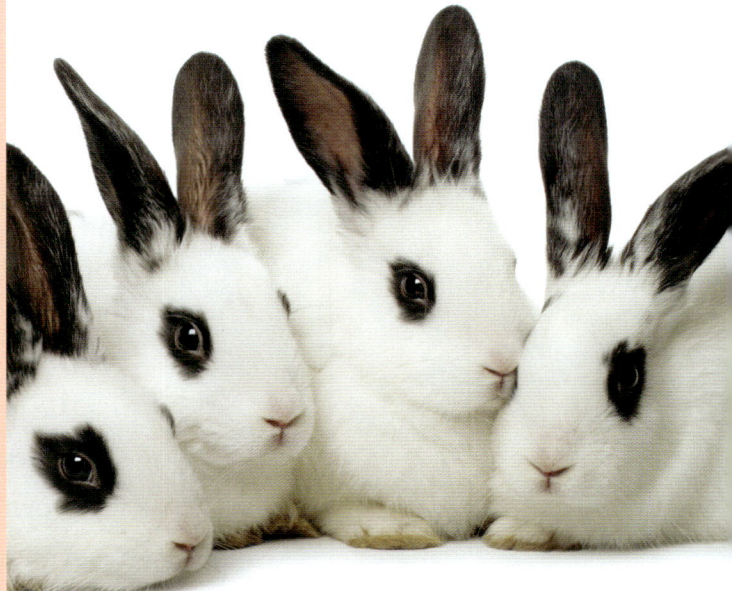

3

wrap-up
continued

Activity Three

1. For this activity, you will work in groups of two or three.

2. Your job is to take one character from Unit Three and place him or her in a different story in Unit Three. How will the character react? How will the others feel? Will this character help solve a problem or will the character cause new problems? Does your character become friendly with the other characters in the story? What information or insight can this character share with the others in the story?

ACTIVITY FOUR

Characters change and learn over the course of a story. Choose a character from one of the stories in this unit and write a paragraph about how the character changed from the beginning to the end of the story. What caused the character to change?

- Was it some event?
- The influence of another character?
- A sudden understanding?
- Growing older?
- A combination of these or other things?
- Did the character change for the better or the worse?

A Change of Place

3. Think through your choice of story and character before you make your decision. Discuss various possibilities with your classmates. Consider, for example, placing one of the Wright brothers into *Heatwave!* or making Eddie a classmate of Cricket and Zoe.

4. Using the answers you have given for the questions in #2, write a small play. You will have to invent a situation that is similar to one in the story you have chosen. Then, write an interesting dialogue for the story's characters and the character you have added to the story. Don't be afraid to be serious, mysterious, or funny!

Poetry

Poetry Is . . .

Sound and Rhythm

Sound, Rhythm, and Rhyme

Saying a Lot in a Few Words

A Picture

Rhyme

Fun to Write

Free

Contents

What Is Poetry?

Poetry Is Sound and Rhythm.

Sound is what we hear when we speak,
when we hear the voices of others,
the noises of the world around us, and
the beating of our own hearts.

Some noises are harsh and hurt our ears.
But poetry is not harsh! Poetry is a song.

Think about this:

When we try to make little children and babies happy, if they are crying or they need a nap, we speak in songs, nursery rhymes, animal sounds, and lullabies.

> *Meow meow woof woof quack quack and mooooo*
>   *of Old MacDonald's Farm,*
> *One Potato Two Potato*
> *Hickory Dickory Dock*
> *rock-a-bye baby—*

These are poetry.

Poetry sounds are
repeated repeated repeated re re re pea pea pea ted ted ted.

Beverly McLoughland

Birds' Square Dance

Swing your partner
Cockatoo
Bluefoot booby
Marabou

5   Cassowary
Heel and toe
Toucan, noddy
Oriole

Chachalaca
10 To the right
Bobolink and
Hold her tight

Kittiwake and
Tap your feet
15 Loon and puffin
Parakeet

Flap your feathers
Curlew, crow
Pipit, tern, and
20 Do-si-do.

Karla Kuskin

Thistles

Thirty thirsty thistles
Thicketed and green
Growing in a grassy swamp
Purple-topped and lean
5   Prickily and thistley
Topped by tufts of thorns
Green mean little leaves on them.
And tiny purple horns
Briary and brambley
10 A spikey, spiney bunch of them.
A troop of bright-red birds came by
And had a lovely lunch of them.

Whirligig Beetles

Paul Fleischman

We're whirligig beetles
we're swimming in circles,
black backs by the hundred.

We're spinning and swerving
as if we were on a
mad merry-go-round.
We never get dizzy
from whirling and weaving
and wheeling and swirling.

The same goes for turning,
revolving and curving,
gyrating and twirling.
The crows fly directly,
but we prefer spirals,
arcs, ovals, and loops.

"As the whirligig swims"

circular
roundabout
backtracking
indirect
serpentine
tortuous
twisty,
best possible
route.

We're whirligig beetles
we're swimming in circles,
black backs by the hundred.
We're spinning and swerving
 as if we were on a
mad merry-go-round.

We never get dizzy
from whirling and weaving
and wheeling and swirling.
The same goes for turning,
revolving and curving,
gyrating and twirling.

The crows fly directly,
but we prefer spirals,
arcs, ovals, and loops.
We're fond of the phrase
"As the whirligig swims"
meaning traveling by
the most circular
roundabout
backtracking
indirect
serpentine
tortuous
twisty and
turny,
best possible
route.

This Is the Key

This is the key of the kingdom:
In that kingdom there is a city.
In that city there is a town.
In that town there is a street.
5   In that street there is a lane.
In that lane there is a yard.
In that yard there is a house.
In that house there is a room.
In that room there is a bed.
10   On that bed there is a basket.
In that basket there are some flowers.

Flowers in a basket.
Basket on the bed.
Bed in the room.
15   Room in the house.
House in the yard.
Yard in the lane.
Lane in the street.
Street in the town.
20   Town in the city.
City in the kingdom.
Of the kingdom this is the key.

Anonymous

THINK about it

1. Read *Birds' Square Dance* to yourself, silently. Then read *Birds' Square Dance* out loud. Now read *Birds' Square Dance* tapping your foot and clapping your hands to the beat. Which sounds did you hear repeated? Write them down.

2. In *Birds' Square Dance*, the poet uses the sound *ooo* (as in *boo hoo*) seven times. Write down the seven words that have the sound *ooo*.

3. *Thistles* is a tongue twister. Your teacher will give you a tongue twister to practice and say before your class. Which consonants are repeated in *your* tongue twister? Write them down.

4. a. Write down the six words in *Thistles* that begin with *th*. (Do not include the word *them*, because it is a different *th* sound.)

   b. Write down the three words (one of these is used twice) that begin *gr*.

   c. Now, write down the words that begin *br* and those that begin *sp*.

5. a. This exercise must be led by your teacher. *Whirligig Beetles* is meant to be read in two groups. During part of the reading, one group is quiet while the other recites. The easiest way to recite in the correct rhythm is to clap your hands and tap your foot as you say the words out loud. In order to keep the rhythm you have to keep clapping and tapping even when it is not your group's turn to read.

   b. Your teacher will assign you to Group One or Two.
   Remember: When your group is not reciting, keep beating time.

6. *This Is the Key* goes forward and back. Which line is at the exact center of the poem? Write down your answer.

7. You are going to write a poem just like *This Is the Key*. Your poem will have only ten lines. Five will go forward and five will go back. Here are some beginning lines to choose from:

   > *This is the door to the house…*
   > *These are the steps to the library…*
   > *This is the gate to the path…*

   You may choose to think of one of your own.

LESSON two

Poetry Is Sound, Rhythm, and RHYME!

Poetry Is Nonsense

Have you ever heard the expression "it tickles my funny bone"? Even if you haven't, you will surely agree that that is what a limerick does! Limericks are not written to teach a lesson or to describe a beautiful scene. They are there just to make you laugh! Part of what makes them so much fun to read and write is that they are all written in the same form. Limericks all have five lines. What else do they all have? (Hint: The answer includes the words rhythm and rhyme.)

Limericks are most enjoyable when read aloud. Reading the limerick correctly is part of the fun. In the examples that follow, the syllables that should be stressed when being recited are italicized.

An *old* man was *seen* in the *park*.
He *raked* leaves from *dawn* until *dark*.
　"I *can't* stand the *noise*,
　Of *dogs*, girls, and *boys*,
But it's *worse* when the *dogs* start to *bark*."

A lot of limericks have the name of a place as the last word in the first line:

A *kid* in my *class* at my *school*,
Could *add* and sub*tract* on a *stool*.
　Where he *stood* on his *head*,
　Till his *face* turned quite *red*,
We *all* thought it *real*ly quite *cool*.

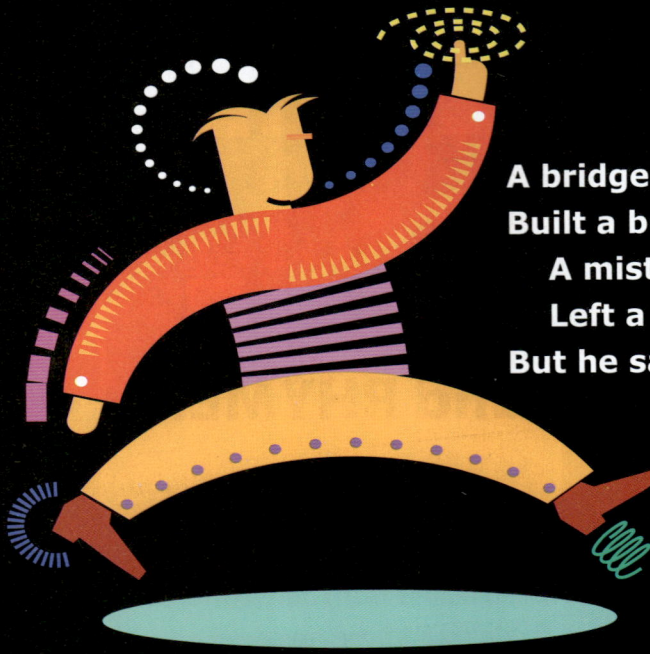

A bridge engineer, Mister Crumpett,
Built a bridge for the good River Bumpett.
   A mistake in the plan
   Left a gap in the span,
But he said, "Well, they'll just have to jump it."

Anonymous

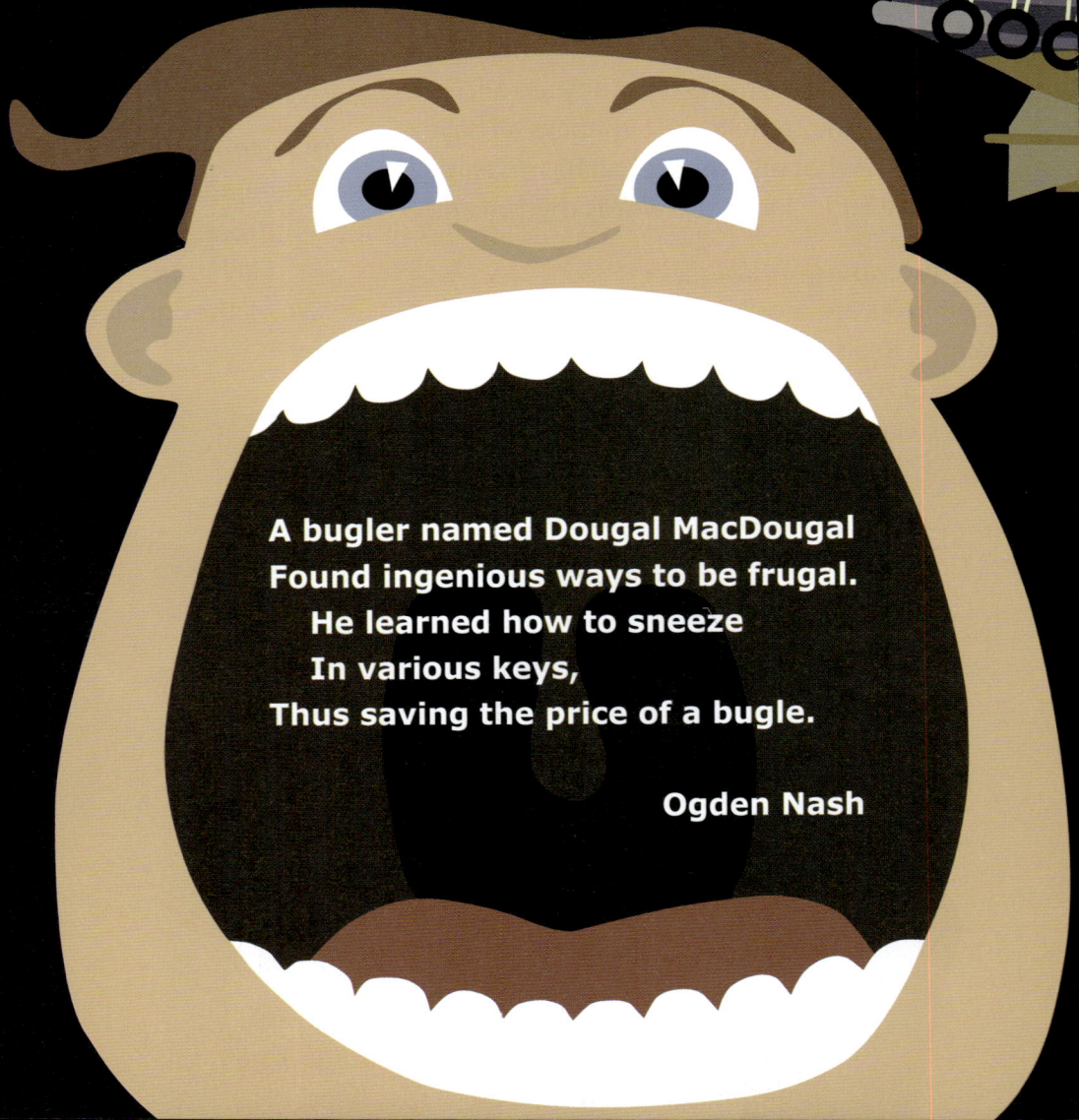

A bugler named Dougal MacDougal
Found ingenious ways to be frugal.
   He learned how to sneeze
   In various keys,
Thus saving the price of a bugle.

Ogden Nash

A funny young fellow named Perkins
Was terribly fond of small gherkins
One day after tea
He ate ninety three
And pickled his internal workings

Anonymous

A native of Chalamazug
Once fell overboard from a tug
He cried, "Ding-dong boller
Doo jango zong zoller"
Which means, "Glug-glug glug
     glug-glug glug"

Graham Lester

A gullible rancher named Clyde
Bought forty-eight gnus "on the side"
Said his wife, "This herd's phony,
All but one is a pony"
"Well, it's all gnus to me" he replied

Graham Lester

Here are four limericks for you to complete!

1. A *sol*dier who *came* here from *France*,
   Had *stripes* down the *legs* of his *pants*,
      His *jack*et was *small*,
      Cause *he* was so *tall*,
   _____.

2. Jane Smith came from *Kal*amazoo,
   Her *pet* was her *dear* cocka*too*.
      Ma*rie* was all *white*,
      _____.

   But her *squawk* made Jane *cry*, "Boo *hoo*!"

3. A young man from Philly, PA,
      (pronounced "pea *ay*")
   _____.
      He *took* off his *coat*,
      Then *he* cleared his *throat*,
   And *said*, "_____."

4. A *child* went to *play* at the *shore*,
   And *found* it was *real*ly a *bore*.
      _____
      _____
   Now *he* never *swims* any*more*.

5. It is time to write your own limerick. Think of your three rhyming words in the 1st, 2nd, and 5th lines before you begin.
   Hint: When you are trying to find rhymes, start with one sound, and then go through the alphabet with it.

   For example: *a*nd, *b*and, *c*anned, *f*anned, *g*rand, *h*and, *l*and, *m*anned, *p*lanned, *s*and, *st*and.

6. Your teacher will pair you with another student. Rehearse one of the five limericks in your book or your *own* limericks, so that the two of you can recite a limerick or two for the class.

Poetry Is Saying a Lot In a Few Words

What do we mean when we say that poetry says a lot in a few words?

Here is an example of what poetry can do. You might say, "The sky is blue today. There are puffy clouds, however. I don't know what the weather is going to be. Therefore, I am not sure where we should go." Or you could write:

Blue sky no rain now
Puffy clouds like cotton balls
Which way will we go?

What is the difference between the four prose sentences and the three-line poem? The three-line poem, called a *haiku*, is softer, more delicate, and quieter. A good haiku will make you feel more like you are seeing a picture than reading words.

Just as limericks have rules, so do haiku, pronounced, hi • **koo**. These are haiku rules:

Usually—

1. A haiku has three lines.
2. Lines 1 and 3 have five syllables.
3. Line 2 has seven syllables.
4. Altogether, a haiku has seventeen syllables.
5. A haiku does not rhyme.
6. Haiku are about things you can see or hear or picture in your mind.

Seasons Haiku
Myra Cohn Livingston

Summer

Wild branches, spilling
over the concrete wall, reach
out to touch the bus...

Autumn

Old rags hold fast to
bare bushes near the freeway,
waving me along...

Piles of ragged leaves,
Flung together, huddle up
against winter's chill

Winter

Here go the willows
again, dragging their long sleeves
into the river...

Spring

THINK about it

1. Go back and reread the four haiku. Count the syllables in each one, line by line. How many syllables are there in each line? How many syllables are in each haiku? Write down your answer.

Examples of Words Divided into Syllables

Now let's make sure you know what a syllable is. It is easy to explain by giving examples. Look at the examples line by line.

One Syllable	Two Syllables	Three Syllables	Four Syllables
car	au•to	Toy•o•ta	au•to•mo•bile
sport	base•ball	bas•ket•ball	to•bog•gan•ing
pleased	con•tent	sat•is•fied	com•fort•a•ble
pain	dis•tress	suf•fer•ing	mel•an•chol•y
flute	cel•lo	pi•an•o	har•mon•i•ca
ape	mon•key	go•ril•la	o•rang•u•tan
red	pur•ple	ma•gen•ta	aq•ua•ma•rine

2. On a piece of paper, draw a chart like the one shown. Your chart should have three columns. Number the columns one through three. Using words of four letters or more, write a list of one-syllable words into the column labeled "1." Write a list of two-syllable words under the column labeled "2." Write one three-syllable word in the third column. The words should be taken from the haiku poems on the previous pages.

3. Write four haiku. First, pick a topic that will provide you with four different pictures. Here are some examples: the seasons, animals, and colors—or think of a category of your own. Remember, your haiku will have three lines with syllables of 5/7/5. Haiku are supposed to be "word pictures." They describe something you can see or hear in your imagination.

LESSON four

Poetry Is a Picture

Poetry usually draws pictures for us—pictures that we see in our imaginations as we read the poem. But in the poems that you are about to read, the words are placed on the page so that they form an *actual* picture. This kind of poem is called a form poem or a concrete poem.

Form poems are for the eyes as well as the ears. The poem has a shape that the reader can recognize. Just by looking at the shape of a concrete poem, we can tell what the poem is about.

A SEEING POEM HAPPENS WHEN WORDS TAKE A SHAPE THAT HELPS THEM TO TURN ON A LIGHT IN SOMEONE'S MIND

POPSICLE

Joan Bransfield

popsicle
popsicle
tickle
tongue fun
licksicle
sticksicle
please
don't run
dripsicle
slipsicle
melt, melt
tricky
stopsicle
plopsicle
hand all
s
t
i
c
k
y

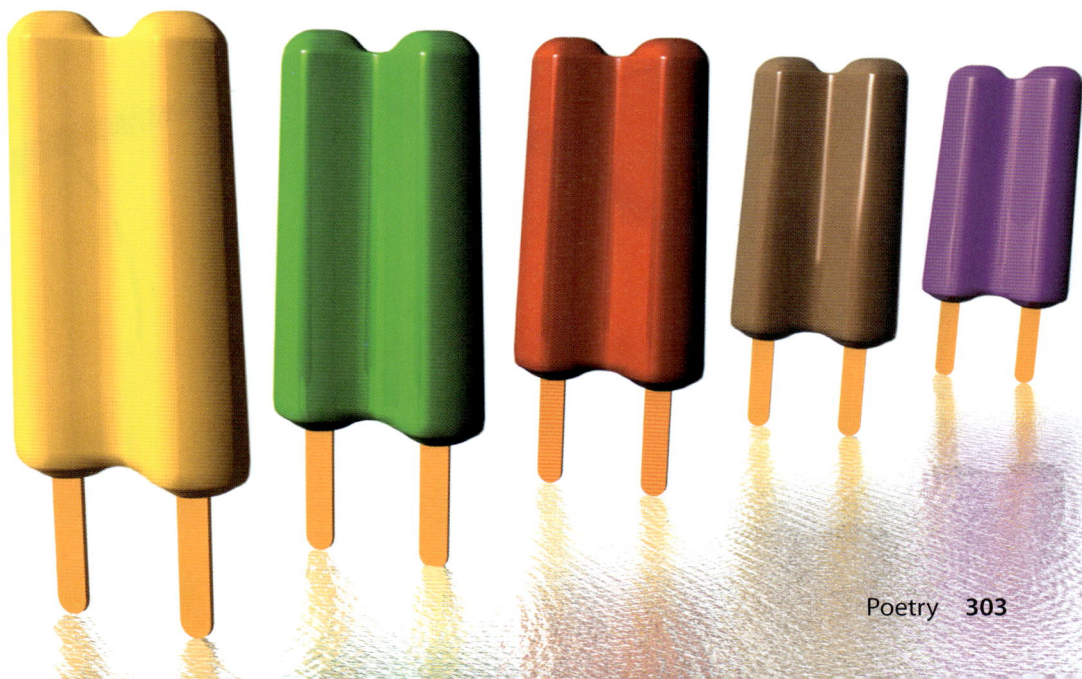

THINK
about it

What shape could a poem have? Here are some ideas:

a square	an animal
a circle	a bed
the sun or the moon	a fruit
ocean waves	a snake
a mountain	a fish

Can you think of some other shapes?

Write your own form poem. Copy it onto a poster board, making it large and clear. Surround your form poem with a collage that illustrates your poem.

LESSON five

Poetry Is Rhyme

You did lots of rhyming with limericks, so you really know what a rhyme is. But what is the definition of the word *rhyme*? When the end sounds of two words are the same, they rhyme. *Good* and *should* rhyme because *-ood* and *-ould* sound the same.

Rhyming poems are written in a variety of ways. Sometimes every two lines rhyme. For example:

Rain, rain go **away**
Come again some other **day**.

Sometimes, the second and fourth lines rhyme. For example:

Let me root, root, root for the home team
If they don't win it's a **shame**
For it's one, two, three strikes you're out
At the old ball **game**

The pattern in which the lines of a poem rhyme is called a **rhyme scheme**. A rhyme scheme shows which lines rhyme with which. Sometimes a rhyme scheme can be tricky. Look at the well-known nursery rhyme *Jack and Jill*.

Jack and Jill
Went up the hill,
To fetch a pail of water.

Jack fell down,
And broke his crown,
And Jill came tumbling after.

In this poem there are three lines in each verse. The first two lines of each verse rhyme:

Jill and *hill*
down and *crown*

The surprise comes in the third line. When we read the first verse, we think the third line is just "lonely," and rhymes with nothing. But we find its match when we read the second verse—it is the third line of the second verse!

water and *after*

THE SHARK

My sweet, let me tell you about the shark.

Though his eyes are bright, his thought is dark.

He's quiet—that speaks well of him.

So does the fact that he can swim.

5 But though he swims without a sound,

Wherever he swims he looks around

With those two bright eyes and that one dark thought.

He has only one, but he thinks it a lot.

And the thought he thinks but can never complete

10 Is his long dark thought of something to eat.

Most anything does, and I have to add

That when he eats his manners are bad.

He's a gulper, a ripper, a snatcher, a grabber.

Yes, his manners are drab. But his thought is drabber.

15 That one dark thought he can never complete

Of something—anything—somehow to eat.

Be careful where you swim, my sweet.

JOHN CIARDI

DUST OF SNOW

ROBERT FROST

The way a crow
Shook down on me
The dust of snow
From a hemlock tree

5　Has given my heart
A change of mood
And saved some part
Of a day I had rued.

THINK about it

1. Robert Frost's *Dust of Snow* and John Ciardi's *The Shark* are very different from each other—except that both poems have rhymes. Create a table like the one below. (You will need extra space for Rhyme Scheme and What Is the Poem About?.) Fill in the table. When you have finished, you will have *compared* and *contrasted* the two poems.

	Dust of Snow	The Shark
Rhyme Scheme (Which lines rhyme?)		
Number of Lines (Don't count the indented lines!)		
Number of Sentences		
Mood of the Poem (Serious? Funny?)		
What Is the Poem About?		
Author		

2. a. The word *rued* means regretted—to be very sorry about something. What does Robert Frost mean when he says, "a day I had rued"? How did the poet feel about the day, if he rued it?

   b. The crow changed the poet's mood. How did he feel after the crow shook snow on him?

308   Poetry

LESSON six

Poetry Is Fun to Write

Have you ever thought that you could write a poem by making a list? Have you ever thought that you could take a list and make it into a poem? You can! Each of the poems you will now read uses a list. *Some Opposites* is a list of opposites. *Tortillas Like Africa* begins and ends with a story about "Isaac and me" making tortillas, but the middle six lines are a list of countries.

The use of lists is a way that these two poems are alike. How are these two *different*?

Some Opposites has a regular rhythm of eight or nine beats per line. Also, every two lines of *Some Opposites* rhyme.

Count the beats in each line of *Tortillas Like Africa*. Do the lines all have the same beat? Now look at the last words of the lines. Do the lines rhyme?

Poems that don't have a regular beat and don't rhyme have a special name: FREE VERSE! *Tortillas Like Africa* is free verse.

What, then, makes free verse poetry? Free verse often has a lot of repetition. Lines may be repeated. Phrases may be repeated. Words may be repeated. Sounds may be repeated.

Free verse poems, like other poetry, may have odd punctuation: no periods, commas where there should be periods, and commas where there should be no punctuation.

Free verse poems may have capital letters in the middle of sentences. It may have very long sentences or no sentences. A line may leave you hanging, on the edge of a cliff, waiting for the next line to complete the idea. You will see how this works in the poetry lesson that follows.

Richard Wilbur

SOME OPPOSITE

The opposite of *standing still*
Is *walking up or down a hill,*
Running backwards, creeping, crawling,
Leaping off a cliff and falling,
5 *Turning somersaults in gravel,*
Or any other mode of travel.

The opposite of a *doughnut*? Wait
A minute while I meditate.
This isn't easy. Ah, I've found it!
10 *A cookie with a hole around it.*

What is the opposite of *two*?
A lonely me, a lonely you.

The opposite of a *cloud* could be
A *white reflection in the sea,*
15 Or *a huge blueness in the air,*
Caused by a cloud's not being there.

The opposite of *opposite*?
That's much too difficult. I quit.

Tortillas Like Africa

When Isaac and me squeezed dough over a mixing bowl,
When we dusted the cutting board with flour,
When we spanked and palmed our balls of dough,
When we said, "Here goes,"
5 And began rolling out tortillas,
We giggled because ours came out not round,
   like Mama's,
But in the shapes of faraway lands.

Here was Africa, here was Colombia and Greenland.
Here was Italy, the boot country,
10 And here was México, our homeland to the south.

Here was Chile, thin as a tie.
Here was France, square as a hat.
Here was Australia, with patches of jumping kangaroos.

We rolled out our tortillas on the board
15 And laughed when we threw them on the *comal*,
These tortillas that were not round as a pocked moon,
But the twist and stretch of the earth taking shape.

Gary Soto

THINK about it

Here's what you have to do…

Take a look in your refrigerator.
What do you see?

> *A brown apple with a bite*
> *Guess it didn't taste quite right.*

Take a look at your dresser drawer.

> *Two pens, some stamps, and, look! six keys!*
> *Some dust that always makes me sneeze.*

Now look in your closet?

> *A white blouse ironed, wrinkle-free,*
> *It has a pocket for my key.*

How about a list of your friends?

> *Benjamin, sometimes angry but wise*
> *A better friend than three other guys.*

How about a list of the animals at the zoo?

> *A zebra like a thunderbolt,*
> *A momma horse with her new colt.*

You have been given these two-line openers so that you can do the following:

1. Write your own list poem of eight or more lines. You can use one of the suggested topics or one you think up yourself. Make this a rhyming poem. Rhyme every two lines or every other line. Remember that this is more than a list. You should include some detailed descriptions, as well as thoughts and feelings.

2. Richard Wilbur's list includes *standing still*, *a doughnut*, *two*, and *a cloud*. Write down his list, and next to each item write its opposite (or opposites, where he gives more than one).

3. What do you think is the opposite of *opposite*?

4. Make a list of the countries in Gary Soto's poem. Write each country on a separate line. Three of the countries have no description. But next to each country that *does*, write the words he uses to describe it.

5. Now is your chance to write a free-verse list poem. You may use the same topic you used for your rhyming poem, one of the other topics that was suggested, or something you have thought of yourself.

Poetry Is Free

What does that *mean—that poetry is free?*

When you write a poem, you let a part of yourself go free. You share some of your thoughts or memories with other people. You let a part of yourself out into the world. Some of your feelings and ideas can go for a long, long walk!

Poetry is also fre*er*. That is, poetry is freer than prose. When you write free verse poetry, you can write in any shape or form. You can let one line hang out like the ledge of a cliff. The next line can be just one word. *You* decide what you want to do with your poem.

You don't have to use punctuation, or you can use punctuation in odd places. You don't have to use capital letters, or you can use MANY capital letters. If you are writing free verse, poetry has very few rules.

Good Hotdogs

For Kiki

Fifty cents apiece
To eat our lunch
We'd run
Straight from school
5 Instead of home
Two blocks
Then the store
That smelled like steam
You ordered
10 Because you had the money
Two hotdogs and two pops for here

Everything on the hotdogs
Except pickle lily
Dash those hotdogs
15 Into buns and splash on
All that good stuff
Yellow mustard and onions
And french fries piled on top all
Rolled up in a piece of wax
20 Paper for us to hold hot
In our hands
Quarters on the counter
Sit down
Good hotdogs
25 We'd eat
Fast till there was nothing left
But salt and poppy seeds even
The little burnt tips
Of french fries
30 We'd eat
you humming
And me swinging my legs

Sandra Cisneros

Jackrabbit

from *Desert Voices*
by Byrd Baylor

The sudden leap,
the instant start,
the burst of speed,
knowing
5 when to run
and when to freeze,
how to become
a shadow
underneath
10 a greasewood bush...

these are things
I learned
almost at birth.

Now
15 I lie
on the shadow-side
of a clump of grass.
My long ears bring me
every far-off footstep,
20 every twig that snaps,
every rustle in the weeds.

I watch
Coyote move
from bush to bush.

25 I wait.
He's almost here.

Now…

Now I go
like a zig-zag
30 lightning flash.
With my ears laid back,
I sail.

Jumping gullies
and bushes and rocks,
35 doubling back,
circling,
jumping high
to see where my enemy is,
warning rabbits
40 along the way,
I go.

I hardly touch
the ground.

And suddenly
45 I disappear.

Let Coyote stand there
sniffing
old jackrabbit trails.

Where I am now
50 is a
jackrabbit secret.

THINK
about it

In *Good Hotdogs*, Sandra Cisneros has written a poem for Kiki about a time when they would eat hotdogs together for lunch.

1. Reread the poem and make a list of the words and phrases that are repeated.

2. What two places in the poem are given special importance by the way the lines end?

3. Write one or two paragraphs about a special time you spent with someone. Your memories may be happy or sad.

4. Now, remove the punctuation and change your prose piece into a free verse poem. Give your poem a title and name the person for whom you are writing the poem.

In *Jackrabbit,* Byrd Baylor uses two columns (in some places) and a zigzag form to make her poem look like the track of the jackrabbit as it runs from the coyote.

5. Write about a bird fleeing a cat, a dog chasing another dog, a deer being followed by hunters—or any other story of one creature trying to escape another. Make your poem look a little like the chase. Your poem can be shorter than *Jackrabbit*.

unit 4

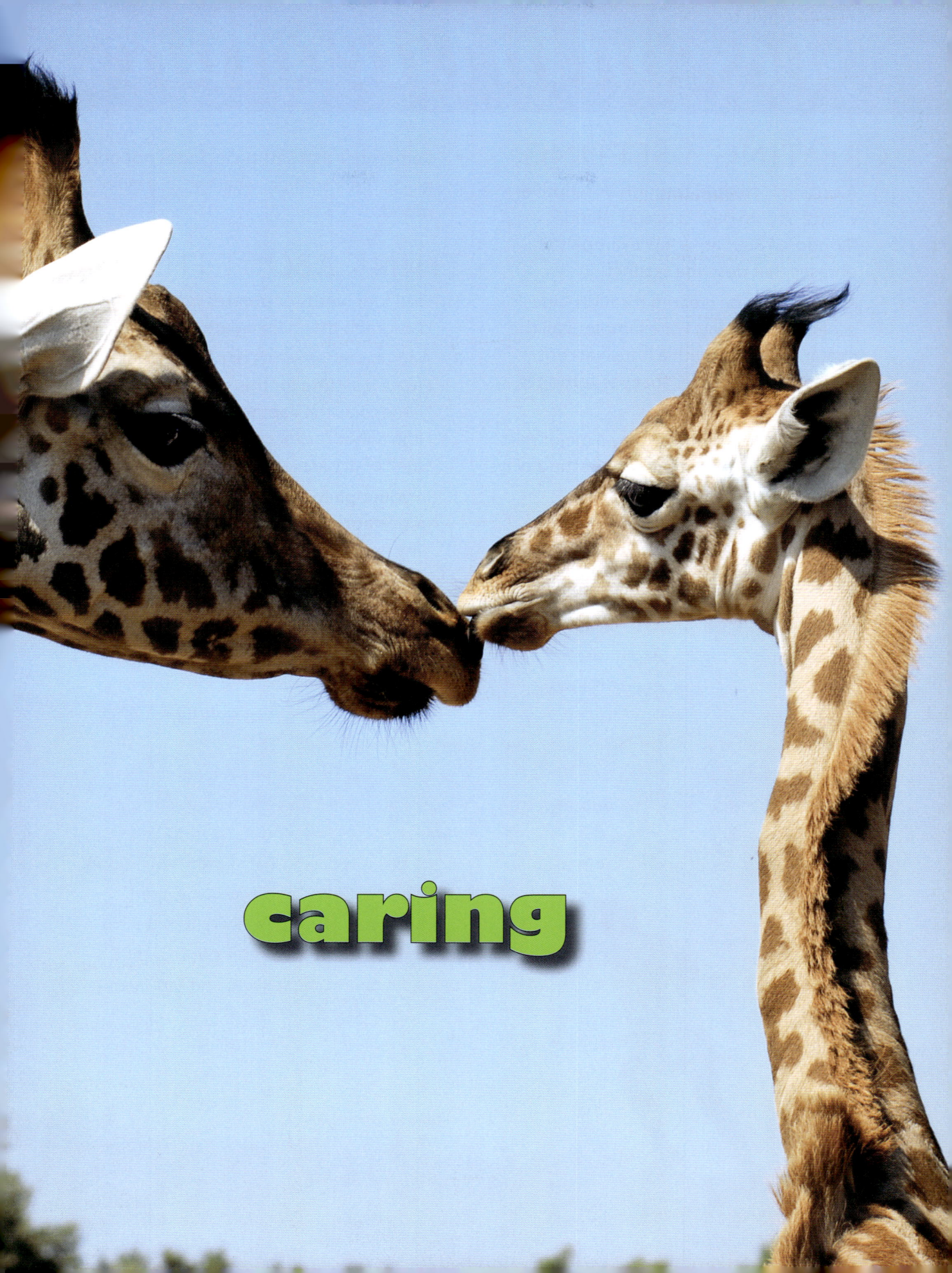

caring

Lesson in Literature...

CREATING A SETTING

- A setting is created through descriptive words. "A cold day," "a desert island," "London, 1880," are a few examples of phrases that describe setting.

- A setting can be created through "clues," especially in a play. For example, if all the characters speak with a British accent, the audience guesses that the setting is England.

- At times, the setting will play a major part in the plot. At other times, the setting plays only a small role in the story.

- Remember that setting includes not only place, but also time, weather, and even mood.

THINK ABOUT IT!

1. Find four words or phrases in the first paragraph that help create the setting.

2. Add two more words or phrases that help create a setting for this story. For example, "James was the captain of the Beechmont High School cross-country team," or, "the smell of dry leaves filled the air."

3. In your opinion, does setting play an important role in this story? Why or why not?

It was a cold, windy day in November when James, the cross-country team's captain, took one last stretch, signaled to the others, and began to run. "This is our last run together," he said over his shoulder. James had instructions from Coach Smith to lead the whole team on a long, slow run on the path through the woods.

But the other runners didn't join in behind James.

"It's too cold," one shouted.

"I'm too tired," another yelled.

Another runner, a senior, announced to the others, "Let's just forget about running today and go home."

James jogged back to his teammates. "How many times have we run this route together?" he asked.

"A thousand," another senior said, joking. "Let's just go home and just say we ran!"

Jogging in place, James wondered what he should do. The team had run together every day the whole season, and James and

CROSS COUNTRY

the other seniors had run together every day for four seasons. Finally, he decided. "It's the right thing to do," he said and jogged off.

The route took him behind the school and down a dirt path that veered left up a hill and into the woods. This is the last run, he thought, and I'm alone. When he entered the woods, he settled into a steady pace, but he felt sad and discouraged that on the last run of the season his teammates were not with him.

But as he passed through a patch of bright sunlight through the trees, he realized he wasn't alone. Each time his foot struck the ground, he was reminded of the many other times he had run this path. He remembered when he was a freshman, running behind the older boys and wondering if he could keep up. He remembered hot days in August when he was already sweaty by the time he reached the hill. He remembered the day he found out about a low grade on a report card and the day he felt sick but didn't want to let the others down. He remembered the day he was elected team captain.

His feet still striking the ground in rhythm, James heard something, something familiar, so he slowed up at a bend in the path but didn't look back. Suddenly, he knew what was coming up behind him. It was the sound of many feet striking the ground in unison, the sound of the strength of a team joining him on the last run of the season.

As each teammate caught up to him, each thanked James. "You were right," one said. "We're a team." "Thanks for your example," another said. "You taught me a lot," a sophomore said. A senior patted him on the back. "James, you were there for us, showing the way. Thanks," he said.

By the time the cross-country team finished their last run of the season, they knew it was a run they would never forget. Their captain, too, knew he would never forget that day, and what he would remember had nothing to do with running.

Blueprint for Reading

INTO . . . *Earthquake Terror*

What is courage? Is it the opposite of fear? If someone is afraid, does that make the person a coward? Many people who act bravely are very frightened at the time. They know they are in danger but they do what has to be done. A firefighter who runs into a burning building to rescue someone knows she is in danger. She may be afraid, but she has a job to do. She enters the building in spite of the danger. That is courage. An officer leading his troops into battle knows he may be killed. He is almost certainly afraid. But he stays in the front, leading his troops. That is courage. In short, it is not how we *feel* that makes us courageous, it is what we *do*.

EYES ON *Creating a Setting*

Dan and his son loved the feel of sand and the misty spray of the water. They spent as much time as possible outdoors, soaking in the sun, the birds, and the lovely view. It was only a short drive from their home in New York, but it was just the place they needed for their vacation.

In these few lines, the author has created a setting. Dan and his son are on a beach near New York on a warm, sunny day. Describing the setting at the beginning of a story is important because it helps the reader picture the story's events as they happen. The time, location, and other details like weather and lighting are all part of the story's setting.

Before the main part of the story begins, the author of *Earthquake Terror* describes the way the woods look and feel. Think about why the setting is such an important part of the story.

An excerpt from
Earthquake Terror

Peg Kehret

Jonathan's family is on vacation on Magpie Island when his mother breaks her ankle and has to go to the hospital. He is left in the woods in charge of his partially paralyzed younger sister, Abby.

In his mind, Jonathan could see his father unhitching the small camping trailer. He pictured the car going along the narrow, winding road that meandered from the campground through the woods. He saw the high bridge that crossed the river, connecting the island campground to the mainland.

He imagined his father driving across the bridge, faster than usual, with Mom lying down in the back seat. Or maybe she wouldn't lie down. Maybe, even with a broken ankle, she would wear her seat belt. She always did, and she insisted that Jonathan and Abby wear theirs.

Moose cocked his head, as if listening to something. Then he ran toward the trail, sniffing the ground.

"Moose," Jonathan called. "Come back."

Moose paused, looked at Jonathan, and barked.

"Come!"

Moose returned but he continued to smell the ground and pace back and forth.

"Moose wants Mommy," Abby said.

Moose suddenly stood still, his legs stiff and his tail up. He barked again.

"Silly old dog," Abby said.

WORD BANK

meandered (mee AN derd) *v.*: wound around gently from one place to another

x

He knows something is wrong, Jonathan thought. Dogs sense things.

He knows something is wrong, Jonathan thought. Dogs sense things. He knows I'm worried about Mom. Jonathan patted Moose's head. "It's all right, Moose. Good dog."

Moose barked again.

"I'm hot," Abby said. "It's too hot to eat."

"Let's start back. It'll be cooler in the shade and we can finish our lunch in the camper."

Maybe he could relax in the camper. Here he felt jumpy. He didn't like being totally out of communication with the rest of the world. Whenever he stayed alone at home, or took care of Abby, there was always a telephone at his fingertips or a neighbor just down the street. If he had a problem, he could call his parents or Mrs. Smith next door or even nine-one-one.

Here he was isolated. I wouldn't do well as a forest ranger, Jonathan thought. How do they stand being alone in the woods all the time?

He rewrapped the uneaten food, buckled the backpack over his shoulders, and put the leash on Moose. The goofy way Moose was acting, he might bolt down the trail and not come back.

WORD BANK

bolt *v.*: suddenly run away

Jonathan helped Abby stand up and placed her walker in position. Slowly, they began the journey across the sand and into the woods, to follow the trail through the trees.

Jonathan wished he had worn a watch. It seemed as if his parents had been gone long enough to get partway to town, but it was hard to be sure. Time had a way of evaporating instantly when he was engrossed in an interesting project, such as cataloging his baseball cards, or reading a good mystery. But time dragged unbearably when he was in the dentist's office or waiting for a ride. It was hard to estimate how much time had passed since his parents waved good-bye and walked away. Forty minutes? An hour?

Abby walked in front of him. That way he could see her and know if she needed help, and it kept him from going too fast. When he was in the lead, he usually got too far ahead, even when he tried to walk slowly.

While they walked Jonathan planned what he would do when they got back to the camper. As soon as he got Abby settled on her bed, he would turn on the radio

WORD BANK

evaporating (ee VAP uh RAY ting) *v.*: disappearing
engrossed (en GROSED) *v.*: occupied; completely involved in
cataloging (CAT uh LOG ing) *v.*: organizing a list of items into groups

and listen to the ball game. That would give him something to think about. The San Francisco Giants were his favorite baseball team and he hoped they would win the World Series.

Jonathan noticed again how quiet it was. No magpies cawed, no leaves rustled overhead. The air was stifling, with no hint of breeze.

Moose barked. Jonathan jumped at the sudden noise. It was Moose's warning bark, the one he used when a stranger knocked on the door. He stood beside Jonathan and barked again. The dog's eyes had a frantic look. He was shaking, the way he always did during a thunderstorm.

"What's wrong, boy?" Jonathan asked. He reached out to pet Moose but the dog tugged toward Abby and barked at her.

"Hush, Moose," Abby said.

Jonathan looked in all directions. He saw nothing unusual. There were still no people and no animals that would startle Moose and set him off. Jonathan listened hard, wondering if Moose had heard something that Jonathan couldn't hear.

WORD BANK

stifling (STYF ling) *adj.*: so hot and still as to make it difficult to breathe

Jonathan looked in all directions. He saw nothing unusual.

Abby stopped walking. "What was that?" she said.

"What was what?"

Jonathan listened. He heard a deep rumbling sound in the distance.

Thunder? He looked up. The sky was bright and cloudless. The noise came closer; it was too sharp to be thunder. It was more like several rifles being fired at the same time.

Hunters! he thought. There are hunters in the woods and they heard us move and they've mistaken us for deer or pheasant. Moose must have seen them or heard them or possibly smelled them.

"Don't shoot!" he cried.

As he yelled, Jonathan felt a jolt. He stumbled forward, thrusting an arm out to brace himself against a tree. Another loud noise exploded as Jonathan lurched sideways.

He dropped the leash.

Abby screamed.

A bomb? Jonathan thought. Who would bomb a deserted campground?

The noise continued, and the earth moved beneath his feet. As he felt himself lifted, he knew that the sound was not hunters with guns. It was not a bomb, either.

Earthquake! The word flashed across his brain as if he had seen it blazing on a neon sign.

The ground shook again, and Jonathan struggled to remain on his feet.

He felt as if he were on a surfboard, catching a giant wave, rising, cresting, and sliding back down again. Except he was standing on dry land.

"Jonathan!" Abby's scream was lost in the thunderous noise. He saw her fall, her walker lunging off to one side as she went down. Jonathan lunged forward, arms outstretched, trying to catch Abby before she hit the ground. He couldn't get there fast enough.

The ground dropped away beneath his feet as if a trapdoor had opened. His legs buckled and he sank to his knees. He reached for a tree trunk, to steady himself, but before his hand touched it, the tree moved.

Jonathan's stomach rose into his throat, the way it sometimes did on a fast elevator.

Ever since first grade, when the Palmers moved to California, Jonathan had practiced earthquake drills in school each year. He knew that most earthquakes occur along the shores of the Pacific Ocean. He knew that the San Andreas fault[1] runs north

---

1. The *San Andreas fault* is in California. A *fault* is a crack in the rock that covers an area of the earth. Earthquakes are more likely to occur along the fault than in other places.

and south for hundreds of miles in California, making that land particularly susceptible to earthquakes. He knew that if an earthquake hit while he was in school, he was supposed to crawl under his desk or under a table because injury was most likely to be caused by the roof caving in on him.

That was school. This was Magpie Island. How should he protect himself in the woods? Where could he hide?

He struggled to his feet again. Ahead of him, Abby lay whimpering on the ground. Moose stood beside her, his head low.

"Put your hands over your head," Jonathan called.

The ground shook again, and Jonathan struggled to remain on his feet.

"I'm coming," he shouted. "Stay where you are. I'm coming!"

But he did not go to her. He couldn't.

WORD BANK

susceptible (suh SEP tih buhl) *adj.*: more likely to be affected by something

The ground heaved, pitching Jonathan into the air.

He staggered sideways, unable to keep his balance. He felt as if he were riding a roller coaster standing up, except the ground rocked back and forth at the same time that it rolled up and down.

A clump of small birch trees swayed like dancers and then fell.

The rumbling noise continued, surrounding him, coming from every direction at once. It was like standing in the center of a huge orchestra, with kettle drums pounding on all sides.

Abby's screams and Moose's barking blended with the noise.

Although there was no roof to cave in on him, Jonathan put his arms over his head as he fell. The school's earthquake drills had taught him to protect his head and he did it the only way he could.

Earthquake.

He had never felt an earthquake before and he had always wondered how it would feel. He had questioned his teacher, that first year. "How will I know it's an earthquake?" he asked. "If it's a big one," the teacher said, "you'll know."

His teacher had been right. Jonathan knew. He knew with a certainty that made the hair rise on the back of his neck. He was in the middle of an earthquake now. A big one.

The ground heaved, pitching Jonathan into the air.

Jonathan hit the ground hard, jarring every bone in his body. Immediately, the earth below him moved, tossing him into the air again.

As he dropped back down, he saw the trunk of a giant redwood tree tremble. The huge tree swayed back and forth for a few moments and then tilted toward Jonathan.

Frantically, he crawled to his left, rushing to get out of the tree's path.

The roots ripped loose slowly, as if not wanting to relinquish their century-long hold on the dirt.

As Jonathan scrambled across the unsteady ground, he clenched his teeth, bracing himself for the impact.

The tree fell. Air whizzed across Jonathan as the tree trunk dropped past, and branches brushed his shoulder, scratching his arms. The redwood crashed beside him, missing him by only a few feet. It thudded down, landing at an angle on another fallen tree. Dirt and dry leaves whooshed into the air, and then settled slowly back down.

WORD BANK

jarring (JAR ing) *v.*: shaking
relinquish (rih LINK wish) *v.*: let go of

Beneath him, the ground swelled and retreated, like ocean waves.

The earth shuddered, but Jonathan didn't know if it was from the impact of the tree or another jolt from the earthquake.

With his heart in his throat, Jonathan crept away from the redwood tree, toward Abby. Beneath him, the ground swelled and retreated, like ocean waves. Twice he sprawled facedown in the dirt, unable to keep his balance. The second time, he lay still, with his eyes closed. How much longer would this go on? Maybe he should just lie there and wait until this earthquake was over.

"Mommy!" Abby's shrill cry rose above the thundering noise.

Jonathan struggled toward her again, his heart racing. When he finally reached her, he lay beside her and wrapped his arms around her. She clung to him, sobbing.

"We'll be okay," he said. "It's only an earthquake."

Only an earthquake. He remembered magazine pictures of terrible devastation from earthquakes: homes toppled, highways buckled, cars tossed upside down, and people crushed in debris. Only an earthquake.

WORD BANK

impact (IM pakt) *n.*: the force with which one thing hits another
retreated (rih TREE ted) *v.*: moved back toward the place it had come from
devastation (DEH vis TAY shun) *n.*: destruction and ruin
debris (duh BREE) *n.*: the remains of anything destroyed

"I want Mommy!" Abby shrieked.

"We have to get under shelter," he said. "Try to crawl with me." Keeping one arm around Abby's waist, he got to his hands and knees and began crawling forward on the undulating ground.

"I can't!" Abby cried. "I'm scared. The ground is moving."

Jonathan tightened his grip, dragging her across the ground. A small tree crashed beside them. Dust rose, filling their noses.

"I want Mommy!" Abby shrieked.

He pulled her to the trunk of the huge redwood tree that had uprooted.

"Get under the tree," he said, as he pushed her into the angle of space that was created because the center of the redwood's trunk rested on the other tree.

When Abby was completely under the tree, Jonathan lay on his stomach beside her, with his right arm tucked beneath his stomach and his left arm thrown across Abby. He pulled himself in as close as he could so that both he and Abby were wedged in the space under the big tree.

"What's happening?" Abby sobbed. Her fingernails dug into Jonathan's bare arm.

"It's an earthquake."

"I want to go home." Abby tried to push Jonathan away.

WORD BANK

undulating (UN dyuh LAY ting) *v.*: moving with a wavelike motion
wedged (WEJD) *v.*: packed in tightly

"Lie still," Jonathan said. "The tree will protect us."

The dry forest floor scratched his cheek as he inhaled the pungent scent of dead leaves. He felt dwarfed by the enormous redwood and tried not to imagine what would have happened if it had landed on him.

"Moose!" he called. "Come, Moose."

Beneath him, the ground trembled again. Jonathan tightened his grip on Abby and pushed his face close to hers. A sharp crack rang out beside them as another tree hit the ground. Jonathan turned his head enough to peer out; he saw the redwood branches quivering from the impact.

What if the earthquake caused the redwood to move again? What if it slipped off the tree it rested on and crushed them beneath it? Anxiety tied a tight knot in Jonathan's stomach.

The earth shuddered once more. Abby buried her face in Jonathan's shoulder. His shirt grew wet from her tears. The jolt did not seem as severe this time, but Jonathan thought that might be because he was lying down.

WORD BANK

pungent (PUN junt) *adj.*: sharp and strong (used only to describe a taste or smell)
dwarfed (DWORFD) *v.*: appeared small by comparison

Moose, panting with fear, huddled beside Jonathan, pawing at Jonathan's shoulder. Relieved that the dog had not been injured, Jonathan put his right arm around Moose and held him close.

As suddenly as it had begun, the upheaval stopped. Jonathan was unsure how long it had lasted. Five minutes? Ten? While it was happening, time seemed suspended and Jonathan had thought the shaking might go on for days.

The woods were quiet.

He lay motionless, one arm around Abby and the other around Moose, waiting to see if it was really over. The air was completely still. After the roar of the earthquake, the silence seemed both comforting and ominous.

Earlier, even though there were no other people in the area, he'd heard the magpies cawing, and a squirrel had complained when Jonathan tossed a rock.

Now he heard nothing. No birds. No squirrels. Not even wind in the leaves.

WORD BANK

upheaval (up HEE vul) *n.*: a great disturbance
suspended (sus SPEND ed) *v.*: temporarily stopped
ominous (AH mih nuss) *adj.*: threatening; hinting that something bad is about to happen

"Is it over?" Abby's voice was thin and high.

He wondered if his parents had felt the quake. Sometimes, he knew, earthquakes were confined to fairly small areas.

Once Grandma Whitney had called them from Iowa. She had seen news reports of a violent California earthquake less than one hundred miles from where the Palmers lived.

"Are you all right?" Grandma cried, when Mrs. Palmer answered the phone. "Was anyone hurt?"

Grandma had been astonished when none of the Palmers knew anything about an earthquake.

After several minutes of quiet, Jonathan eased out from under the tree. He sat up and looked around. Moose, still trembling, licked his hand.

Jonathan put his cheek on the dog's neck and rubbed his ears. He had chosen Moose at the animal shelter, more than six years ago. The Palmers had planned to get a small dog but the moment Jonathan saw the big golden retriever, who was then one year old, he knew which dog he wanted.

Mrs. Palmer had said, "He's too big to be a house dog."

Mr. Palmer said, "I think he's half moose."

Jonathan laughed and said, "That's what I'll name him. Moose."

His parents tried unsuccessfully to interest Jonathan in one of the other, smaller dogs, before they gave in and brought Moose home.

Despite his size, Moose was a house dog from the start, and he slept beside Jonathan's bed every night. They played fetch, and their own version of tag, and Jonathan took Moose for long walks in the country park. In the summer, they swam whenever they had a chance.

When Abby had her accident and Jonathan's parents focused so much of their attention on her, Moose was Jonathan's comfort and companion.

Now, in the devastation of the earthquake, Jonathan again found comfort in the dog's presence. He let go of Moose and looked around. "Wow!" he said, trying to keep his voice steady. "That was some earthquake."

"Is it over?" Abby's voice was thin and high.

"I think so."

He grasped Abby's hand and pulled her out from under the tree. She sat up, apparently uninjured, and began picking leaves out of her hair.

"Are you okay?" he asked.

"It's all right," he said. "If that tiny little scrape is all you got, you are lucky, and so am I."

"My knee is cut." She touched one knee and her voice rose. "It's bleeding," she said, her lips trembling. "You pushed me under the tree too hard."

Jonathan examined her knee. It was a minor cut. He knew that if he made a fuss over it, Abby would cry. He had seen it happen before; if his mother showed concern about a small injury, Abby got practically hysterical, but if Mom acted like it was no big deal, Abby relaxed, too. It was as if she didn't know whether she hurt or not until she saw how her parents reacted.

"It's all right," he said. "If that tiny little scrape is all you got, you are lucky, and so am I. We could have been killed."

"We could?" Abby's eyes grew round.

Quickly Jonathan said, "But we weren't, and the earthquake is over now."

ABOUT THE AUTHOR

In her book, *Small Steps*, **Peg Kehret** tells how she had polio when she was a girl growing up in Austin, Minnesota. During that difficult time, she was hospitalized and nearly died. She recovered and later married Carl Kehret, and together they adopted a son and a daughter. Peg writes books for children, radio commercials, plays, and magazine stories. For many years Peg and Carl traveled around the country in a motor home so that she could speak at schools, libraries, and children's literature conferences. Today, Peg lives in Washington State and writes, reads, and visits with her grandchildren.

Poetry
is not afraid to be afraid

MICHAEL IS AFRAID OF THE STORM

Gwendolyn Brooks

Lightning is angry in the night.
Thunder spanks our house.
Rain is hating our old elm—
It punishes the boughs.

5   Now, I am next to nine years old,
And crying's not for me.
But if I touch my mother's hand,
Perhaps no one will see.

And if I keep herself in sight—
10 Follow her busy dress—
No one will notice my wild eye.
No one will laugh, I guess.

Studying the Selection

QUICK REVIEW

1. Describe the setting at the start of the story.
2. Why was Jonathan left alone with his sister Abby?
3. Where did Jonathan and Abby take shelter during the earthquake?
4. Did anyone get hurt?

FOCUS

5. Was Jonathan frightened during the earthquake? Support your answer.
6. Describe the scene after the earthquake.

CREATING AND WRITING

7. Write about a time when you (or someone you know) reacted with bravery to a frightening or challenging situation.
8. Write the ending of the story. You may include how Jonathan and Abby made their way back to the camper, what happened to Mom at the hospital, whether Mr. and Mrs. Palmer experienced the earthquake, and how Jonathan's parents reacted to the way he handled the situation.
9. Put together an emergency kit. Imagine being stranded in a woodsy area and think of what you would need to have on hand for a day. Do not include food in your kit, but you may include some bottled water. You should have eight to ten items in your kit. If, for example, you would like to include a flashlight, but don't have one at home, you may use an index card with the word "flashlight" on it. You may do this for no more than two of your items.

Jill's Journal:
On Assignment in New Madrid

What would *you* do if you were a journalist and you needed to write about earthquakes? Me, I decided that I had to go to the site of a famous earthquake. Then I could describe what occurred. Otherwise, how would I know what an earthquake is like? How could *I* try to tell *you* about something I had never seen?

First, I thought of visiting the earthquake in San Francisco, California on April 18, 1906. But other writers have already described that terrible event. So I chose New Madrid, Missouri, on December 16, 1811. That was so long ago, Missouri wasn't even a state. The New Madrid earthquakes were the worst earthquakes in American history.

I'm here in New Madrid, now. I'm nervous, but I mustn't act nervous. I'm not so sure this was such a good idea. For tonight, I'm staying in a log cabin with Eliza Bryan and her family. They know I am just passing through and will leave in the morning.

A log cabin is a small place with a dirt floor, but the Bryans' little home is very clean, cheerful, and snug. The children played a card game earlier as Mr. Bryan played the fiddle. Red and white gingham curtains hang in the windows. A large, braided rug covers the floor. My bed is filled with furs and fresh hay. The sun has gone down and logs are burning brightly in the huge fireplace. A calico cat sleeps on the orange bricks of the hearth.

Mrs. Bryan and I spoke before we went to bed. What can I tell you about her? She has worked hard all her life. She is patient with the children. She is thirty-five years old and proud of her home, I think. Guess what? She can read and write! Not many people in this place and time can read and write. I hear the clock chime eight times, as my eyes close. I fall asleep thinking that it is good that New Madrid has such a small population, given what is to come.

The clock strikes 2:00 A.M. Oh! There is a great shaking of the earth! The earth feels like the ocean! It moves in waves! By the light of the fire I see the large fine dining table thrown into the air! The chairs are thrown about and overturned. I've been thrown from the bed! I feel broken glass and splintered wood under my hand. I feel about the floor. Their beautiful clock is shattered and in pieces!

There is a roar so loud my ears are hurting. I hear terrible screams of people and animals outside. We try to stand but are thrown to the floor again. What is that terrible roaring sound? It sounds like a storm but I know it is not a storm. Mrs. Bryan—I think it is Mrs. Bryan—tries to throw water into the fireplace. She screams, "Don't let the fire spread!"

I am afraid the walls will collapse. I crawl on my hands and knees to the door and push it open. Will the shaking and roaring ever stop? It sounds like thunder. I hear cracking as trees fall. The birds are shrieking in terror. The Mississippi River is roaring. How close are we to the riverbanks?

The air clears a bit and I see people fleeing in every direction. The earth is torn to pieces. There is a huge crack in the earth close to the cabin. Sand and water and something black is boiling up. The crack is huge. This is truly horrible.

The terrible roaring stops and there is silence. Then there is sobbing and the sounds of people comforting each other. I hear the cat meow.

It is nearly dawn. Mr. and Mrs. Bryan and their children are setting out to search for their two cows and three horses. I hear them calling to the animals, mooing and neighing as people do. I bid the Bryans goodbye. I must return to my own time. I am so relieved no one was hurt.

POWER SKILL:
The Five W's of Reporting: Who, What, When, Where, Why

Newspaper reporters must always be certain of their facts. After all, newspaper articles are supposed to report facts, not opinions. What is the difference between facts and opinions? A *fact* is a piece of information about something that has actually happened. A fact is supposed to be the truth. A fact can be supported by actual evidence. However, an *opinion* is a view or judgment formed in someone's mind about a particular matter. People can say why they have a particular opinion—they can give good reasons for their opinion—but that does not make it a fact.

When a reporter writes about an event, she must be sure to tell *who* was involved, *what* occurred, *where* it occurred, *when* it occurred, and *why* it

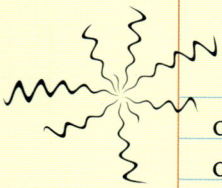

occurred. These are *the five w's* of reporting. They don't necessarily go in that order. Sometimes reporters will write the where and when first, the what and the who next, and close with the why. Often, why an event occurred is anybody's guess, or people may have different ideas about why the event occurred. So for the last *w*, more opinion may be involved than fact.

Exercise

Imagine you are a journalist or a reporter. It is time to write your news article. Your deadline is fast approaching. So what are you going to write about? These are your guidelines. Write about events that actually occurred in your life—events that you actually witnessed. It can be what happened at breakfast this morning at home (but it must be told in a way that is interesting!), or an event in your town, or at school, or in some other part of your life. Don't forget to include the five w's. Make up a good headline. When you are finished, on a separate sheet of paper, write down each of your w's, just to make certain you included them all. Your article should be at least one page long.

Lesson in Literature...

WHAT IS IMAGERY?

- An **image** is a picture created with words. *A red barn, a single flame, a mangy dog,* are all examples of images.

- Images help us picture the settings and characters of stories. They boost our imaginations.

- A skillful writer will look at someone or something and be able to describe it in a way that creates a powerful picture.

- A writer may compare one thing to another: *His fur was like velvet*. This kind of comparison is called a **simile**.

THINK ABOUT IT!

1. The author provides the reader with an image of Coach Fred in a wheelchair. But what does the room he is sitting in look like? What is Coach Fred wearing? Is there a good smell in the room from the desserts brought over? Write three sentences with images that describe the setting of this story.

2. The young teacher describes his run in the woods. Based on the images in the paragraph, what season do you think it is?

3. The young teacher describes the way the woods looked. Use a simile to add to his description.

When Coach Fred, who was the gym teacher at the school, came home from the hospital in a wheelchair, everyone from the school was sad and surprised. As a gym teacher, he pushed the children to do their best in their physical activities, but he also inspired them with words of wisdom to do the right things in their lives. Although he was probably as old as most of the children's grandfathers, Coach Fred loved physical fitness. His favorite exercise was a daily jog.

As soon as Coach Fred came home from the hospital, many people visited him and his wife Lois at their house. His daughter and grandsons brought dinners and books. His neighbors came over, bringing desserts and amusing stories about the neighborhood. Teachers from the school arrived offering good wishes and get-well cards. Many of the students who came by told Coach Fred that his high standards and wise words had made a difference in their lives.

Coach Fred loved all his visitors. But one young teacher who visited never brought food or get-well cards. He didn't share stories either. Instead, the young teacher just sat in a chair next to Coach Fred's wheelchair and listened as Coach Fred told him stories and memories from his life.

It wasn't long before the young teacher began to wonder if he should bring something like everybody else.

"Do you want me to bring you dinner, Coach?" he asked.

"No," Coach Fred answered. "I have my daughter's help."

A Run In the Woods

"Do you want me to tell you the news from the school? Or funny stories?"

"No," Coach Fred said with a wink, "you aren't that funny."

The young teacher smiled. "Isn't there anything I can bring you?"

Coach Fred looked at him. "Yes, there is something you can bring me," he said.

"What?" The young teacher couldn't guess what it was.

"Go for a run in the woods."

"That's it?" the young teacher asked.

Coach Fred explained, "The next time you visit you can describe it. More than anything else I miss my daily jogs."

At his next visit the young teacher used vivid detail to describe his experience of running in the woods. He described a warm breeze behind him and a late afternoon sun glowing ahead of him. He described the strain in his legs as he ran up a hill and the bounce in his step as he ran back down. He described the excitement of running fast around a corner and the joy of running slow enough to observe the birds in the trees.

When the young teacher was finished, Coach Fred smiled. "Thank you for the gift of your strong legs and powerful words. I felt like I was out there running with you."

"No," the young teacher said humbly, "thank you, Coach Fred, for the gift of asking me to share a part of myself with you."

"That's the best gift of all," Coach Fred said with wisdom in his eyes.

Blueprint for Reading

"Oh, he's my best friend!"

"My friends are coming over after school today."

"I invited only my closest friends to a sleepover this weekend."

"She's not really my friend."

Have you heard comments like these in the classroom or the hallway? Have some of these comments been addressed to you, or have you made them yourself? Have you taken time to consider what makes a friendship real? As you read the following story, try to understand why two such different people become such loving friends.

EYES ON *Imagery*

Sam was happy to be at Grandpa's house once again. It always made him feel good. The farm was nice and he was busy all day. He rode the tractor with Grandpa and visited the animals.

Sam slipped under the cool, satiny covers on the guest room bed. The cozy feeling was the perfect ending to a perfect day. Earlier in the day, when he saw the white picket fence and green meadows as he rode up to Grandpa's farm, Sam had felt really excited. He had spent the day picking ripe strawberries, riding the big tractor, and visiting the animals. The aroma of Grandma's fresh strawberry pie was still in the air as Sam drifted off to sleep, tired and content.

Which paragraph paints a clearer and more inviting picture? Which one helps you to imagine the scene better? The second one provides more details using sensory images. **Sensory images** are words that make us use one of our five senses in our imaginations. They tell us to *picture*, *smell*, *hear*, *feel*, or *taste* something in a story. As you read *The Gift*, notice how the images add to the story.

The Gift

Helen Coutant

Anna left the house at the usual time that morning. It would take her five minutes to run down the hill to where the school bus waited. If she was fast, she could stop by old Nana Marie's house. By now, Nana Marie might be back from the hospital. She had disappeared without warning more than a week ago. For two days, no one had answered when Anna knocked on the door after school. By the third day, Anna could scarcely eat she was so worried. Had they taken Nana Marie to one of those homes for very old people? But the next afternoon the daughter-in-law, Rita, who took care of Nana Marie, had opened the door an inch. It was just enough so that Anna could hear her voice over the blare of the radio. "You here to see Nana Marie? She's in the hospital." That was all Anna found out.

Now, rounding a bend in the road, Anna could see Rita standing by the gate in front of Nana Marie's house. Rita's loud voice rang out. "She's coming home today! Home from the hospital! Nana Marie!"

Nana Marie was coming home. Anna's heart gave a joyful leap.

"We're throwing a little party," Rita went on. "Just a few neighbors on the hill to welcome her back, cheer her up. Drop by after school. She'll be looking for you."

A party. That meant Anna would have to share Nana Marie with everyone else. Rita's voice, suddenly lower, caught Anna's attention.

"She won't really be looking for you, Nana Marie won't. But come to see her anyway. She'll need your company now that she's blind..."

Blind? Rita's voice rattled on, but Anna heard nothing more. Her heart seemed to have stopped on the word *blind*. How could Nana Marie suddenly be blind? There had been nothing wrong with Nana Marie's eyes. In fact, it was those extraordinary warm eyes, a cornflower blue, that had drawn Anna to Nana Marie in the first place. A small, choking noise escaped from Anna's throat.

Rita cocked her head and looked down, waiting for Anna to speak; then resumed her monologue. "Just happened, just like that," she said, shaking her head. "It's a pity. It's terrible. But you come by this afternoon for the party. We'll cheer her up, give Nana Marie some little presents to help her forget. Can I count on you?"

Count on her! Had Anna ever missed a chance to visit Nana Marie in the last six months, ever since the two had discovered each other one balmy September afternoon?

"So you come!" Rita repeated, her voice rising.

Anna couldn't answer. She pulled back, nodding, and turned away. She walked carefully around the puddles in the road. Her whispered "good-bye" floated up unheard by Rita, who was already going in the house, shivering from the February cold.

When the door banged, Anna took off, propelled by anger and sorrow. Her heart was pumping "blind, blind, blind" faster and faster. Blind without any warning. How could it happen? And yet it had.

She got to the foot of the hill just in time to see the school bus disappear around the curve. It had gone without her. The tears she had been holding back came to her eyes. There was no way she could get to school. Her mother was already at work.

WORD BANK

monologue (MAH nuh log) *n.*: a long speech made by one person, with no answer or interruption from the listener
balmy (BAH mee) *adj.*: mild and refreshing weather
propelled (pruh PELD) *v.*: moved; driven

Not wanting to go back to the empty house, Anna headed for her favorite path, which led upwards into the woods. The day was hers to do as she pleased.

There must be something she could do for Nana Marie. Rita had said something about a present. But what present could ever console a person who had become blind?

Anna remembered a time she had imagined being blind. Once in the middle of the night she had opened her eyes thinking it was morning. The unexpected blackness pressed down on her. She turned

WORD BANK

console (kun SOLE)
v.: comfort

her head this way and that and saw nothing, as if she had been buried. Just when she was ready to scream, her hand shot out and touched the light, nudging it on. The brightness, which then appeared so suddenly, dazzled her eyes. The patchwork quilt shone. The yellow walls glistened as if they had been freshly painted, and the air rushed out of her lungs in relief. Now she wondered how Nana Marie had felt waking up blind.

Anna broke into a trot. Ahead was a place she often came, a small, deep spring in the woods. When she knelt to gaze into the bottomless pool, at first she saw nothing but darkness. Then as the sun came out, the water seemed to open up, reflecting the bark of silver beeches, shining like armor. The reflection of luminous silver reminded her of Nana Marie. She sat back on her heels, remembering.

Six months ago, at the end of summer, Anna and her parents moved to the house just up the hill from Rita's. A week later Anna started school. She didn't know anyone and found it hard to make friends with the other fifth graders. She was very lonely until one afternoon when she had looked up and saw Nana Marie's welcoming smile.

There was a small moving van outside Rita's house that day. From a safe distance, half concealed by bushes, Anna watched it being unloaded. There were only a half dozen pieces of furniture, all a lovely dark wood, highly polished. Rita stood by, directing the operations. Anna could see the simple delight on Rita's face and wondered where this furniture was coming from.

As Anna watched, Rita's husband got out of his car, walked around it, and opened the door by the front seat. Then there was a long wait. Finally a white head emerged. Haltingly, as though every movement took a great deal of thought, a very old woman rose and holding on to her son's arm, began to walk toward the house. Halfway to the steps, she paused for breath. Then, as if she felt Anna's eyes on her, the old woman looked up. Their eyes met, and Nana Marie smiled.

The next afternoon when Anna came home from school, she saw Nana Marie sitting in a rocking chair on the front porch.

Slowly Anna approached, her school shoes raising little puffs of dust. The moment Nana Marie saw her she smiled, and the next thing Anna knew she was sitting cross-legged at Nana Marie's feet. Then they began to talk as if they had known each other for years. On and on till supper time they talked, "like old friends reunited," Nana Marie said. They even found out they had birthdays the same month and only two days apart.

Every day after that, when the school bus let Anna off at the bottom of the hill, she raced up to Rita's house to keep Nana Marie company. As long as the afternoons were warm they sat on the porch until twilight. They never ran out of things to talk about.

Nana Marie pointed out the fat groundhog scavenging for corn in the stubble of the field below Rita's house, and the flock of wild geese whose perfect "V" cut the sky as they flew south with haunting cries. And always, if she told Anna to listen, from far away would come the hollow *clack-clack* of a woodpecker at work on a tree. Anna would linger, enchanted, until there was just enough light left for her to run home. Sometimes an autumn moon, perfectly round, lit her way.

When cold weather arrived, Anna climbed the steep stairs to Nana Marie's room. Sitting by the window, they could see the world just as well as from the porch. They watched the trees on the top of the mountain turn bare and black, while there was still a wide strip of deep yellow at the foot of the mountain. Day by day this strip shrank until one day, after heavy rains, it was gone. Next came the snow, pure magic seen from Nana Marie's window.

Although most of Nana Marie's polished furniture was downstairs in Rita's living room, it was still cozy in Nana Marie's room. There was a bed, a table, a large chest of drawers, and a trunk. As soon as Anna arrived, she would put her books on the trunk and boil water on the hot plate in one corner. Then the two of them would have tea and share the events of the day. As the weeks passed, Anna learned that every object in Nana Marie's room had a meaning and a story. One by one, Anna learned the stories.

The silver hairbrush and matching hand mirror that lay on the chest of drawers had been an engagement present from Nana Marie's husband. A large *MK* with many curlicues was engraved on the back of each piece. Next to the hairbrush was a battered red and yellow cigar tin that said *The Finest Turkish*. When Anna opened the lid, she found a large round watch that dangled from a chain. The watch ticked once or twice when Anna moved it, then stopped. It had belonged to Nana Marie's father. An Indian figure carved out of wood gazed thoughtfully at the box. On the trunk was a very shiny bright-blue clay bowl overflowing with

WORD BANK

scavenging (SKAH vun jing) *v.*: taking or gathering something useable from among unwanted things

linger (LEENG er) *v.*: to stay somewhere longer than necessary because one does not want to leave

odds and ends. One side of the bowl was crooked, and it tipped when Anna touched it. It had been a present from Nana Marie's grandson when he was seven. Boxes of letters and photographs completely covered the table. Anna loved best the teapot with its two Chinese pheasants.[1] Its spout was stained brown from all the tea that had been poured, and Nana Marie said the teapot was six times as old as Anna.

Finally, what at first had seemed to Anna only a small, cluttered room expanded to become a history of Nana Marie's life, of her joys and sorrows and memories stretching over almost a century.

Gazing deep into the shining pool again, Anna decided that Nana Marie was like this spring. Each day of her old age she had quietly caught and held a different reflection. Stored in her depths were layers

---

1. *Pheasants* are large long-tailed birds that are considered a delicacy.

of reflections, shining images of the world. Many of these she had shared with Anna. But now that she was blind, would these images be gone, the way water became dark when there was no light? What would her days be like?

Anna's thoughts moved to the party that Rita would hold in the afternoon. She knew what the neighbors were likely to bring: candy, scarves, flowers. She could do the same, yet none of these gifts would express what she felt for Nana Marie. And could any of them really make Nana Marie feel better?

Lost in thought, Anna continued to follow the path up the mountain. Even though her sneakers were wet from the soft thawing soil of the woods, she decided to stay there until school was out. Maybe by then she would know what to bring Nana Marie.

Slowly the world about her drew Anna in, just as if she had been with Nana Marie. The wan February sun was swallowed by a thick mist, which the mountain seemed to exhale with each gust of wind. Although the air was damp, it had an edge of warmth that had been absent in the morning. It felt almost like the beginnings of spring. As the hours passed, Anna picked up objects she thought Nana Marie would like: a striped rock, a tiny fern, a clump of moss, an empty milkweed pod. None of them, on second thought, seemed a proper gift for Nana Marie. Other days, she would have loved them. But now Anna thought they could easily make her sad, for in touching them, Nana Marie would be reminded of the things she would never see again. There had to be a way to bring the whole woods, the sky, and the fields to Nana Marie. What else would do? What else would be worthy of their friendship?

Suddenly Anna knew what her gift would be. It would be like no other gift, and a gift no one else could bring. All day long Anna had been seeing the world the way Nana Marie had shown her. Now she would bring everything she had seen to Nana Marie.

Her wet feet, her damp skirt and jacket, no longer mattered. Eagerly she turned and began the long trudge back to Nana

WORD BANK

wan (WAHN) *adj.*: pale and weak

Marie's house. Her hands were empty in her pockets. But the gift she carried in her head was as big as the world.

Just as the sun went over the mountain, Anna emerged from the woods. Ahead of her was the road and Nana Marie's house. She looked at Nana Marie's room, the window directly over the front door. A light should be on by now. But the blinds were down as they had been all week, and the window was so dark it reflected, eerily, the reddish glow of twilight. Everyone must be downstairs at the party. Probably Rita hadn't even bothered to go upstairs and raise the blinds. Yet downstairs the windows were dark too. What had happened? Where was Nana Marie?

Anna stopped to catch her breath. Her entire body was pounding. She ran around Rita's car to the kitchen door. She hesitated, biting her lip, before she rapped softly on the glass part of the door. There was no answer. She could see a light in the living room, something was turned on. She knocked again, louder, then put her hand on the doorknob. It opened from the other side, and Rita stood there in her bathrobe. The kitchen table was covered with the remains of the party: tissue paper, stacked plates and cups. So the neighbors had come and gone. Anna was too late for the party, but Nana Marie must be there!

"Well, here at last," Rita said. "I figured you went home and forgot. The party ended half an hour ago. I told Nana Marie it wasn't any use waiting up for you longer. I expect she's asleep by now. She was real disappointed you didn't come, though she got lots of nice things from everybody. Why don't you come back tomorrow when she's rested."

"Please, I can't," Anna said. She bent, tearing at her wet shoelaces. "I have a present for Nana Marie. It won't take long. I'll take my shoes off and go upstairs to her room."

Rita shrugged. She seemed anxious to get back to her show. At the door to the living room she called back, "Don't go waking her up. I just got her settled. You can leave the present on her table. I'll tell her about it tomorrow."

Nodding, Anna headed for the stairs on tiptoe. The world of Rita dropped away as she climbed toward Nana Marie's room. The landing at the top of the stairs was dark, and the door to Nana Marie's room was closed. Anna paused and let her breath out slowly. What did blind people look like? What if the doctors had taken out Nana Marie's eyes and only two black holes were left? Anna's hand hesitated on the doorknob.

Then she opened the door and shut it behind her.

Nana Marie's room was pitch black. There was no sound at all. Was the room empty? The window was straight ahead. Anna ran to it, groping for the cords. The blinds clattered up, crashing in the darkness. Rita was sure to come up. Then a faint light flowed into the room. Outside, in the winter twilight, a small frozen moon was wandering upward.

"Anna," Nana Marie was calling her name. She was not asleep after all. "Anna," Nana Marie said, and now there was surprise and joy in her voice. Nana Marie was sitting in her rocking chair. Her eyes were open and as blue as they had always been, like the sky on a summer morning.

"Oh, Nana Marie!" Anna exclaimed. She patted the old warm skin of Nana Marie's cheek.

"You came," Nana Marie said. "I thought maybe you were getting tired of having such a very old lady for a friend."

"I brought you a present," Anna said. "I'm late because it took me all day to get it."

"Gracious," said Nana Marie. "You shouldn't have done that! All the nice people who came this afternoon brought me presents as if I could see and were still of some use to someone!" She chuckled, gesturing toward the table and a new stack of boxes.

"Mine is different," Anna said. "I brought you a last day."

"A last day..." Nana Marie's voice trailed off. At the hospital someone had arranged her hair in soft waves. She put her hand up as if to touch them, but halfway there her fingers stretched out, reaching for Anna. She took Anna's hand and held it firmly.

"You didn't have a last day to look at the world," Anna said. "So I brought it to you. Everything I saw today. Just as if you saw it with me. The way you would see it. And tomorrow I'll bring you another—and the next day another. I'll bring you enough seeing to last forever. That's my present, Nana Marie."

Nana Marie was silent for a minute. Then she added softly, almost to herself, "Oh, child, how did you ever think of that?" She leaned back in the rocking chair. One hand held on to Anna's. With the other she gestured toward a chair. "Pull it up right here, Anna," she said, "so we can look out over the valley and the moonlight together. The moon is out, isn't it, Anna? I can feel it." She closed her eyes.

Anna pulled Nana Marie's hand into her lap and held it with both of her own as she described the silver beeches reflected in the spring, the yellow mist breathing in and out, the pale sun—everything she had seen that day.

When Anna was finished, Nana Marie sat up and turned toward her. Nana Marie's blue eyes shone with contentment. "Thank you, Anna," she said. "That was beautiful." She paused briefly and when she continued it was almost as though she was speaking to herself. "*This* is a day I'll always remember."

Anna sat holding on to Nana Marie's hand until the moon disappeared over the house. Even though something as terrible as going blind had happened to Nana Marie, she really hadn't changed. She could still marvel at the world, she could still feel the moonlight. Anna knew she was going to be all right.

ABOUT THE AUTHOR

Helen Coutant, like so many authors of children's books, is a teacher. *The Gift* is her second book. Her first book was the award-winning *First Snow*. In addition to teaching and writing, Mrs. Coutant works with her husband as a translator. They have translated short stories from Vietnamese to English.

For You

Here is a building
I have built for you.
The bricks are butter yellow.
Every window shines.
5   And at each an orange cat is curled,
lulled by the summer sun.
The door invites you in.
The mat is warm.
Inside there is a chair
10   so soft and blue
the pillows look like sky.
In all the world
no one but you
may sit in that cloud chair.
15   I'll sit near by.

Karla Kuskin

Poetry is giving

Studying the Selection

QUICK REVIEW

1. Where did Nana Marie go when she 'disappeared' and why?
2. Who informed Anna about the blindness and the welcoming party?
3. When did Anna and Nana Marie meet?
4. What were some things Anna and Nana Marie spoke about?

FOCUS

5. What was unusual about the friendship between Anna and Nana Marie?
6. Explain how Anna used images to make a "gift" for Nana Marie.

CREATING AND WRITING

7. What are five important qualities you look for in a friend? Explain why these qualities are so important to you.
8. Write about the kind of gift you usually give to close friends or relatives.
9. Choose an adult friend or relative and ask the person to share a memory of some important event with you. Tell this person that you would like the event to be described in detail, with many images. Write down three or four of the images the person shares with you. Your job is to gather three or four objects that represent these images and make them into a collage. Attach the objects to a poster board and bring it to class. You will be asked to show your collage to the class and explain the meaning of each object.

Lesson in Literature...

COMPARING SETTINGS

- Many stories and plays have more than one setting.
- A story may take place in two or more different places or two or more different time periods.
- The change in setting signals a change in the plot or the characters.
- A change in setting will be indicated by the story's narrator or through the characters' dialogue.

THINK ABOUT IT!

1. The first setting—the country, is different from the second setting—the ocean. List four ways these settings are different.
2. Does the main character change when the setting changes?
3. The author uses many images to create the two settings for the story. Find four images used to describe either setting and write them down.

Laurel lived with her parents in the country. Their house was near the top of a hill and at the edge of a pine forest. She loved her country home. She loved its quiet and its beauty. She loved the smell of the pine trees when the wind blew. She loved the sound of the birds when she walked beside a stream. She loved the big garden in the backyard where her mother planted flowers and vegetables. She loved watching deer and foxes appear out of the forest. She loved climbing the hill behind her house and looking out at the rolling countryside. She loved the blue sky above the fields and the trees, too. It reminded her of the color of

the water at the beach. She loved everything about her home in the country, but as soon as school ended each year she couldn't wait to leave it all behind.

Laurel couldn't wait to leave because at the beginning of each summer, she and her parents left the country for another place they loved: the beach. Each summer as the car rolled down the hill where they lived, she just couldn't wait to get to the beach. She watched out the window with anticipation as farms and fields changed to bays and bridges. She watched with excitement as the scenery changed from country roads to sandy roads, from feed stores to bait-and-tackle shops, and

THE COLOR OF WATER

from farmers' markets to seafood restaurants. As they got closer to the beach, she squeezed her eyes shut in the bright sun. When the car climbed the last bridge onto the narrow shore, through the open car window she could hear the sound of the waves and smell the salt air.

They were at the beach!

She couldn't wait until her father pulled the car right up to the shore. She sprang from the back, racing as fast as she could up and down the beach. She chased and dodged waves at the waterline. She rolled around in the sand as if it were snow. When she took a walk, she made deep footprints, burying her toes in the cool sand. She waded up to her knees in the cold surf. She loved the beach! She could stay all day having fun. She loved the beauty of the beach, too. Everything was so white and so blue. The sand was bone-white and sparkling in the sun, and the ocean was as blue as the sky in the country.

At the end of each summer, Laurel watched out the car window with fond memories of a summer at the beach, but she also watched closely for the turn onto the country road that led up to her house on the hill. By the end of the summer, she couldn't wait to get home to the country. She loved the excitement of the beach, but the quiet of the country was home.

Blueprint for Reading

INTO . . . *Toto*

Imagine you are a soccer player and you notice a sign on the bulletin board. "Interested in being captain of our soccer team? Please inform the gym teacher." You are thrilled. You race toward the gym teacher's office—and then it happens. Your hands start feeling cold and your stomach feels a little funny. You slow down. "What if they don't choose me? What if my friends think I'm not good enough to be captain?" Suddenly, you are afraid to take the risk. The gym teacher walks out of his office and sees you. You hesitate and tell the teacher what you've been thinking. The teacher smiles and says, "I don't know if you'll be chosen. I don't know what your friends will think. But I *do* know that if you don't try for the job, you *won't* be chosen and your friends *won't* have a chance to support you. If you *do* try, chances are you'll succeed!"

Learning more and experiencing new things requires taking risks. To grow, we have to take a chance on something new. As you read *Toto*, you will see that the two main characters both leave what is familiar to them and try something new. Ask yourself what they have lost by this, and what they have gained.

EYES ON *Comparing Settings*

What is the setting of *Toto*? Is it Suku's village? Is it the valley, where Toto and the other elephants roam? The answer is: it is both; the story has two settings. *Toto* is built around the two settings and the characters who live in them. As the story develops, each main character leaves the safety of his home and ventures into the other's home. As they learn about the world outside their homes, they become wiser and more mature. What lessons—and it is not the same one—do Suku and Toto learn?

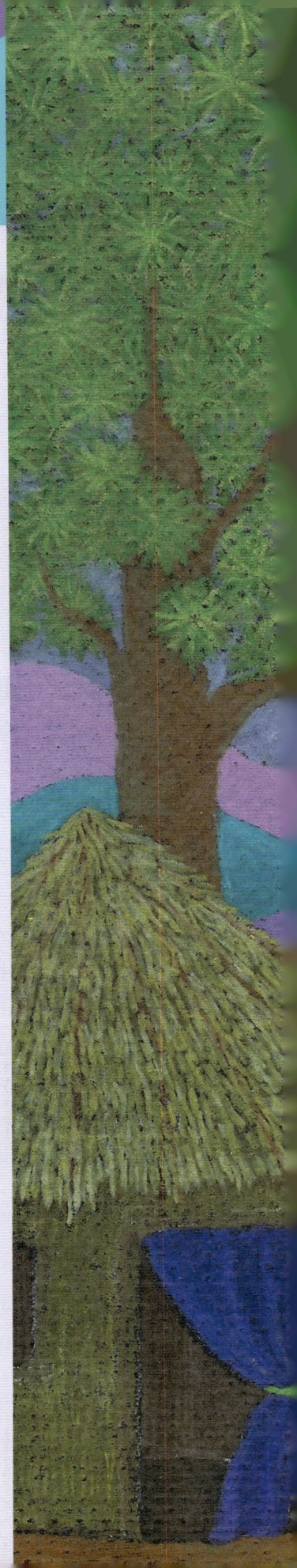

Toto

Marietta D. Moskin

Deep in Africa, on the outer slopes of a gently rolling ring of hills, lived a timid young boy named Suku. His round thatched hut stood in a busy village where his tribe had always lived. Just a short distance away, on the other side of the blue and purple hills, was a quiet valley set aside for animals to live without fear of being hunted by men. Suku had often climbed to the top of the tallest hill and had watched the herds of animals moving through the grasslands far below.

WORD BANK

timid (TIH mid) *adj.*: shy and easily frightened

thatched *adj.*: having a roof made of straw

But that was as far as he ever went. His own world was outside the protected game reserve[1]—with his family, in the safe, familiar village.

On a saucer-shaped plain sheltered by the ring of blue and purple hills lived a curious little elephant. His name was Toto—the little one—because he was the youngest and smallest elephant in the herd. With his large family he roamed across the silvery plains of his valley, feeding on the juicy grasses and bathing in the broad green river that twisted through the land. It was a good life for elephants and for the many other animals with whom they shared their peaceful valley.

Day by day the little elephant in the valley and the boy in the village grew stronger and bigger and learned the things they had to know.

Toto learned which berries and roots were good to eat and which ones would make him sick. He learned to recognize danger by smells in the air and sounds in the distance. He stood patiently while his mother doused him with water from her trunk, and he paid attention when she showed him how to powder himself with red dust to keep the insects away.

When his mother warned him never to stray outside their peaceful valley because there were dangers beyond the hills, Toto listened. Most of the time he was happy to play with his cousins among the thorn trees and with his friends, the antelope and the baby baboons. But sometimes Toto looked toward the blue and purple hills in the distance and wondered what lay behind their rounded crests.

Suku too learned a great many things a boy growing up in an African village had to learn. He carried water for his mother from the river and he collected dung to burn in the fire on which she

---

1. A *game reserve* is a large area of land where animals, which might normally be hunted, are protected by the law.

cooked their midday meal. In the evening he helped his father and the other men to pen the tribe's cattle and goats within the village compound. But in the morning, when the boys and young men of the village went out to herd their cattle on the rich grazing lands in the valley, Suku did not go with them. He watched when the herd boys walked jauntily out of the village, brandishing their wooden staffs and shouting to their charges. At seven he was old enough to go, but Suku was frightened when he thought of the herd boys walking through the bush with nothing but a stick or crude iron spear to protect them from lions.

"Our ancestors were famous lion hunters," his mother scolded. "The men of our tribe have always walked fearlessly through the bush."

"Give Suku time," his father counseled. "Courage sometimes comes with need."

So Suku went on doing women's chores around the village and avoiding the boys who teased him.

And inside the ring of gently rolling purple hills, Toto, the little elephant, roamed with the herd across the grasslands. But whenever he saw the young weaverbirds flying from their hanging straw nests, he watched enviously as they sailed off into the sky far, far beyond the circle of hills.

One night Toto followed the elephant herd to the edge of their valley where the river flowed onto the plain through a gap in the hills. There, in a clearing between the trees, the young males of the herd fought mock battles with each other in the moonlight.

Sheltered by his mother's bulk, Toto watched for a while. Then, looking up at the velvety sky, he saw that the moon had traveled across the valley and was about to dip down below the highest hill.

I wonder where she goes, Toto thought. Perhaps I'll just follow the river a little ways and see. Not very far—just to where the river curves.

Slowly Toto moved away from the group of elephants. Nobody noticed. Not even his mother. But once he was in the shadows of trees, the moon was no longer there to guide him.

"Elephants have no enemies—Mother said so," he told himself bravely. Only the lion might stalk an unprotected elephant child—but the lions had had their kill

WORD BANK

jauntily (JAWNT ih lee) *adv.*: in a lively, carefree, and slightly proud way
brandishing (BRAN dish ing) *v.*: waving and displaying
crude *adj.*: rough; not well-designed
mock *adj.*: pretend; make-believe

earlier that night. Toto had seen them at their meal.

Toto walked on through the darkness. Sometimes he could see the moon reflected on the river, and he hurried to catch up with it. But he didn't look back, and so he didn't realize that the hills lay behind him now. He didn't notice either that he could no longer hear the loud trumpeting of the other elephants at play. He didn't know that he was already in that mysterious world beyond the hills he had longed to discover.

Suddenly Toto felt a sharp pain in his right front leg. Something hard and sharp had fastened around his foot. Toto pulled and pulled, but he couldn't free his foot. Each time he pulled, the pain got sharper.

Nothing his mother had told him about danger had prepared Toto for this. In fear and pain he trumpeted loudly. But he had walked too far to be heard. There was no answering call from his mother or from any of the other elephants. For the first time in his life, Toto was alone.

In the round thatched hut in the village, Suku slept on a woven mat next to his parents. Suku was a sound sleeper, but something—some noise—awoke him before dawn. It sounded like an elephant trumpeting, Suku thought sleepily. But elephants rarely strayed this far out of the game reserve in the valley. He must have been dreaming, Suku told himself. He couldn't have heard an elephant this close.

But Suku could not go back to sleep. When the first sunshine crept through the chinks under the door, he got up and slipped into his clothes. He had promised his mother he would cut some papyrus[2] reeds at the river today so that she could mend their torn sleeping mats. Now that he was awake he would do it before the day grew hot.

Quietly, so as not to waken the rest of his family, Suku tiptoed out of the hut. Outside, no one stirred. Even the cattle were still asleep.

---

2. *Papyrus* (puh PY rus) is a marsh plant with tall, thin stems.

Clutching his sharp reed knife, Suku followed the winding path down the hill to the riverbank, searching for a good stand of feathery papyrus.

Suddenly the silence at the river was broken by a loud rustling sound. The sound came again—not just a rustling this time, but a snapping of twigs and a swishing of the tall grasses. Carefully, and a little fearfully, Suku moved around the next curve in the path. And then he stopped again.

Before him, in the trampled grass, lay a very young elephant. Around one of the elephant's legs the cruelly stiffened rope of a poacher's trap had been pulled so tight that the snare had bitten deeply into the flesh. The elephant had put up a fierce struggle, but now he was exhausted. He lay quietly on his side, squealing softly from time to time.

Anger exploded inside Suku—anger at the cruel poachers who had set their cunning trap so close to the game reserve. He approached the trapped elephant carefully. His father had taught him to be aware of wounded animals who could be far more dangerous in fear and pain. But the little elephant seemed to sense that Suku wanted to help him, and he held very still. Grasping his knife, Suku slashed at the thick, twisted rope. It took time to free the elephant's leg, but finally the last strand of the rope gave way. The boy jumped out of the way quickly, and the small elephant slowly got to his feet. Then he just stood there on the path, staring at Suku.

"Shoo, shoo, little elephant—quickly, run back into the valley," Suku urged. The poachers who had set the trap could be back at any time. But Toto, who had spent the night by himself, would not leave that strange two-legged creature with the oddly dangerous smell but the warm, comforting sounds. When Suku turned to walk back to the village, Toto started after him.

"Please, little one, please, hurry home," Suku pleaded.

But the little elephant didn't budge.

"What are we going to do?" Suku asked in despair. "Will I have to lead you back to your family, you foolish little one?"

Suku didn't want to go into the bush. But he looked at the elephant baby and knew that there was no choice.

Suku began to walk, and the small elephant followed. He walked slowly and painfully, limping on the leg that had been cut so badly by the poacher's snare.

It was easy for Suku to find the way Toto had left the reserve. Trampled grass and elephant droppings formed a perfect track. After a while the boy and the elephant came to the clearing where the herd had watched the fight between the young bulls the night before. The clearing was empty, but a trail of droppings showed that the herd had moved on across the open bush.

Suku was so busy following the trail that he hadn't thought much about what he was doing. Suddenly he realized he was walking all by himself across the open grasslands. Just like the herd boys. And he didn't even have an iron spear for protection—nothing but a small reed cutting knife!

He walked on, trying not to think about the dangers. By now the sun was high in the sky, and at home they were surely wondering what had happened to him.

They walked and walked. Suku, who hadn't had any breakfast that morning, began to feel hungry and thirsty. Toto hadn't had breakfast either, but there was no time to stop and eat.

Suddenly Toto stopped. He raised his head and listened, trembling a little. Young as he was, Toto recognized the smells and sounds of danger.

Suku looked around to see what had frightened Toto. And then he saw the danger too. A few paces away, half-hidden in the silvery-tan grass, stood an enormous brown-maned lion.

The lion looked from the elephant to the boy, almost as if he were measuring which one would make the easier victim. He looked haughty and strong and very big. Suku's fist tightened around

the handle of his knife. He wasn't sure at all whether the knife would do him any good, but he was prepared to defend himself if the lion attacked. Behind him he could sense the little elephant stiffen. Even though the lion looked awfully big to him too, Toto had raised his trunk and spread his ears the way the big elephants did when they were ready to attack.

"Oh, please, make him go away, make him go away," Suku prayed silently. His hand around the knife handle felt clammy and stiff. It seemed to him that he and the elephant and the lion had stood there facing one another, forever.

It was Toto who broke the silence. He took a step toward the lion, and he trumpeted a warning.

The next moment—almost like an echo—another elephant call sounded across the bush. Then another and another. Turning his head, Suku saw a large herd of elephants advancing from behind a nearby stand of thorn trees. Toto's family had come to rescue their littlest one!

Then Suku heard another, more familiar sound. It was the rattling and roaring sound of a car traveling fast across rough ground. A second later the game warden's battered white Landrover appeared over the next small hill. Suku recognized the warden at the wheel, and next to the warden Suku saw his father standing up in the car with a gun in his hand.

"Stand still, Suku—just don't move," his father shouted. He aimed his gun at the lion, waiting to see what the lion would do.

The lion looked at his two young victims. Then he looked at the menacing group of elephants on his right and at the men in the car to his left. Mustering what dignity he could, he stalked slowly and deliberately away. Within moments he had disappeared into the tall dry grass.

Another loud, single call sounded from the elephant herd. Toto was being summoned. His mother was coming to take him back to the herd.

Slowly Toto raised his trunk to the boy who had brought him home. Then, still limping badly, he turned and followed his mother.

WORD BANK

menacing (MEN uh sing) *adj.*: threatening
mustering (MUST uh ring) *v.*: gathering; calling upon

The warden had waited for the elephants to withdraw. Now he drove the Landrover over to where Suku stood.

"Get in, Suku—let's go," the warden said.

"You came just in time," Suku said.

"We found the cut snare and the elephant tracks—and someone in the village had seen you going down to the river early this morning," his father explained.

"The poachers would have killed him for his hide," Suku said.

"You did right, Suku," the warden said. "I get so angry too when I catch these poachers. You would make a good game ranger some day, Suku. You love animals, and you are brave."

The warden's words made Suku feel good. He knew that he hadn't felt brave, but he had walked in the footsteps of his ancestors: he had gone into the bush, and he had faced a lion!

Now he would never feel shy of the village boys again. He knew he had earned his place in the tribe.

Under the leafy canopy of the forest, Toto nuzzled up close to his mother's flank. He had eaten his fill of crisp greens at the riverbank, and his mother had bathed his cut foot and smeared it with healing red mud. Now the herd was resting quietly in the shade near the river.

It was good to be home, Toto thought contentedly. Let the moon and the sun and the birds travel beyond the hills if they wished. His place was here.

ABOUT THE AUTHOR

Born in Austria before World War II, **Marietta Moskin** spent many of her teenage years imprisoned in a concentration camp. Even during that terrible time, she wrote poems and stories on precious bits of paper. After the war, while still in Germany, Marietta taught herself English by reading English books. She made her way to the United States, where she finished high school and went on to write books both in English and in other languages. Marietta hopes to acquaint her young readers with ways of living, feeling, and thinking that may be different from their own.

In This Jungle

Myra Cohn Livingston

In this jungle
I will search an elephant,
A huge elephant, gray, with pink eyes.

It is quiet now,
5   But I understand
That if I listen carefully,
If I crouch very still,

If I wait patiently,
He will come.

10   Boughs break.
Feet thunder
Branches fly.
And there will be a world of trumpeting

When he comes,
15   When my elephant comes.

Poetry is quiet and strong

Studying the Selection

QUICK REVIEW

1. How old was Suku and where did he live?

2. Who was Toto?

3. What did both Suku and Toto dream about sometimes?

4. What did Suku discover when he followed the noise early in the morning?

FOCUS

5. What made Suku go to Toto even though he was afraid? Would he have gone just out of curiosity?

6. Was it difficult for you to follow two different plots and settings in one story? Why or why not?

CREATING AND WRITING

7. Suku and Toto both took risks in this story. As a result, they both grew and learned more about themselves. Write about a time you took a risk. What were the results? If you cannot think of an example, write about something that you would like to try but are afraid to do because of the risk involved.

8. Imagine what it might have been like when Suku's father was a young boy and went out into the bush. Was he brave? Was he afraid, as Suku was? Did he have to face an elephant or a lion? Did he go alone or with a group? Write a few paragraphs about this.

9. Follow your teacher's instructions for a special risk-taking activity.

Lesson in Literature . . .

WHAT IS MOOD?

- Part of setting is **mood**. Mood is the atmosphere in which a story takes place.

- Mood can be created by narration: *tension filled the air.*

- Mood can be created by setting: *outside, lightning and thunder filled the black night.*

- Mood can be created by dialogue: *"Good morning! What a wonderful day it is!"*

THINK ABOUT IT!

1. What would you say is the mood of this poem? Choose three words or phrases from the poem that gave you this feeling.

2. In one sentence, describe the beach. In one sentence, describe the boy. Is the mood of the setting similar to or different from the boy's emotions?

3. At the end of the poem, the boy pictures a house. What is the mood he pictures?

DRIFTWOOD

On the beach at night
midwinter

Dad and I gather
driftwood

for fires we'll set
together.

We search cold
gray sand

find planks, boards,
two-by-fours.

Here, he says,
piling wood

into my open arms
until the stash

scrapes my chin.
He walks ahead

his own woodpile
stacked high.

Wind whips.
Winter waves

crest and break.
I do not move.

It's a face-chapping night.
I'm too cold now

for driftwood.
I drop the pile

cold hands
against cold face

squat in dark sand
wishing I hadn't.

Moonlight litters
the shipwrecked beach.

As Dad helps home
my driftwood and me

I wish I were a son
who set blazing fires

flames crackling salt
thick wood smoke rising

the whole house
burning with pride.

Blueprint for Reading

INTO . . . *Owl Moon*

Have you ever gotten up before the sun rose to leave on a trip? Have you ever had a secret meeting with your friend to go exploring just before dark? Did you and your brother ever arrange to get up in the middle of the night to work on some mysterious project? If you have, then you know that tingly feeling of being awake when the entire world is asleep. You remember the hush that blankets everything, that makes you want to whisper even if no one can hear you. When you are alone in the dark, you hear every noise, you sense every movement, and your eyes, ears, skin, and sense of smell are on high alert. As you read *Owl Moon*, walk through the woods with a young girl and her father, and watch for the great, dark owl to cast his shadow over the big, yellow moon.

EYES ON *Mood*

It was a dark and stormy night. The fireplace had only a small fire and the gloomy, old room was damp and drafty. Outside, the wind howled and the branches beat at the windowpane.

How would you describe the mood created by this description? Is it cheery? Does it sound warm and friendly? How about spooky? The **mood** of a poem or story means the feeling that is there, in the background, as you read. Another word for mood is *atmosphere*. In stories, many things help to create a mood, just as they do in real life. Light has a lot to do with mood. Surroundings create mood, as do sound and music. Extremes of temperature—very hot or freezing cold—affect mood. *Owl Moon* uses all of these: light, surroundings, sound, and temperature to create a mood. Can you think of anything else that adds to the mood of the poem?

OWL MOON

JANE YOLEN
Illustrated by
JOHN SCHOENHERR

It was late one winter night,
long past my bedtime,
when Pa and I went owling.
There was no wind.
The trees stood still
as giant statues.
And the moon was so bright
the sky seemed to shine.
Somewhere behind us
a train whistle blew,
long and low,
like a sad, sad song.

I could hear it
through the woolen cap
Pa had pulled down
over my ears.
A farm dog answered the train,
and then a second dog
joined in.
They sang out,
trains and dogs,
for a real long time.
And when their voices
faded away
it was as quiet as a dream.

We walked on toward the woods,
Pa and I.
Our feet crunched
over the crisp snow
and little gray footprints
followed us.
Pa made a long shadow,
but mine was short and round.
I had to run after him
every now and then
to keep up,
and my short, round
shadow
bumped after me.
But I never called out.
If you go owling
you have to be quiet,
that's what Pa always says.
I had been waiting
to go owling with Pa
for a long, long time.

We reached the line
of pine trees,

black and pointy
against the sky,
and Pa held up his hand.
I stopped right where I was
and waited.
He looked up,
as if searching the stars,
as if reading a map up there.
The moon made his face
into a silver mask.
Then he called:
"Whoo-whoo-who-who-who-whooooooo,"
the sound of a Great Horned Owl.
"Whoo-whoo-who-who-who-whooooooo."

Again he called out.
And then again.
After each call
he was silent
and for a moment we both listened.
But there was no answer.
Pa shrugged
and I shrugged.
I was not disappointed.
My brothers all said
sometimes there's an owl
and sometimes there isn't.

We walked on.
I could feel the cold,
as if someone's icy hand
was palm-down on my back.
And my nose
and the tops of my cheeks
felt cold and hot
at the same time.
But I never said a word.
If you go owling
you have to be quiet
and make your own heat.

We went into the woods.
The shadows
were the blackest things
I had ever seen.
They stained the white snow.
My mouth felt furry,
for the scarf over it
was wet and warm.
I didn't ask
what kinds of things
hide behind black trees
in the middle of the night.
When you go owling
you have to be brave.

Then we came to a clearing
in the dark woods.
The moon was high above us.
It seemed to fit
exactly
over the center of the clearing
and the snow below it
was whiter than the milk
in a cereal bowl.

I sighed
and Pa held up his hand
at the sound.
I put my mittens
over the scarf
over my mouth
and listened hard.
And then Pa called:
"Whoo-whoo-who-who-who-whooooooo.
Whoo-whoo-who-who-who-whooooooo."
I listened
and looked so hard
my ears hurt
and my eyes got cloudy
with the cold.
Pa raised his face
to call out again,

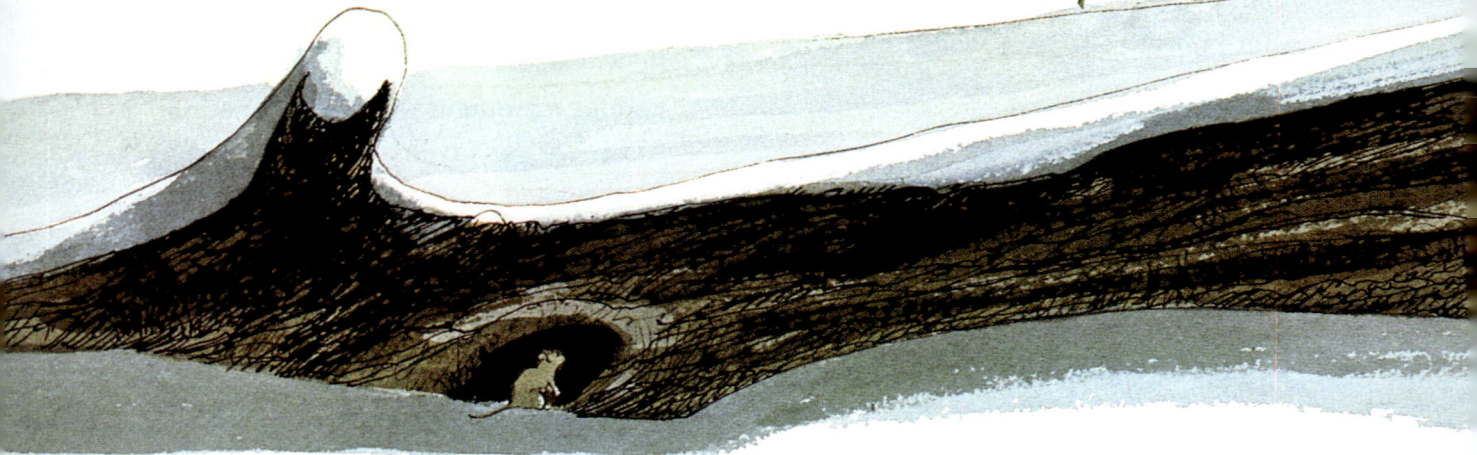

but before he could
open his mouth
an echo
came threading its way
through the trees.
"Whoo-whoo-who-who-who-whooooooo."

Pa almost smiled.
Then he called back:
"Whoo-whoo-who-who-who-whooooooo,"
just as if he
and the owl
were talking about supper
or about the woods
or the moon
or the cold.
I took my mitten
off the scarf
off my mouth,
and I almost smiled, too.

The owl's call came closer,
from high up in the trees
on the edge of the meadow.
Nothing in the meadow moved.

All of a sudden
an owl shadow,
part of the big tree shadow,
lifted off
and flew right over us.
We watched silently
with heat in our mouths,
the heat of all those words
we had not spoken.
The shadow hooted again.

Pa turned on
his big flashlight
and caught the owl
just as it was landing
on a branch.

For one minute,
three minutes,
maybe even a hundred
minutes,
we stared at one
another.

Then the owl
pumped its great wings
and lifted off the branch
like a shadow
without sound.
It flew back into the forest.
"Time to go home,"
Pa said to me.
I knew then I could talk,
I could even laugh out loud.
But I was a shadow
as we walked home.

When you go owling
you don't need words
or warm
or anything but hope.
That's what Pa says.
The kind of hope
that flies
on silent wings
under a shining
Owl Moon.

ABOUT THE AUTHOR

Jane Yolen has written so many books, she has lost count! This author of more than 280 books was born in New York City in 1939. When she was still a little girl, she and her brother wrote a newspaper for their big Manhattan apartment building. They sold the newspapers for five cents a copy! Jane published her first book of poems when she was only 22 years old. Jane married David Stemple, and they had three children. When she is not visiting her vacation home in Scotland, Jane Hyatt Yolen lives in Massachusetts near her daughter, Heidi.

Studying the Selection

FIRST IMPRESSIONS

The father and daughter were careful not to disturb the silence of the woods and did not talk to each other at all. What might they have said, had they spoken aloud?

QUICK REVIEW

1. Why was the narrator so eager to go owling?

2. What was one very important rule of owling?

3. What does one do to attract owls?

4. What happened once Pa and the narrator actually saw an owl? What did they do and how did they feel?

FOCUS

5. Choose three words that describe the way the narrator felt about her father. The words can describe three different feelings.

6. What lines in the poem created the mood of *anticipation*, or waiting for something important to happen?

CREATING AND WRITING

7. The author describes an experience in a natural, outdoor setting. Write about an experience you had somewhere outdoors. Make sure you describe the setting as well as the experience itself.

8. Write a paragraph that summarizes the story from the owl's point of view. Your story may be humorous, if you wish.

9. Your teacher will give you pictures of beautiful outdoor scenes. Look at your picture closely, and write down four sentences that describe it. Glue the picture onto a piece of poster board, then "frame it" by writing one of your four descriptive sentences on each side of it. If you are artistic (or even if you're not!), you may write the sentences in flowing or fancy letters.

SANDRA DAY O'CONNOR

WHAT IS BIOGRAPHY?

- One form of nonfiction is **biography**. Biography is the true story of one person's life told by another person.

- A biography can take the form of a short story, a book, or even a play.

- A biography may cover the person's entire life or only one part of the person's life.

- When someone writes a book about their own life, the book is called an *auto*biography.

THINK ABOUT IT!

1. Why was a biography written about Sandra Day O'Connor?

2. At what point in Sandra Day O'Connor's life does the story open? Why?

3. This is a very short biography about Sandra Day O'Connor. What part of her life would you like to learn more about? List three topics that would make the story of her life more interesting for you.

Sandra Day O'Connor, the first woman to serve on the Supreme Court of the United States, served as an Associate Justice from 1981 until her retirement from the bench in 2005. In this excerpt, she contemplates the historic significance of her first day "on the bench."

Sandra Day O'Connor stood where she had never stood before. In fact, she stood where no woman in history had ever stood before. It was September 1981, and she stood at the doors of the Supreme Court of the United States about to enter as its first woman justice. She was nervous. Everything around her was new and a little strange. The eight other justices in long robes were new and a little strange to her. The big city of Washington, D.C., with its fast pace and important people, was new and a little strange

to her. All the media interest in her life and career was also new and very strange. But she was excited. She stood where she had never stood before. She was about to make history.

As she waited to enter the Supreme Court for the first time, she couldn't help but think about her life. Had any of her experiences prepared her for this historic role? She was born March 26, 1930, in El Paso, Texas. Her parents, Harry and Ada Mae, owned a 198,000 acre cattle ranch, called the Lazy B Cattle Ranch, in southeastern Arizona, where

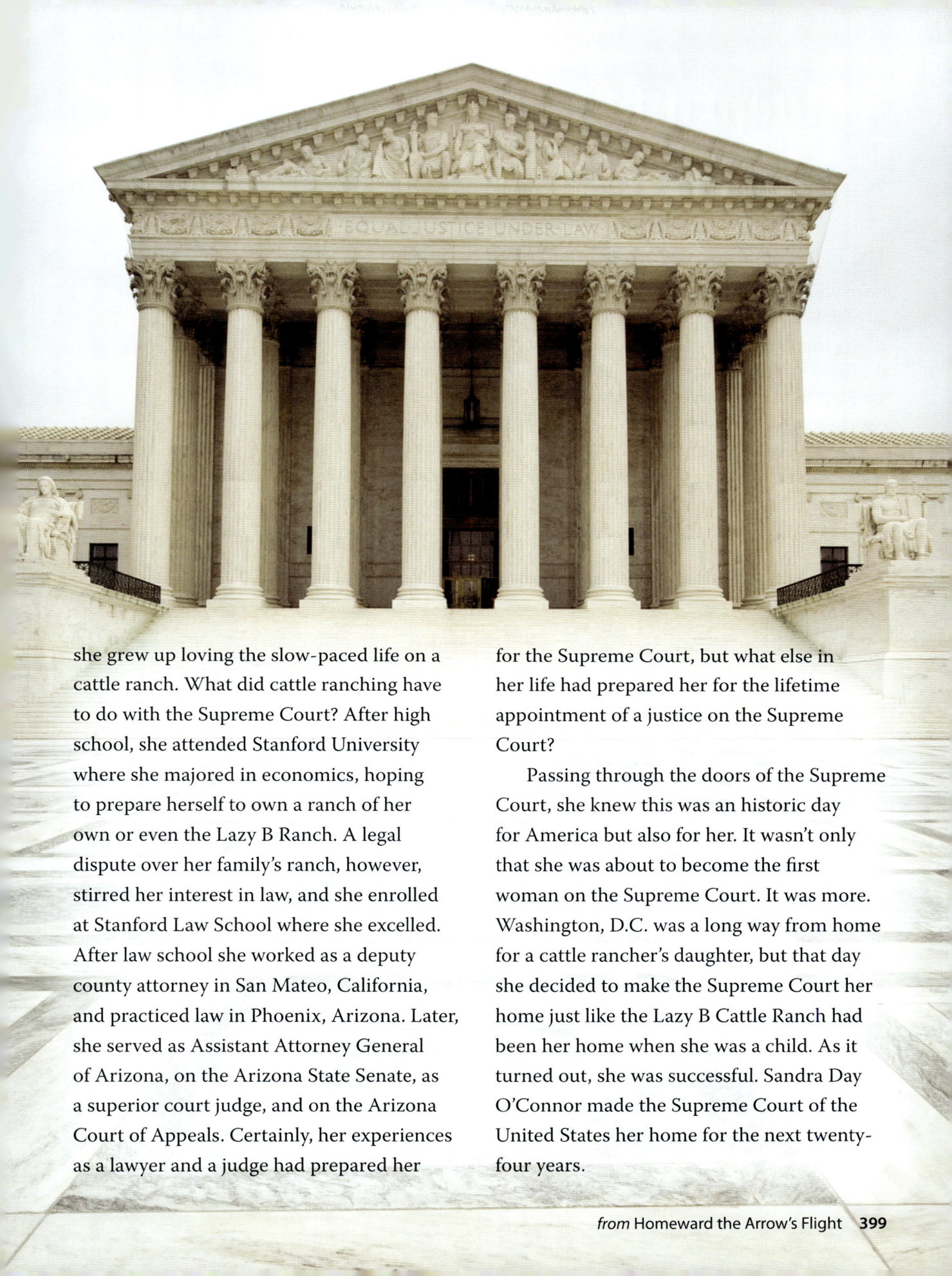

she grew up loving the slow-paced life on a cattle ranch. What did cattle ranching have to do with the Supreme Court? After high school, she attended Stanford University where she majored in economics, hoping to prepare herself to own a ranch of her own or even the Lazy B Ranch. A legal dispute over her family's ranch, however, stirred her interest in law, and she enrolled at Stanford Law School where she excelled. After law school she worked as a deputy county attorney in San Mateo, California, and practiced law in Phoenix, Arizona. Later, she served as Assistant Attorney General of Arizona, on the Arizona State Senate, as a superior court judge, and on the Arizona Court of Appeals. Certainly, her experiences as a lawyer and a judge had prepared her for the Supreme Court, but what else in her life had prepared her for the lifetime appointment of a justice on the Supreme Court?

Passing through the doors of the Supreme Court, she knew this was an historic day for America but also for her. It wasn't only that she was about to become the first woman on the Supreme Court. It was more. Washington, D.C. was a long way from home for a cattle rancher's daughter, but that day she decided to make the Supreme Court her home just like the Lazy B Cattle Ranch had been her home when she was a child. As it turned out, she was successful. Sandra Day O'Connor made the Supreme Court of the United States her home for the next twenty-four years.

Blueprint for Reading

INTO . . . from *Homeward the Arrow's Flight*

Have you ever gotten so caught up in some project that it took all of your free time? Perhaps you know a teenager or adult who is very involved with a certain idea, hobby, or organization. When that idea or project is one that helps others, we call the person who works at it an *idealist*. We admire the idealist who puts others' needs first. As you read about Susan La Flesche Picotte, notice how she gives more and more of herself to the people of the reservation. How does she feel about having so little time for her own needs? How does she react to the fact that there is not even enough money to pay her for all her work?

EYES ON *Biography*

A **biography** is the true story of one person's life and accomplishments. A biography is usually about someone whose life story will be interesting to others. When somebody helps us, interests us, or entertains us, we usually want to know more about that person. We want to know when and where the person lived, went to school, and worked. We are also curious about the person's personality and opinions. A good biography will include all of those things. By the time you have finished the story, you will feel as though you know the person whose biography you have just read.

An excerpt from

Homeward the Arrow's Flight

The Story of Susan La Flesche

Susan La Flesche Picotte was the first female
Native-American doctor in the United States.
After she graduated from medical school she
returned to her home, on the Omaha Reservation
in Nebraska, to begin work as the doctor at the
reservation school. In this excerpt we learn that
her application to become doctor to the entire
reservation has been accepted. We read about
her first weeks as both doctor to the school, and
to all the families on the Omaha Reservation.

by Marion Marsh Brown

Susan wrote a letter of application on the very night that she told Rosalie, her sister, she wanted the position of reservation physician. Then she waited anxiously for a reply.

At last the letter arrived. She tore it open eagerly. "Well, finally," she sighed. She carried it to the kitchen where her mother was preparing supper. "I got the appointment," she said. "I don't get any more money though."

Her mother looked up. "So much more work and no more pay?" she asked.

"That's what the letter says: 'As there are no funds available except for your present salary as physician to the government school, we will be unable to pay any additional monies for your additional services as reservation physician.' Well, anyway I have the title. Now to see what I can do with it."

That same night, the first snow of the winter fell. Susan was soon inundated with a siege of colds, grippe, and pneumonia. It was as if the first snowstorm had been a signal for winter illnesses to attack.

She had laid her plans carefully before entering into her new contract to do two jobs for the price of one. She would spend mornings at the school and would make house calls in the afternoons. The only problem, she soon discovered, was that there weren't enough hours in the day.

"I don't know why babies always want to get born in the wee hours of the morning," she said to Rosalie, stopping at her sister's house one day on the way to school. She'd been up since midnight and would not have time to go home before she was due at school. She was glad to have a place to clean up and get a cup of coffee.

"Sue, you can't go on this way," her sister said. "You'll ruin your own health."

Susan sighed. "But what else can I do, Ro?"

It was a bad winter, one of the worst Nebraska had seen in many a year. The north wind blew in icy gusts, finding its way around poorly fitted window frames and under ill-hung doors

WORD BANK

appointment *n.*: position; job
inundated (IN un DAY tud) *v.*: flooded
siege (SEEJ) *n.*: a serious attack, as in illness
grippe (GRIP) *n.*: influenza

into the Omahas' houses. Many of the houses were getting old and they had not been kept in repair.

When Susan rode up to one in which a windowpane was out, the hole stuffed carelessly with old rags, anger flared in her. Inside, she knew, lay a child on the verge of pneumonia.

"Tom," she said, when she had entered, "there's no excuse for that." She pointed at the window. "When you get your next allotment, buy a piece of glass and some putty and replace that pane."

"You're just like Iron Eye," he said, and Susan detected resentment in his tone. "Always trying to tell us how to live."

Susan bit her tongue and went about her task of examining the sick child. Was it hopeless, she wondered, trying to teach them? But her father, Iron Eye, had never given up.

One morning when she started for school, the wind was particularly vicious. Reluctantly, she turned Pie, her horse, into it. When they reached the schoolgrounds, she immediately put him into the shed that was provided for bad days. As she turned

WORD BANK

allotment (uh LOT ment) *n.*: the portion of something that is assigned to someone
resentment (ree ZENT ment) *n.*: a feeling of displeasure with someone who, one believes, has caused injury or unhappiness
vicious (VISH uss) *adj.*: harsh and cruel

to the schoolhouse, she noted that the sky looked ominous. It took all her strength to wrench the door open against the wind. "I think we're going to get snow," she called to Marguerite, the middle sister, as she entered.

Marguerite turned back, and Susan saw the worried look on her face. "Oh, dear, I hope not. Charlie's sick again. He has an awful cough, Sue, and he was so hot last night, I know he has fever. And he went out to look after the stock this morning. I was hoping you could go by and see him this afternoon."

"Of course I'll go. A little snow won't stop me," Susan replied with a smile, hoping to cheer her sister.

As the morning progressed, the wind howled and the snow grew heavier. In a moment's lull in her work, Susan glanced out the window and discovered she could no longer see the row of trees that formed a windbreak for the school building. She felt a little tug of concern. Some of the children lived quite a distance from school. Perhaps they should be getting home.

WORD BANK

ominous (AH mih nuss) *adj.*: threatening; foretelling of some harm
lull *n.*: a temporary calm

It wasn't long until the teachers were consulting her. "Do you think we should dismiss school? If it keeps this up…"

"I think it would be wise to get the children on their way. It certainly isn't getting any better."

So an early dismissal was agreed upon.

Susan was helping the teachers bundle the children into coats and overshoes, tying mufflers over mouths and noses, and giving instruction to the older ones to keep a tight hold on the hands of younger brothers and sisters, when the outside door burst open and a man stumbled in. He was so caked with snow that at first she didn't recognize him.

"Dr. Susan!" he cried. "Come quick! My Minnie…"

"Oh, it's you, Joe," she said. "Has your wife started labor?"

He nodded. "But she's bad, Doctor. Not like before."

"Come on in and warm up, then go home and put lots of water on the stove to heat. I'll be along shortly."

Joe didn't linger. As soon as the children were on their way and she had straightened up her office, Susan sought out Marguerite. "I'll have to wait to see Charlie until after I deliver Minnie Whitefeather's baby. Joe says she's having a bad time, so I may be late."

"All right. Be sure to bundle up," Marguerite said. "It looks like the storm's getting worse."

"That I will. I always come prepared!" Susan assured her. She pulled her stocking cap down over her ears and donned the heavy wool mittens her mother had knit for her.

"I hope you'll be all right," Marguerite said. "It's a long way over there."

"Don't worry. You can depend on Pie!" Susan waved a cheery good bye and plunged out into the storm. She had to fight her way to the shed.

Already drifts were piling high. "I hope the children are all safely home by now," she thought. Her pony was nervous. "Good old Pie," she said, patting the sleek neck as she mounted. "When you were a young one and we went racing across the hills, you

WORD BANK

consulting (kun SULT ing) *v.*: asking advice of
donned (DAHND) *v.*: put on

didn't think you were going to have to plow through all kinds of weather with me when you grew old, did you?"

The Whitefeathers lived on the northernmost edge of the reservation. Susan turned Pie onto the road, and he plodded into the storm. "Good boy!" she said encouragingly. But she couldn't hear her words above the violent shrieking of the wind. Nor, shortly, could she tell whether they were following the road; she could only trust Pie.

It seemed to her that the storm grew worse by the minute. Suddenly Pie stopped, turning his head back as if asking Susan what he should do. She tried to wipe the caked snow from her eyes to see what was wrong and found that her fingers were stiff. But she saw Pie's problem. A huge drift lay across their path. "We'll have to go around it, Pie." She pulled him to the left until they reached a point where the drift tapered off.[1] Pie moved around it, and Susan thought, "Now can we find the road again— if we were on the road?" She pulled on the right rein. But she

---

1. To *taper off* means to grow smaller and smaller.

couldn't tell whether they were going north, for now the storm seemed to be swirling around them from all directions.

Soon another drift blocked their way. But this time Pie wallowed through with a strange, swimming motion. How did he know he could get through that one and not the other, she wondered. Suddenly, having maneuvered the drift, the pony stopped.

"Get up, Pie! We have to go on!" she urged. He did not move. She slapped the stiff reins on his neck, but to no avail.[2] She tried kicking his sides with feet she discovered were numb. "We'll freeze to death! Go on!" Still Pie refused to move.

At length she dismounted. If she could walk on her numb feet, perhaps she could lead him. Stumbling, she made her way to Pie's head.

Then she saw, and she caught her breath in terror. For Pie stood with his head directly over a bundle in the snow—a bundle that she knew instantly was a child.

_____

2. An effort that is made *to no avail*, means that the effort failed.

WORD BANK

wallowed (WAH lode) *v.*: rolled about in a clumsy way
maneuvered (muh NOO vurd) *v.*: moved about and changed direction as required

"Oh, my!" she cried. She lifted the bundle into her arms. It was a boy, one of the little ones they had turned out of school to find his way home. "What were we thinking of?" Susan railed at herself. "Jimmy! Jimmy!" she cried, shaking the child. She scooped the snow off his eyelids. He stirred, and then his eyelids lifted. "Jimmy! It's Dr. Sue. You were asleep, Jimmy. You have to wake up now." She hoisted him in front of her on the pony, and holding him close to give him warmth from her body, she beat on his arms.

The minute she was back in the saddle, Pie moved on. "Pie! Bless you. You probably saved Jimmy's life."

As Pie pressed on, Susan continued to talk to Jimmy, working on him as she talked—rubbing his hands, cradling his face against her. "We have to warm up your nose," she told him. He began to cry. "You mustn't cry. Your tears will make cakes of ice!"

She strained her eyes ahead, but she could see nothing against the driving snow. She had no idea how long they had been in this frozen white nightmare. Surely if they were going in

Word Bank

hoisted (HOYS tid) *v.*: raised

the right direction, they should have reached the Whitefeathers' by now. "Pie's going to take us where it's nice and warm," she soothed Jimmy. And to herself she said, "If he doesn't, it's the end of all of us, you and me and him. And maybe Minnie Whitefeather and her child too."

She tried to keep Jimmy awake, finding to her consternation that she herself was growing drowsy. She well knew that to go to sleep was a sure way to freeze to death.

She must have dozed briefly, for she started when Pie suddenly stopped. She roused herself to urge him on.

"Get up, Pie! We can't stop now! We have Jimmy!" She kicked his sides, but the pony refused to move. The snow had again caked her eyelids and she pawed at it with unfeeling fists. She supposed they'd come to another drift Pie couldn't manipulate.

As she blinked hard to see, she was suddenly aware of a sound that was not born of the storm. Pie had whinnied. She even felt the ripple-like movement of his neck. What did it mean?

WORD BANK

consternation (KAHN stur NAY shun) *n.*: a sudden alarming amazement or dread

manipulate (muh NIP yoo layt) *v.*: handle with skill

Then she saw! They were by the side of a building, sheltered from the wind. It was a barn!

"Pie! Pie! You did it!" she cried.

As she tried stiffly to dismount with Jimmy, strong arms were supporting her. It was Joe.

"We are so glad you're here, Dr. Sue. We were afraid you would not make it."

"So was I," Susan said. "Please take care of Pie. We wouldn't be here except for him."

Susan delivered a baby girl that night, but she did not get to Marguerite and Charlie's.

Nor did she get to her sister's home for the two days following, because the storm raged on fiercely through the night, wrapping the reservation in a tight white cocoon that could not be penetrated. There was no way to return Jimmy to his home or to let his parents know that he was safe. Susan agonized over this, but there was nothing she could do.

There were two other Whitefeather children, and Susan noticed that they came to have their hands washed before a meal. She noticed other things too: the family's clothes were clean, and so were the blankets on the beds. "You're doing well with your little family," she praised Minnie.

Minnie smiled. "Remember the summer you were home from school when you rode around trying to teach people to wash their hands before meals? We believed you—about germs and all."

"And now you're teaching your children," Susan said approvingly. "That's fine, Minnie. It means the upcoming generation will have a better time of it."

When Susan eventually got to Charlie and Marguerite's, she found Charlie in bed in the throes of a violent chill. His cough was frightening. She left medicine and tried to reassure him, but as her sister saw her to the door, Susan shook her head. "His lungs are weak, Marg. You'll have to be very careful."

"I know," Marguerite replied quietly.

"I wonder if she does know," Susan thought as she went on her snow-clogged way. There was no question in her mind that Charlie was consumptive,[3] as his mother had been. Susan had been doing all she could for him, but she feared he would be one she couldn't save—gentle Charlie, who was so good to everyone, especially to Marguerite.

By early February he was continuously confined to his bed, and there was no more Susan could do. Marguerite had to take leave from her teaching position to care for him.

He died quietly, as he had lived, just before the month was out.

"I thought maybe if he could make it till spring…" Marguerite said desolately.

---

3. Consumption is an old-fashioned word for tuberculosis, a lung disease. A *consumptive* person was one who was ill with tuberculosis.

WORD BANK

agonized (AG uh NYZD) *v.*: worried unhappily
confined (kun FYND) *v.*: restricted; kept from leaving a place
desolately (DESS uh lit lee) *adv.*: very sadly

"Why don't you come home and live with Mother and me?" Susan suggested. "It would be too lonely for you here."

They sent word of Charlie's death to his family in Dakota, and his brother, Henry, came. "We wanted the family represented at his funeral," he said.

"Henry's different," Susan remarked to Rosalie. "Yet he reminds me of Charlie. Sort of a more cheerful, livelier version!"

"He's more worldly," Rosalie said.

Susan smiled. It had taken Ro, who had less "worldly" exposure than the rest of them, to see straight through to the point. "Yes, you're right," she agreed.

With the funeral over, Henry gone, and Marguerite back in the home where she and Susan had grown up, things settled down into a certain routine. Marguerite went back to teaching, and Susan went on with her doctoring.

"It's like the old days," Susan said one evening when she and Marguerite and their mother sat down to supper.

"Only different," Marguerite said.

"Yes," Susan agreed, thinking of how it had been when Nicomi, her grandmother, and Iron Eye and Rosalie had all been at that table. "Things don't stay the same, do they, Mother?"

Her mother shook her head.

"We have to learn to accept change. That was one of the things Father tried to teach us long ago."

Spring was late that year, but when it finally came, it was so beautiful that Susan at times thought she couldn't bear it. Sometimes when she was riding home from a call in early evening, she would dismount and let Pie graze while she gazed down on the greening of the willows that fringed the river like a band of chartreuse[4] lace. If it weren't too late, she would venture into the woods to look for wild flowers—violets and Dutchman's-breeches and the shy lady's-slipper.

"What a wonderful place to live," she thought. And more and more she could see that her work was bearing fruit. "I'm

---

4. *Chartreuse* is a clear, light-green color.

WORD BANK

venture (VEN chur) *v.*: to go carefully into an unknown or dangerous place

not accomplishing miracles," she told Rosalie one evening, "but I am beginning to see some of the results of better hygiene and health habits. And we're losing fewer babies and fewer cases to infection."

"You don't need to convince me," Rosalie said. "I can see it on every hand. How pleased Father would be."

ABOUT THE AUTHOR

Marion Marsh Brown was born on a Nebraska farm in 1908. Her education started in a one-room schoolhouse and she learned so rapidly that she started college when she was only fifteen. She later taught English at the college level. In 1937, Marion married Gilbert Brown and they had a son, Paul. As Paul grew, she noticed that there were very few interesting books for grade school children. Marion decided to devote her efforts to writing books for elementary and junior high school students. From 1949 on, she wrote a book almost every two years until the early 1990s. Her outstanding work earned her many awards.

Studying the Selection

QUICK REVIEW

1. Where did Susan La Flesche Picotte grow up?

2. What were Susan's jobs?

3. Who was Pie and how did he help Susan?

4. What were some of Susan's accomplishments?

FOCUS

5. What did Susan do for the people of the reservation aside from provide them with medical care?

6. What parts of Susan's life are described in this excerpt from her biography?

CREATING AND WRITING

7. What cause interests you so much that you would want to devote time and effort to it? Write about what you would choose, why it would mean a lot to you, and how you would be dedicated to that cause.

8. Write about a family that is forced to stay inside for several days due to a fierce snowstorm. How do they entertain each other without arguing or becoming bored? How do they create fun during the snowstorm?

9. Native Americans are known for their use of herbs as medicine and other home remedies. For homework, ask your family and neighbors to tell you about home remedies they or their parents and grandparents have used. Did these remedies really work? Share what you have learned with the class.

Jill's Journal:

On Assignment in Britain to Speak with the Lady with the Lamp

I am going to have the privilege of visiting Florence Nightingale! She is the most extraordinary person. In case you don't know, she is the famous British nurse and humanitarian. What is a humanitarian, you ask? A *humanitarian* is a person who works very hard to help others. Florence Nightingale is actually a *pioneer* of nursing care for soldiers and poor people. A pioneer develops something new and prepares a way for others to follow.

Florence Nightingale grew up in a world of servants, royalty, and luxury. She could have had an easy life. Yet she wanted to work with the sick, and she taught herself how to be a nurse. She learned how a hospital ought to be run. By the time she was 30, she was the one and only expert on the subject of nursing and hospitals in all of Europe.

Today is June 18, 1859. I visited a hospital in London this morning. It was very dirty and smelled very bad. I left quickly. One day in the future, Florence Nightingale will show the world that ninety percent of the people who go to hospitals here die. In fact, they are worse off if they go than if they don't.

In these times, where poor people live, there is no running water. They have no way to bathe or wash their clothes. They live in tiny rooms and have no disinfectants with which to clean. Of course, there is no electricity yet. It would be hard for any of us to go into these homes as Florence Nightingale did—we would probably feel sick to our stomachs. I guess that sometimes, being brave means working in dirty places where people are suffering.

I will be visiting Ms. Nightingale at the Burlington Hotel in London. When she returned from the Crimean War in Turkey in 1857, she moved there from her family's estate. Unfortunately, she then became very ill with a fever and remained in her rooms for quite some time. (Doctors today think she had an illness called brucellosis, or Crimean fever, that she would have contracted during the war.)

Despite her illness, this great woman is now spending her own money to set up the Nightingale Training School at St. Thomas' Hospital, to teach young women how to be nurses. (Would you believe that the school still exists today—150 years later?)

A servant welcomes me in. Ms. Nightingale is reclining on a divan with a large knit shawl draped over her shoulders. Her dress is dark purple taffeta with velvet stripes. She motions me to a chair and says kindly, "Please sit. I want visitors to be comfortable in my home." I curtsy and sit down. I look about the room. The marble floor is covered with beautiful rugs from Turkey. Heavy drapes hang in the windows. There is a fireplace, and magnificent candelabras sit on either end of the mantelpiece.

"I hope your journey went well," she says. "Traveling by boat is sometimes not so easy! Now, tell me. What is your interest in coming here to speak with me?" She says this gently, like the gentlewoman she is.

"I understand," I tell her, "that more than 4,000 men died in hospitals during the Crimean campaign. How did you get through it? It must have been terrible!"

She nods wisely. "Of course it was terrible. But I wanted so much to help them. I trained thirty-eight brave women volunteers as nurses—including my aunt, Mai Smith—and, if nothing else, we made that hospital clean. I learned so much about what we need to do to care for the wounded and the sick.

"You know, I am very busy, even here in my rooms. I am working on a small book that I will simply title, *Notes on Nursing*. It is to be published next year. I expect it to be the main curriculum at the Nightingale School. If many copies are sold, then perhaps these ideas will spread to the general public." She shows me a pie chart. It may surprise you to learn that, like Mrs. Wright, Florence Nightingale has great mathematical abilities. She even invented the pie chart! A pie chart is a table that is in the shape of a circle.

Florence Nightingale has the nickname "The Lady with the Lamp." In *The London Times*, a reporter wrote about her work during the Crimean War. He said that when she moved quietly down the corridors of the hospital, each soldier's face softened with gratitude when he saw her. When all the medical officers were asleep for the night, silence and darkness settled down upon rows of sick men. Florence Nightingale could be seen all alone, checking each patient, with a little lamp in her hand. And so she came to be called The Lady with the Lamp.

"When I returned from the Crimea, I began collecting evidence to show the Royal Commission on the Health of the Army that most of the soldiers at the hospital died because conditions there were so poor. I will never stop reminding people of the importance of cleanliness. My dear, if you ask why I do this, I have to say that it has been my one and only desire to nurse."

POWER SKILL:
Making a Pie Chart

A pie chart is a way of showing information. It is easier to understand than simple words, because it is a picture that we can see with our eyes. The idea behind a pie chart is this: The whole pie, or circle, equals 100%. Half the pie or circle is 50%. A quarter slice is 25%. If you add one half and one quarter, you get 75% of the pie.

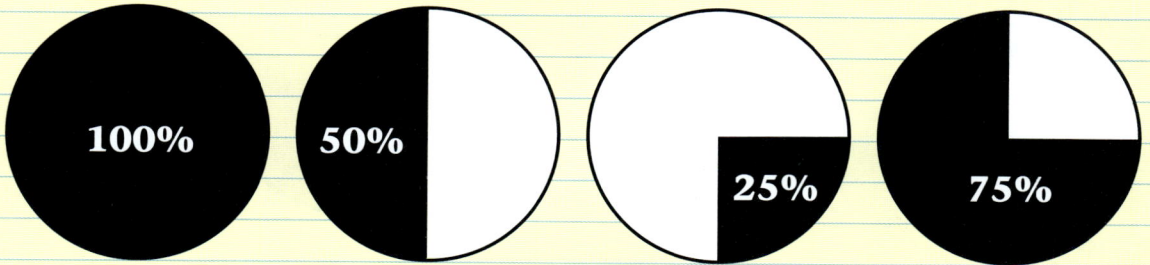

Let's look at some examples. You have a big bowl of fruit. There are twenty pieces of fruit in the bowl. The whole bowl (or all of the fruit) equals the whole pie—so the whole circle can be labeled *All the Fruit*.

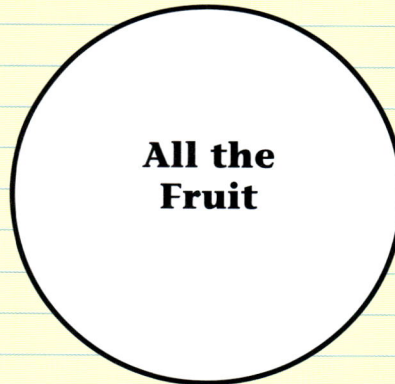

Now, let's say that half of the fruit, or 10 pieces, are apples. So half of the circle or pie can be labeled *Apples*.

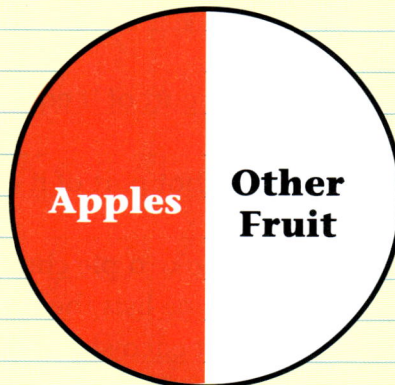

Now, let's say that another 5 pieces of fruit are plums. Five is one-quarter of 20. So now half of the circle is labeled *Apples*, one-quarter is labeled *Plums*, and one-quarter is labeled *Other Fruit*.

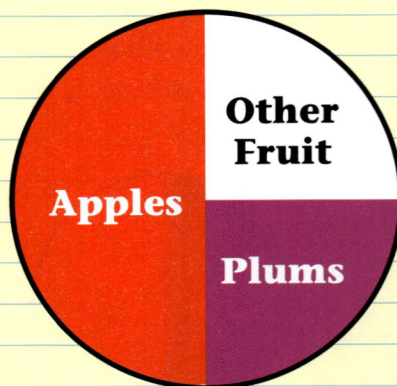

The last 5 pieces of fruit are pears. Once again, remember that 5 is one-quarter of 20. So the last quarter of the circle is labeled *Pears*.

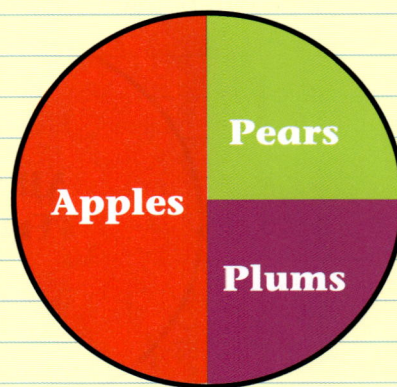

This is an easier way to show the percentages of different kinds of fruit in the bowl than by describing it with words.

Exercises

1. Draw a big circle. What part of it equals 50% or one-half? Color that part red.
2. Draw a second circle. What part of it equals 25% or one-quarter? Color that part blue.
3. Now it is your turn to make a pie chart from some information in a table. The table on the next page lists the names of 12 students. It also shows the ice cream flavor that each student likes best from four choices (vanilla, chocolate, coffee, strawberry).

12 Students	Vanilla	Chocolate	Coffee	Strawberry
Miriam			X	
David		X		
John	X			
Carol		X		
Sarah			X	
Keith				X
Joshua				X
Nancy		X		
Bob	X			
Laurie	X			
Debbie				X
Mark			X	
Totals:	**3**	**3**	**3**	**3**

a. How many of the children like vanilla best?

b. How many of them like chocolate the most?

c. How many of them pick coffee ice cream?

d. How many prefer strawberry?

In each case, the answer is three. How are you going to show this information on a pie chart? The most important thing for you to know is that three goes into twelve four times. That means that it takes four 3s to make twelve. Take a sheet of paper and tear off twelve small scraps. Now, arrange the twelve small scraps of paper in four equal piles. Each pile will end up having three small scraps of paper. That means that three is ¼ of twelve.

Now let's go back to our pie chart. The whole pie is equal to all of the ice cream choices.

All Flavors

Now we want the pie chart to show how many students like vanilla. Draw a circle. Divide it in half. Then divide the halves in half. Now you have a pie chart with four quarters. You can write vanilla in one quarter, since ¼ of the students like vanilla. Now label the other three quarters.

unit

wrap-up

caring

ACTIVITY ONE

Choose a nature scene from any of the stories in the unit. As you know, the settings of each story are very different. Using a variety of craft materials, create the scene as you pictured it in your mind. You may add figures that represent some of the human or animal characters in the story.

Earthquake Terror

The Gift

Toto

Owl Moon

Homeward the Arrow's Flight

ACTIVITY TWO

Your teacher will divide the class into groups. Each group will discuss one of the questions listed in this activity. Your teacher will assign a question to your group. Each student must contribute to the discussion.

1. Which two main characters do you think were the bravest? Support your opinion.

2. Choose two main characters and describe what they will be like when they grow up. What career do they choose? Where do they live? What are three personality traits that they have as adults? Do they have families?

3. If you could be friends with one of the main characters, which one would you choose? Why? Are you like that character? Do you have similar or different personality traits? What about shared interests?

unit

ACTIVITY THREE

Your teacher will divide you into groups for the game of charades. The groups will be given a few minutes to choose one scene from any story in the unit for their charade. Try to include everyone, even if it means someone is a bird chirping or a big tree standing silently. When the preparation time is up, each group will perform their charade for the rest of the class. The first student to guess what scene is being acted out wins the round.

ACTIVITY FOUR

The overall theme of Unit Four is *Caring*. Select a character that cared about another person, an animal, or even a part of nature. If you wish, you may choose a minor character. Write two paragraphs in which you describe how this character thought, felt, and behaved in a way that was caring.

unit 5

Determination

Lesson in Literature . . .

AUTHOR'S PURPOSE

- An author writes a book, story, poem, or drama for a variety of reasons.

- The author may write to *interest* the reader.

- The author may write to *inform* the reader.

- The author may write to *persuade* the reader.

THINK ABOUT IT!

1. This story is interesting, it informs, and it persuades the reader. Write a sentence about one part of the story that was interesting.

2. Write a sentence about one part of the story that informed you of something.

3. Write a sentence about one part of the story that persuaded you to feel or think a certain way.

DEER CROSSING
NEXT 2 MILES

ON A DARK COUNTRY ROAD

Late one night I was driving home by myself on a dark country road when a pair of big bright eyes appeared directly in front of my car's headlights. "Oh no!" I shouted to myself. I slammed on the brakes and held the steering wheel as tightly as I could.

I was too late. Or so I thought.

As the car skidded, I looked into the pair of startled, scared eyes staring back at my headlights. Staring back, I bet my eyes looked scared, too. Then the two eyes in the middle of the dark country road squinted as if to ask me a question. I wondered what question those eyes were asking.

A second later the car's bumper struck the deer, the car stopped, and everything was suddenly silent. I opened the car door. After the screeching of the brakes and the thud of the crash, the complete silence was eerie.

At the front of the car, I stood over the deer as it lay on its side, still breathing, and its eyes looked up at me. This time the eyes' question was clear.

Why?

I knelt beside the injured deer and touched its warm side. I wanted to answer its question. "It was an accident," I said softly, "and I'm so sorry you are hurt." Its legs moved a little but then its eyes slowly closed.

I wondered what I was supposed to do next.

I stood, imagining that the woods around this scene watched my every move. Should I roll the dead deer off the road? I didn't want another driver to come along late at night, swerve to miss the remains of a dead deer, and end up in an accident.

So I decided.

Inside my car I found a flashlight, shone it into the woods at the edge of the road, and chose a spot where I could drag the deer.

But when I returned to the front of the car, something had changed. The deer's eyes were opened, and its legs were moving back and forth as if it was imagining it was running away.

"Are you okay?" I asked.

At that instant the deer scrambled up, wobbly on its four legs, looked at me with one more question, and bounded off into the woods.

I looked on in awe and happiness. Perhaps, I thought, the impact of the collision stunned the deer more than injured it, or perhaps its sudden recovery was something else. Perhaps, I thought, my few words of apology gave the deer just enough strength to get up again. I don't know. I'll never know. I do know that I won't soon forget the terrible sounds of the crash, and I won't soon forget those big bright eyes looking back at me before they disappeared into the woods. I don't know the question they asked, but they may have been asking whether I would make it home safely, too.

Blueprint for Reading

INTO . . . *Underwater Rescue*

Communication is a very important part of life. Whether we are expressing our feelings, sharing information, or simply saying hello or good-bye, we are communicating. Communication is our link to everyone and everything that exists outside ourselves. Without it, we could not have any relationships. What people sometimes forget is that communication is not limited to speaking and writing. Communication through motions, gestures, and signs, such as a hug or a wave, are also important ways to connect. As you read, think about how communication plays an important role in *Underwater Rescue*.

EYES ON *Author's Purpose*

Why do people write nonfiction stories? There are many reasons. Most people enjoy recalling something unusual that happened to them or to another person. One way of doing that is to write about it. Many of us want to share an experience with others; writing a story or book allows us to share experiences with a great number of people. Sometimes, writing about an experience helps us to understand it better. Other times, we feel we have an important message, so we write as a way of passing that message on to others. Last but not least, some of us are born entertainers! We like to amuse or puzzle others. All the reasons we have given for writing nonfiction are what we call the **author's purpose**. Can you add some reasons to the list?

UNDERWATER RESCUE

Wayne Grover

Geared up and ready to dive, I held the end of the rope in my hand, and when we got to the place I felt was right, I rolled over the side of the boat and into the water.

As I drifted down, I had the distinct feeling that something was happening over which I had no control. I tried to relax, but the feeling would not go away.

After swimming along the deep outer reef edge at eighty feet, I suddenly heard a loud clicking noise in the water. It grew louder with each passing second.

I stopped and held on to a large rock as I tried to see what was making the noise. I looked in every direction.

The clicking became so loud, I could feel it against my eardrums. There was something familiar about the noise, but I could not place it.

Then I saw them!

WORD BANK

reef *n.*: a ridge of rocks or sand near the surface of the water

Racing
through the clear water,
three dolphins were coming from the
deep side of the reef, knifing through the water
with graceful speed.

I had been diving for many years, but never before had
wild dolphins come near me in the water.

As I watched, the three swam closer to me.

There was a large male, a smaller female, and a baby dolphin. As
the three circled me, I could see the baby was bleeding from a deep
wound near its tail where a long string of clear plastic fishing line
trailed for several feet behind.

The male and female dolphins were making a clicking noise as
they swam nearer to me. Then they stopped and hovered.
The clicking noise also stopped.

The baby was between its mother and father. All three
looked at me with their little eyes over upturned
mouths, reminding me of a human grin.

I could see the baby had
become

tangled in a fishing line with a big hook that had snagged it between the dorsal fin[1] on its back and the tail fluke.[2] The shaft of the hook was sticking out of the bleeding wound, making a trail of green in the depth.

Because all colors are filtered out in the ocean depth, the baby's red blood looked green eighty feet below the surface. My first reaction was one of awe. My second thought was worry for the baby. I knew it would either get snagged and drown or be tracked down and eaten by a shark.

Dolphins are very intelligent and are abundantly happy in their wild domain. They are loving and loyal and have close family ties, taking care of their young and their older, less able peers.

They seldom approach people in the sea and with good reason. Humans are dangerous and can cause them harm. But these dolphins were desperate.

---

1. The *dorsal fin* is located on the back of the dolphin.
2. Each lobe, or section, of a dolphin's tail is called a *fluke.* Like the dorsal fin, flukes have no bone or muscle inside.

WORD BANK

hovered (HUV urd) *v.*: waited nearby
shaft *n.*: the long, straight stem of something
abundantly (uh BUN dunt lee) *adv.*: very much
domain (doe MAYN) *n.*: a region inhabited by a certain type of wildlife
peer *n.*: one who is the equal of another

The baby dolphin looked scared and in pain. Its little eyes rolled in their sockets as it watched me. It was afraid of me, but its parents had brought it near. I looked into the eyes of each of them as they hovered just three feet away, and thought about all the dolphins that had been needlessly killed by fishermen and their nets or caught on their hooks. All my life I have loved animals and have done my best to see they are respected and protected. Perhaps the dolphins had sensed that I was a friend. There were four other divers in the water, all armed with weapons. I was alone and unarmed.

Now we were face-to-face. This dolphin family had an injured baby. Could they have come to me for help?

I knew something most unusual was happening.

The baby dolphin would probably die without help, but what could I do? How could I do anything about the fishing hook and the plastic line?

I had only my big diving knife and no one to help me. If I didn't help, the baby was doomed. I decided I must try.

I reached out to touch the big male, who was nearest me, and all three suddenly shot away, swimming out of sight.

I felt a great surge of disappointment, thinking I'd never see them again. Had I done something wrong?

Then, within seconds, they were back. They swam around me, clicking again, but more softly. They kept their eyes on me every moment. Now I was convinced the dolphins had chosen me to help them.

I tied the rope from the float ball to a nearby rock and let myself sink to the seafloor, where I sat on my knees.

I could sense the dolphins were trying to communicate with me. As I sat there on the sea bottom looking at the three creatures, I knew it was a rare moment. They were trusting me and I was trusting them. With their great speed and strength, they could easily injure me.

They needed help, but they could not speak. I wanted them to know I would help, but I could not communicate in their dolphin language. There must be a way, but how?

The clicking increased in frequency and then stopped. The three dolphins moved very slowly toward me. With their strong tail flukes barely moving up and down, they inched nearer and nearer until they were close enough for me to reach out and touch them.

The mother and father dolphin were slightly above the baby and were holding it between their flippers as they tried to place it on the sand right in front of me. At last they pushed the baby to the bottom.

The baby was frightened, and I could see it trembling. Its eyes never left mine. I slowly reached out to touch it, but when I did, it freed itself and swam rapidly away. The two parent dolphins immediately swam after it. In moments they were back, holding the baby tightly between them.

The father dolphin, hovering just inches from me, placed his nose under my arm and pushed up. My arm lifted, and I let it fall back in place. Again the big dolphin lifted it. I looked at his upturned mouth and bright eyes and couldn't help smiling. The impatient father dolphin wanted me to "get to work."

I took off my diving gloves and slowly reached out to touch the trembling baby. Its skin was smooth and silky as I ran my hand from just behind its breathing hole on the top of its head to the base of its dorsal fin in the middle of its back. I used my fingers to stroke its nose very gently, then ran them up and between its eyes.

The trembling stopped as the little dolphin began to sense that I had no intention of harming it. After petting it for a couple of minutes, I slowly ran my hand to the wounded area near its tail. The clear fishing line was wrapped around the thin part of its body, embedded into the skin, causing blood to ooze out.

The shaft of the fishhook stuck out from a bloody hole in its back that had been ripped open when the baby broke the line, freeing itself from the fisherman above.

It was in great pain and frightened. Instinctively it understood that a shark could sniff along the blood trail and find it. That would be the end of the baby dolphin, and all four of us knew it.

I knew that getting the hook out and the line loose would be painful for the baby, but it had to be done.

All I had to work with was the big diving knife I wore strapped to my right leg. It was about a foot long, and it was not very sharp.

I gently touched the hook shaft, and the baby made a high-pitched cry. It was going to be hard to help it.

Suddenly all three dolphins swam away, climbing toward the surface above. I had forgotten they had to breathe every few minutes.

Within a minute they were right back to me, this time with the baby coming along on its own. I knew I had to work fast so they could breathe when they needed to.

I gently held the baby on the sea floor, then cut the trailing fishing line free until all that was left was the part embedded under the baby's tender skin. Getting it out with as little pain for the baby as possible was going to be the hard part.

Then, bit by bit, I started pulling the embedded line loose so I could cut it with my knife. As I pulled it up, more blood flowed out.

I looked around for sharks, not wanting to get in the way if the parent dolphins needed to protect their baby from an attack.

Seeing no sharks, I gently continued to pull some line free.

The baby cried out in pain, and the big dolphin clicked several times. It seemed as though the parent dolphins were working with me, encouraging their baby to cooperate.

Finally, all the line was cut free except for a short piece attached to the hook. This was going to be the hardest part. I touched the hook shaft, and the baby jumped and trembled. I carefully ran my finger into the deep wound, feeling its body heat within the flesh. The baby struggled to get away, but I placed my left hand on its back and pushed it down against the sand.

I felt so bad to be hurting it, but I knew if I didn't help, it would probably die.

Holding the baby dolphin with my left hand, I stuck one finger down the hook shaft until I felt the place where it turned up to form the barbed hook. It was stuck tight, hooked into the muscle tissue in the baby's tail.

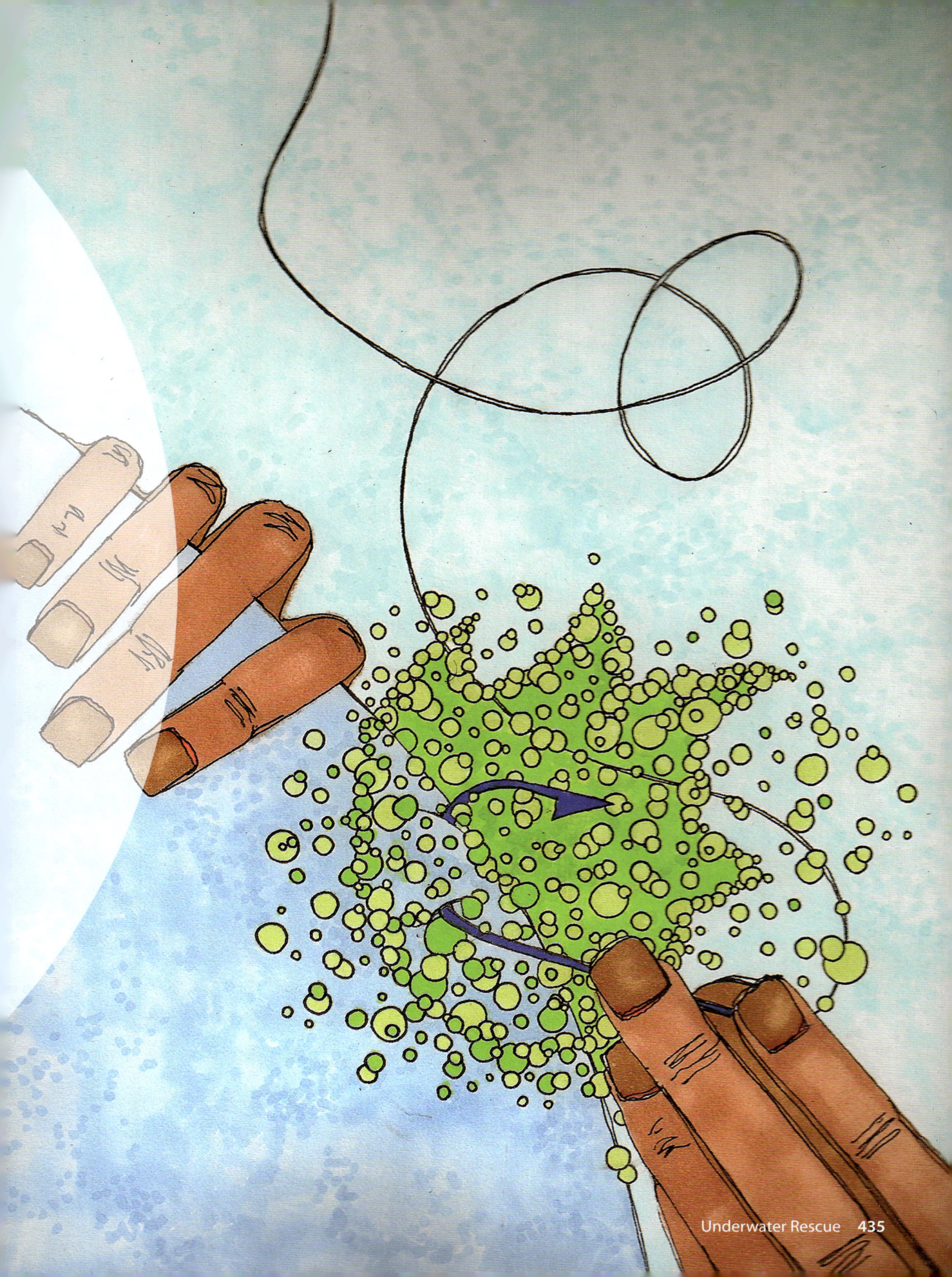

I tried to wiggle it free, but it would not budge.

As the baby cried out, the mother dolphin used her nose to stroke the baby, calming its struggle. She watched my hands closely and it seemed like a nurse hovering over a doctor at the operating table.

The hook had to be cut free, and I dreaded using the big diving knife to do it, but there was no choice. Placing the blade between my fingers the way you would hold a pencil to write, I very carefully put the point into the hole above the embedded hook.

The baby cried and struggled. I could not hold it with my hand, so I placed my left leg over its body and held it down gently. I stroked its whole body for a few moments, trying to calm it.

Impatient, the big dolphin again nudged me with his bottle nose. They would need to breathe soon.

Taking a deep breath from the regulator in my mouth, I slipped the knife into the wound and gently ran it down along the hook shaft. I used my left hand to feel into the wound as I pushed the knife in. Then I hit the muscle tissue that held the hook in place. It was now or never.

I cut the barb loose, and the hook was free. I withdrew the knife and took the hook out. Blood flowed from the baby's tail, and I pushed my palm down hard on the open wound to slow the bleeding.

The two big dolphins clicked excitedly about me. I felt a great surge of relief. I had done it. My heart was filled with joy. I was unbelievably happy.

Then the big dolphin suddenly darted away downcurrent. Something had caught his attention. A pair of bull sharks were coming straight for the baby, sniffing the blood trail as it flowed toward them in the fast Gulf Stream.

The father dolphin saw them and raced for them head-on. He was so fast that even the speeding sharks could not get out of his way.

Wham! The father dolphin hit the bigger shark right behind its gill slits, knocking it aside.

Wham! He hit it again. The shark swam away with a trail of blood pouring from its gills. It wanted no more fight with the protective father dolphin.

The other shark continued swimming straight toward the baby and me. The mother dolphin exploded into action. She tore through the water and met the shark with a fierce bump to its side.

A second later the father dolphin hit it from the other side. It swam away, also trailing blood.

The father dolphin followed, making repeated attacks, ensuring they would not return to harm the bleeding baby.

The sharks were no match for the enraged parent dolphins who had saved their baby and probably me, too.

I lifted my hand from the baby, and the bleeding had almost stopped. The mother dolphin had returned. She looked at the hole in its body and then at the hook lying on the sand nearby. She clicked loudly, and I heard more clicking from farther away. It was the father dolphin coming back.

He had chased the sharks far away. He was there in an instant, swimming rapidly back to his family.

I let the baby up, and it joined the parent dolphins. They all swam around me, making clicking sounds.

The father dolphin swam right up to me and looked into my eyes behind the diving mask. He nodded his head up and down in a rapid motion and then gently pushed me with his nose.

I reached out to touch his head, and he let me do so. For that brief moment, whether it was my imagination or it was really happening, I had the strong impression that he was thanking me, one father to another.

WORD BANK

enraged (en RAYJD)
adj.: extremely angry

Then
he made the clicking
sound again, and the three swam
rapidly toward the surface, leaving me
alone on the bottom. I knew it was time for
them to breathe again.

I looked at my air gauge and saw I had enough air
to swim awhile longer. The experience that I will never
forget had all happened in about ten minutes.

I kept looking for the dolphins to return that day,
but they didn't.

As I climbed into the boat after I surfaced,
I felt a happiness that I have never known
before. The dolphins had left me with
a sense of peace and a strong
feeling of love.

All the way back from the day's dive, I could not stop feeling the dolphins were still communicating with me from someplace out there in the sea.

For the next couple of weeks I kept thinking about the baby dolphin, wondering if the sharks had gotten it or if it had survived. I couldn't get the dolphins out of my mind.

Then Amos called to see if I wanted to dive the next morning, and I said yes.

It was a different kind of morning from that last time. The sky was overcast, and the sea was much rougher with a cool northeastern wind blowing whitecaps toward shore. Only Amos and one other diver were along as we sped down the coast to our selected diving area.

I was working on my diving equipment when Amos shouted, "Hey, look over there. Dolphins!"

I looked up, and sure enough, several dolphins were racing with our boat, jumping from the water right by our bow wake. Suddenly I had that same feeling I had experienced on the day I helped the dolphin family.

Then I saw a small dolphin. It was in the midst of six other dolphins with a scar clearly visible on its back. It was the baby I had helped. I cheered and laughed until the tears rolled down my cheeks. The baby dolphin had survived.

It swam close to the boat, easily keeping pace with our speed, jumping high out of the water. It seemed its upturned mouth had an even bigger grin on it than before.

For a few minutes the dolphins stayed with us. Then they swam away, jumping and enjoying just being alive in the sea.

As I watched them go, I knew I had experienced something very special.

It's been some time now since my dolphin adventure, but I often think about that dolphin family. I shall never forget the feeling of happiness I felt in their presence.

I look forward to swimming with the dolphins again. It could happen anytime now.

ABOUT THE AUTHOR

Wayne Grover wants people to know they can make a difference. That is why he writes about conservation and ecology. Historical wrecks and marine research are two more subjects that fascinate him. He has loved animals all of his life and wants to ensure that they can live and grow in a healthy environment. Mr. Grover's articles are published in newspapers and magazines. One of his favorite subjects is the dolphin, and three of the four books he has written feature these smart and gentle creatures.

Today the Dolphins Came to Play

Wayne Marshall

Today the dolphins came to play
I watched them jump for joy
It seemed just then, they were wise old men
and I, a foolish boy

5 Atop the mighty waves they danced
to the rhythms of the moon
in harmony with the song of the sea
they played in perfect tune

Behind me fast cars rushed on by
10 towards some other time and place
What wonders do we never see
that stare us daily in the face?

Today the dolphins came to play
I never felt so small
15 and yet so grand, bare feet in the sand
a vital part of the all

Studying the Selection

QUICK REVIEW

1. What happened to the author for the first time after many years of diving?

2. What caused the dolphins to approach the diver?

3. What did the diver think the first time the dolphins swam away? What was the true reason?

4. How did the adult dolphins help the diver save the injured baby dolphin?

FOCUS

5. When the dolphins first approached the diver, what made him stay instead of swimming away?

6. How would the story have been different if one of the people on the boat or a friend of the author had told it?

CREATING AND WRITING

7. Nowadays, modern technology has provided us with many new ways to communicate, such as faxing and e-mailing. Do you think this improves connections and relationships between people? Why or why not?

8. Write an original story about how a person helped an animal in trouble. If you prefer, you can write about a person who is helped by an animal.

9. Together with a classmate, create a code using clicking sounds.

Jill's Journal:

On Assignment Exploring the Mesoamerican Reef

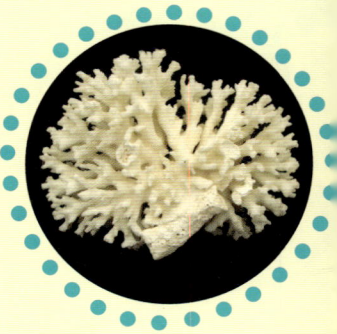

Do you know what a *reef* is? It's a long mound of rocks or sand in the ocean that reaches almost to the surface of the water. When I say long, I mean *long*. Why, one famous reef is *seven hundred* miles long! But before we talk about that particular reef, let's talk a little more about reefs in general. Although many reefs are made of rocks or sand, other reefs are made of something called coral. Now, even though coral looks like a kind of stone, it is really made of the skeletons of millions of little sea-animals called coral polyps. This may sound a little creepy to you, but coral is beautiful. If you've ever seen a piece of coral, you know that it looks like a little tree with a lot of soft branches, and feels cool and smooth. Coral reefs grow very slowly over time but, as everyone knows, little bits of things can add up and grow into something very big—which brings us to the Mesoamerican Reef.

That name may look hard to say, but if you break it up into parts, you'll have no trouble with it. Mezz-oh American. See? It's easy. This reef is the seven hundred mile one I mentioned earlier. It's located in the Caribbean Sea and is made up of a lot of smaller reefs and an assortment of different colored, beautiful corals.

A reef is a little like an underwater jungle. All kinds of sea animals are attracted to it and live in and around it. The Mesoamerican Reef is home to all sorts of magnificent tropical fish, like the queen angelfish, and the queen triggerfish. Mammoth whale sharks also lurk there. Then, there's the saltwater crocodile, different kinds of turtles, a variety of dolphins, and lobsters, conches, shrimp, groupers, and snappers. Don't you wish you could sell tickets to this unbelievable "aquarium"?

Not only do fish and other sea-creatures swim around the reef, the air above it is full of exotic birds like the frigate bird, the red-footed booby, the brown pelican, and the brown noddy. One of my favorite animals, the manatee, also lives there.

If you know me, you know that once I heard about this wondrous reef, I just *had* to see it. So to a town near the Caribbean Sea I went, and enrolled in a scuba diving class. We were taught to dive and given a list of rules. Some of the rules are designed to protect us ("Stay at least 10 feet away from whale

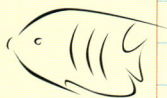

sharks at all times"—that's one rule I think I'll keep!). Others are designed to protect the reef (avoid walking on corals; don't spear any living things). I've completed the class and am ready to dive. Here goes!

POWER SKILL:
Learning to Write Setting

If you want to be a writer, or if you want to write well, it will help if you learn how to write setting. A good setting forces the writer to include many details. Learning to write more carefully about what you see will also make it possible for you to share the pictures in your mind with a friend.

Compare these two passages about the Mesoamerican Reef. It is obvious which one describes the setting best!

- The Mesoamerican Reef bustles with life, color, and sound. The water is a clear blue, the sand sparkles. I see the dolphins playing, splashing water. The reds, blues, yellows, and greens of the tropical fish catch the sun as they dart through the gentle waves. Above us, tropical birds fly through the perfect, blue sky.
- The Mesoamerican Reef is very pretty. The water is blue. There are dolphins here.

You can practice including detail in your writing. Fold your arms on your desk or a table. Shut your eyes and put your head down on your folded arms. Now, in your mind's eye, go someplace you have been before—anyplace. Again, in your mind's eye, review all of the details of what you see. Now, open your eyes and write down what you saw—even the little things.

Exercises

1. Wherever you are now sitting, without looking around, write down a description of what is around you.
2. Now, take a good look at what is around you. Close your eyes and review what you saw. Write down this detailed description.
3. Compare your two descriptions of setting. How are they different?

Lesson in Literature . . .

WHAT IS STATED THEME?

- The **theme** is the main idea of the story; it is often the reason the story was written.

- Every piece of literature—short stories, novels, poems, essays, and plays—has a theme.

- Sometimes, the author expresses the theme very clearly. We call this a **stated** theme.

- The stated theme may be found at the beginning or end or, sometimes, even the middle of the piece. But it will be clear to the reader that *this* is the theme.

THINK ABOUT IT!

1. What is the theme of *My Dog Is Best*?

2. The author uses a character to state the theme. Which character is it?

3. What does the character do to prove the point that the author wishes to make?

On Somerton Road everyone thought their dog was the very best dog on the street. The Wilson family thought their collie Trixie was the best. "Trixie is so intelligent," Rita Wilson told her neighbors. "She's the best dog on Somerton." Billy Delaney thought his Golden Retriever was the best, and he didn't mind telling people. "You should see how my dog Rusty obeys me. He's the best!" Mary Maguire thought her white poodle Candy was the best dog. "Candy's the prettiest and the best dog on Somerton," she told all her friends. Eddie Wentworth liked to brag about Willie, his Doberman Pinscher. "Willie's the fastest dog on Somerton," he said to anyone who listened. "He can outrun any dog. No dog is equal to Willie." Even Josh Levine, who owned a quiet Basset Hound named Oliver, thought his dog was the only exceptional dog on Somerton. "Oliver knows tricks that the other dogs on Somerton can only dream about!" he said. Sometimes he took Oliver out on his front lawn to show off his tricks.

When Susan Cohen moved into a house on Somerton, she was surprised by all her neighbors' boasting about their dogs. Didn't they know that all their dogs were equal? Her dog Moxie was a mutt, middle-sized, black,

My Dog Is Best

furry, and friendly. Moxie wasn't the best at anything at all. He wasn't the best looking or the most intelligent or the best behaved or the most athletic. But he was the best dog because he was a good pet.

One day as she and Moxie walked up the sidewalk on Somerton Road, Susan wondered how she could convince the other dog owners that the only thing that mattered was whether a dog was a good pet or not. How could she convince them that all their dogs were equal?

She had an idea. The next morning she stuffed flyers into all her neighbors' mailboxes. She knew that all her neighbors loved their dogs not because they were the smartest or the prettiest or the fastest but because they were good pets. Susan's flyer read: "If your dog is the best pet on Somerton Road, come to the park today at noon."

As Susan and Moxie approached the park at noon, she wasn't surprised by what she saw. The Wilsons' Trixie chased a Frisbee. Billy Delaney's Rusty held a stick in his mouth, and Candy, Mary Maguire's poodle, chewed on a dog toy. Eddie Wentworth's Doberman Pinscher ran around the park as fast as he could, while Josh Levine's Oliver performed tricks in the grass. When Moxie joined the menagerie, every dog from Somerton Road was there, and every dog owner was proud to own the best pet on Somerton Road.

Susan smiled. On Somerton Road all the dogs were equal, and, it seemed, all their owners loved their pets equally.

Blueprint for Reading

INTO . . . *The Seven Children*

For some people, working as part of a team is as natural as breathing. For others, it is one of the most challenging skills they will ever have to learn in their lives. Since working in a group is an almost unavoidable part of growing up, the sooner we learn how to work with others, the better off we will be. What makes a good team member? What makes a poor one? As you read *The Seven Children*, see if you can name some of the qualities that make working with others pleasant and easy.

EYES ON *Stated Theme*

The theme of a story is the main idea that runs through it. When the author tells you what the story's main idea is, the story has a **stated theme**. The stated theme is often presented near the beginning of the story. In *The Seven Children*, the theme is presented on the very first page. Can you find the line that clearly describes the story's theme?

THE SEVEN CHILDREN

A FABLE ABOUT UNITY

LINDA & CLAY GOSS

A farmer and his wife had seven children. Now, folks from neighboring farms were always telling them how well-blessed they were to have such fine, healthy children.

But sometimes the farmer and his wife didn't feel quite so lucky because the seven children constantly argued and fought with each other. They yelled and screamed at the top of their

voices. They threw stools and bowls across the room. Sounds of screams and things crashing into walls could be heard all day and sometimes even all night. At suppertime, when the family gathered at the table, the seven children made faces at one another and kicked at each other's feet. There was no peace in the farmer's home.

One evening, for supper, the farmer's wife cooked everyone's favorite meal—chicken and dumpling stew. She placed the big pot of stew in the middle of the long table and announced, "It's time to eat."

The farmer and the seven children rushed to the table as they always did, and blessed the food. Slowly, the mother served the farmer his bowl of stew. The farmer served a bowl of stew to his wife. None of the seven children could wait their turn for a bowl of stew. They grabbed the pot, yanked it this way and that,

and flung it to the wall. All the delicious-looking chicken and dumplings spilled out onto the floor.

The farmer pounded on the table and shouted, "Enough is enough! Clean up the mess you have made and go to bed." The seven children began to cry and blame one another.

Later that night, the farmer and his wife couldn't sleep. "I'm worried about our children," said the wife.

"They are certainly a wild bunch, but I believe buried in their heart is kindness," said the farmer.

"You are right, my wise husband, but we need a way to dig up that treasure buried beneath their hearts," said the wife.

Early the next morning, the farmer woke up each of the seven children. "Hurry and do your chores, children, for we are going on a journey through the woods," said the farmer.

The seven children were full of anticipation. They loved walking through the woods. Quickly, they did their chores and ran to the table to eat their morning meal.

But, instead of finding seven bowls of hot rice, they saw seven neatly tied bundles lying on the table. "Where is our food?" asked the seven children.

"It's time to go on our journey," said the father. "We will eat fruits and berries along the way."

"Oh, goody," shouted the children.

"And take these bundles with you," said their mother. "Don't open them now, for you will need them later." She gave each of the seven children a bundle and a hug. And so, off they went.

The farmer led his seven children through a part of the forest that was unfamiliar to them. There were no clear-cut walkways. They saw one fruit tree, but it bore very little fruit. They saw only one sweet berry bush, but it was surrounded by a thicket of thorns. Mosquitoes buzzed around their ears. Snakes glided across their path. They walked all day long.

When they came to a clearing, the farmer and the seven children stopped to rest. The farmer said to them, "My dear children, I must return home at once. There is something out

WORD BANK

thicket (THIK it) *n.*: many bushes growing close together

here your mother and I want all of you to find. When you have it, you will be able to return home."

"But, Father," said one of the seven children, "the sun is going down."

The farmer said no more and walked away.

"What shall we do now?" said one of the seven children.

"I will decide, because I am the oldest," said the oldest child.

"But I am the smartest. I should decide what we should do," said the child next to the oldest one.

"I'm hungry," said the child before the child in the middle.

"I'm thirsty," said the child in the middle.

"I'm scared," said the child after the child in the middle.

"My legs hurt," said the child next to the youngest child.

"I want to go home," said the youngest child, and he cried as loudly as he could.

The seven children began arguing over which direction to take and what should be done next and who should be doing it!

One of the seven children claimed that he knew what their mother and father wanted them to find, but he wasn't going to tell any of them.

Each of the seven children was curious about what was in the others' bundles, but no one wanted to share the contents with anyone else. Finally each of the seven children ran off into the woods in a different direction, hoping to get as far away from the others as possible.

When she was safely away, the oldest child opened up her bundle and found two flint stones. The child next to the oldest child opened up his bundle and found kindling, bits and pieces of dry sticks and twigs.

One of the seven children found a net made of tiny strings in his bundle. Another one of the children unfolded a large quilted blanket that was inside her bundle. The middle child discovered a canteen of water in her bundle. The child next to the youngest child had a bundle wrapped within a bundle within a bundle. Inside the last bundle she saw a loaf of banana bread. The youngest child was very confused because he had found a piece of cloth inside his bundle. Something was drawn on the cloth

WORD BANK

flint stones *n.*: hard stones used to produce a spark
kindling (KIHND ling) *n.*: material that ignites easily, used to start a fire

but he could not tell what it was because the woods had become dark and strange animal sounds could be heard. The youngest child screamed out in terror. The other children, fearing that their brother was in danger, ran through the woods to help him. Then he showed them what he had found in his bundle.

"We will need to make a fire with my flint stones so we can see what is on the piece of cloth," said the oldest child.

"I will help you, my sister. I have some kindling," said the child next to the oldest child.

After they had made the fire, they set the net up like a tent so the mosquitoes wouldn't bite them. They passed the canteen around so each of them could drink some water. The child next

to the youngest child gave each of her brothers and sisters a piece of banana bread. They looked at the piece of cloth and realized that it was a map showing them how to get back home.

Feeling somewhat better, they lay under the blanket and went to sleep. The next morning, the seven children woke up. They felt strong and happy. They were glad they had stayed together and were able to make it through the night without harm coming to any of them.

The seven children followed the directions on the map and returned home through the woods safely.

The farmer and his wife were pleased to see their children. Holding hands, the family formed a circle and gave thanks. Then the children told their mother and father how each one of their brothers and sisters had shared what was in the bundles.

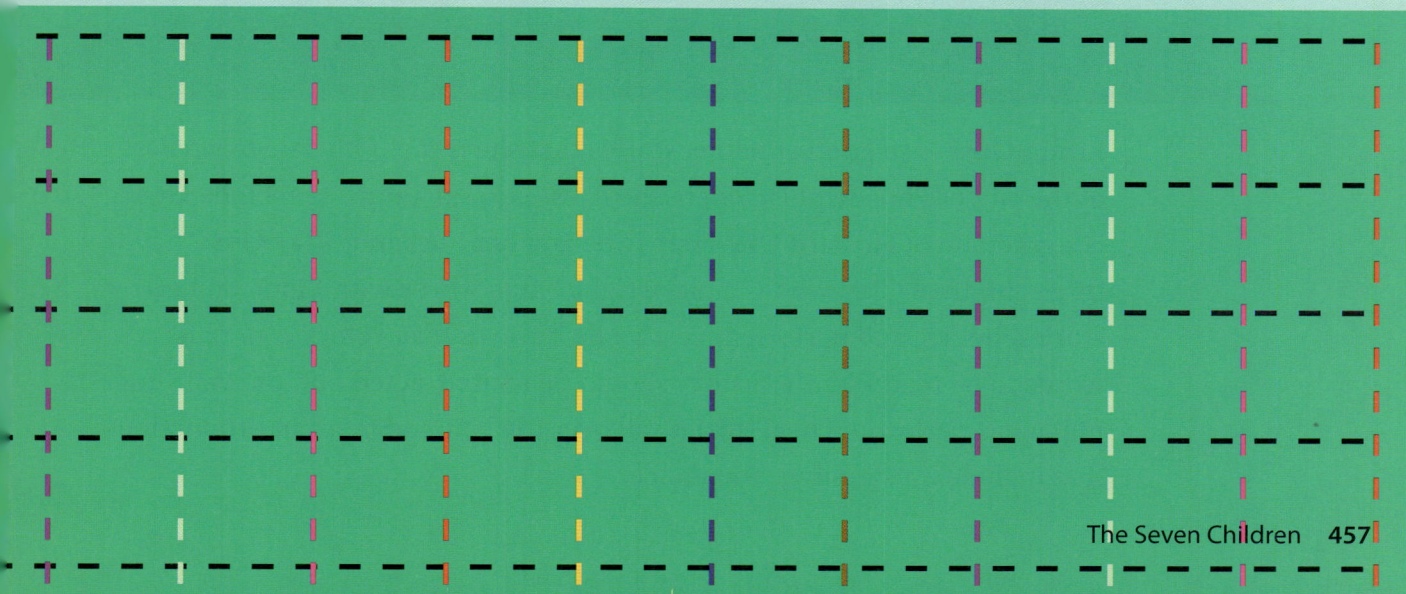

"Oh, children, did you find the thing your dear mother and I wanted you to find?"

"Yes, Father," said the oldest of the seven children. "Together we used what we had been given and found our way out of the forest. We found unity."

The youngest of the seven children spoke up. "Yes, but we also found Mother's delicious banana bread!"

The father, mother, and all the children laughed. The father looked around at his family enjoying each other and feeling happy that they were together again. He said, "We are together as a family; this is our strength. Together we have found unity."

ABOUT THE AUTHORS

Linda Goss is so good at telling stories that she is the "Official Storyteller" of the city of Philadelphia, where she lives. Born in Tennessee, Linda Goss is a graduate of Howard University. She and her husband, **Clay Goss**, have three children. Clay, who is a playwright, often works with Linda on her stories, books, and performances. Linda believes that a story is not just words to be read silently; a story should be recited, acted out, or even sung. Linda has performed her "stories" all over the United States, in productions that include music, song, and dance.

Studying the Selection

FIRST IMPRESSIONS

Did you think that the children were going to be able to 'find' or learn the lesson of unity in the woods or that they would run into problems?

QUICK REVIEW

1. Why did people often tell the farmer and his wife they were blessed and what caused them to feel otherwise at times?

2. What was the situation that finally made the parents do something drastic about their children's behavior?

3. What were the children provided with for the trip?

4. How did the children feel when they woke up in the woods?

FOCUS

5. The parents of the seven children believed that, deep down, their children were good. How did this belief help the parents make their plan? What would they have done if they had not thought their children were really kindhearted?

6. The theme of *The Seven Children* is the importance of working together. Write one sentence to show how the following parts of the story all contribute to the theme:

   a. "All the delicious-looking chicken and dumplings spilled out onto the floor."

   b. " 'I'm worried about our children,' said the wife."

   c. "The oldest child opened up her bundle and found two flint stones. The child next to the oldest child opened up his bundle and found kindling…"

CREATING AND WRITING

7. Write about a group project you enjoyed working on. Describe how being part of the group made the work easier and more interesting. Instead, you can choose to write about an experience you had in which you found it difficult and unpleasant to work with a group. Try to explain why the experience was not a good one.

8. Write a short story about someone who taught another person a lesson in a creative way, just like the parents did in this selection.

9. Your teacher will divide the class into groups. Each group must think of five to seven items that when put together will solve a problem. When your group has created or gathered the items, exchange them with another group. Your group will be given another group's items and a problem to solve.

Lesson in Literature...

WHAT IS IMPLIED THEME?

- To imply is to hint at something.
- An **implied** theme can be hard to find.
- In a story with an implied theme, a reader must work at discovering what the author wishes to say.
- Uncovering an implied theme is a little bit like solving a mystery. The reader must find clues, develop a theory, and arrive at an answer.

THINK ABOUT IT!

1. Which of the following is an implied theme of the story? Remember, the theme is the main idea of the story, not one detail of it.

    a. Respect for parents is very important.

    b. Learning to obey school rules is an important part of growing up.

    c. Planting seeds for the future is so important that it is worth risking punishment to do it.

2. Which of the following lines does not hint at the theme of the story?

    a. "That night both boys promised their mothers they wouldn't be late to school again. Ever."

    b. "Timmy crouched beside him, digging his own row of holes and dropping seeds into them."

    c. "Thanks to them, someday there would be an apple orchard in the vacant lot and apples for everybody!"

3. Replace the story's title with one of your own. Your new title may either state or imply the story's theme.

SEEDS

The two boys were late to school every day.

"Jimmy, your teacher called," his mother said sternly when he came home from school one afternoon. "Why were you and Timmy late to school again today?"

"I don't know," Jimmy answered as he opened the refrigerator looking for an afternoon snack.

At Timmy's house when he got home his mother asked him the same question. "Timmy, why were you and Jimmy late to school again today? You left on time this morning, and the walk to school isn't far at all."

"I don't know," Timmy said. He was hungry, too. He opened a kitchen cabinet hoping to find something to eat.

That night both boys promised their mothers they wouldn't be late to school again. Ever.

But the next morning Jimmy and Timmy did the same things they did every other morning. First, each said good-bye to his mother and each took an apple for the walk to school. Next, Jimmy headed over to Timmy's street where his friend waited for him on the sidewalk in front of his house. Then the two friends walked the four blocks up Main Street to their elementary school. As they walked, they talked. They talked about school and sports, teachers and friends, weekend plans and summer vacations. When they came to each intersection, the boys looked both ways before they crossed the street.

Halfway up Main Street, they took out their apples, and both boys chomped on them as they walked along. Other students passed them and waved. One girl walked by and said, "Don't be late!"

When Jimmy and Timmy reached the third intersection, both were enjoying their apples. Jimmy bit hard into his. "I'm eating this apple to its core," he said. "Me too," Timmy said. Then, as they did most mornings, they sat on the curb in front of a vacant lot, eating their apples and talking— but they talked about apples, not themselves.

"How many seeds do you have?" Timmy asked. "I have six."

"Five," Jimmy said.

"Where did we plant yesterday?" Timmy asked.

Jimmy went over to a spot in the middle of the vacant lot. "Here," he said and dug in the dirt, making small holes every few feet and dropping apple seeds into them. Timmy crouched beside him, digging his own row of holes and dropping seeds into them.

When they had planted all their apple seeds, the two boys looked at each other, satisfied, and continued their walk to school. Still half a block away, they heard the last school bell ringing, telling them that they were late to school again. But this morning, just like other mornings, the boys didn't mind. Thanks to them, someday there would be an apple orchard in the vacant lot and apples for everybody!

Blueprint for Reading

INTO . . . *The Garden of Happiness*

When things don't go our way, how do we keep going? We *hope* things will get better. We *dream* of better days ahead. We *try* to help ourselves. We *work* at solving the problem. We *wait* for our efforts to pay off. And then, when our hopes, dreams, efforts, work, and waiting are done—something wonderful happens! Imagine a group of people who live in an old, run-down neighborhood. They would like to have something green and growing and beautiful to enjoy. They get together and plant some seeds in a little patch of earth. They work and they wait. After a while, the small corner in the old neighborhood turns into a spot of beauty in their lives, a place to relax and to dream, a real Garden of Happiness. And how did it all start? With a little bit of hope.

EYES ON *Implied Theme*

In *The Seven Children*, we discussed stated theme. The author of that story tells the reader what the story's theme is. In *The Garden of Happiness*, there is an **implied theme**. That means that the author does not *openly* state what the theme is, she only hints at it. You, the reader, have to work a bit to figure out what it is. Of course, all the different parts of the story—plot, characterization, and setting—help to develop the theme. But it is up to you to put the pieces of the puzzle together. As you read, ask yourself: What is the main idea of the story? Don't decide on a final answer until you get to the surprise ending!

The Garden of Happiness

Erika Tamar

O n Marisol's block near East Houston Street, there was an empty lot that was filled with garbage and broken, tired things. It had a funky smell that made Marisol wrinkle her nose whenever she passed by.

One April morning, Marisol was surprised to see many grown-ups busy in the lot. Mr. Ortiz carried a rusty refrigerator door. Mrs. Willie Mae Washington picked up newspapers. Mr. Singh rolled a tire away.

The next afternoon, Marisol saw people digging up stones. Mr. Ortiz worked with a pickax.

"*¿Qué pasa?*"[1] Marisol asked.

Mrs. Willie Mae Washington leaned on her shovel and wiped her forehead. "I'm gonna grow black-eyed peas and greens and sweet potatoes, too," she said. "Like on my daddy's farm in Alabama. No more store-bought collard greens for me."

---

1. *Qué pasa* (KAY POSS ah) means "what's happening?" in Spanish.

"We will call it The Garden of Happiness," Mr. Singh said. "I am planting *valore*[2]—such a beautiful vine of lavender and red. Yes, everyone is happy when they see this bean from Bangladesh."[3]

On another day, Marisol watched Mr. Castro preparing the ground. Mrs. Rodriguez rolled a wheelbarrow full of peat moss. Marisol inhaled the fresh-soil smell of spring.

"Oh, I want to plant something in The Garden of Happiness!" Marisol said.

"Too late, *niña*,"[4] Mr. Ortiz said. "All the plots are already taken."

Marisol looked everywhere for a leftover spot, but the ground was crisscrossed by markers of sticks and string. She looked and looked. Just outside the chain-link fence, she found a bit of earth where the sidewalk had cracked.

"¡*Mira*![5] Here's my patch!" Marisol called. It was no bigger than her hand, but it was her very own. She picked out the pebbles and scraped the soil with a stick.

Marisol noticed a crowd of teenagers across the street from the lot. They were staring at a brick wall. It was sad and closed up, without windows for eyes. Marisol crossed over to ask what they were doing.

"City Arts is giving us paint to make a mural on the wall," a girl told her.

"What will it be?" Marisol asked.

"Don't know yet," one of the big boys said. "We haven't decided."

"I'm making a garden," Marisol said. "I haven't decided, either, about what to plant."

In The Garden of Happiness, the ground had become soft and dark. Mr. Castro talked to his seedlings as he placed them in straight rows. "Come on now, little baby things, grow nice and big for me."

---

2. *Valore* (vah LOH reh) is a type of bean.
3. *Bangladesh* is a small country east of Pakistan.
4. *Niña* (NEEN yah) means "girl" in Spanish.
5. *Mira* (MIH rah) means "look!" in Spanish.

> ## WORD BANK
>
> **mural** (MYOOR ul) *n.*: a large picture painted directly on a wall or ceiling

Marisol had no seedlings or even small cuttings or roots. *What can I do,* she thought, *where can I find something to plant?*

She went to the corner where old Mrs. Garcia[6] was feeding the pigeons. Marisol helped herself to a big flat seed. The birds fluttered about angrily. "Only one," she told them, "for my garden."

Marisol skipped back to her patch. She poked a hole with her finger, dropped in the seed, and patted the soil all around. And every single day that spring, Marisol carried a watering can to the lot and gave her seed a cool drink.

Before long, a green shoot broke through in Marisol's patch. Even on rainy days, she hurried to the lot to see. Soon there were two leaves on a strong, straight stalk, and then there were four. It became as high as Marisol's knee!

Green things were growing all around in The Garden of Happiness. Mr. Castro's tiny seedlings became big bushy things with ripe tomatoes shining like rubies.

"What's *my* plant?" Marisol asked. Now it reached to her shoulder. "What's it going to be?"

"Dunno," Mrs. Willie Mae Washington answered. "But it sure is *somethin'*!"

Marisol pulled out the weeds in the late afternoons, when it wasn't so summer-hot.

Sometimes she watched the teenagers across the street. They measured the wall. They talked and argued about what they would paint.

---

6. *Garcia* (gar SEE yah)

Often Marisol saw Mr. Ortiz in his plot, resting in a chair. "I come back from the factory and breathe the fresh air," he said. "And I sit among my *habichuelas*,[7] my little piece of Puerto Rico."

"Is *my* plant from Puerto Rico? Do you know what it is?" Marisol asked.

Mr. Ortiz shook his head and laughed. "¡*Muy grande*! Maybe it's Jack's beanstalk from the fairy tale."

---

7. *Habichuelas* (ah bee CHWELL ahs) are kidney beans in Spanish.
8. *Muy grande* (muh wee GRAHN day) means "very big" in Spanish.

By the end of July, Marisol's plant had grown way over her head. And then, at the very top, Marisol saw a bud! It became fatter every day. She couldn't wait for it to open.

"Now don't be lookin' so hard," Mrs. Willie Mae Washington chuckled. "It's gonna open up behind your back, just when you're thinkin' about somethin' else."

One morning, Marisol saw an amazing sight from halfway down the block. She ran the rest of the way. Standing higher than all the plants and vines in the garden was a flower as big as a plate! Her bud had turned into petals of yellow and gold.

"A sunflower!" Mrs. Anderson exclaimed as she pushed her shopping cart by. "Reminds me of when I was a girl in Kansas."

Mrs. Majewska was rushing on her way to the subway, but she skidded to a stop. "Ah, słoneczniki!⁹ So pretty in the fields of Poland!"

Old Mrs. Garcia shook her head. "No, no, *los girasols*¹⁰ from Mexico, where they bring joy to the roadside."

"I guess sunflowers make themselves right at home in every sun-kissed place on earth," Mrs. Willie Mae Washington said.

"Even right here in New York City," Marisol said proudly.

The flower was a growing circle, brighter than a yellow taxi. *A flower of sunshine*, Marisol thought, *the happiest plant in The Garden of Happiness*.

All summer long, it made the people on the street stop and smile.

Soon the air became cool and crisp with autumn. Mr. Castro picked the last of his tomatoes. Mr. Singh carried away a basket full of beans. Mrs. Rodriguez picked her *tomatillos*. "To dry and cut up for *salsa*," she said.

Mrs. Willie Mae Washington dug up orange potatoes.

"I can almost smell my sweet potato pie." She winked at Marisol. "I'm gonna save an extra big slice for a good little gardener I know."

---

9. *Słoneczniki* means "sunflower" in Polish.
10. *Los girasols* (loss hee rah SO less) are sunflowers in Spanish.

But something terrible was happening to Marisol's flower. Its leaves were turning brown and dry. Marisol watered and watered until a stream ran down the sidewalk. But her flower's leaves began to fall.

"Please get well again," Marisol whispered.

Every day, more golden petals curled and faded.

"My flower of sunshine is sick," Marisol cried. "What should I do?"

"Oh, child," Mrs. Willie Mae Washington said. "Its season is over. There's a time to bloom and a time to die."

"No! I don't want my flower to die!"

"*Mi cariño*,[11] don't cry," Mrs. Rodriguez said. "That's the way of a garden. You must save the seeds and plant again next spring."

Marisol's flower drooped to the ground. The Garden of Happiness wasn't happy for her anymore. The vines had tumbled down. The bushy green plants were gone. She collected the seeds and put them in her pocket, but spring was much too far away.

_____

11. *Mi cariño* (mee kah reen YOH) is "my dear" in Spanish.

Marisol was too sad to go to the empty lot anymore. For a whole week, she couldn't even look down the block where her beautiful flower used to be.

Then one day she heard people calling her name.

"Marisol! Come quick!"

"Marisol! ¡*Apúrate*![12] Hurry!"

A golden haze shone on the street. There was a big crowd, like on a holiday. Music from the *bodega*[13] was loud and bright. And what she saw made Marisol laugh and dance and clap her hands.

---

12. *Apúrate* (ah POOR ah tay) means "hurry up!" in Spanish.
13. A *bodega* (bo DAY gah) is a grocery store in Spanish.

ABOUT THE AUTHOR

Born in Austria, Erika Tamar came to the United States when she was four years old. Her parents were refugees who had escaped death at the hands of the Nazis. Like so many immigrants, the family settled in New York. She later married and had a family. When her children brought home books for young adults, she decided it was time for her to write. She has since published many books for young adults and elementary school children.

Poetry plants seeds

Johnny Appleseed

Rosemary and Stephen Vincent Benét

Of Jonathan Chapman
Two things are known,
That he loved apples,
That he walked alone.

5   At seventy-odd
He was gnarled as could be,
But ruddy and sound
As a good apple tree.

For fifty years over
10   Of harvest and dew,
He planted his apples
Where no apples grew.

The winds of the prairie
Might blow through his rags,
15   But he carried his seeds
In the best deerskin bags.

From old Ashtabula
To frontier Fort Wayne,
He planted and pruned
And he planted again.

20   He had not a hat
To encumber his head.

He wore a tin pan
On his white hair instead.

He nested with owl,
25   And with bear-cub and possum,
And knew all his orchards
Root, tendril and blossom.

A fine old man,
As ripe as a pippin,
30   His heart still light,
And his step still skipping.

Why did he do it?
We do not know.
He wished that apples
35   Might root and grow.

He has no statue.
He has no tomb.
He has his apple trees
Still in bloom.

40   *Consider, consider,*
Think well upon
The marvelous story
Of Appleseed John.

Studying the Selection

We know that Marisol was hopeful, but at what point in the story did you believe that her one sunflower seed i a sidewalk crack would grow?

QUICK REVIEW

1. What surprise did Marisol find on her block one April morning?

2. After Marisol discovered that all the plots were taken, where did she find a place to plant?

3. What kind of plant did Marisol grow and where did she get the seed?

4. How did Marisol care for her plant?

FOCUS

5. "And what she saw made Marisol laugh and dance and clap her hands." What do you think it was that caused Marisol to feel this way at the end of the story?

6. Find three places in the story that *imply* (hint at) the theme of "hope," even though they do not state it clearly.

CREATING AND WRITING

7. Think about something that you are hopeful about. Is it a realistic hope or more of a dream? Write about a hope that you believe will really happen one day.

8. Write a short story about someone who grew not in size, but in character. Describe a situation that caused the person to develop greater understanding and maturity. Your story may be true or fictional.

9. Follow your teacher's instructions for a gardening activity.

Jill's Journal:
On Assignment in Crista's Garden

I have a friend named Crista who is a Master Gardener. In fact, she lives around the corner from me. Her backyard is right next to mine. We share the tall, slatted wood fence that marks the boundary. We began as neighbors and now we are friends.

Crista's backyard is not just a yard. It is a little world—a secret garden that no one can see from the street. It has taken me a while to realize that when I am in Crista's garden, all of my worries fall away. Let me describe what I see when I step out her back door. Here there is so much that is green. Towering trees that reach to the sky. Moss. Plants of many varieties. Old stone benches. Eight flat clay dishes to hold water for the birds. And two more cement birdbaths that are fancier and sit on stands. In the tall grasses sleep several young cats.

Crista introduces her garden to me. Here is a big plant with velvety golden-yellow blooms and little white ones. "This is a popcorn plant," she says. "Earl and I found it in a garden in a little town in North Carolina." Earl is Crista's husband. He is an astronomer. "We take the popcorn plant indoors in winter."

"Look over here," she points. I see a tall plant with bright red blossoms. "These are canna lilies. They bloom like this for about two months a year, in August and September." We step deeper into the garden.

"Now, smell these herbs!" she says excitedly. In a large, clay pot, rosemary and flat basil and catnip grow in big bunches. "Of course," she adds, smiling, "the catnip is for the cats. But they hardly give it a chance to grow before they've jumped up here and eaten it!" We both laugh.

"And this is our pond," she explains. She points toward the circle of water that is about six feet wide and three feet deep. "We used to keep our goldfish in there, but they really got too big!" Crista and her husband actually made the pond themselves.

Crista tells me that the very tall tree to my right is called a sweet gum. "In autumn, sweet gums produce the brightest colors: Orange, red, and yellow appear together on every leaf. When the tree goes to seed, little balls about one inch wide hang from small stalks on the branches.

"See this smaller tree here—small, because it is young. It will grow large. Notice how the leaves are shaped like little fans. This is a ginkgo tree. This one is a boy tree." I am surprised. I didn't know that trees could be boys or girls. "Yes," she assures me. "Like people and animals, trees have a gender.

"We often don't pay attention to the natural world. We are so busy that we tend to take things for granted." She shakes her head a little sadly. "Look at these spider plants, for instance. Do you know that if you have them in your home, they filter the air and remove unhealthy particles?" I admit that I did not know this. She lifts a potted spider plant from one of the stone benches and places it in my arms.

"If you are writing for young students, tell them that dirt—soil—is not dirty. That to grow a little garden and be part of nature makes a person feel more alive. There is joy in seeing things grow. That is why I have this garden. I know that if there are trees around the house, they provide shelter for squirrels and birds. The trees and plants and flowers provide nourishment for birds and bees and butterflies. If I have a garden, it makes me more a part of the circle of life."

I walk home holding the spider plant, thinking over what my friend has just said.

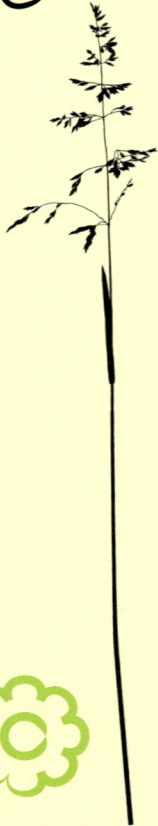

POWER SKILL:
Conducting an Interview

Interviews are a good tool for gathering information. Although most information can be found in books, talking to people who have firsthand experience in the topic you are studying can be exciting and satisfying. Older people may have a wealth of knowledge and wisdom. Therefore, it is important to think about what makes a good interview.

When you are preparing to interview someone, try to learn something about the topic you will be asking about. Also, make sure you know a little about the person you are interviewing. If you are not asking about a special skill or knowledge that the person has, but instead, about the person's life, read a little about the events that have occurred during his or her lifetime. This way you will understand the person better.

Make a list of questions. Remember, good questions build on the question before. Your questions should make the person being interviewed think. Don't ask questions that can be answered with a yes or no. Also, avoid questions that may be too personal and questions whose answers you already know.

Exercises

1. Imagine that you are going to interview a cat or some other animal of your choice. Write out ten questions you are going to ask the animal. His or her name would be a good place to start.

2. Do you have a grandparent or another older relative or family friend you could interview? Your first job is to think of such a person. Your second job is to think about what you want to know about them. Third, make your list of questions.

Lesson in Literature...

DRAWING CONCLUSIONS

- As we read a story, we wonder how the conflict will end. We search for clues.
- We look for hints about what will happen, what the main character will do to solve the problem, or what surprises may be in store for us.

- We begin to *draw conclusions*.
- When we use all of the information provided by the author to predict what will happen, we are *drawing conclusions*. When we use only some of the information and make a hasty guess, we are *jumping* to conclusions!

The park at the end of Steve and Samantha's street closed abruptly at the beginning of the summer. A big, handwritten sign outside the park entrance read:

CLOSED FOR THE SEASON— IN NEED OF MAJOR REPAIRS

So one day as Steve and Samantha rode their bikes past the closed park entrance, they both wondered sadly if they, or anyone else in their neighborhood, would ever enjoy Forestdale Park again.

"I miss Forestdale every day," Samantha said, pedaling slowly.

Forestdale used to be a very nice park. When they were young, they took walks to the park with their parents, played on the playground, ate sandwiches at picnic tables, and watched ducks swimming happily in

FORESTDALE FOREVER

THINK ABOUT IT!

1. What is the story's conflict?

2. Choose one line in the middle of the story from which you can draw conclusions about how the story will end.

3. Read the second to last paragraph. If you passed the group, what clues would help you draw the right conclusion about why they were there?

the pond. When they were older, they rode their bikes to the park, swam in the pool for hours, and played Frisbee on the grassy fields. Every summer Forestdale's well-kept baseball diamond was home field for Steve's baseball and Samantha's softball games.

Now Forestdale was closed. They both knew the story of its closing. "It is still a very nice park but no one takes care of it," their father told them, "and the city can't afford to fix it up." Steve and Samantha knew the park's problems too well. Last summer the pool's filter broke, and the water turned green. The playground's swing set broke, too. Picnic tables fell apart. The grass grew high in the baseball field's outfield. Even the ducks disappeared from the dirty pond.

"What can the two of us do?" Steve asked, riding his bike close to his sister's.

"We," Samantha said, stopping her bike, "can't do much alone. But what if we each asked a friend to help us clean up the park? And what if those friends asked their friends? And those friends asked other friends? Don't you see, Steve?"

Steve loved Samantha's idea.

The next day he explained the plan to his friend Kevin, who agreed to ask a friend. Samantha asked her friend Renee who also agreed to ask a friend. Within a few days four friends turned into eight friends, eight into sixteen, sixteen into thirty-two and so on until Steve and Samantha announced the last Saturday in July as "Forestdale Forever Day."

On the appointed day the number of children who volunteered to clean up the park was close to a hundred. The crowd attracted attention. Parents stopped what they were doing and joined the cause. Police and firemen stopped by. Soon city council and the mayor showed up with rolled up shirtsleeves. All afternoon people raked leaves, cut grass, and fixed wooden tables. A handyman repaired the pool filter. Others cleared the pond of leaves. At the end of the day, the mayor hired carpenters, electricians, and groundskeepers for upkeep of the park and declared Forestdale open for the summer!

For Steve and Samantha, the reopening of Forestdale was a lesson in numbers—and a lesson in friendship.

Blueprint for Reading

INTO . . . *One Grain of Rice*

Have you ever stood in front of a very tall building and wondered how it was built? The answer is easy—from the bottom up! On the first day of work, one row of bricks was laid on the ground. On the second day, two rows of bricks were laid on top of those. On the third day, four rows were laid on top of those—and so on, until a skyscraper was standing. There is a famous saying, "A journey of a thousand miles starts with one step." When we think of doing great things, we tend to think of the finished job and wonder how we can ever achieve something so grand. If we were to realize that many small steps add up to one giant achievement, we would be eager to roll up our sleeves and get to work! In the following story, the people are starving. They need a tremendous amount of food. Who could possibly provide all the help they need? What possible good could come of one grain of rice?

EYES ON *Drawing Conclusions*

Have you ever been in the middle of telling your friend a good story when, much to your annoyance, your friend interrupts and tells you what the end of the story must be? It is worse yet, when your friend is right! Don't be too annoyed. The fact that your friend could guess the end of the story says that you are a very good storyteller. You were able to give the facts in such a clear and organized fashion that your friend was able to **draw conclusions** and figure out what would happen at the end. As you can see, the expression "to draw conclusions" means to take all the information that has been given and predict how things will turn out. *We* predict that, as you near the end of *One Grain of Rice*, you will come to the right conclusion about how it ends!

One Grain of Rice

A MATHEMATICAL FOLKTALE   Demi

Long ago in India, there lived a raja who believed that he was wise and fair, as a raja should be.

The people in his province were rice farmers. The raja decreed that everyone must give nearly all of the rice to him.

"I will store the rice safely," the raja promised the people, "so that in time of famine, everyone will have rice to eat, and no one will go hungry."

Each year, the raja's rice collectors gathered nearly all of the people's rice and carried it away to the royal storehouses.

WORD BANK	**raja** (RAH zha) *n.*: the title of a chieftain or prince in India and areas of southeast Asia
	decreed (dih KREED) *v.*: ordered; commanded
	famine (FAM in) *n.*: a hunger; a major food shortage

For many years, the rice grew well. The people gave nearly all of their rice to the raja, and the storehouses were always full. But the people were left with only just enough to get by.

Then one year the rice grew badly, and there was famine and hunger. The people had no rice to give to the raja, and they had no rice to eat.

The raja's ministers implored him, "Your highness, let us open the royal storehouses and give the rice to the people, as you promised."

"No!" cried the raja. "How do I know how long the famine may last? I must have the rice for myself. Promise or no promise, a raja must not go hungry!"

Time went on, and the people grew more and more hungry. But the raja would not give out the rice.

One day, the raja ordered a feast for himself and his court—as, it seemed to him, a raja should now and then, even when there is famine.

A servant led an elephant from a royal storehouse to the palace, carrying two full baskets of rice.

A village girl named Rani saw that a trickle of rice was falling from one of the baskets. Quickly, she jumped up and walked along beside the elephant, catching the falling rice in her skirt. She was clever, and she began to make a plan.

WORD BANK
implored (im PLORD) *v.*: begged

At the palace, a guard cried, "Halt, thief! Where are you going with that rice?"

"I am not a thief," Rani replied. "This rice fell from one of the baskets, and I am returning it now to the raja."

When the raja heard about Rani's good deed, he asked his ministers to bring her before him.

"I wish to reward you for returning what belongs to me," the raja said to Rani. "Ask me for anything, and you shall have it."

"Your Highness," said Rani, "I do not deserve any reward at all. But if you wish, you may give me one grain of rice."

"Only one grain of rice?" exclaimed the raja. "Surely you will allow me to reward you more plentifully, as a raja should."

"Very well," said Rani. "If it pleases Your Highness, you may reward me in this way. Today, you will give me a single grain of rice. Then, each day for thirty days you will give me double the rice you gave me the day before. Thus, tomorrow you will give me two grains of rice, the next day four grains of rice, and so on for thirty days."

"This seems still to be a modest reward," said the raja. "But you shall have it."

And Rani was presented with a single grain of rice.

The next day, Rani was presented with two grains of rice.

And the following day, Rani was presented with four grains of rice.

On the ninth day, Rani was presented with two hundred and fifty-six grains of rice. She had received in all five hundred and eleven grains of rice, only enough for a small handful.

"This girl is honest, but not very clever," thought the raja. "She would have gained more rice by keeping what fell into her skirt!"

On the twelfth day, Rani received two thousand and forty-eight grains of rice, about four handfuls. On the thirteenth day, she received four thousand and ninety-six grains of rice, enough to fill a bowl.

On the sixteenth day, Rani was presented with a bag containing thirty-two thousand, seven hundred and sixty-eight grains of rice. All together she had enough rice for two full bags.

"This doubling adds up to more rice than I expected!" thought the raja. "But surely her reward won't amount to much more."

On the twentieth day, Rani was presented with sixteen more bags filled with rice.

On the twenty-first day, she received one million, forty-eight thousand, five hundred and seventy-six grains of rice, enough to fill a basket.

On the twenty-fourth day, Rani was presented with eight-million, three hundred and eighty-eight thousand, six hundred and eight grains of rice—enough to fill eight baskets, which were carried to her by eight royal deer.

On the twenty-seventh day, thirty-two Brahma bulls were needed to deliver sixty-four baskets of rice.

The raja was deeply troubled. "One grain of rice has grown very great indeed," he thought. "But I shall fulfill the reward to the end, as a raja should."

On the twenty-ninth day, Rani was presented with the contents of two royal storehouses.

On the thirtieth and final day, two hundred and fifty-six elephants crossed the province, carrying the contents of the last four royal storehouses—five hundred and thirty-six million, eight hundred and seventy thousand, nine hundred and twelve grains of rice.

$$200 + 56 = 256$$

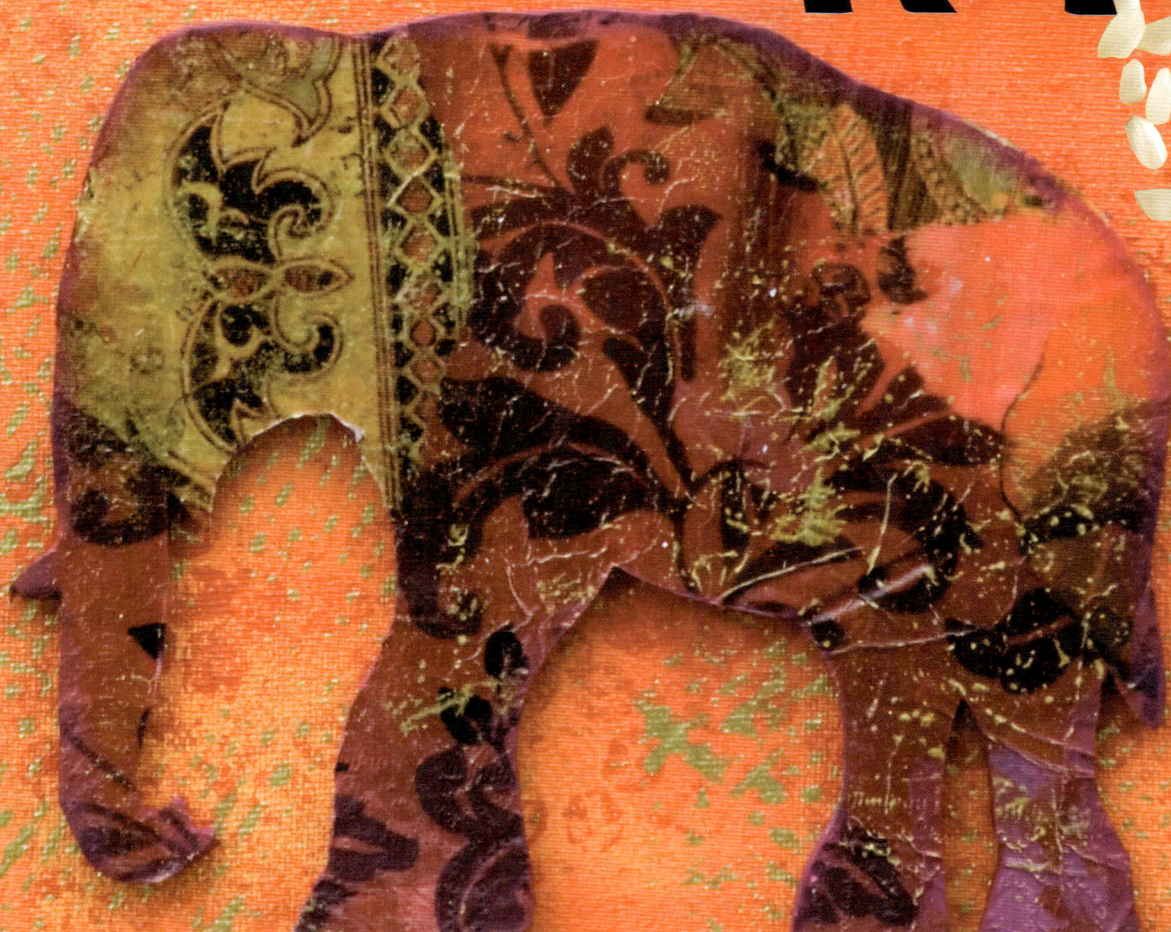

All together, Rani had received more than one billion grains of rice. The raja had no more rice to give. "And what will you do with this rice," said the raja with a sigh, "now that I have none?"

"I shall give it to all the hungry people," said Rani. "And I shall leave a basket of rice for you, too, if you promise from now on to take only as much rice as you need."

"I promise," said the raja.

And for the rest of his days, the raja was truly wise and fair, as a raja should be.

ABOUT THE AUTHOR

"Life is magic. To capture life on paper is magic." These are the words that **Demi**, born Charlotte Dumaresq Hunt, uses to explain her work as an artist and a writer. Demi has spent years "capturing life on paper" both by painting pictures and by writing stories. In the field of art, she is especially interested in Chinese art and silk painting. In the field of writing, she specializes in turning Chinese folktales into children's books. In addition to the more than 130 books she has written, Demi paints murals, makes jewelry, works with ceramics, and spends time with her husband, Tze Si Huang, and their son.

Studying the Selection

FIRST IMPRESSIONS
Do you think the raja was a wise and fair ruler?

QUICK REVIEW

1. When and where does the story take place?

2. Why did the rice farmers give most of their rice each year to the raja?

3. What did the raja do with the rice the year there was a famine?

4. How did Rani have the opportunity to speak to the raja about rice?

FOCUS

5. What was so creative about Rani's idea for her reward?

6. At what point did you conclude that Rani's request was not silly, but wise, creative, and kind?

CREATING AND WRITING

7. Write about someone you know who started a group, project, or business with almost nothing and turned it into something very big and successful. If you don't know anyone who has done this, you may make up a story about someone's astonishing success.

8. Write a fictional story about a king who is selfish and proud. Tell how a child saves the nation from the king's thoughtlessness and teaches him a lesson. Make the king selfish, but not cruel, so that he can change his ways at the end of the story.

9. Find at least one good recipe that uses a staple food such as rice, potatoes, bread, or yams and bring a copy of it to class. You may ask your family or anyone else you know for an old favorite. When the recipes are collected you will make a class "staples" cookbook.

Lesson in Literature ...

IN THE EYES OF THE BEHOLDER

Laura and her older sister Helen loved to draw and paint, but they especially loved writing poetry. But since Helen was two years older than Laura, she was the one who always wrote the better poems. Their mother liked to say, "My daughter Helen has an eye for poetry." Helen's teachers always complimented her when they returned her writing assignments, especially her poetry. After one teacher read Helen's poem about the lovely flowers that bloomed in their family's garden, she wrote, "Everything you write is so beautiful, Helen." Another teacher wrote "This is A+! I love your poetry!" after Helen submitted a poem about a beautiful

sunset at the beach. Even Laura loved Helen's poetry. Sometimes she asked her sister, "Would you read me that poem again about the pretty castle in the woods?"

Laura's problem was that when she sat down to write, she couldn't think of anything to write about flowers or sunsets or castles. She loved her sister's poems, but she couldn't write them. When she tried to write about those topics, her poems lacked the details. Her other problem was that when she sat down to write, she always wrote about things that weren't good topics for poetry. One time she started to write a poem about a hooting train whistle, but she didn't finish

COMPARE AND CONTRAST

- When we **compare** two things, we look for *similarities* between them.
- *He was such a great baseball player that they compared him to Babe Ruth.*
- When we **contrast** two things, we look for *differences* between them.
- *Although both Florida and California are hot in the summertime, Florida is very humid while California is not.*

THINK ABOUT IT!

1. Compare Laura and Helen. In what two ways are they alike?
2. Contrast Laura and Helen. In what two ways are they different?
3. What lesson did Laura learn about poetry?

it. Who ever wrote a poem about a noisy train? Another time she started a poem about a spider she found under a rock. She liked writing about the spider, but was a poem about a spider a real poem? She even thought about writing a poem about a tree stump in her family's backyard, but she didn't write it. Who ever read a poem about a tree stump? So Laura decided she wouldn't write any more poetry, because poems were supposed to be about beautiful things like flowers and sunsets.

One day, though, Laura took a walk in the woods beside a stream and had an idea for a poem about her favorite amphibian, the salamander. Her poem described a shady scene, a quietly flowing stream, a buzzing fly, a big log across the stream, and a black salamander with yellow spots and a long tongue. As she wrote, she didn't describe the fly, log, and salamander as beautiful like Helen's flowers and sunsets; instead, she described them exactly as she saw them on her walk.

As Helen read the poem, Laura watched her sister's eyes grow wide with happiness. "Laura," Helen said, "your poem is so good. Your words make everything so real. I can picture the setting and the salamander. I love it!" As Laura listened to her sister's complimentary words, she realized she wanted to write more poems about all the things she noticed in the world like a train whistle, a spider, and a tree stump. She realized there was poetry everywhere as long as she looked for it.

Blueprint for Reading

INTO . . . *Maria's House*

What makes us feel embarrassed? Saying the wrong thing? Doing poorly at something that we'd like to be good at? Being shorter, taller, richer, poorer, or *different* in some way from our friends? Many people are anxious to be "like everybody else," and work hard at hiding something about themselves that makes them stand out. As you read *Maria's House*, ask yourself why she feels she must hide the truth about where she lives. Would you feel that way? *Should* you feel that way? What life lessons does Maria learn about herself and others at the end of the story?

EYES ON *Compare and Contrast*

Which do you like better, summer or winter? How are alligators and crocodiles different from one another? Why do you like arithmetic more than history? To answer any of these questions, you will have to **compare** and **contrast** two things. When we compare two things, we are finding ways in which two things are alike. "Summer and winter both have such great outdoor sports," we might say. When we contrast two things, we are finding ways in which two things are different. "Summer is warm and sunny, but winter in our town is cold and drab." As you read *Maria's House*, compare and contrast the characters and the settings to one another. This will help you to understand each one better.

MARIA'S HOUSE

FROM THE BOOK BY JEAN MERRILL

"Maria, Maria!"

Mama looked in the door of Maria's room.

"Today is Saturday," Mama said. "Wake up. You will be late for the art class."

Maria lay in bed staring at a crack in the ceiling. She did not want to go to her art class today.

Could she tell Mama that she was sick?

No. Mama would know.

Usually, Maria could not wait for Saturday morning. She loved her art class at the museum. And she loved Miss Lindstrom, her wonderful art teacher.

Usually, Maria was so excited on Saturday morning that she woke up even before the Sanitation Department started banging down the garbage cans outside her window. She would be up and dressed before Mama had set the table for breakfast.

She would brush and braid her hair. Then it would take a long time to decide which of her three smocks she would wear.

Mama had made her three smocks for the art class—a blue one, a yellow one, and a tan one. "Art coats" Mama called them. They were exactly like the smocks Maria's art teacher wore. Except that all Miss Lindstrom's smocks were blue.

When Maria came into the kitchen on Saturday morning, Mama would look up to see which smock she was wearing.

"Ah, pretty," Mama would say. "Pretty color on you."

Mama always said "pretty"—no matter which of the three smocks Maria chose.

Maria knew that Mama looked forward to Saturday as much as she did. Mama always looked very pleased with herself as she brought out the old brown teapot in which she kept the money she earned from ironing shirts for the Overnite Laundry.

Every Saturday morning it was the same. Mama would count out three quarters from the teapot—two for Maria's bus fare to the museum, and an extra one "just in case of something."

Mama would hand the quarters to Maria. Then she would stand at the kitchen door, holding Maria's portfolio, while Maria put on her coat.

"Art bag" Mama called the portfolio. Mama had bought the portfolio at an uptown art store for Maria's birthday.

"Special art bag, so pictures should not be damaged on the way to art class," Mama had explained.

Only two other girls in the class had portfolios. Two other girls and Miss Lindstrom. Maria was very proud of her portfolio.

Everything about Saturday morning made it seem a special day—the clean smock, the three quarters in her coat pocket, Mama's handing her the portfolio. Maria always felt taller than usual as she walked down to the corner of Market Street to get the bus to the museum.

Her friends, in their Saturday clothes, would be playing on the street as Maria, scrubbed and neat, hurried past, carrying her portfolio. Her friends would stare curiously at her.

Most of them did not understand why anyone would want to go to a class on Saturday. But they were not artists.

Maria even liked the long bus ride across town to the museum. She liked watching the city change from block to block.

First there were the streets near the river. Busy and noisy. People sitting on steps. Boys playing stickball in the street.

Then there were the clean, modern buildings with wide glass windows in the uptown shopping district. And finally the bus would turn up a quiet tree-lined avenue of old houses that were set far back from the street. This was the part of town where the museum was.

Yes, everything about Saturday was wonderful. And knowing that Saturday was coming made the rest of the week wonderful, too.

All week Maria could dream that the next Saturday might be the day that Miss Lindstrom would stop at her easel and

WORD BANK

portfolio (port FO lee oh) *n*.: a flat, portable case for carrying loose papers, drawings, and the like

admire the drawing there. Might even choose her drawing to go on the bulletin board that ran around two sides of the large room in which the art class was held.

That hadn't happened yet. Maybe it wouldn't for a long time.

Miss Lindstrom was always kind and encouraging. But she praised you only when your work was very, very good. If one small detail in a drawing pleased Miss Lindstrom, it was enough to make Maria happy all week.

Once Maria had drawn purely for the fun of it, filling notebook after notebook with pictures. Decorating the margins of her school books, and making birthday cards for her friends.

But since Mama had been sending her to the classes at the museum, Maria had begun to draw with one purpose—to make a painting or drawing that Miss Lindstrom would find beautiful.

That was why she could not make herself get out of bed this Saturday. Maria did not want to show Miss Lindstrom the picture that she had finished last night.

The Saturday before, Miss Lindstrom had given the class an assignment to do at home. Usually, Maria was very happy when Miss Lindstrom suggested assignments to be done outside of class.

Such assignments gave Maria a whole week to plan the beautiful picture she would draw for Miss Lindstrom. Drawing or painting in class, Maria never felt she had enough time to make a picture as perfect as she would have liked. She often had a better idea on the bus going home.

Then, too, when there were outside assignments, Miss Lindstrom would come around to her easel at least twice during class. Once to look at the work she'd done at home. Then again to see what she was doing in class.

So Maria had been pleased last week when Miss

Lindstrom gave them a special assignment. It wasn't until she got off the bus at Market Street that she realized that she could not do it.

Miss Lindstrom had asked the class to make paintings or drawings of the houses where they lived. As Maria walked down Market Street after class, she saw suddenly that she could not take Miss Lindstrom a picture of the building in which her family and fourteen other families lived.

Miss Lindstrom had said to draw a house. Maria did not think of the building in which she lived as a "house."

It was just an ugly, old building. Squeezed into the middle of a block of ugly buildings, each one as tired and worn-out looking as the next. How could she make a beautiful picture of 79 Market Street?

Inside the building, the apartment where Maria lived looked bright and fresh. Mama and Papa scrubbed the kitchen floor every day and put new paint on the walls every year.

"Can't put up beautiful pictures on dirty walls," Mama said. Mama had Maria's best paintings and drawings pinned up in every one of the apartment's three rooms.

The apartment looked nice enough. But from outside, the building looked terrible.

Maria was sure that when Miss Lindstrom said to draw a house, that she was thinking of a house where one family lived, a neat, freshly painted building

set apart from other houses by grass, gardens, and shade trees. The kind of house that would have a front yard and a backyard with flowering bushes planted here and there. A house with a private driveway, and even a private sidewalk leading from the city sidewalk up to the front door.

The other children in the art class probably all lived in such houses. Out on the edge of the city, just before you came to the country.

Why, of course. That was why the parents of many of them drove them to the museum on Saturday morning.

Maria had been thinking that their parents brought them to the museum because they did not trust them, as Mama trusted her, to take the bus by themselves.

That wasn't it at all. It was that they lived so far from the center of the city. The city buses didn't run from there.

Of course. They all lived miles and miles from the noisy, dirty streets of the city. In beautiful houses. On streets that looked like parks.

None of them lived in buildings like those on Market Street. Nobody on Market Street sent their children to art classes at the museum. Except Mama.

Miss Lindstrom probably thought Maria lived in the same sort of house as the rest of the class. When Maria walked into the museum on Saturday, she was always neatly dressed, and she had her beautiful portfolio. How would Miss Lindstrom know that she lived on Market Street?

Maria had worried all week about the assignment. How could she do it? There was no way of making a rundown tenement building look beautiful, if you drew it the way it was.

Could she make a little watercolor painting of the inside of the apartment? Perhaps of the sunny corner of the kitchen where Mama had her spice shelf and the pots of basil and parsley growing?

WORD BANK

tenement (TEH nuh munt) *n.*: a run-down and often overcrowded apartment house

But she would have to explain to Miss Lindstrom why she had drawn the inside of a house, instead of the whole house.

Maria had put off doing the assignment all week. Then last night, Friday night, she had opened her drawing pad on the kitchen table.

She had a new set of colored markers that Mama had bought her. She wanted to do a drawing with the markers.

She tried all the colors on the cover of the pad. Then she sat for a long time, staring at a clean sheet of drawing paper. Finally, she started to draw.

She drew a large white house with picture windows. The windows looked out over a wide lawn that sloped down to a pond.

Maria sketched in a winding driveway with birch trees on either side. To one side of the house, she drew a stone terrace and colored in some chairs, covered in a gay, striped cloth.

She wondered if she should put a car in the driveway. Or a station wagon.

No, she decided. Miss Lindstrom might have seen her getting off the Eastside bus in front of the museum.

At the far end of the driveway, Maria drew a figure of a girl on a bicycle.

Mama, who was ironing one of Maria's smocks, looked over at the drawing.

"Pretty," Mama nodded. "Like a picture in the magazines. But what are you drawing for the art class?"

"This is for class," Maria said.

"A *magazine* picture?" Mama said.

Mama had learned a lot about art, and she knew by now that art was not like a picture in a magazine. So when she asked about the house, Maria could not lie to her.

"We have to draw a house this week," she said.

"Just a house," Mama said. "Any house? Just a plain house?"

Maria did not answer for a minute. Then she told Mama, "It's supposed to be a picture of the house where we live."

"Oh," Mama said. She looked at Maria's picture again.

"Our house?" she said.

"No," Maria said. "I can't draw our house."

"Can't *draw* it?" Mama said. "Before you ever went to art class, you could draw a whole block of houses burning down and five fire engines and ten cops and a hundred people in the picture. Now you can't draw one house?"

"That's not what I mean," Maria said.

Maria tried to explain to Mama that a three-room apartment on Market Street wasn't the same as a house. And so to do the assignment, she would have to imagine a house.

"But a three-room apartment is *in* a house," Mama said. "So it's a big house. Apartment house. Your teacher means draw where you live."

Maria jabbed a pencil into the kitchen table.

"Oh, Mama!" she said. "This house is no good to draw. How can I make a beautiful picture of this house? I was trying to make a beautiful picture."

Mama looked down at the house Maria had drawn and shook her head.

"It's nice art should be beautiful," Mama said. "But it should also be true. Your teacher asks you to draw what you know."

Maria did not say anything. What was wrong with using her imagination? An artist should be able to imagine things, too.

But the picture did look like a magazine picture. Mama was right about that.

Maria tore the picture from her drawing pad and slipped it into her portfolio. She started another drawing.

She sketched in the outline of the house she lived in. With angry slashes of a marker, she drew the rusted fire escape zigzagging down the front of the building. She drew the sagging window frames and the crumbling cement steps leading up to the front door.

There were the broken windows in Mrs. Sedita's apartment on the ground floor. The landlord had refused to fix them, and Mrs. Sedita had had cardboard tacked over the missing panes for a year.

On the windowsill outside the Durkins' apartment, Maria drew three milk cartons. The power company kept turning off the Durkins' electricity, and Mrs. Durkin had to put her milk on the windowsill to keep it cool.

Maria drew Mrs. Katz leaning out of a third-floor window, screaming at a bum slumped on the steps below.

Then she took a marker and lettered on the front of the building the words some kids had painted there in a nasty green color a long time ago.

She was drawing very fast. Putting in all the things that made the building look so sad, old, tired, dirty, and ugly. Mama would see that she could not take a picture like this to Miss Lindstrom.

Maria paused and looked at her drawing.

It was 79 Market Street all right. And she hadn't had to go out and look at the building. She knew exactly how it looked.

Except that she had forgotten to put in the carved stone heads. They were the only thing she really liked about the building.

Between the first and second floors, just above the first-floor windows, were four carved stone heads. When the building was built, eighty or ninety years ago, the four stone heads had been set into the brickwork to decorate the building.

Under the heads were four names carved into the stone bases: BACH,[1] MOZART,[2] BEETHOVEN,[3] and WAGNER.[4] Mr. Bocci,[5] the super,[6] had told Maria that they were the names of four famous musicians.

"This was probably some fancy building when it was built," Mr. Bocci said.

If the man who built it could see it now, Maria thought as she chose a gray marker and carefully drew in the stone heads.

She knew the exact expression on each musician's face, and how each musician's hair was carved. She was just finishing Bach's funny little sausage curls when Mama came over to look.

Mama studied the picture for a long time.

"It's true," she said finally. "It's Market Street."

Mama sighed. "You take to art class?"

"Mama! I can't."

---

1. *Bach* (BAHKH)
2. *Mozart* (MOE tzart)
3. *Beethoven* (BAY toe ven)
4. *Wagner* (VAHG ner)
5. *Bocci* (BAHCH ee)
6. *Super* is short for superintendent, a building manager.

It *was* true. It *was* Market Street. And Maria was afraid she was going to cry.

She ripped the picture off her pad and stuffed it into her portfolio. She put away her markers and pencils, washed, and went to bed.

Maria heard Mama come into her room much later to hang a freshly ironed smock in her closet. Mama stood at the foot of her bed for a minute, as if she wanted to say something. But Maria pretended to be asleep.

What difference would it make which drawing she showed Miss Lindstrom? Miss Lindstrom would not know that the first drawing was an imaginary house. Only Mama knew.

Only Mama. Mama, who never complained about the hours she spent ironing for the Overnite Laundry. Working sometimes until long after Papa and Maria were asleep.

But last night Maria had not been able to sleep. Even so, morning had come too fast. And now she lay in bed listening to the Sanitation Department throwing the garbage cans down on the sidewalk, and could not make herself get up.

Maria heard Mama calling her for the second time.

No, she could not tell Mama she was sick.

Maria dressed, braided her hair, and put on her yellow smock.

When Mama said, "Pretty," as Maria came into the kitchen, Maria could not look Mama in the eye.

Mama did not say much at breakfast. And when she took down the brown teapot and fished out the three quarters, Maria wanted to say, "Please, Mama, try to understand."

But she couldn't say it. And when Mama went to wake up Papa, Maria knew what she had to do.

She opened up her portfolio and took out the drawing of the white house with the picture windows. She looked at the drawing for a minute. Then she tore it up and put it in the garbage can.

Mama must have known. She nodded her head in a proud stern way as Maria went out the door.

Maria felt better as she walked to the bus stop. But once on the bus, she began to think about Miss Lindstrom again, and wished she had stayed home.

She hunched down in her seat and stared out the window. The city streets flashed by in the crazy way they do in a dream that is going too fast and is going to end in a terrible way. And suddenly the bus was at the museum.

Maria walked quickly through the big entrance room. Usually, she walked very slowly through this room. She loved its high ceilings and the sunlight slanting down through windows placed high on the outside walls. The sound of her footsteps echoing from the stone walls and the serious faces of the six lions who guarded the hallway that led to the art class made Maria feel as if she were a distinguished person arriving at a great palace for an important occasion.

But this morning Maria hurried past the lions without a glance.

Most of the kids in the class were already at their easels when Maria came in, and were pinning up the drawings they had done during the week.

If only she'd come a few minutes earlier, Maria thought, she might have gone up and explained quietly to Miss Lindstrom that she'd forgotten to bring her drawing. Had forgotten to do the assignment even.

Coming in late, though, Maria felt as if everyone was watching her. Quickly, she opened up her portfolio and took out her drawing.

Her hands were clumsy as she tacked the drawing to her easel, afraid someone might laugh. But no one did.

Glancing over her shoulder, Maria saw that the other students were looking at their own work, some of them adding a few lines to their pictures. Or trying to smudge out bits they didn't like.

Miss Lindstrom was already walking around, looking at what everyone had done. At one easel, she would nod and smile. At another, she would ask a question. Now and then she would call the whole class to look at something unusual in someone's drawing.

Maria trailed behind the others, hardly hearing what the silvery voice was saying.

Most of the drawings on the easels were of houses with yards and trees as Maria had expected. But many of the houses pictured were less grand than she'd imagined. None as grand as the one she'd wanted to draw for Miss Lindstrom.

And there was one picture that surprised Maria because the house in it looked quite old and shabby. The house was set in a big yard and had a funny tower on one side, which perhaps had made it look very handsome at one time. But the house looked now as if it needed painting, and there was one very messy-looking corner of the yard with a lot of boards and boxes scattered around.

A redheaded boy named Jasper had painted the picture. Jasper pointed to the house in the painting.

"This is where I live," he told Miss Lindstrom. "But over here is where I'm *going* to live." He pointed to the boards and boxes.

"That's the most important part of the picture," he explained. "I'm building my own house out here. I'm designing it myself, and it's going to be really beautiful."

Miss Lindstrom laughed. "Is it going to have a tower?"

"Certainly not," Jasper said. "It's going to be a very modern house. With see-through walls that you can walk through to get outdoors."

The whole class laughed, and then Miss Lindstrom talked a little about how it was clear from the way Jasper had placed the house off to one side in the picture that the messy pile of boards *was* the most important part of the picture.

There was always something funny in Jasper's paintings, a kind of crazy way of looking at things. But Miss Lindstrom seemed to like Jasper's work.

Maria was puzzling over this when Miss Lindstrom moved over to her easel. Maria's hands felt cold. Her mouth felt dry. She wanted to run down the hall to the washroom and hide. But she just stood there by Jasper's easel, watching Miss Lindstrom.

Maria caught the brief look of surprise on Miss Lindstrom's face and wished she could sink through the floor.

Miss Lindstrom did not say anything for a minute. Then she looked around for Maria.

"Maria," she called. "Come." She put an arm around Maria's shoulder.

"Everyone come here," she called.

The rest of the class crowded around Maria's easel.

"Maria didn't quite understand the assignment," Miss Lindstrom was saying. "But it doesn't matter. Look what she's done."

Miss Lindstrom stepped back so that everyone could see.

"I'd meant for you to draw your own house," Miss Lindstrom said to Maria. "But what you've done is very interesting."

Miss Lindstrom asked the class whether any of them had ever driven through Carpenter Street, Market Street, or Water Street—the old part of town down near the river.

"I have," Jasper said. "My uncle goes there to buy fish."

"If any of you have," Miss Lindstrom said, "you will see how perfectly Maria has caught the feeling of the crowded tenements in that part of town.

"Look." Miss Lindstrom bent over Maria's drawing. "See here," she said, "—and here—and here—" The art teacher's beautiful hands touched the paper lightly.

"So many beautiful things," she said.

Miss Lindstrom pointed to Mrs. Katz's laundry strung across the fire escape on the third floor. To the cats fighting over a spilled garbage can in front of the house. To a tired figure leaning on a windowsill. To the milk cartons on another sill.

"I can almost hear the kids yelling in the street," Miss Lindstrom said. "I can hear people yelling, laughing, and crying inside the apartments. I can smell spaghetti cooking. And chicken soup."

"Not me," Jasper said. "I smell fish."

Miss Lindstrom laughed. "You're right, Jasper. I can smell that, too. There's so much going on in this house."

"And these heads," she said. "Look at these. When this building was built years ago, someone lovingly carved those heads, and Maria has drawn them so lovingly that you can feel the care the stonecutter took in carving them."

"Hey, that's Beethoven!" Jasper said, pointing to one of the heads.

"How did you know?" Maria asked in surprise. Because she had not put the musicians' names under the heads.

"I saw his picture in a book once," Jasper said.

Miss Lindstrom asked the class if they knew that there was an exhibition of carved stone heads, like those in Maria's drawing, on the top floor of the museum. They were taken from old buildings in the city, before the buildings were torn down, she said.

Maria looked at her drawing. Would Bach, Mozart, Beethoven, and Wagner be in the museum someday? She tried to imagine their faces looking down on museum visitors instead of her friends on Market Street.

Miss Lindstrom was talking to the class again.

"Does everyone see what is so good about Maria's drawing?" she asked.

"All those little details," one girl said. "The heads, the cats, the milk cartons, and the writing on the front of the building."

"No," another girl said. "All those bits are nice. Maria can draw anything. But what's really good is that her picture isn't just a picture of a building. You feel as if you know the people who live in it."

"Yes," Miss Lindstrom said. "That's it. It's a beautiful drawing, Maria. Full of life and feeling. The nicest thing you've done this year." She gave Maria a hug and moved on to another easel.

Maria stood staring at her picture.

Miss Lindstrom had hugged her and told her that her picture was beautiful. But it wasn't Miss Lindstrom with her spun-gold hair that Maria was seeing as she stared at her picture.

She was seeing Mama. Mama standing dark and stern over the ironing board. Mama saying stubbornly, "Art must be true." Mama standing and nodding gravely as Maria would tell her what Miss Lindstrom had said about her drawing today...

Then Maria heard Miss Lindstrom say her name again.

"Maria's picture gave me an idea for next week's assignment," Miss Lindstrom was saying.

"Next week," she said, "I want each of you to visit a part of the city where you have never been before and to draw a picture of the houses there—or the stores—or the street.

"Except Maria," said Miss Lindstrom.

"Since you have already done that, Maria," she said, "maybe you would like to draw your own house next week."

Maria felt as if Mama's grave eyes were on her as she looked up at her art teacher and said in a clear, sure voice, "But that *is* my house in the picture."

ABOUT THE AUTHOR

Young **Jean Merrill** grew up in Webster, New York, along the shores of Lake Ontario. She loved the long afternoons spent reading outside so much that she decided to write some books of her own. Before she became an author, she worked for four years as an editor for Scholastic Magazines. Soon afterwards, she began to write children's books and stories. In 1952, Ms. Merrill traveled to India to study Indian folklore. She later wrote several books based on the folklore of China, Japan, India, and Burma (Myanmar). Other books written by Jean Merrill have a wide variety of subjects and settings. Jean Merrill currently lives in Vermont.

City I Love

Lee Bennett Hopkins

In the city
I live in—
city I love—
mornings wake
5   to
swishes, swashes,
sputters
of sweepers
swooshing litter
10 from gutters.

In the city
I live in—
city I love—
afternoons pulse
15 with
people hurrying,
scurrying—
races of faces
pacing to
20 must-get-there
places.

In the city
I live in—
city I love—
25 nights shimmer
with lights
competing
with stars
above
30 unknown heights.

In the city
I live in—
city I love—
as dreams
35 start to creep
my city
of senses
lulls
me
40 to
sleep.

Poetry shows us our world

Studying the Selection

FIRST IMPRESSIONS

Do you think that Maria's feelings about her family and her home changed by the end of the story?

QUICK REVIEW

1. How were Maria's Saturdays different from those of her friends?

2. Describe Maria's art teacher, Miss Lindstrom.

3. Why did Maria think that her building was not what Miss Lindstrom had had in mind when she asked her students to draw pictures of their houses?

4. What were some of the details Maria included in her drawing of the imaginary house?

FOCUS

5. Both Maria and Miss Lindstrom jumped to the wrong conclusions. What mistake did each one make about the other?

6. Choose one of the following activities:

   a. Compare and contrast Maria's first and second drawings and the way in which she drew them.

   b. Compare and contrast the inside and outside of Maria's building.

CREATING AND WRITING

7. Write about something that makes you proud of yourself or someone in your family.

8. Write a short story about an artist. The term "artist" includes a painter, a musician, a dancer, a weaver, a sculptor, a singer, or any other type of skilled or talented person. In your story, a problem arises that keeps the artist from completing a work of art. Describe the problem and how it is solved.

9. Draw a detailed picture of the home you live in as best as you can. Then, write a paragraph to explain what you like most about it. You may love some actual feature of the house, like a round window or big attic, or you may choose something that has meaning only to you, like the view from your bedroom window or the warm corner you like to curl up in.

5

unit

wrap-up

determination

ACTIVITY ONE

Draw a sample of a T-shirt that you are going to design. The T-shirt should have a saying or a slogan that expresses the theme of one of the stories in this unit. For example, if the theme you chose was kindness, you might use "Practice random acts of kindness," or "Actions speak louder than words." If the theme was having a positive attitude, you could use "Look for the silver lining." Make your sample creative and interesting.

Practice random acts of kindness

Underwater Rescue

The Seven Children

The Garden of Happiness

One Grain of Rice

Maria's House

ACTIVITY TWO

Each of the stories in this unit takes place in a different setting: underwater, a forest, an ancient Far Eastern country, and two New York neighborhoods. Imagine that these plots and settings were switched. How would the stories be affected? What if the seven children faced a test in the city of New York? Suppose The Garden of Happiness was in an ancient country of the Far East? Choose a plot from one story and the setting from another and put them together to create a new story. You may change details as needed. Read your story to the class and wait for the applause!

5

unit

ACTIVITY THREE

For this exercise, your teacher will divide the class into five groups and assign one of the stories in the unit to each group.

In all but one of the stories in this unit, the main character is a young person. In most of the stories the main character has a particular skill or talent. (In the case of the seven children, a few talents are described.) Imagine that the years have gone by and each of these main characters has grown up. Each one must open a business, using his or her special abilities. Decide what sort of business the main character of your story will open. Write a short description of the business on a piece of paper. Then, create a sign for your character's business. The sign may be a drawing or something crafted. Have one member of the group read the description of the business while other members of the group present the sign to the class.

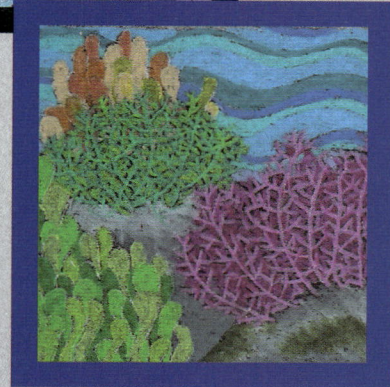

ACTIVITY FOUR

The theme of this unit is *determination*. Determination is a strong, unshakable will to reach a goal. Think about something that you are determined to do even if it requires a lot of hard work. Your goal may be something that is far in the future, such as becoming a doctor or a teacher, or something that can be achieved in the very near future, such as learning to ice skate. Write an essay that describes what you are determined to accomplish and what you will do to reach that goal.

unit 6

The Grand Finalé

Lesson in Literature ...

ELEMENTS OF FICTION

- **Plot** is the story line; when we ask what the story's plot is, we are asking, *what happened in the story*?
- **Characters** are the people in a story; when we discuss the characters in a story, we are talking about all *the people or animals in the story*.
- **Setting** is when and where the story takes place; when we ask what the story's setting is, we are asking *how we should picture the scene* in our imaginations.
- **Theme** is the idea that the story as a whole wishes to teach the reader; when we discuss the story's theme, we are talking about *the idea, message, or lesson* that the story gave us.

THINK ABOUT IT!

1. List all of the characters in the story. Include even those who are only mentioned.
2. Use five words or phrases to describe parts of the story's setting. For example, if the story took place in Alaska, you could use snow, ice, cold, white, and blue sky.
3. What message does the author wish to deliver to the reader?

My brother Mark and I love to swim in the ocean. We love wading into the surf and diving under the waves. We love swimming out as far as the breakers, but most of all we love body surfing in to the shore.

Every time we go swimming our mother warns us, "Don't swim beyond the ropes." It's what our father tells us, too. It's also what lifeguards yell whenever anyone swims near the ropes. There's even a sign next to the lifeguard stand that reads:

**NO SWIMMING ALLOWED
BEYOND THE ROPES**

My brother Mark loves swimming, but he also loves an adventure. So one day he asks our mother, "Why can't we swim beyond the ropes?"

"It's dangerous," our mother says sternly. "If there's an undertow, you could be carried out to sea just like that." Our mother snaps her fingers to show us how fast an ocean current could carry us out to sea if we got caught in an undertow.

The next day I decide not to go swimming. Instead I stay on the beach thinking about the undertow. Mark doesn't care, though, and dives in. Imagining he's an Olympic swimmer practicing the backstroke, he swims fast—not just toward the ropes but beyond them until he's headed directly toward some large rocks.

From the shore I yell, "Mark, watch out!" But he doesn't hear me. He's too far away.

"Help! That's my brother!" I yell, looking up at the lifeguard stand. I expect to see a lifeguard waving his arms and blowing a whistle, but the lifeguard isn't there.

Where is he?

BEYOND THE ROPES

I look around on the beach. No one else notices that Mark is in trouble.

I panic. What should I do? Should I run up the beach for help? Or should I swim beyond the ropes to save my brother?

I decide. Imagining the lifesaving tactics of a real lifeguard, I run into the surf and swim out. But as I approach the ropes, I stop and tread water. Ahead, my brother backstrokes off-course toward the dangerous rocks.

"Mark!" I yell.

I try for help. Waving my arms toward the shore, I catch the attention of a lifeguard jogging up the beach. Before long, two lifeguards with rescue equipment swim out to Mark.

Within minutes, they help him back within the ropes.

I'm waiting for him. "Are you okay?" I ask.

"I'm okay," he says, but in his eyes I see that he's scared and grateful I'm there.

As we swim in together, he tells me he can't believe he didn't listen and swam beyond the ropes. "It's dangerous," he says. "I learned a lesson."

I learned a lesson, too. I would have crossed the ropes to rescue my brother, but first I looked for help and found it just in time, and I was there to swim back to shore with my brother. The ropes taught both of us big lessons.

Blueprint for Reading

INTO . . . *The Bridge Dancers*

Most of us have a picture in our minds of the kind of person we would like to be. Perhaps we would like to be terrific at sports or good leaders. We might imagine ourselves as one day being friendlier or a little less loud than we are now. Having an ideal to work towards is a good thing. But sometimes, the person we would like to be is just too different from who we really are. It is important for us to have goals that can be reached with our *own* abilities—not someone else's. The narrator of *The Bridge Dancers*, Maisie, admires her daring older sister, Callie. As you read the story, you will find that all of your attention is drawn to Callie. But turn your thoughts to Maisie, and follow her progress. You will see how a young girl begins to discover and value her own strengths.

EYES ON *Realistic Fiction*

Fiction is literature that has imaginary plots and characters. **Realistic fiction** has real life problems; the events in the story did not happen, but they *could have* happened. The characters have realistic character traits and may even be based on real people. Many parts of realistic fiction may be true. For example, a story may include events that actually took place or characters who really lived, even though most of the story is invented. As you read *The Bridge Dancers*, think about what parts of it are fiction and what parts, if any, are true.

BY CAROL FISHER SALLER

MAMA GIVES THE COMB A YANK through the mess of Callie's long, wild hair, and Callie gives a yell like you've never heard before. That's not to say I've never heard it before; I've heard it plenty. Callie says when she grows up she's going to the city to live, where she'll start a new style. All the ladies will come to her and pay a lot of money to get their hair tangled up in knots, and she'll get rich and never comb her hair again.

I'm not a lot like Callie. My hair doesn't fly around much, and I like it combed, and I don't often think about leaving this mountain. Callie's going to be thirteen soon. I'm only eleven, and I've never even been across the bridge.

When Callie's all combed, we go down the path to the bridge. It's our favorite place to play when our chores are done. The dirt path is steep from our house down the twisty old hill. We like to run down fast, bouncing off the little trees in a crazy zigzag, but when we reach the edge of the gorge, the path levels off and we run alongside it. To folks way down below on the river we must look like two little pokeberries, up high on the mountain's edge.

What we call the bridge isn't the real bridge, where horses and buggies can get across, that's a few miles off along the path. Our bridge is just a shaky old skeleton, a tangle of ropes and boards that ripples and swings in the breeze. Our house is the closest one to this bridge. The next nearest is the Ketchums' place, another mile up the mountain. Most of our neighbors live across

WORD BANK

gorge (GORJ) *n.*: a small canyon through which a stream runs

the gorge; Mama says there are seven houses within the first half hour's walk. Mama often has to cross the bridge, but we're not allowed.

On this day, the wind is strong and the bridge is rocking like a boat in a storm. We make clover chains and toss them into the gorge, watching them blow away and then down, down. We count the seconds till they hit the water far below. Callie stays by the edge, but I spy some yellow-eyed daisies growing up the hill a ways, and I know Mama will want them. If you boil daisies—stalks, leaves, and all—it makes a tea that's good for coughs, or a lotion for bruises and sores. Mama doctors most of the folks on this mountain, and we always keep a store of dried plants for medicine. I pull the best ones and put them in my apron pocket.

Later, when the sun is behind the mountain and I'm getting cold and hungry, I start back up the path, but Callie doesn't want to go. "Maisie! I dare you to stand on the bridge!" she calls, just like she does every time we're here. I don't answer, but I stop and turn to look. She knows the thought of it scares me.

Now she skips up the hill a little ways and stands on her toes like a dancer, her skirt ballooning in the wind. In the gloomy light of sundown she is ghostlike and beautiful. "Announcing… Calpurnia the Great!" She twirls and leaps and strikes a pose with one toe pointed forward: "Calpurnia—the Daring Bridge Dancer!"

I laugh. I'm pretty sure she's only teasing. Callie dances toward the bridge, humming a tune that she imagines sounds like a circus. When she gets to the part of the bridge that sits on land, she holds on to one post and points her foot out toward the gorge, leaning back in a swoop. Then she grabs both posts and slides both feet out onto the bridge. She starts to slip, but before I can cry out, she turns back, laughing. My heart is jumping. I'm getting ready to run and pull her away from the bridge when she skips aside quick as lightning and starts chewing a piece of clover. In a second I see why.

Mama is huffing down the path. She's lugging her doctoring bag and has to watch her step. If she'd seen Callie fooling around on the bridge we'd both have caught it. "Girls, I've got to attend

to Mrs. Gainie," Mama says, putting her bag down for a rest. "She thought the baby would come last night, but tonight's the full moon. It'll come tonight." She looks us over and frowns across the gorge. "I might be gone till sunup, so get yourselves some supper, and don't forget to bolt the door, you hear?" She points at some dark clouds moving fast across the sky. "Hurry on up. I've already made a fire—there's a storm blowing." We nod. She starts for the bridge.

"Mama?" I call, and she stops and turns. "Is Mrs. Gainie going to be all right?" Mama nods. "She's a strong woman." She reaches for the bridge rail with one hand.

"Wait!" I call.

Mama stops again. "What is it, Maisie?"

"Have you got the tansy I picked?" I ask. Tansy is supposed to help a baby come, but if it doesn't do that, at least it keeps the bugs away.

Mama says, "I've got it, but I don't expect to need it this time." She smiles at me. "I'll mind my steps on the bridge, Maisie." Mama knows I'm afraid.

When Mama crosses the bridge, I never let go of her with my eyes. She's a big, heavy woman, and when she steps off the land part, the whole bridge from one side to the other dips into a sharp V with Mama at the bottom point. She goes slow, holding the ropes with one hand and her bag with the other, and she walks in a careful rhythm, giving the bridge time to bounce just right between steps. Callie says, "She won't fall if you look away," but I never look away. On the other side it's already dark, but we can just see Mama turn and wave. We wave back, and Mama disappears around the side of the mountain down the path to the Gainies'.

"Come on, Callie," I say, starting up the path. I know that there's supper to get and more wood to gather and plenty else to do. But Callie isn't of a mind to work. She throws her blade of grass to the wind and runs ahead of

me, her arms flung wide. "Burst into jubilant song!" she cries. "The everlasting chains are loosed and we are free!" Callie gets a lot of big words from reading the Bible. "Let us soar into the heavens, never to be enchained again!"

With that, she scampers off the path into the brush, and is soon just a flutter of white in the dusk, dancing and dodging among the trees. I feel the first drops of rain, and in a moment Callie is back.

"Maisie, I know what let's do," she says, blocking the path. She has to raise her voice now against the wind.

"What?" I ask with a frown. Callie's smile looks like it's hiding a bad idea, and I'm not sure I want to know.

"Let's get the ax and split a log for the fire," she says, wrapping her skirt around her and skipping along beside me. "There's a big storm. Let's have a fire that will last us all night."

I'm not sure. A fire would be good on a cold, stormy night, and I know there's only kindling left in the box. But Mama's the one who chops the wood. She takes down that big old ax from its pegs high on the wall and tells us to stand away. She's never told us not to touch it, but I have a feeling that we're not supposed to. I shake my head. "Callie, I don't hardly think you could even lift that ax. You're likely to get yourself killed." But my words blow away with the wind, and Callie is already halfway up to the house. I start to run, too, but I've never yet stopped Callie from doing what she wants to do. I figure the best I can do is be there when she needs help.

When I get to the door, Callie has the lantern lit and is dragging the rocking chair over to the wall. "Don't stand on that—it's too tottery!" I cry, and I run to hold the rocker while Callie climbs up and waits for the wobbling to stop. When the chair is still, she reaches up both hands to lift the ax from its pegs. It's heavy, all right; I can see by the way Callie's muscles stand out on her arms. Just when she's got it lifted off the pegs, the wind blows the door shut with a powerful "bang!" and we both jump in fright. The rocker pitches, and Callie falls.

WORD BANK
jubilant (JOO bih lunt) *adj.*: full of joy
soar (SORE) *v.*: fly high into the air
pitches *v.*: falls sharply

For a long moment it seems like nothing happens. My thoughts stop; even my heart seems to stop. Then Callie is crying out with pain and fear. It's her leg, cut deep by the ax. She clutches hold of my arm, tight, and gasps with the force of the pain. "Maisie, hurry and get Mama!" she whispers. "Callie…" I start to say, thinking about the wind, the dark, the bridge. Callie sees how I don't want to go, and she looks at me, begging with her eyes. "Maisie, I'm sorry—but you've got to go! You're the only one who can help me!"

I don't want to think about what Callie is saying. Instead I grab one of the clean cloths Mama uses for straining her herb medicines, and with shaky fingers, tie it right around Callie's leg. I take a quilt from the bed and put it over her, then run to the kindling pile and throw an armload of sticks on the fire. Callie is crying; the wind is crying. I light another lantern and wonder how I can cross the bridge, in the night, in the storm.

Outside, the wind and trees are whipping at the sky. I hold my skirt in one hand, the lantern in the other, and stumble in the quivery light down the path to the bridge. With my whole heart I wish there was some other way to fetch Mama. I think of Mama with her jars and packets, her sure hands and her healing ways. She'll stop the bleeding with a poultice of yarrow;[1] she'll make an herb tea that will

---

1. *Yarrow* is a plant with fernlike leaves and yellow or white flowers.

WORD BANK

quivery (KWIH vuh ree) *adj.*: shaky
poultice (POLE tiss) *n.*: a small moist bandage of cloth or herbs

help Callie sleep. But Mama is far across the valley—how will I ever cross that bridge… Near the bottom of the hill, I can hear it before I see it, ropes groaning and boards creaking, as it tosses in the storm.

I stand at the edge of the gorge, my lantern lighting the first few steps of the rain-slicked bridge. The fear in me is so powerful it stings my eyes, and I know I don't have the courage for even the first step. But I remember what Callie said—"Maisie, you're the only one who can help me"—and I step onto the bridge with both feet.

The bridge pitches and plunges. I grab for the ropes, and the lantern flies from my hands. "No!" I shriek, as it rolls away and drops into the darkness. On my hands and knees, I crawl back to the edge of the gorge, sobbing in the terrible black night, crying for Callie, crying for Mama. How can I cross the bridge…how can I help Callie…think what to do, Maisie, think what to do. With my face near the ground, I make myself take slow breaths. I can smell clover, damp with rain.

Suddenly, I know what to do. I pick myself up and start back up the path, feeling my way in the darkness, guided by the small light in the house at the top of the hill. I remember all the times I've watched Mama with her bag, with her poke leaves for burns, her chickweed for tummyache. It's the yarrow plant that stops someone bleeding, and I can make the poultice myself. Near the top I begin to run.

WORD BANK

plunges (PLUNJ iz) *v*.: falls down suddenly

When I burst in through the door, I see that Callie's face is pale. "Maisie—Mama!" she says, weakly. "There, Callie, don't fret; it's going to be fine," I comfort her. "I know what to do. Mama will come later, but I know just what to do."

My hands shake a little as I set the kettle on to boil—the fire is still burning strong. Then I go to Mama's cupboard of crushed and dried plants. I find some yarrow and wrap it in a clean muslin cloth to make the poultice. My fingers are sure now—Mama does it exactly so. Then I take a handful of dried feverfew and put it in a pot, for tea. Callie is moaning, so I sit by her and talk. "Yarrow is just the thing—and I remember I picked this myself! It has such pretty little flowers, and so many funny names: thousand-leaf, angel flower, bunch-a-daisies, sneezewort. It won't take but a minute, once that water's boiled. Don't you worry, Callie. Maisie can take care of you."

When the water is boiling, I pour some into the teapot with the feverfew and put it near the window to cool. Then I put the wrapped-up yarrow into the kettle and put the kettle back on the fire—not too long, just long enough for the water to soak in and soften the yarrow. Then I scoop out the poultice with a ladle, and after a minute, while it's still hot, I put it carefully on Callie's leg. I know it will hurt, so I keep talking. "Listen to that rain! It's really starting to pour now. You know, this is a pretty bad cut, Callie, and it hasn't stopped bleeding yet. The poultice will stop it. Can you smell how sweet?" But Callie yells when the poultice touches her leg.

When the tea is cool, I pour some into a cup, and hold up Callie's head for her to drink. "That's good," I tell her. "This will ease the pain. Maybe you can sleep a little; sleep till Mama comes." I rest her head in my lap, leaning my back against the wall. Rain thrashes the roof as I stroke her hair, all tangled and wild. I talk on and on, about ox-eye daisies and Queen Anne's lace, chickweed and tansy, the names like song words, lulling her to sleep at last.

WORD BANK
thrashes *v.*: beats against
lulling (LULL ing) *v.*: putting to sleep by quiet, soothing means

When Mama came home early the next morning, she found us sleeping on the floor. She unwrapped the cloths and washed out the cut—Callie hollered like anything—and said I'd done just what she'd have done herself. She never scolded about the ax—she knew there was no need—but she did ask why I hadn't come to fetch her. I was ashamed, telling Mama how I'd been too afraid to cross the bridge. "You've got good sense, Maisie," she answered. "I guess there's more than one way to cross a bridge."

It's been three months since Callie was hurt, and she's healed as much as she ever will. There's a fearsome scar on her leg, but Callie says that when she goes to live in the city she'll wear long pants like the men and no one will ever know.

Ever since I took care of Callie, Mama has let me help her with the doctoring. From the time I was little, I've helped her find and dry the flowers, but now I go along and watch when she tends to sick folks. When Callie talks about the city, I sometimes think I might visit her there. But for me, I think the mountain will always be my home. I like the way the mountain needs Mama. Someday I think it's going to need me, too.

ABOUT THE AUTHOR

Carol Fisher Saller has written several books for children, including biographies of Florence Kelley and George Washington Carver and a book about working children. She lives in Chicago near Lake Michigan and works as a manuscript editor at the University of Chicago Press.

In her spare time, Ms. Saller sings with a barbershop quartet, tends her small garden, and skates along the lake.

Studying the Selection

QUICK REVIEW

1. Why does Maisie say that their bridge is not a real bridge?
2. Why did Mama frequently cross the bridge?
3. What always made Maisie fearful?
4. What caused Callie's accident?

FOCUS

5. What was the meaning of Mama's words, "I guess there's more than one way to cross a bridge"?
6. What parts of the story's plot and characterization are realistic?

CREATING AND WRITING

7. Each person has different talents and skills. Write about one or more things that you feel you are very good at and what you can do with that talent.
8. Write about a situation where an individual 'crossed a bridge.' They were able to overcome a fear, learn something about themselves, and change for the better.
9. The class will be divided into groups of three or four. Each group will make a model of a bridge out of string, Popsicle sticks, toothpicks, and glue. Before you begin, draw a plan of the bridge on paper, showing where everything goes.

Lesson in Literature...

ELEMENTS OF NONFICTION

- Nonfiction comes in as many forms as fiction does. It may take the form of a story, a drama, a poem, or an essay.
- A nonfiction piece has the same literary elements as a fiction piece. For example, a nonfiction story, like a fiction story, will have plot, characters, setting, and theme.
- Although we usually think of nonfiction as being written to inform us, it can be written simply to entertain us.
- The real world is so full of fascinating things that people will often remark, after reading a true story, that it is *stranger than fiction*!

THINK ABOUT IT!

1. In one sentence, state the topic of this nonfiction essay.
2. The essay is informative and presents a lot of information. What fact in the essay was new to you?
3. Choose one of the types of storm described in the essay. Imagine that you wanted to write a story with that type of storm as its setting. Use the descriptions in this essay to help you write three opening sentences for your story. If you like, you can even place a character or two in your setting.

The sky grows dark. Rain falls. Wind blows. Lightning strikes. Thunder cracks. What is the weather forecast? Is it a thunderstorm? Or is it a hurricane? Is it a typhoon or a cyclone? Or is it a tornado?

Every summer, weather reports in many parts of the country include a forecast for a severe storm. Usually, in the summer, if a storm is in the forecast, it's a summer thunderstorm. A summer thunderstorm can be identified by a dark sky, heavy rain, flashes of lightning, and the sound of distant thunder. If the forecast is for a summer thunderstorm, everyone knows the first thing to do is to find the nearest shelter from the lightning and rain.

Sometimes, though, the forecast is for a much more severe storm called a hurricane. Hurricanes can be identified by very heavy rain and powerful winds that rotate in a counterclockwise direction. Most hurricanes begin as storms in tropical oceans and stay over the sea, but, occasionally, hurricanes do come ashore. Because of its flooding rains and whirling winds, a hurricane is capable of causing serious damage to life and property.

News of the sighting of a hurricane is not a cause for alarm, but a cause for preparation. Meteorologists keep track of the movement of a hurricane and inform people of its exact location, path, and intensity. They issue a "hurricane watch" if a hurricane is possible and a "hurricane warning" if a hurricane is expected. The National Hurricane Center offers safety instructions for people to follow during a hurricane, including staying informed of the latest news, knowing evacuation routes

IS IT A HURRICANE?

and sites of shelters, checking emergency equipment, stocking up on supplies and food, and either finding shelter in a basement or interior closet or obeying orders for evacuation. A severe hurricane can be destructive, but people can safeguard themselves and their property by taking safety measures.

Once people know about hurricanes, they also know about typhoons and cyclones, because the three names are different labels for the same storm. If a storm begins over the North Atlantic Ocean, the Caribbean Sea, the Gulf of Mexico, or the Northeast Pacific Ocean, it is called a hurricane. If it occurs in the Northwest Pacific Ocean, it is called a typhoon. If it forms near Australia and in the Indian Ocean, it is referred to as a cyclone. A tornado, though, is not the same storm as a hurricane, typhoon, or cyclone. Instead of beginning over a tropical ocean, a tornado begins over dry land and can be identified by its rotating, funnel-shaped cloud of winds. Like a hurricane, typhoon, or cyclone, a tornado can cause serious damage, so everyone must be knowledgeable about and prepared for all kinds of severe storms. So, is there a severe storm in the forecast? Is it a thunderstorm? Or is it a hurricane or a tornado? Now you know more about what's on the horizon.

Blueprint for Reading

INTO . . . *Dancing Bees*

"Dancing Bees? I've heard of stinging bees, buzzing bees, honey bees, and truthfully, I wouldn't mind skipping bees altogether—but dancing bees?" you may ask. Well, here's a question for you: Have you ever taken a good look at a bee? Have you watched a group of bees in motion? You probably haven't. But if you were a scientist, that's just what you would have done. Part of science is *observing*— that is, watching carefully and noticing small details. As you read this selection, you will be amazed at what people can learn if they have the time and patience to watch and wait, and watch and learn.

EYES ON *Nonfiction*

Who doesn't like a story? Whether it is true or imaginary, most of us can't resist anything that starts out "did you ever hear the story about…" Yet, a lot of what we read is *informative nonfiction*. **Informative** means it gives information. **Nonfiction** means it is true. Articles about health, science, and other topics are interesting even though they are not stories. In school, your history and science textbooks are filled with informative, nonfiction writing. What people find difficult about reading informative writing is that they often have trouble remembering a lot of new information.

What is the key to following and remembering the information in a nonfiction piece like *Dancing Bees*? The answer is a word called **association**. To associate one thing with another is to find a connection between the two. If you saw a tall man named Mr. Thomson and wanted to remember his name, you might think to yourself the **T**all man's name is Mr. **T**homson. You would associate the new information, Thomson, with something you already knew, that he is tall. When you learn about something new, try to connect it with something you already know. It will make it easier for you to understand it and to remember it.

Dancing Bees

from *Bees Dance and Whales Sing*
Margery Facklam

When a honeybee
discovers a rich supply
of nectar, it flies back
to the hive to tell the other bees
exactly where the food is. The bee even
tells them what kind it is, and how good it
is. How can an insect with a brain no bigger than a
grass seed describe all this information?

Dr. Karl von Frisch was the first person to find out.
He put a dot of red dye on a worker bee and watched
as she flew off and returned to the hive. (Worker bees are
always female.) As he watched thousands of bees, Dr. von
Frisch discovered how they sent their messages. They danced!
He called it the "waggle dance." The pattern of a bee's dance
is a figure eight. She repeats it over and over again as her
sister bees watch. The most important part of the dance is the
straight run through the middle of the figure eight. That shows
the direction from the hive to the food. If the bee is dancing outside
the hive on a flat surface, she lines up with the sun, then
turns to point toward the food. If the bee is inside, on

the wall of the dark hive, her head points up, as if the sun were overhead. Then she turns right or left to show where the food is.

As she runs through the figure eight, the bee waggles her head and tail from side to side. The farther away the food is, the faster she dances. Different kinds of bees have different waggle signals. For German honeybees, one waggle means the food is about fifty yards away. Italian bees, which are favored by beekeepers in the United States, use one waggle to mean about twenty-five yards.

As she dances, the bee's wings vibrate so fast that they buzz. The other worker bees touch the dancer with their antennae to feel the vibrations. They also sample a drop of the nectar she has found. In a few minutes, the first bees to figure out where the food is fly away. Then the others move up to touch the dancer bee, and they leave the hive as soon as they know the directions, too. Before each bee flies off, she lines up facing the sun and turns in the direction that the waggle dancer pointed.

The information given by a dancing bee is so accurate that scientists can follow the bee's directions and find the same flowers.

In 1988, a team of scientists from Denmark and Germany built a tiny electronic robot honeybee that was run by a computer. The robot bee was designed to "talk" to

a hive full of bees and give them instructions to fly to a specific spot. The robot doesn't look much like a real bee, but it doesn't have to, because a bee hive is dark. All the robot has to do is send signals the bees can understand—and offer a sample of the food.

Before the scientists could test the robot, they had to get real bees to taste the peppermint-scented sugar water they would use as bait. They put a dish of sugar water almost a mile away from a hive, and let a worker bee from that hive taste it. (They had marked the worker bee so they could recognize her.) When the worker bee flew back to the hive, she danced and gave samples of the food, and almost three hundred bees followed her instructions. They found the peppermint-scented sugar water a mile away.

The next step was to program the robot bee to dance the directions to the sugar water, which had been moved to a new spot. In the hive, the bees gathered around and paid attention to the robot bee. But could they follow the robot's directions? That was the big test. When the dancing robot bee buzzed and waggled and gave samples of the food (the scientists released a drop of the sugar water through a tiny brass tube above the robot's head), almost a hundred

bees found the sugar water. The robot wasn't quite as successful as the real bee—but the robot was obviously working.

Then they tried some other experiments. For example, when the robot gave samples but didn't dance, only ten bees found the food. When the robot danced but didn't give samples, or when it danced and gave samples but didn't whir its wings, very few bees found their way to the sugar water. Finally the scientists knew that the bees needed the whole message— the waggle dance, the whirring wings, and a taste of the food.

The keepers of the robot bee can hardly wait to find out what else it will tell them. They are ready for surprises.

About the Author

As a young girl, **Margery Facklam** spent every Saturday at the Buffalo Museum of Science in Buffalo, New York. During high school, she worked in the reptile house at the Buffalo Zoo. After graduating from college, she married and raised five children. When the youngest of her five children was grown, she went back to working with animals in a zoo. At the same time, she began to write books on scientific topics, sometimes with her husband, Howard Facklam, or her daughter, Margaret Thomas. Several of her books were illustrated by her son, Steven, making her writing career a real family affair!

Studying the Selection

FIRST IMPRESSIONS

Did you think that the robot bee would be able to mimic the real worker bee?

QUICK REVIEW

1. What does a bee do when it discovers a rich supply of nectar?

2. What discovery was made by Dr. Karl von Frisch?

3. What are some of the ways the worker bees communicate about food sources?

4. What did scientists create to help them learn more about honeybees?

FOCUS

5. Can you think of any way that the knowledge about the way bees communicate could be useful in today's world?

6. What are some things you can do to help you remember the facts you read in a nonfiction piece of writing?

CREATING AND WRITING

7. Choose two other things in nature that seem as amazing as the dance of the bees. Write a few sentences about each of your choices telling why you find it amazing.

8. Write a story about a worker bee's life from the bee's point of view. Include a small adventure on a trip to find nectar.

9. With a partner, choreograph (make up) a dance that has some sort of message. Write down the meaning of each move.

Lesson in Literature ...

ELEMENTS OF DRAMA

- Drama is *different* from all other literary genres in these two ways: it is written entirely as dialogue and is meant to be performed, not read silently.

- Drama is *similar* to fiction and nonfiction stories in every other way. It has plot, characters, setting, and theme.

- Drama can be written in prose or in poetry. It is sometimes written to music.

- A drama offers the viewer the ability to actually see the characters, hear the dialogue, and "live" in the setting.

THINK ABOUT IT!

1. List the characters in this drama. In one or two sentences, describe the setting.

2. What do the woman, man, and boy have in common? What do the old man and the girl have in common?

3. Do you think this drama would be more or less interesting if it were written as a story? Explain your answer.

Time: *Present*
Setting: *A Park Bench*

At Rise an OLD MAN sits alone on a park bench as pedestrians walk by. His wheelchair is just out of his reach.

OLD MAN (*To himself*): What a beautiful day to be alive!

A Woman enters. She is well-dressed and in a hurry.

WOMAN (*Upset*): Sir, where's the bus stop?

OLD MAN: Hello. It's a beautiful day to be in the park, isn't it?

WOMAN (*In a hurry*): You think so? Not for me. Is the bus stop around here or not?

OLD MAN (*Pointing*): Over there. But can you help me...?

Woman exits.
A Man enters. He is dressed in a business suit and in a hurry.

MAN: Hey, you, where's 41st and Vine?

OLD MAN: It's a beautiful day for a walk, isn't it?

MAN (*In a hurry*): Not for me. Do you know where it is or not? I'm late!

OLD MAN (*Pointing*): Two blocks north. But can you give me a hand...?

Man exits.
A Boy enters, running.

BOY (*Upset*): Hey, mister, have you seen my kite?

OLD MAN (*Smiling*): What a beautiful day to fly a kite!

BOY (*Ignoring OLD MAN*): Wait, I see it! Hey, somebody stole my kite! Hey, you, give me back my kite!

Boy exits, running.

OLD MAN (*To himself*): It's a beautiful day to be alive, but...

A BEAUTIFUL DAY

A Girl enters.

OLD MAN: Hello, little girl. It's a beautiful day, isn't it?

GIRL (*Upset*): It was.

OLD MAN: It was?

GIRL (*Sniffling*): Have you seen my dog? I took her for a walk in the park today because it's so beautiful, but she ran away. Can you help me find her?

OLD MAN: I can try.

GIRL: Thank you. I asked a woman, but she was in a hurry to catch a bus. I asked a man, but he was late for a meeting. I asked a boy with a kite but he ignored me.

OLD MAN (*Trying to stand up*): It's been the same with me. I've been sitting on this bench all afternoon and I can't get up. I tried asking for help but no one had the time. Can you help me?

GIRL: I can try.

OLD MAN: Can you reach my wheelchair for me?

GIRL: (*She moves his wheelchair closer and helps him.*) How's that?

OLD MAN (*Sitting in his wheelchair*): Thank you, young lady. You're the kindest person I've met in the park today. Now what does this dog look like?

GIRL (*Smiling*): She's small and black with brown paws and a white streak on her front. Her name is Roxy.

OLD MAN (*In a loud voice*): Roxy!

GIRL (*Pushing the OLD MAN in his wheelchair away from the bench*): Roxy! Roxy!

OLD MAN: Roxy! (*A dog barks offstage.*)

GIRL: It's Roxy!

OLD MAN (*To himself*): I just knew this would turn out to be a beautiful day. I just knew it.

THE END

Blueprint for Reading

INTO . . . *Name This American*

What makes someone famous? Think of the famous people you know. This may include a president, an inventor, an author—the list is long. Do famous people have anything in common? Yes. Each one has, in one way or another, given something to other people. One famous person may have been a great leader; another, a wonderful entertainer; yet another, an outstanding scientist.

Name This American is about five Americans who made important contributions to the people of their country. As you read, think of how these men and women left their mark on the United States of America.

EYES ON *Drama*

How is a play different from a written story? The main difference is a play is meant to be performed and a story is meant to be read. Because an audience will see and hear a performance, **dialogue**—what the actors are saying—is the most important part of a play. When we read, the story tells us what someone is thinking, what has happened in the past, or how things smell or feel. But when we watch a play, we must learn all those things by listening carefully to the dialogue. Yet, there are certain things that we learn more easily in a play than we do in a story. Can you name some of those things? What are they, and how does an audience learn them?

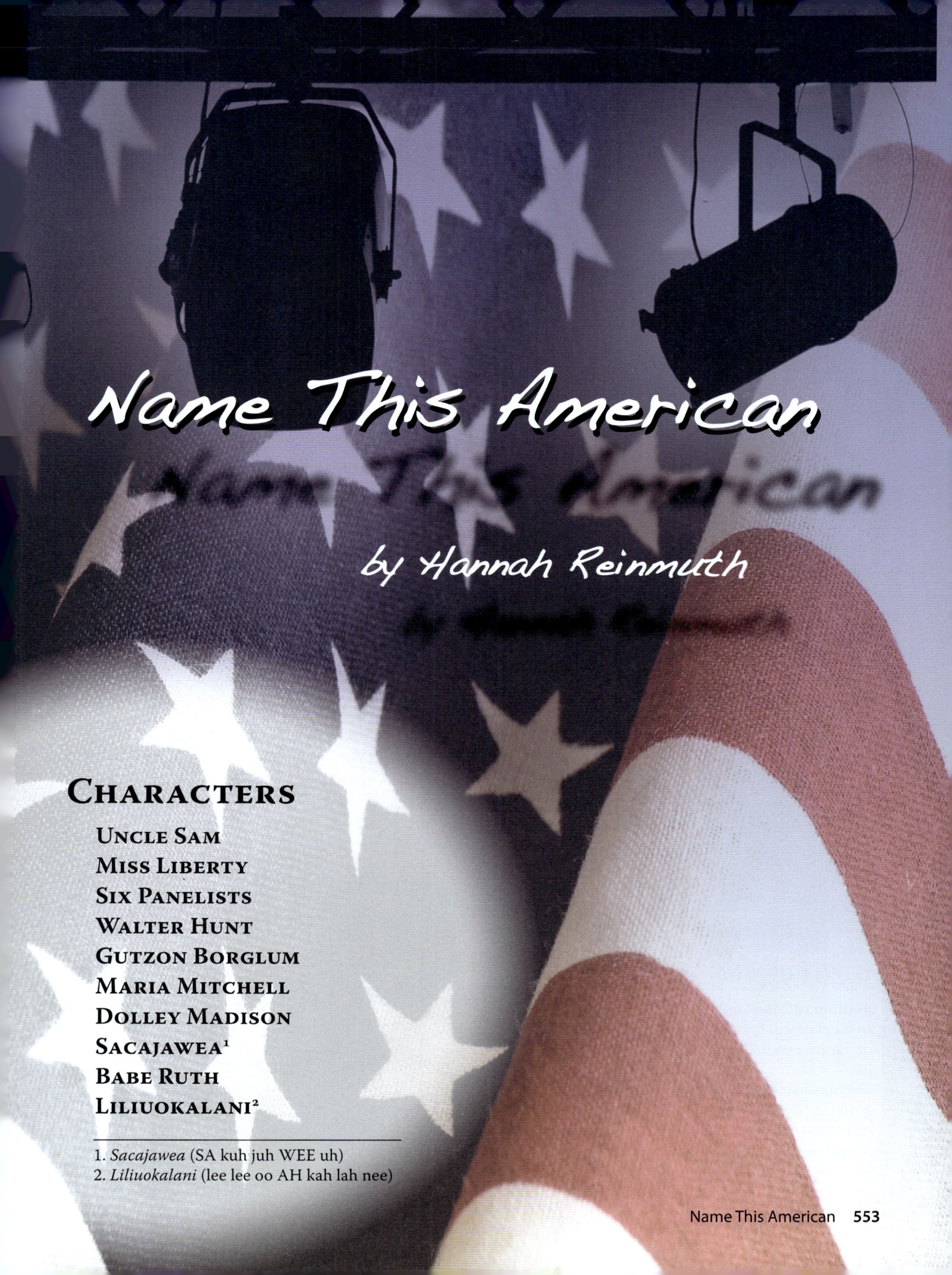

Name This American

by Hannah Reinmuth

CHARACTERS

UNCLE SAM
MISS LIBERTY
SIX PANELISTS
WALTER HUNT
GUTZON BORGLUM
MARIA MITCHELL
DOLLEY MADISON
SACAJAWEA[1]
BABE RUTH
LILIUOKALANI[2]

---

1. *Sacajawea* (SA kuh juh WEE uh)
2. *Liliuokalani* (lee lee oo AH kah lah nee)

Quiz Show
KEEPS PANELISTS GUESSING.

TIME: *Present.*

SETTING: *The stage of a quiz program. Podium is center. Next to it is music stand. Long table with blindfolds on it and six chairs are right. Desk and chair are left.*

AT RISE: SIX PANELISTS *are seated at long table.* UNCLE SAM *stands at podium.* MISS LIBERTY *stands behind music stand.*

UNCLE SAM: Good afternoon, everyone, and welcome to Name This American! We are honored to have as our guests a number of remarkable Americans. Some you may know, and some you may not know, but I guarantee you'll know them all by the time the show's over. To help us identify these special guests is our panel of distinguished scholars. Let's give them

WORD BANK

podium (PO dee um) *n.*: a small platform for a speaker, orchestra conductor, or the like
distinguished (dis TEENG wishd) *v.*: important and respected

all a hand. (*He and* LIBBY *clap.* PANELISTS *wave and smile.*) Now, my assistant, Miss Liberty, will explain how the game works. (*Gesturing*) Libby?

LIBBY: Thank you, Uncle Sam. The panel will question our guests and the guests will answer yes or no. If a question has a yes answer, the panelist may continue the questioning. If the answer is no, we move on to the next panelist, and the mystery guest receives $50. If our guest stumps all the panelists, he or she wins $500.

SAM: Thank you, Libby. Now, let's begin by bringing in our first guest. (LIBBY *beckons offstage and* WALTER HUNT *enters and sits at desk.*) Welcome to our show.

HUNT: Thank you.

SAM: Panelist number one, please begin the questioning.

1ST PANELIST: Are you famous?

HUNT: No, not really.

SAM: Mystery guest, you've already won $50. (LIBBY *puts $50 sign on stand. Throughout game,* LIBBY *props scores up on stand.*) Let's continue with the next panelist.

2ND PANELIST: Did you discover something?

HUNT: (*Giving* SAM *questioning look*): I suppose you could say so.

SAM: Actually, I'm afraid a yes would be misleading, so we will have to say no and move on to our third panelist.

3RD PANELIST: Let me see…Were you the first to do something?

HUNT: Yes.

3RD PANELIST: Did you, perhaps, invent something?

HUNT: Yes.

SAM: Now we're on the right track.

3RD PANELIST: Is it something you would find around the house?

WORD BANK

misleading (miss LEED ing) *adj.*: words or actions that lead people to believe something that is not true

HUNT: Yes.

3ʳᵈ PANELIST: Is it electrical?

HUNT: No.

SAM: That's another $50. Panelist four, your turn.

4ᵀᴴ PANELIST: Is it bigger than a bread box?

HUNT: No.

5ᵀᴴ PANELIST: Is it small enough to carry in your pocket?

HUNT: Yes.

5ᵀᴴ PANELIST: Is it a comb?

HUNT: No.

SAM: Panelist six, you're our last chance.

6ᵀᴴ PANELIST (*Pleased*): I think I've got it. Did you invent the pen?

HUNT: No, I did not.

SAM: Mystery guest, congratulations. You stumped our panel of experts. (*All applaud as* LIBBY *puts out the $500 card.*) We are all eager to hear about your invention. Please tell us who you are and what you invented.

HUNT: My name is Walter Hunt. Few people have heard of me, but everyone has used my invention. I am quite proud of my safety pin. (PANELISTS *express surprise.*) I had thought about it for a long time, but it took me only about three hours to make. I had it patented[3] in April, 1849.

---

3. When an inventor *patents* an invention, it means that, by law, no one else may manufacture or sell that invention for a certain number of years.

SAM: We are certainly honored to meet you, Mr. Hunt. Thank you for playing Name This American.

HUNT: Thank you. (*All applaud as he exits.* GUTZON BORGLUM *enters and sits.*)

SAM: Here's our next challenger, so let's begin.

1ST PANELIST: Are you not very well known?

BORGLUM: Yes, that's true. Few people know my name.

1ST PANELIST: Oh, another hard one! (*Thinks a moment*) Are you involved in the scientific field?

BORGLUM: No.

SAM: That's your first no, panel, and our guest's first $50. Next panelist.

2ND PANELIST: Are you an artist?

BORGLUM: Yes.

2ND PANELIST: Are you a painter?

BORGLUM: I've done some painting, but that's not what I'm known for.

SAM: We'll have to count that as a no and go on to the next panelist.

3rd Panelist: Are you a musician?

BORGLUM: No.

4TH PANELIST: An entertainer?

BORGLUM: No.

5TH PANELIST (*Thinking, at a loss*): Are you—a sculptor?

BORGLUM: Yes, I am.

5TH PANELIST (*Pleased*): Have I seen your work?

BORGLUM: I'm sure you have.

5TH PANELIST: Have you sculpted any of our presidents?

BORGLUM: Yes.

5TH PANELIST: Do you have any work displayed in Washington, D.C.?

BORGLUM: Yes.

5TH PANELIST (*Knowingly*): And at Mt. Rushmore?

BORGLUM: Yes.

5TH PANELIST: Then you must be Gutzon Borglum.

OTHER PANELISTS (*Ad lib; surprised, to* 5TH PANELIST): Who? I've never heard of him. (*Etc.*)

SAM: Yes, this is Gutzon Borglum, the artist who designed and carved Mt. Rushmore. Mr. Borglum, please tell us more about yourself.

BORGLUM: My full name is John Gutzon de la Mothe Borglum. I was born in 1867 in Idaho. In 1916, I completed plans to make a Confederate memorial on Stone Mountain near Atlanta, Georgia, but I had a disagreement with my sponsors and by the time it was settled, I had begun the Mt. Rushmore Memorial. I died before it was finished, so my son completed it.

SAM: We certainly admire your work. Now more of us will remember your name. Thank you for joining us.

BORGLUM: I enjoyed it. (*All applaud as he exits and* MARIA MITCHELL *enters, sits.*)

SAM (To MITCHELL): Welcome to Name This American. Are you ready to play?

MITCHELL (*Smiling*): I'm ready.

SAM: Panelist number one, begin.

1ST PANELIST: We've had an inventor and an artist. Could you be in politics?

MITCHELL: No. Politics never interested me.

2ND PANELIST: Were you involved in something related to science?

MITCHELL: Yes, I was.

2ND PANELIST: Are you in the field of medicine?

MITCHELL: No.

3RD PANELIST: Are you involved in the earth sciences?

MITCHELL: No.

4TH PANELIST: Astronomy.

MITCHELL: Yes.

4TH PANELIST: I can't think of any astronomers. (*Thinks a moment, then gets an idea*) Did you, by any chance, grow up on Nantucket Island, Massachusetts?

MITCHELL: Yes.

4TH PANELIST: Are you Maria Mitchell?

MITCHELL: Yes, I am. (*All applaud.*)

SAM: Congratulations, panel. Miss Mitchell, please tell us about your interest in astronomy.

MITCHELL: It was unusual for a woman in the mid 1800s to become an astronomer, but I was always interested in the stars—and in the sun, too. I did a lot of research on sun spots. (*Enthusiastically*) In 1847 I discovered a new comet, which was very exciting!

SAM: Thank you, Miss Mitchell. You were way ahead of your time. I'm sorry you didn't win more from our panel.

MITCHELL (*Rising*): I'm sorry, too.

(*All applaud. She exits as* DOLLEY MADISON *enters.*)

SAM: Welcome to Name This American.

MADISON: Thank you, Uncle Sam.

SAM: Panelist one, let's start right in.

1ST PANELIST: Your dress makes me think you may have lived about 200 years ago. Is that correct?

MADISON: Yes, that's correct.

1ST PANELIST: Were you involved in the Revolutionary War?

MADISON: I was very young, but yes, I remember it.

SAM: I'm afraid I must count that as a no, since she was only a child at the time.

2ND PANELIST: Were you a seamstress who worked on our first flag?

MADISON: No.

3RD PANELIST: Were you married to one of our presidents?

MADISON (*Smiling*): Yes, I was.

3RD PANELIST: Are you Martha Washington?

MADISON (*Slightly offended*): No, she was much older than I am.

4TH PANELIST: Are you Abigail Adams, the wife of the second president, John Adams?

MADISON: No.

5ᵀᴴ Panelist: Let's try the next president. Are you Mrs. Jefferson?

Madison: No.

6ᵀᴴ Panelist (*Embarrassed*): I can't remember who was the fourth president. Are you Mrs. Monroe?

Madison: No.

Sam: Too bad, panel. Our fourth president was James Madison. Let me present that famous first lady, Dolley Madison. (*All applaud.*) Tell us about yourself, Mrs. Madison.

Madison: I was born in North Carolina in 1768 but grew up in Virginia. My first husband, John Todd, was a lawyer. We had two sons, but one of them and my husband died in 1793. I met and married Congressman James Madison a year later and was thrilled to become the first lady in 1809. (*Enthusiastically*) I loved entertaining at the White House. One of my favorite days was when I introduced ice cream to my guests for the first time. What a party! (*More seriously*) I suppose my greatest accomplishment was during the War of 1812. I managed to save a lot of my husband's papers and a portrait of George Washington before the British burned down the White House.

Sam: Mrs. Madison, our country is indebted to you. Thank you for coming today.

Madison: It was my pleasure. (*All applaud as she exits.*)

Sam: Now, Libby, why don't you explain how the second part of our program works?

Libby: I'd be glad to, Uncle Sam. This is the time we ask our panelists to wear blindfolds, as we welcome special celebrities who would be too easy to identify by sight. (PANELISTS *put on blindfolds.*)

WORD BANK

indebted (in DET ed) *adj.*: owing; obligated to repay something
celebrities (suh LEB rih teez) *n.*: well-known or famous people

Courtesy of the Library of Congress.

SAM: Thank you, Libby. Panel, no peeking, and, audience, no hints. Blindfolds in place? (PANELISTS *nod*.) Then let's bring in our next guest. (LIBBY *motions offstage and* SACAJAWEA *enters*.) Welcome, mystery guest. Are you ready to play?

SACAJAWEA (*Sitting; in deep voice throughout following*): I'm ready.

1ST PANELIST: Are you from the 20th century?

SACAJAWEA: No.

2ND PANELIST: The 19th century?

SACAJAWEA: Yes and no.

SAM: Actually only part of this person's life took place in the 1800s.

2ND PANELIST: Then, I assume, the other part was in the 1700s?

SACAJAWEA: Yes.

2ND PANELIST: And with that voice, I assume you're a man.

SACAJAWEA (*In regular voice*): No, I'm not.

2ND PANELIST (*Surprised*): What? You tricked us.

SACAJAWEA (*Laughing*): I'm sorry. I really am a woman.

3RD PANELIST: If you lived around 1800, did you have anything to do with the westward movement?

SACAJAWEA: Yes.

3RD PANELIST: I can't think of any women of the West except Annie Oakley and Calamity Jane. Are you either of them?

SACAJAWEA: No.

4TH PANELIST: Did you move west with the settlers?

SACAJAWEA: No.

5TH PANELIST (*Thinking*): Were you an explorer?

SACAJAWEA: No.

6TH PANELIST (*Shaking head*): This is a hard one! (*Pause*) Did you help an explorer?

SACAJAWEA: Yes.

6TH PANELIST (*Pleased*): Oh good, now we're getting somewhere! (*Thoughtfully*) Are you an Indian?

SACAJAWEA: Yes.

6TH PANELIST: Are you Sacajawea?

SACAJAWEA: Yes.

SAM: Good work, panel. You may remove your blindfolds (*They do so.*) and take a look at the famous Indian guide for Lewis and Clark, Sacajawea. (*All applaud.*) Please tell us about yourself.

SACAJAWEA: My name, Sacajawea, means Bird Woman in Shoshone. I was captured by enemy Indians and sold to a French-Canadian trader. We joined Lewis and Clark's famous expedition to explore the Louisiana Territory in 1804. I helped as an interpreter with the local Indians and was their principal guide.

SAM: And they would not have made it without you. That's why a river, a mountain peak, and a mountain pass have been named after you, not to mention numerous monuments and memorials. (SACAJAWEA *smiles and nods modestly.*) Thank you for joining us today. (*All applaud, as* PANELISTS *put on blindfolds and* SACAJAWEA *exits.* BABE RUTH *enters.*)

SAM: Welcome, challenger. (BABE *sits.*) Let's begin.

1ST PANELIST: Are you in politics?

BABE: No, I am not a politician.

2ND PANELIST: Are you involved in sports in any way?

BABE: Yes.

2ND PANELIST: Is that sport football?

LEWIS AND CLARK TRAIL

BABE: No.

3ʀᴅ PANELIST: Is it basketball?

BABE: No.

4ᴛʜ PANELIST: What about baseball?

BABE: That's the one.

4ᴛʜ PANELIST: Two great players come to mind when I think of baseball, Babe Ruth and Lou Gehrig. Are you one of them?

BABE: Yes.

4ᴛʜ PANELIST: Well, I have a 50-50 chance. Are you Babe Ruth?

BABE: Yes. (*All applaud.* PANELISTS *remove blindfolds.*)

SAM: Good work, panel. Babe, tell us about some of the highlights of your amazing baseball career.

BABE: I love everything about the game. I set records both from the mound and at the plate. For years I held the record with my total of 714 career homeruns. And in 1936 I was among the first ballplayers elected to the Baseball Hall of Fame.

SAM: Thank you for being part of our show. (*Applause.* PANELISTS *restore blindfolds.* BABE *exits and* LILIUOKALANI *enters.*) It's time for our final contestant. (*To* LILIUOKALANI) Welcome. Are you ready? (*She nods, sits.*) I'm going to help you out, panel, by telling you this is a woman. Now you won't waste any questions on that, and I'm going to give her $50 to start with. (LIBBY *puts up $50 card.*) Panelist number six, let's begin with you.

6ᴛʜ PANELIST: Thank you. Mystery guest, do we need blindfolds because we would recognize your face or would the clothes you are wearing give you away?

LILIUOKALANI: Which question do you want me to answer?

6TH PANELIST: I'm sorry. Would your clothes give us a clue to your identity?

LILIUOKALANI: Yes, I'm sure they would.

6TH PANELIST: Would a man wear the same outfit?

LILIUOKALANI (*Giggling*): I certainly hope not.

5TH PANELIST: Are you an entertainer?

LILIUOKALANI: No.

4TH PANELIST: Let's get back to the clothes idea. Do they have anything to do with the part of the United States where you live?

LILIUOKALANI: Yes.

4TH PANELIST: Are you from the western part of our country?

LILIUOKALANI: Yes.

4TH PANELIST: The northwest?

LILIUOKALANI: No.

3RD PANELIST: Then it must be the southwest, maybe New Mexico, California, or Arizona.

LILIUOKALANI: No—farther southwest.

2ND PANELIST (*Knowingly*): Are you a famous Hawaiian?

LILIUOKALANI: Yes.

2ND PANELIST: Are you Queen Liliuokalani?

LILIUOKALANI: Yes, I am.

SAM: Good work, panel. (*Applause.* PANELISTS *remove blindfolds.*) Tell us a little about yourself.

LILIUOKALANI: As a child, I loved to write songs. When I got older I wrote the national anthem of Hawaii, but it was never as popular as my song "Aloha Oe." My older sister was supposed to be queen, but she married an American and decided to give up the throne. Then my brother became King Kalakaua. When he died in 1891, I became Queen Liliuokalani, ruling until 1893, when the United States took over. Hawaii became the 50th state in 1959.

SAM: And a beautiful state it is!

LILIUOKALANI (*Graciously*): It is only one of many.

SAM: Ladies and gentlemen, I'm afraid our time is up, but we are glad you could join us in honoring a few famous Americans. After all, it takes special people to make a great nation like ours. Before we go, we would like to bring out all our contestants. (*Everyone enters.*) Please join us in singing "This Land Is Your Land."

(*All sing. Curtain*)

THE END

Studying the Selection

QUICK REVIEW

1. What are three of the game show rules?
2. List three of the mystery guests and describe their accomplishments.
3. Which guests stumped the panelists completely?
4. Why did the panelists have to wear blindfolds for certain guests?

FOCUS

5. Do you think the game show format is a good way to learn history? Why or why not?
6. What is gained by presenting these historical personalities in a play?

CREATING AND WRITING

7. Write about a historical figure who either influenced your way of thinking or had an impact on your daily life.
8. Imagine being a panelist on a show like this one, twenty years from now. Who would be the mystery guest? What would the questions be like? Write about the experience.
9. Choose a famous individual. Do a bit of reading in an encyclopedia or other source if you are not familiar with that person's accomplishments. Then, using magazines, stickers, or other materials, cut out pictures or words that represent that person. Create a collage and present it to the class. See if your classmates can identify the famous person you have chosen based on what you have included in the collage.

Lesson in Literature . . .

FICTIONALIZED BIOGRAPHY

- Fictionalized biography is a story that is partly fiction and partly nonfiction.
- Usually, the setting and the main characters are true, while parts of the plot and some of the characters are fictional.
- When a character is a person who really existed, the character's lines in the story are supposed to express that person's ideas, even if the person did not ever speak those exact words.
- Fictionalized biography is an enjoyable way to learn about a famous person or a period of history.

THINK ABOUT IT!

1. Sometimes, an author of fictionalized biography will describe the setting of an event that actually happened. The author imagines what the weather, lighting, sounds, and so forth were like and "makes up" a setting. In two sentences, describe the setting of the accident between the car and the carriage that is described in the second paragraph.

2. Often, an author of fictionalized biography will invent the dialogue in an otherwise true story. Make up six lines of a dialogue that is held between Garrett Morgan and his brother when they hear about the explosion under Lake Erie.

3. In fictionalized biography, an author will often invent minor characters. Choose one of the scenes in the story and summarize what happened. Add a minor character to your summary. The minor character may be used to add a bit of humor, sadness, or history to the story.

It was a day like any other day for Garrett Morgan of Cleveland, Ohio. He had worked a full day, half in his sewing machine repair shop and half in his tailor shop. Driving home in his model-T car, he looked around as bicycles, horse-drawn carriages, and gas-powered automobiles passed him by on a busy street. This city, Garrett Morgan thought, is changing fast. Ever since Henry Ford's invention of the assembly line for making automobiles, Cleveland's streets had been busier than ever.

At the next intersection Garrett Morgan watched as an automobile

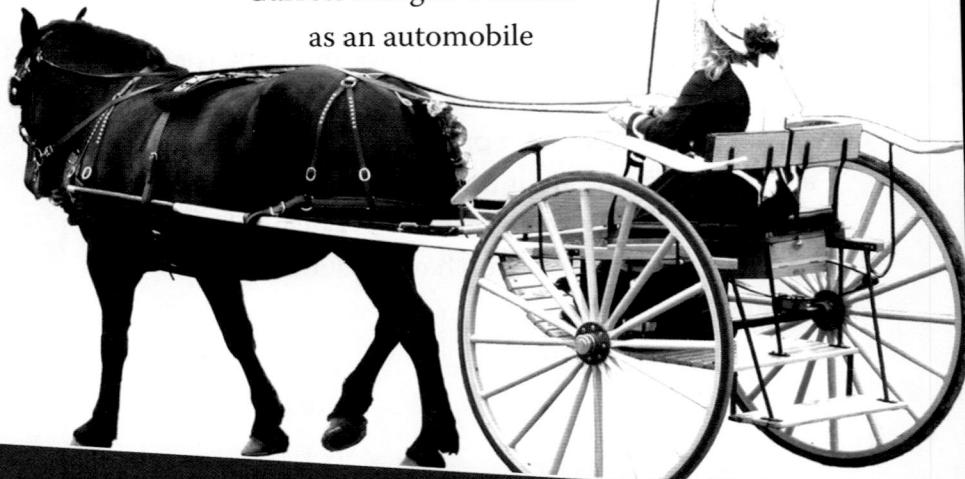

BEWARE OF HORSE DRAWN TRAFFIC

collided with a horse and carriage. Everyone stopped. A doctor in the crowd rushed to the aid of the automobile driver who had been knocked unconscious. Garrett Morgan found out later that the injured horse had to be destroyed.

He couldn't forget what he saw.

Ever since he was a boy on his parents' farm in Kentucky, he had been fascinated by the way things work. When he moved to Cincinnati as a teenager, he worked as a handyman fixing things. After he moved north to Cleveland in 1895, he went to work as a sewing machine repairman. In 1907 he opened his own sewing machine store, selling new machines and repairing old ones. In 1909 he expanded the business to include a tailoring shop that made coats, suits, and dresses using machines he designed.

But he didn't forget his love for invention. A few years before he witnessed the traffic accident, he invented a hood to be worn over a person's head with tubes for breathing in and out. He called it a safety hood, but it later came to be known as a gas mask.

On July, 25, 1916, his gas mask saved lives. After an explosion under Lake Erie filled a tunnel with smoke, dust, and poisonous gases and trapped thirty-two workers, Morgan, his brother,

and several other rescuers, wearing gas masks, went into the tunnel and saved the workers. After the rescue, Morgan became a national hero, and his company received requests from fire departments around the country who wished to purchase the new masks. The Morgan gas mask was later refined for use by the U.S. Army during World War I.

At home after the traffic accident, Garrett Morgan wondered if there wasn't a better design for the hand-operated traffic signals at intersections. What if, he wondered, he developed an automatic traffic signal with clear signs? He tinkered, but it didn't take long. The Morgan traffic signal was a T-shaped pole unit that featured three positions: Stop, Go, and an all-directional stop position. This third position halted traffic in all directions to allow pedestrians to cross streets more safely. Soon, because of Garrett Morgan's invention, the streets of Cleveland were safer for everyone.

The son of former slaves, Garrett Morgan also founded a newspaper known as the *Cleveland Call* (later the *Call and Post*), but he is most remembered as the inventor of the Morgan T-shaped traffic signal.

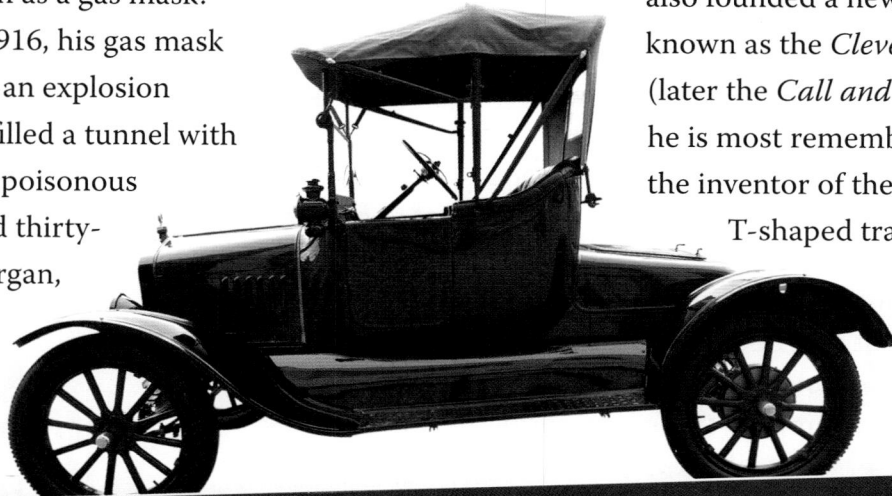

Blueprint for Reading

INTO . . . *Boss of the Plains*

Some people are good at many things. Others are good at only a few things. But being good at even one thing can bring surprising success. Are you a fast runner? Why feel bad that you weren't chosen for the school choir? You could probably be great at winning races. You would certainly be first choice for running to get help in an emergency! The secret to success is using your particular talent or skill to its utmost.

John Stetson had dreams of making it in the Wild West. But he was not cut out to be a cowboy or a gold miner. When his efforts at discovering gold failed, instead of giving up, he decided to use a skill that he already had—hatmaking. In the end, he got his gold—just not the way he had planned!

EYES ON *Fictionalized Biography*

This story is a fictionalized biography. Don't those two words sound like opposites? Fiction is not true. Biography *is* true! How can there be a fictionalized biography? The story itself is true. John Stetson was a real person who *did* make the Stetson hat and sell it to people in the West. The main character and plot of the story are true.

What part of it, then, is not true? One part of the story that the author makes up is the dialogue. Did a traveler actually say the words, "Sure wish we had a snug tent"? Somebody might have said something like that, but the author made up the line. Another part that is not actual fact is the description of what people thought or their gestures. The story says, "John Stetson smiled." Do we know that he smiled at that moment? No, but he might have. The author made up that line, because it tells you what might have happened. A **fictionalized biography** is a true story whose dialogue and descriptions are mostly the inventions of the author.

Boss of the Plains

The Hat That Won the West

Laurie Carlson

Slouch Hat

At first, settlers and travelers in the American West wore whatever hats they had worn back home: knit caps, wool derbies,[1] or straw sombreros.[2] Some wore old sea captain's caps; others wore army hats, calico sunbonnets, homburgs,[3] slouch hats,[4] or even silk high hats.

Everyone wore some kind of hat, though, because the weather was likely to be either burning sunshine, drenching rain, whipping wind, or swirling snow. A hat was important protection.

One hat would come along that was particularly well suited to frontier life. This is the true story of that amazing hat—the hat that won the West.

In the 1840s, while explorers pushed on through new territory and pioneers tamed the mountains and plains of the West, twelve-year-old John Batterson Stetson sat on a high wooden stool, working along with his father and his eleven

---

1. A *derby* is a man's stiff felt hat with a rounded crown and a narrow brim. It is also called a *bowler*.
2. A *sombrero* is a broad-brimmed, tall-crowned hat of straw or felt worn especially in Mexico and the southwestern U.S.
3. A *homburg* is a man's felt hat with a soft crown dented lengthwise and a slightly rolled brim.
4. A *slouch hat* is a soft hat often made of felt and having a soft, usually broad brim.

brothers and sisters in the family's tiny, damp hatmaker's shop in Orange, New Jersey.

The Stetsons made hats the same way hatters had done it for years: by pressing felt, made from wet fur and wool, over a wooden form to shape it.

John sat at the worktable and dreamed of the West he'd heard customers and neighbors talk about.

Out west there were clear skies, roaming buffalo, and the promise of adventure. Everyone seemed to be going there. Everyone except hatmakers.

It wasn't until years later, when the dampness and steam of the shop had weakened his lungs and he became sick with tuberculosis, that John Stetson decided to go west himself. If he wanted to see the West, he couldn't wait. So he headed to the town where the West began: St. Joseph, Missouri, the jumping-off point where people bought gear and supplies for their journey to the goldfields.

It was 1859, and St. Joe's streets were bustling and crammed with wagons, mules, pack dogs, and adventurers bound for the frontier.

Determined to start a new life in St. Joe, John looked around for some way to make his mark. It was only when he met up with a group of travelers heading to Colorado Territory that opportunity presented itself.

"Why not come to Pikes Peak with us?" they asked. "There's gold there, and fortunes to be made."

That was all John Stetson needed to hear.

It was a 750-mile trip, and the long days of walking in the dry prairie air soon improved John's

Derby

Knit Cap

WORD BANK

WORD BANK

huddled (HUH dld) *v.*: gathered closely together
pelts *n.*: animal skins that have not been prepared for use in clothing or other items
sapling (SAP ling) *n.*: young tree

health. Before long his legs grew strong and he hardly ever coughed.

One night the Pikes Peakers huddled around their campfire.

"Sure wish we had a snug tent," one of the travelers commented. "Maybe we could make one out of the rabbit skins we've been saving."

"Won't work," someone else replied. "The skins will shrink up and get hard unless they're properly tanned."

John Stetson smiled. "Fur can be made into cloth without tanning,"[5] he announced.

"Can't be done!" the others scoffed.

But John knew that it could. He'd been making hats that way for years. So he spread out a blanket and gathered the dried rabbit pelts, along with a hatchet, a canteen of water, and a hickory sapling. He put the kettle on to boil.

He carefully shaved the fur from the first hide and piled it in the center of the blanket.

Then he sliced a strip of hide off the rabbit skin and tied each end of the strip to the hickory stick. It looked like an Indian's bow.

---

5. *Tanning* means converting an animal hide into leather by soaking it in a mixture of water and tanbark, the bark of an oak tree.

Sea Captain's

Next he flicked the bow, blowing puffs of fur up in the air to settle back down on the blanket until they made an even layer.

As everyone watched, John took a swig from the canteen and gently sprayed water through his teeth onto the fur until it matted.

With a gleam in his eye, he carefully lifted the corner of the fur; it came up off the blanket in one piece. Then he walked to the campfire and dipped the piece of matted fur in and out of the boiling water until it shrank into a little blanket.

"Felt!" he proclaimed. "Thick, warm, and stronger than a piece of cloth." It had worked!

Soon John and his friends were sleeping warm and snug in a new felt tent.

Over a month later, the Pikes Peakers reached the gold hills of Colorado. They eagerly went from diggings to diggings, trying their luck.

The scorching sun blistered John's face, and the whipping wind blinded him. The short brim of his derby hat, so stylish back in New Jersey, gave him no protection at all.

WORD BANK

swig *n.*: a mouthful of liquid
matted (MAT ed) *adj.*: thick and tangled

Cap

Before long John decided to make a better hat for himself. "Big and picturesque," he declared, and set to work, using the same technique he'd used to make his tent. It felt good to be making a hat again.

At first the other miners teased John about his funny hat. It certainly was different from the hats back home and the ones they wore. It had a wide brim and a tall crown and was made of thick fur felt. But it worked. The brim kept the sun out of John's eyes and the rain off his back. And when it got dirty, the tough felt could be brushed or thumped to knock the dust off.

One day a horseman rode into camp. When he saw John's unusual hat, his eyes lit up with excitement.

WORD BANK

distinctive (dis TINK tiv) *adj.*: unusual; having a special style

To everyone's amazement, he reached into his pocket, pulled out a five-dollar gold piece, and offered to buy the hat right off John's head!

Delighted, John pocketed the coin. Back in New Jersey, even the finest hat sold for just two dollars. He grinned and waved as the stranger rode out of camp wearing his distinctive hat.

Pickings in the Colorado goldfields were slim, and after a year of digging, John had little money to show for it. But he still had a trade and a talent. He decided to move to Philadelphia to do the one thing he really knew how to do: make hats.

At first he made the styles that were most popular back east, but so did all the other hatters. John wanted to make something unique, something special—a hat that everyone would notice. He even made up styles of his own and wore the hats to drum up orders, but no one in the city was interested.

John Stetson was determined to succeed. He remembered the horseman out west who had thought that his high-crowned, wide-brimmed hat was just right. Maybe other Westerners would like it, too—bullwhackers, who drove oxen; mule skinners, who led mule teams; and drovers, who herded cattle or sheep. He'd make a hat for the wranglers[6] and cowboys of the West. And he knew just what he'd name his new hat: Boss of the Plains.

John spent what little money he had left from mining gold on materials for sample hats. He made them all the same: of light tan felt, with a wide brim, a high crown, and a plain band. He packed sample hats and order forms in special boxes and sent one to every clothing store and hat dealer in the West. Then he waited.

---

6. A *wrangler* is a cowboy who is in charge of saddle horses.

Boss of the

Two weeks passed. Nothing happened. John sat in his empty shop thinking about the gamble he had taken. Had he wasted his time and all his money? Had he been foolish to think anyone would buy his unusual hats?

But then, all at once, orders began pouring in. Each day's mail brought more. People wanted the hats. In fact, they wanted them right away, and they had stuffed money into the envelopes to make sure they got them quickly.

Plains

John used the money to buy supplies and began turning out hats as fast as he could. Out west, cowboys tossed away their knit caps, sombreros, and derbies. In no time, John B. Stetson's Boss of the Plains became the most popular hat west of the Mississippi.

Even though the Boss of the Plains cost a cowboy a whole month's wages, it was worth it.

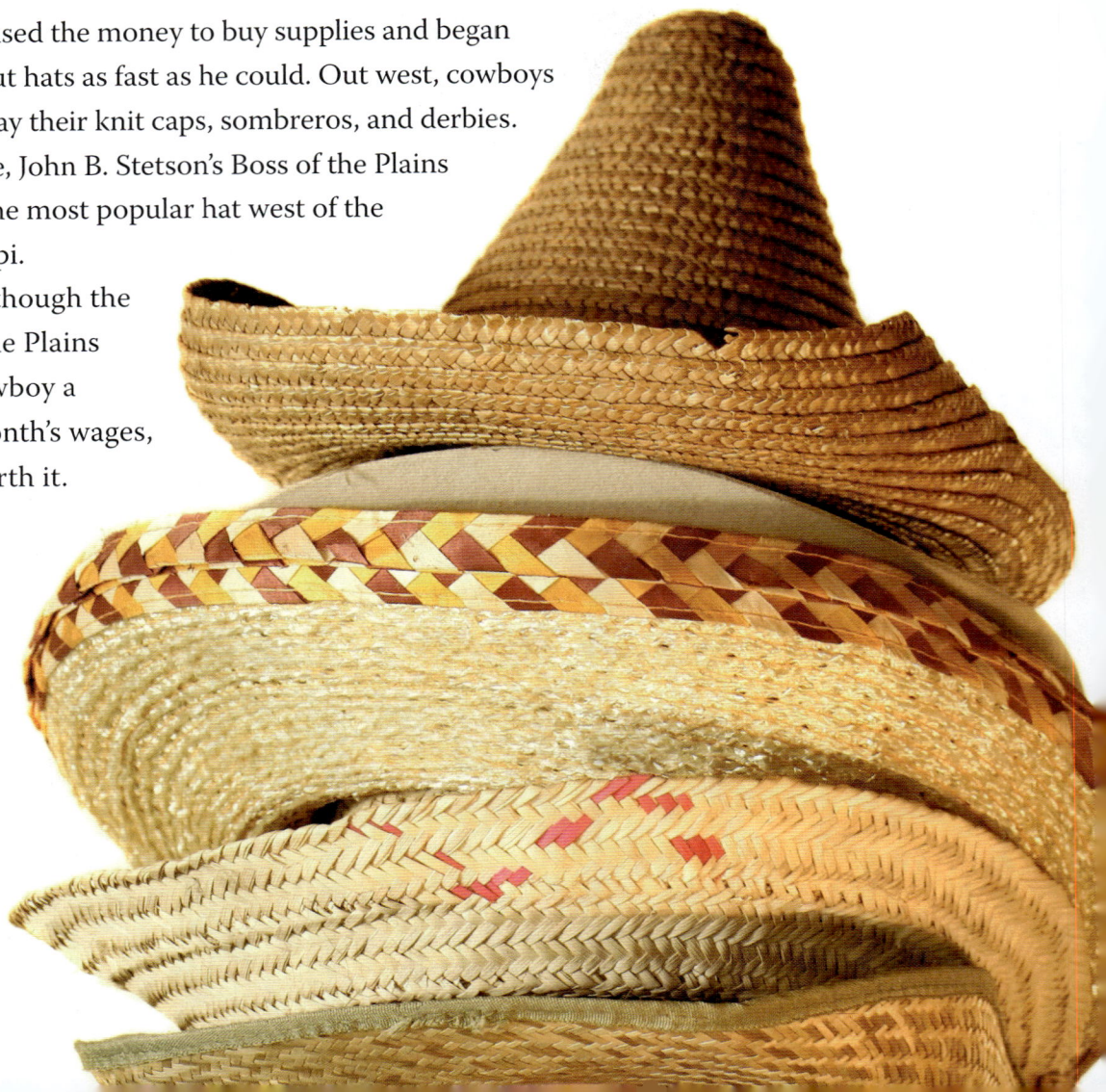

It shielded a cowpoke's eyes from blinding sun and caught the rain before it trickled down his back.

It could wave cows into a corral…or fan the flames of a newly lit campfire.

It could be used to carry oats to feed a horse or to scoop up a refreshing drink of water from a cold mountain stream.

It could come in handy when the sweetest huckleberries were ready to be picked.

It was the perfect decoy when a cowboy was in trouble... and made a soft cushion for a cowboy's head at the end of a hard day.

Westerners laughed about this hat they liked so much. They often said, "It gets so you can smell it across a room, but you just can't wear it out."

John Stetson had become an important part of the great American adventure called the West. Others had done it by striking gold, blazing trails through unknown territory, or taming a wild land. He made his mark with a hat.

Stetson

ABOUT THE AUTHOR

Laurie Carlson has lived in the western United States for most of her life— maybe that's why she enjoys wearing a Stetson hat! Born near the Sierra Nevada Mountains, young Laurie occasionally saw rattlesnakes near her home. She graduated from college and, while teaching elementary school in Arizona, began writing children's books. Soon after, Ms. Carlson branched out into such areas as history and science writing. Laurie Carlson and her husband, Terry, live on a big farm. They have a son, John, and a grandson, Brian, not to mention two goats, Opal and Sapphire!

Studying the Selection

FIRST IMPRESSIONS
How did John use his skill creatively?

QUICK REVIEW

1. What was the Stetson family business?
2. What did John dream of as he worked with felt in his family's shop?
3. What did John do between working with his family in New Jersey and starting a successful business in Philadelphia?
4. Why did people like John Stetson's Boss of the Plains hat so much?

FOCUS

5. How do you think that the name "Boss of the Plains" helped make the hat a success?
6. Draw a line down the center of a piece of paper, making two columns. At the top of one, write FACT. At the top of the other, write FICTION. Under the FACT column, write five facts found in the story. Under the FICTION column, write five descriptions or lines of dialogue which you think the author made up.

CREATING AND WRITING

7. Choose an object or article of clothing and, in two or three paragraphs, describe three different ways it could be used. Humor is a plus! Creativity is a must!
8. Write a fictional story about someone who had an idea that at first was mocked and rejected and then later became a huge success.
9. Draw or design a hat that would be worn for a particular activity.

Lesson in Literature ...

PULLING IT ALL TOGETHER

- We now know that every story has a **plot**, a **setting**, a cast of **characters**, and a **theme**.
- Every story is a unique combination of the four literary elements. A story can be strong in one area and weak in another. For example, the plot may be complicated and the characters very simple.
- We have also learned that **narration** and **dialogue**, both internal and external, move the story along.
- Finally, a good story has a **mood**. When you remember the story, you immediately enter into the mood that the story created in your mind. Even before you remember the plot or characters, you may remember that the story made you feel happy, sad, or frightened.

THINK ABOUT IT!

1. In your opinion, what two elements are the strongest in this story? Defend your answer.
2. In two sentences, describe the setting for this story.
3. What mood does the first part of the story create? What about the second part?

Sometimes at night when Chris looked out of his bedroom window, the big tree in the backyard looked like a big tree, but sometimes at night when he looked out of his window, the big tree looked like a monster.

Chris didn't mind. Monsters didn't scare him. Nothing scared him. When he fell off his bike and scraped his knee, he just got up and rode off. When his older brother teased him about his height, Chris just walked away. When his family moved into their new house, Chris told his father he didn't care about leaving his friends and school behind.

Chris was tough.

He didn't mind living with a monster outside his window.

On moonless nights he saw the monster's big hairy body. On those nights he closed the blinds. When the moon was low, he saw the monster's long hairy arms raised over his head. On those nights he closed the blinds and left the night-light on. When the moon was full, he saw the monster's red bloody eyes staring at him out of the darkness. On those nights he closed the blinds, left the night-light on, and asked his big sister to sleep on the floor in his bedroom.

One night, though, the monster moved. Its hairy body gasped for air, and its long arms pounded on the bedroom window. Chris sat up straight in bed, closed the blinds, turned on the night-light, shut the bedroom door, and slept on the floor in his big sister's room down the hall.

When he told his father, his father handed him a flashlight. "Use this to scare the monster away," he said.

Monster

A few nights later when the monster's chest shook, his arms clawed at his window, and his red eyes glowed in the darkness, Chris switched on the flashlight, shining its bright light into the monster's ugly eyes.

All that stood outside the window was a big tree with leaves and branches blowing in the wind. The monster's big hairy body was nothing more than the tree's thick coat of leaves, and the monster's big hairy arms were nothing more than the tree's long branches. Chris even saw that the monster's red bloody eyes were nothing more than the moonlight reflecting off the red taillights of his father's car parked behind the house.

That night Chris invited his sister into his room. The two of them sat on his bed, turned the flashlight on and off, and laughed hard at the monster's big ears, gigantic nose, and silly toothless smile until they both fell asleep at the end of the bed. While they slept, the flashlight stayed on all night, lighting up the leaves and branches of a big old oak tree blowing in the breeze of a summer night.

Blueprint for Reading

INTO . . . *Stone Fox*

This is a story about the quality of *determination*. Each of the two main characters has a goal that he is determined to reach. Neither character is discouraged by what people think or say. Both of the characters are good people with good goals. The story is about a struggle between two good, two strong, and two very determined people. Who will win? Who will lose? It is not until the very end that we understand who is the winner and if there really is a loser.

EYES ON *Narrative Elements*

You have learned a great deal about the narrative elements of a story. As you read the last selection, *Stone Fox*, see if you can identify the **plot**, **characterization**, **setting**, and **theme**. This story has a lot of detail that will help you identify each of those important story elements. When you identify them, congratulate yourself. You've learned a lot!

An excerpt from

Stone Fox

John Reynolds Gardiner

Little Willy needs five hundred dollars to save his grandfather's farm. The winner of the big dogsled race, held every year in Jackson, Wyoming, wins a five hundred dollar prize. He knows he can win the prize!

Little Willy went to see Mayor Smiley at the city hall building in town to sign up for the race.

The mayor's office was large and smelled like hair tonic. The mayor sat in a bright red chair with his feet on his desk. There was nothing on the desk except the mayor's feet.

"We have a race for you youngsters one hour before." Mayor Smiley mopped sweat from his neck with a silk handkerchief, although little Willy thought it was quite cool in the room.

"I wanna enter the *real* race, Mr. Mayor."

"You must be funning, boy." The mayor laughed twice and blotted his neck. "Anyway, there's an entrance fee."

"How much?"

"Fifty dollars."

Little Willy was stunned. That was a lot of money just to enter a race. But he was determined. He ran across the street to the bank.

"Don't be stupid," Mr. Foster told little Willy. "This is not a race for amateurs. Some of the best dog teams in the Northwest will be entering."

"I have Searchlight! We go fast as lightning. Really, Mr. Foster, we do."

Mr. Foster shook his head. "You don't stand a chance of winning."

"Yes, we do!"

"Willy…the money in your savings account is for your college education. You know I can't give it to you."

"You have to."

"I do?"

"It's *my* money!"

Little Willy left the bank with a stack of ten-dollar gold pieces—five of them, to be exact.

He walked into the mayor's office and plopped the coins down on the mayor's desk. "Me and Searchlight are gonna win that five hundred dollars, Mr. Mayor. You'll see. Everybody'll see."

Mayor Smiley counted the money, wiped his neck, and entered little Willy in the race.

When little Willy stepped out of the city hall building, he felt ten feet tall. He looked up and down the snow-covered street. He was grinning from ear to ear. Searchlight walked over and stood in front of the sled, waiting to be hitched up. But little Willy wasn't ready to go yet. He put his thumbs in his belt loops and let the sun warm his face.

He felt great. In his pocket was a map Mayor Smiley had given him showing the ten miles the race covered.

WORD BANK

stunned (STUND) *v.*: shocked
amateurs (AM uh churz) *n.*: beginners lacking in skill and experience; not experts

Down Main Street, right on North Road—little Willy could hardly hold back his excitement.

Five miles of the race he traveled every day and knew with his eyes closed. The last five miles were back into town along South Road, which was mostly straight and flat. It's speed that would count here, and with the lead he knew he could get in the first five miles, little Willy was sure he could win.

As little Willy hitched Searchlight to the sled, something down at the end of the street—some moving objects—caught his eye. They were difficult to see because they were all white. There were five of them. And they were beautiful. In fact, they were the most beautiful Samoyeds[1] little Willy had ever seen.

The dogs held their heads up proudly and strutted in unison. They pulled a large but lightly constructed sled. They also pulled a large—but by no means lightly constructed—man. Way down at the end of the street the man looked normal, but as the sled got closer, the man got bigger and bigger.

The man was an Indian—dressed in furs and leather, with moccasins that came all the way up to his knees. His skin was dark, his hair was dark, and he wore a dark-colored headband. His eyes sparkled in the sunlight, but the rest of his face was as hard as stone.

The sled came to a stop right next to little Willy. The boy's mouth hung open as he tilted his head way back to look up at the man. Little Willy had never seen a giant before.

"Gosh," little Willy gasped.

The Indian looked at little Willy. His face was solid granite, but his eyes were alive and cunning.

"Howdy," little Willy blurted out, and he gave a nervous smile.

But the Indian said nothing. His eyes shifted to Searchlight, who let out a soft moan but did not bark.

The Giant walked into the city hall building.

---

1. A *Samoyed* (se MOI id) is a medium-sized Siberian dog with long, straight white or cream hair that forms a ruff around the neck.

Word that Stone Fox had entered the race spread throughout the town of Jackson within the hour, and throughout the state of Wyoming within the day.

Stories and legends about the awesome mountain man followed shortly. Little Willy heard many of them at Lester's General Store.

Little Willy learned that no white man had ever heard Stone Fox talk. Stone Fox refused to speak with the white man because of the treatment his people had received. His tribe, the Shoshone, who were peaceful seed gatherers, had been forced to leave Utah and settle on a reservation in Wyoming with another tribe called the Arapaho.

Stone Fox's dream was for his people to return to their homeland. Stone Fox was using the money he won from racing to simply buy the land back. He had already purchased four farms and over two hundred acres.

That Stone Fox was smart, all right.

In the next week little Willy and Searchlight went over the ten-mile track every day, until they knew every inch of it by heart.

Stone Fox hardly practiced at all. In fact, little Willy only saw Stone Fox do the course once, and then he sure wasn't going very fast.

The race was scheduled for Saturday morning at ten o'clock. Only nine sleds were entered. Mayor Smiley had hoped for more contestants, but after Stone Fox had entered, well…you couldn't blame people for wanting to save their money.

It was true Stone Fox had never lost a race. But little Willy wasn't worried. He had made up his mind to win. And nothing was going to stop him. Not even Stone Fox.

It was Friday night, the night before the race, when it happened.

Grandfather was out of medicine. Little Willy went to see Doc Smith.

"Here." Doc Smith handed little Willy a piece of paper with some scribbling on it. "Take this to Lester at the drugstore right away."

"But it's nighttime. The store's closed."

"Just knock on the back door. He'll hear you."

"But…are you sure it's all right?"

"Yes. Lester knows I may have to call on him any time—day or night. People don't always get sick just during working hours, now, do they?"

"No, I guess they don't." Little Willy headed for the door. He sure wished he could stay and have some of that cinnamon cake Doc Smith was baking in the oven. It smelled mighty good. But Grandfather needed his medicine. And anyway, he wouldn't think of staying without being asked.

"One other thing, Willy," Doc Smith said.

"Yes, ma'am?"

"I might as well say this now as later. It's about the race tomorrow."

"Yes, ma'am?"

"First, I want you to know that I think you're a darn fool for using your college money to enter that race."

Little Willy's eyes looked to the floor. "Yes, ma'am."

"But, since it's already been done, I also want you to know that I'll be rooting for you."

Little Willy looked up. "You will?"

"Win, Willy. Win that race tomorrow."

Little Willy beamed. He tried to speak, but couldn't find the words. Embarrassed, he backed over to the door, gave a little wave, then turned quickly to leave.

"And, Willy…"

"Yes, ma'am?"

"If you stay a minute, you can have some of that cinnamon cake I've got in the oven."

"Yes, ma'am!"

Later, on his way to town, little Willy sang at the top of his lungs. The sled's runners cut through the snow with a swish. This was a treacherous road at night, but the moon was out and Searchlight could see well. And, anyway, they knew this road by heart. Nothing was going to happen.

WORD BANK

treacherous (TRECH uh russ) *adj.*: very dangerous

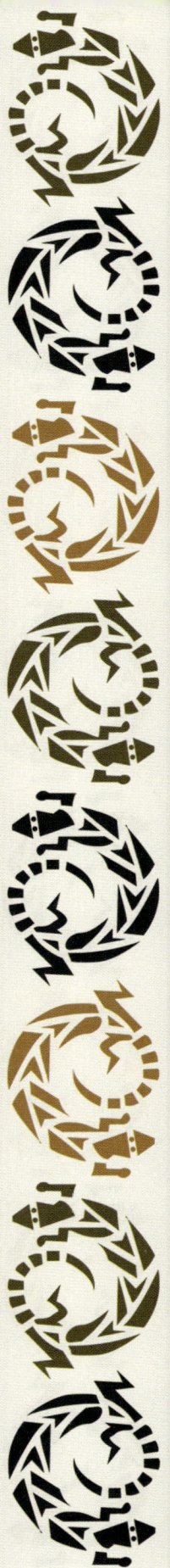

Lester gave little Willy a big bottle of what looked like dirty milk.

"How's your grandfather doing?" Lester asked.

"Not so good. But after I win the race tomorrow, he'll get better. Doc Smith thinks so too."

Lester smiled. "I admire you, Willy. You got a heap of courage, going up against the likes of Stone Fox. You know he's never lost, don't you?"

"Yes, I know. Thank you for the medicine."

Little Willy waved good-bye as Searchlight started off down Main Street.

Lester watched the departing sled for a long time before he yelled, "Good luck, son!"

On his way out of town, along North Road, little Willy heard dogs barking. The sounds came from the old deserted barn near the schoolhouse.

Little Willy decided to investigate.

He squeaked open the barn door and peeked in. It was dark inside and he couldn't see anything. He couldn't hear anything either. The dogs had stopped barking.

He went inside the barn.

Little Willy's eyes took a while to get used to the dark, and then he saw them. The five Samoyeds. They were in the corner of the barn on a bed of straw. They were looking at him. They were so beautiful that little Willy couldn't keep from smiling.

Little Willy loved dogs. He had to see the Samoyeds up close. They showed no alarm as he approached, or as he held out his hand to pet them.

And then it happened.

There was a movement through the darkness to little Willy's right. A sweeping motion, fast at first; then it appeared to slow and stop. But it didn't stop. A hand hit little Willy right in the face, sending him over backward.

"I didn't mean any harm, Mr. Stone Fox," little Willy said as he picked himself up off the ground, holding a hand over his eye.

Stone Fox stood tall in the darkness and said nothing. Searchlight barked outside. The Samoyeds barked in return.

Little Willy continued, "I'm going to race against you tomorrow. I know how you wanna win, but…I wanna win too. I gotta win. If I don't, they're gonna take away our farm. They have the right. Grandfather says that those that want to bad enough, will. So I will. I'll win. I'm gonna beat you."

Stone Fox remained motionless. And silent.

Little Willy backed over to the barn door, still holding his eye. "I'm sorry we both can't win," he said. Then he pushed open the barn door and left, closing the door behind him.

In the barn, Stone Fox stood unmoving for another moment; then he reached out with one massive hand and gently petted one of the Samoyeds.

That night little Willy couldn't sleep—his eye was killing him. And when little Willy couldn't sleep, Searchlight couldn't sleep. Both tossed and turned for hours, and whenever little Willy looked over to see if Searchlight was asleep, she'd just be lying there with her eyes wide open, staring back at him.

Little Willy needed his rest. So did Searchlight. Tomorrow was going to be a big day. The biggest day of their lives.

The day of the race arrived.

Little Willy got up early. He couldn't see out of his right eye. It was swollen shut.

As he fed Grandfather his oatmeal, he tried to hide his eye with his hand or by turning away, but he was sure Grandfather saw it just the same.

After adding more wood to the fire, little Willy kissed Grandfather, hitched up Searchlight, and started off for town.

At the edge of their property he stopped the sled for a moment and looked back at the farmhouse. The roof was covered with freshly fallen snow. A trail of smoke escaped from the stone chimney. The jagged peaks of the Teton Mountains shot up in the background toward the clear blue sky overhead. "Yes, sir," he remembered Grandfather saying. "There are some things in this world worth dying for."

WORD BANK

jagged (JAG ud) *adj.*: rough, sharp, and uneven

Little Willy loved this country. He loved to hike and to fish and to camp out by a lake. But he did not like to hunt. He loved animals too much to be a hunter.

He had killed a bird once with a slingshot. But that had been when he was only six years old. And that had been enough. In fact, to this day, he still remembered the spot where the poor thing was buried.

Lost in his thoughts, little Willy got to town before he knew it. As he turned onto Main Street, he brought the sled to an abrupt halt.

He couldn't believe what he saw.

Main Street was jammed with people, lined up on both sides of the street. There were people on rooftops and people hanging out of windows. Little Willy hadn't expected such a big turnout. They must have all come to see Stone Fox.

Searchlight pulled the sled down Main Street past the crowd. Little Willy saw Miss Williams, his teacher, and Mr. Foster from the bank, and Hank from the post office. And there were Doc Smith and Mayor Smiley. The city slickers[2] were there. And even Clifford Snyder, the tax man, was there. Everybody.

Lester came out of the crowd and walked alongside little Willy for a while. It was one of the few times little Willy had ever seen Lester without his white apron.

"You can do it, Willy. You can beat him," Lester kept saying over and over again.

They had a race for the youngsters first, and the crowd cheered and rooted for their favorites. It was a short race. Just down to the end of Main Street and back. Little Willy didn't see who won. It didn't matter.

And then it was time.

The old town clock showed a few minutes before ten as the contestants positioned themselves directly beneath

---

2. *City slicker* is a slightly insulting phrase used by country dwellers to describe those who live in the city. The word "slick" hints that the people are smooth-talking and tricky.

WORD BANK

abrupt (uh BRUPT) *adj.*: sudden

the long banner that stretched across the street. They stood nine abreast. Stone Fox in the middle. Little Willy right next to him.

Little Willy had read all about the other contestants in the newspaper. They were all well-known mountain men with good racing records and excellent dog teams. But, even so, all bets were on Stone Fox. The odds were as high as a hundred to one that he'd win.

Not one cent had been bet on little Willy and Searchlight.

"What happened to Willy's eye?" Doc Smith asked Lester.

"Bumped it this morning when he got up, he told me. Just nervous. Got a right to be." Lester was chewing on his hand, his eyes glued on Stone Fox. "Big Indian," he whispered to himself.

Although little Willy's eye was black, puffy, and swollen shut, he still felt like a winner. He was smiling. Searchlight knew the route as well as he did, so it really didn't matter if he could see at all. They were going to win today, and that was final. Both of them knew it.

Stone Fox looked bigger than ever standing next to little Willy. In fact, the top of little Willy's head was dead even with Stone Fox's waist.

"Morning, Mr. Stone Fox," little Willy said, looking practically straight up. "Sure's a nice day for a race."

Stone Fox must have heard little Willy, but he did not look at him. His face was frozen like ice, and his eyes seemed to lack that sparkle little Willy remembered seeing before.

The crowd became silent as Mayor Smiley stepped out into the street.

Miss Williams clenched her hands together until her knuckles turned white. Lester's mouth hung open, his lips wet. Mr. Foster began chewing his cigar. Hank stared without blinking. Doc Smith held her head up proudly. Clifford Snyder removed a gold watch from his vest pocket and checked the time.

WORD BANK

abreast (uh BREST) *adv.*, *adj.*: side by side
clenched (KLENSHT) *v.*: held closed tightly

Tension filled the air.

Little Willy's throat became dry. His hands started to sweat. He could feel his heart thumping.

Mayor Smiley raised a pistol to the sky and fired.

The race had begun!

Searchlight sprang forward with such force that little Willy couldn't hang on. If it weren't for a lucky grab, he would have fallen off the sled for sure.

In what seemed only seconds, little Willy and Searchlight had traveled down Main Street, turned onto North Road, and were gone. Far, far ahead of the others. They were winning. At least for the moment.

Stone Fox started off dead last. He went so slowly down Main Street that everyone was sure something must be wrong.

Swish! Little Willy's sled flew by the schoolhouse on the outskirts of town, and then by the old deserted barn.

Swish! Swish! Swish! Other racers followed in hot pursuit.

"Go, Searchlight! Go!" little Willy sang out. The cold wind pressed against his face, causing his good eye to shut almost completely. The snow was well packed. It was going to be a fast race today. The fastest they had ever run.

The road was full of dangerous twists and turns, but little Willy did not have to slow down as the other racers did. With only one dog and a small sled, he was able to take the sharp turns at full speed without risk of sliding off the road or losing control.

Therefore, with each turn, little Willy pulled farther and farther ahead.

Swish! The sled rounded a corner, sending snow flying. Little Willy was smiling. This was fun!

About three miles out of town the road made a half circle around a frozen lake. Instead of following the turn, little Willy took a shortcut right across the lake. This was tricky going, but Searchlight had done it many times before.

Little Willy had asked Mayor Smiley if he was permitted to go across the lake, not wanting to be disqualified. "As long as you leave town heading north and come back on South Road," the mayor had said, "anything goes!"

None of the other racers attempted to cross the lake. Not even Stone Fox. The risk of falling through the ice was just too great.

Little Willy's lead increased.

Stone Fox was still running in last place. But he was picking up speed.

At the end of five miles, little Willy was so far out in front that he couldn't see anybody behind him when he looked back.

He knew, however, that the return five miles, going back into town, would not be this easy. The trail along South Road was practically straight and very smooth, and Stone Fox was sure to close the gap. But by how much? Little Willy didn't know.

Doc Smith's house flew by on the right. The tall trees surrounding her cabin seemed like one solid wall.

Grandfather's farm was coming up next.

When Searchlight saw the farmhouse, she started to pick up speed. "No, girl," little Willy yelled. "Not yet."

As they approached the farmhouse, little Willy thought he saw someone in Grandfather's bedroom window. It was difficult to see with only one good eye. The someone was a man. With a full beard.

It couldn't be. But it was! It was Grandfather!

Grandfather was sitting up in bed. He was looking out the window.

Little Willy was so excited he couldn't think straight. He started to stop the sled, but Grandfather indicated no, waving him on. "Of course," little Willy said to himself. "I must finish the race. I haven't won yet."

"Go, Searchlight!" little Willy shrieked. "Go, girl!"

Grandfather was better. Tears of joy rolled down little Willy's smiling face. Everything was going to be all right.

And then Stone Fox made his move.

One by one he began to pass the other racers. He went from last place to eighth. Then from eighth place to seventh. Then from seventh to sixth. Sixth to fifth.

He passed the others as if they were standing still.

He went from fifth place to fourth. Then to third. Then to second.

Until only little Willy remained.

But little Willy still had a good lead. In fact, it was not until the last two miles of the race that Stone Fox got his first glimpse of little Willy since the race had begun.

The five Samoyeds looked magnificent as they moved effortlessly across the snow. Stone Fox was gaining, and he was gaining fast. And little Willy wasn't aware of it.

Look back, little Willy! Look back!

But little Willy didn't look back. He was busy thinking about Grandfather. He could hear him laughing…and playing his harmonica…

Finally little Willy glanced back over his shoulder. He couldn't believe what he saw! Stone Fox was nearly on top of him!

This made little Willy mad. Mad at himself. Why hadn't he looked back more often? What was he doing? He hadn't won yet. Well, no time to think of that now. He had a race to win.

"Go, Searchlight! Go, girl!"

But Stone Fox kept gaining. Silently. Steadily.

"Go, Searchlight! Go!"

The lead Samoyed passed little Willy and pulled up even with Searchlight. Then it was a nose ahead. But that was all. Searchlight moved forward, inching *her* nose ahead. Then the Samoyed regained the lead. Then Searchlight…

When you enter the town of Jackson on South Road, the first buildings come into view about a half a mile away. Whether Searchlight took those buildings to be Grandfather's farmhouse again, no one can be sure, but it was at this time that she poured on the steam.

Little Willy's sled seemed to lift up off the ground and fly. Stone Fox was left behind.

But not that far behind.

The crowd cheered madly when they saw little Willy come

WORD BANK

effortlessly (EFF urt less lee)
adv.: easily

into view at the far end of Main Street, and even more madly when they saw that Stone Fox was right on his tail.

"Go, Searchlight! Go!"

Searchlight forged ahead. But Stone Fox was gaining!

"Go, Searchlight! Go!" little Willy cried out.

Searchlight gave it everything she had.

She was a hundred feet from the finish line when her heart burst. She died instantly. There was no suffering.

The sled and little Willy tumbled over her, slid along the snow for a while, then came to a stop about ten feet from the finish line. It had started to snow—white snowflakes landed on Searchlight's dark fur as she lay motionless on the ground.

The crowd became deathly silent.

Lester's eyes looked to the ground. Miss Williams had her hands over her mouth. Mr. Foster's cigar lay on the snow. Doc Smith started to run out to little Willy, but stopped. Mayor Smiley looked shocked and helpless. And so did Hank and so did the city slickers, and so did Clifford Snyder, the tax man.

Stone Fox brought his sled to a stop alongside little Willy. He stood tall in the icy wind and looked down at the young challenger, and at the dog that lay limp in his arms.

"Is she dead, Mr. Stone Fox? Is she dead?" little Willy asked, looking up at Stone Fox with his one good eye.

Stone Fox knelt down and put one massive hand on Searchlight's chest. He felt no heartbeat. He looked at little Willy, and the boy understood.

Little Willy squeezed Searchlight with all his might. "You did real good, girl. Real good. I'm real proud of you. You rest now. Just rest." Little Willy began to brush the snow off Searchlight's back.

Stone Fox stood up slowly.

No one spoke. No one moved. All eyes were on the Indian, the one called Stone Fox, the one who had never lost a race, and who now had another victory within his grasp.

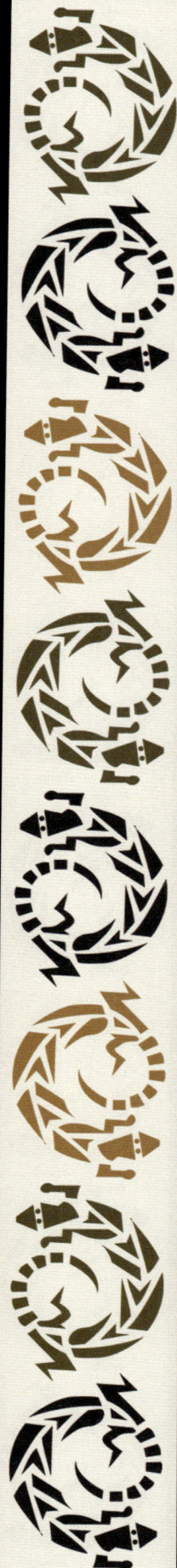

But Stone Fox did nothing.

He just stood there. Like a mountain.

His eyes shifted to his own dogs, then to the finish line, then back to little Willy, holding Searchlight.

With the heel of his moccasin Stone Fox drew a long line in the snow. Then he walked back over to his sled and pulled out his rifle.

Down at the end of Main Street, the other racers began to appear. As they approached, Stone Fox fired his rifle into the air. They came to a stop.

Stone Fox spoke.

"Anyone crosses this line—I shoot."

And there wasn't anybody who didn't believe him.

Stone Fox nodded to the boy.

The town looked on in silence as little Willy, carrying Searchlight, walked the last ten feet and across the finish line.

A Postscript from the Author

The idea for this story came from a Rocky Mountain legend that was told to me in 1974 by Bob Hudson over a cup of coffee at Hudson's Café in Idaho Falls, Idaho. Although Stone Fox and the other characters are purely fictitious and of my creation, the tragic ending to this story belongs to the legend and is reported to have actually happened.

ABOUT THE AUTHOR

Unlike almost every author in this book, **John Reynolds Gardiner** hated to read! Born in California in 1944, he did not read a novel until he was nineteen years old. His grammar was bad and his spelling was atrocious. However, he did love stories. He loved hearing them and he loved telling them. His brother convinced him to enroll in a writing class. He did, but could not sell anything he wrote. Finally, he sent a story to a book publisher. That story was called *Stone Fox*; thousands of copies of it were sold. Mr. Gardiner lived in California with his wife and three daughters until his death in 2006.

Studying the Selection

FIRST IMPRESSIONS
At the beginning, did you think it was foolish of Willy to insist on entering the race? Were you surprised at the ending?

QUICK REVIEW

1. What was unusual about Willy's entry into the race?
2. Why were so few people registered for the race?
3. Why couldn't Willy sleep the night before the race?
4. What made Stone Fox speak to white people for the first time after his long silence?

FOCUS

5. Why do you think Stone Fox let Willy win the race?
6. How do you think the story would have been different if it had been told from Stone Fox's point of view?

CREATING AND WRITING

7. Both Willy and Stone Fox had good reasons for wanting to win the race. Explain what motivated each of them to win. Do you think one's reason was better than the other?
8. Write a paragraph to answer one of the following questions.
   a. What happened to Grandfather and the farm after the race?
   b. Did Willy get another dog and did he race again?
   c. Did the relationship between Stone Fox and the white people change or remain the same?
9. Design the front page for the *Jackson Daily Times* newspaper for the day after the race. Write an article and draw pictures about the event. Which aspect of the race will you focus on? Try to have several different features that will be interesting to different types of readers.

6

unit

wrap-up
the grand finalé

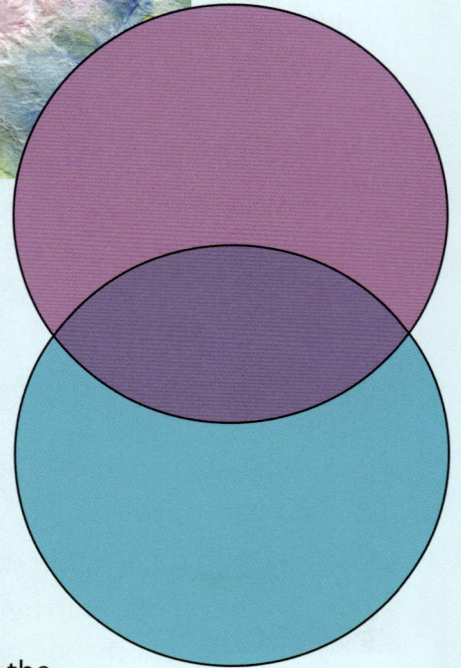

ACTIVITY ONE

Choose two characters from different stories to compare and contrast. Create a Venn diagram out of cardboard. Draw a figure of each character and attach one to either side. Then fill in with the details about those characters. Remember the circles should intersect and the common information should be in the center.

The Bridge Dancers

Dancing Bees

Name This American

LEWIS AND CLARK TRAIL

Boss of the Plains

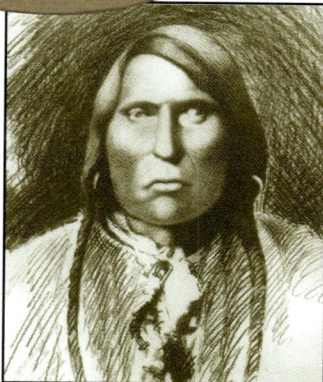

Stone Fox

ACTIVITY TWO

Do you think little Willy would be more likely to be friends with Callie or with Maisie (the two sisters in _The Bridge Dancers_)? Write down a few points to support your opinion and present them to the class.

ACTIVITY THREE

Your teacher will divide you into groups. Together, you are going to create a game show similar to _Name This American_. The show will be about narrative elements. Write down the rules of the game, then divide the questions into four categories: plot, character, setting, and theme. There should be at least five questions for each category. When you are all ready, the groups can take turns playing the games with the entire class.

ACTIVITY FOUR

Write a short essay about how nature and geography play important roles in at least two stories in this unit.

Mosdos Press Literature

- GLOSSARY
- ACKNOWLEDGMENTS
- INDEX OF AUTHORS AND TITLES

glossary

A

abreast (uh BREST) *adv., adj.*: side by side

abrupt (uh BRUPT) *adj.*: sudden

absurd (ub ZURD) *adj.*: ridiculous

abundantly (uh BUN dunt lee) *adv.*: very much

affected (uh FEK tid) *v.*: influenced

agonized (AG uh NYZD) *v.*: worried unhappily

allotment (uh LOT ment) *n.*: the portion of something that is assigned to someone

amateurs (AM uh churz) *n.*: beginners lacking in skill and experience; not experts

anticipation (an TISS ih PAY shun) *n.*: happily looking forward to something

appointment *n.*: position; job

apprentice (uh PREN tiss) *n.*: a person who works for another in order to learn a trade

B

balmy (BAH mee) *adj.*: mild and refreshing weather

basking (BASS king) *v.*: lying in something pleasantly warm (like the sun)

battered (BAT erd) *adj.*: damaged by rough and careless treatment

beacon (BEE kun) *n.*: a light used as a warning signal

bolt *v.*: suddenly run away

brandishing (BRAN dish ing) *v.*: waving and displaying

budge (BUHJ) *v.*: move even slightly

bustling (BUSS ling) *v.*: full of activity

C

calico (KAL ih ko) *n.*: a plain cotton fabric printed on one side

cataloging (CAT uh LOG ing) *v.*: organizing a list of items into groups

celebrities (suh LEB rih teez) *n.*: well-known or famous people

chiseled (TCHIH zuld) *v.*: carved with a *chisel*, a tool with a cutting edge designed to carve a hard material

chores (TSHORZ) *n.*: the everyday work around a house or farm; a small job that must be done regularly

churned *v.*: shook and beat milk to turn it into butter

chute (SHOOT) *n.:* a narrow, sloping passageway for delivering items from a higher to a lower level

clenched (KLENSHT) *v.:* held closed tightly

club (KLUB) *n.:* a heavy stick

clutched (KLUCHD) *v.:* held onto tightly

cobblestone (KOB ul stone) *n.:* a small, naturally rounded stone, used in paving roads

commercial (kuh MUR shul) *n.:* made by companies to be sold in stores; not homemade

commotion (kuh MO shun) *n.:* noise and disturbance

composed (kum POZED) *v.:* made up of

confined (kun FYND) *v.:* restricted; kept from leaving a place

console (kun SOLE) *v.:* comfort

consternation (KAHN stur NAY shun) *n.:* a sudden alarming amazement or dread

consulting (kun SULT ing) *v.:* asking advice of

corroded (kuh RODE id) *adj.:* worn away

crammed (KRAMD) *v.:* crowded; stuffed

craned (KRAYND) *v.:* stretched out their necks (to see)

crest *n.:* the highest part of a hill

crude *adj.:* rough; not well-designed

cultivate (KUL tih vayt) *v.:* to help the plants grow by tending to the soil around them

D

debris (duh BREE) *n.:* the remains of anything destroyed

decreed (dih KREED) *v.:* ordered; commanded

delegate (DELL uh gut) *n.:* one person sent by a group of people to represent them at a convention

dense (DENSS) *adj.:* thick and tightly packed together

desolately (DESS uh lit lee) *adv.:* very sadly

devastation (DEH vis TAY shun) *n.:* destruction and ruin

devour (dih VOW ehr) *v.:* to swallow hungrily

distinctive (dis TINK tiv) *adj.:* unusual; having a special style

distinguished (dis TEENG wishd) *v.:* important and respected

domain (doe MAYN) *n.:* a region inhabited by a certain type of wildlife

donned (DAHND) *v.*: put on

doused (DOWST) *v.*: threw water on

dwarfed (DWORFD) *v.*: appeared small by comparison

E

eaves (EEVZ) *n.*: the overhanging lower edges of a roof

eerie (IH ree) *adj.*: strange and somewhat frightening

effortlessly (EFF urt less lee) *adv.*: easily

embedded (em BED ed) *v.*: set deeply into

engrossed (en GROSED) *v.*: occupied; completely involved in

enraged (en RAYJD) *adj.*: extremely angry

evaporating (ee VAP uh RAY ting) *v.*: disappearing

executive (egg ZEK yoo tiv) *n.*: a person who has a position of leadership in a business or company

expedition (EX puh DISH un) *n.*: a journey or voyage made to a distant place for a certain purpose

F

famine (FAM in) *n.*: a hunger; a major food shortage

flaw *n.*: a defect; an imperfection

flint stones *n.*: hard stones used to produce a spark

G

gingerly (JIN jur lee) *adv.*: with great care

glistened (GLISS und) *v.*: shone

gorge (GORJ) *n.*: a small canyon through which a stream runs

grim *adj.*: serious and unpleasant

grippe (GRIP) *n.*: influenza

gullies (GULL eez) *n.*: small valleys or ravines made by running water

H

habitat (HAB ih TAT) *n.*: the place where a plant or animal is naturally found

haltingly (HALT ing lee) *adv.*: slowly, with hesitation

haughty (HAW tee) *adj.*: snobbish; arrogant

hearth (HARTH) *n.*: the floor of a fireplace

herded (HURD id) *v.*: drove or led (cows)

hoisted (HOYS tid) *v.*: raised

horizon (huh RY zun) *n.*: the place in the distance where the earth and sky seem to meet

hovered (HUV urd) *v.*: waited nearby

huddled (HUH dld) *v.*: gathered closely together

I

impact (IM pakt) *n.*: the force with which one thing hits another

implored (im PLORD) *v.*: begged

income (INK um) *n.*: the money an individual or business makes during a given time period

indebted (in DET ed) *adj.*: owing; obligated to repay something

inspired (in SPY ehrd) *v.*: filled with a sense of purpose

instinctively (in STINK tiv lee) *adv.*: without thinking; from an inborn knowledge, not as a result of having been taught

interchangeable (IN tur CHAYNGE uh bul) *adj.*: two things that can be used in place of one another

inundated (IN un DAY tud) *v.*: flooded

J

jagged (JAG ud) *adj.*: rough, sharp, and uneven

jarring (JAR ing) *v.*: shaking

jauntily (JAWNT ih lee) *adv.*: in a lively, carefree, and slightly proud way

jubilant (JOO bih lunt) *adj.*: full of joy

K

kindling (KIHND ling) *n.*: material that ignites easily, used to start a fire

L

linger (LEENG er) *v.*: to stay somewhere longer than necessary because one does not want to leave

lull *n.*: a temporary calm

lulling (LULL ing) *v.*: putting to sleep by quiet, soothing means

luminous (LOO mih nuss) *adj.*: reflecting light

M

magistrate (MADJ iss trayt) *n.*: a government worker who enforces the law

maneuvered (muh NOO vurd) *v.*: moved about and changed direction as required

manipulate (muh NIP yoo layt) *v.*: handle with skill

matted (MAT ed) *adj.*: thick and tangled

meandered (mee AN derd) *v.*: wound around gently from one place to another

menacing (MEN uh sing) *adj.*: threatening

miscalculated (mis KAL kyuh LAY tid) *v.*: judged incorrectly

misleading (miss LEED ing) *adj.*: words or actions that lead people to believe something that is not true

mock *adj.*: pretend; make-believe

monologue (MAH nuh log) *n.*: a long speech made by one person, with no answer or interruption from the listener

monument (MAHN yoo munt) *n.*: a building, statue, or the like, built in memory of a person or event

mural (MYOOR ul) *n.*: a large picture painted directly on a wall or ceiling

mustering (MUST uh ring) *v.*: gathering; calling upon

N

needlessly (NEED luss lee) *adv.*: unnecessarily

O

ominous (AH mih nuss) *adj.*: threatening; hinting that something bad is about to happen

ornery (OR nuh ree) *adj.*: mean

P

parchment (PARCH ment) *n.*: a stiff, heavy, ivory-colored paper made from the skins of sheep or goats

pare (PAIR) *v.*: to cut off the outer layer

passion (PASH un) *n.*: an enthusiasm for something

peer *n.*: one who is the equal of another

pelts *n.*: animal skins that have not been prepared for use in clothing or other items

persimmon (pur SIH mun) *n.*: a large, plumlike orange fruit that is sweet when very ripe

picturesque (PIK chur ESK) *adj.*: pleasing, interesting, and noticeable

pirouettes (PEER oo ETS) *n.*: a dance step in which the dancer whirls about on one foot

pitch *n.*: a black, sticky tar

pitches *v.*: falls sharply

plain *n.*: a large flat area of land

plucked (PLUKD) *v.*: pulled out, like feathers from a bird

plunges (PLUNJ iz) *v.*: falls down suddenly

poacher (POE chur) *n.*: a person who hunts or fishes in an area where it is illegal for him or her to do so

podium (PO dee um) *n.*: a small platform for a speaker, orchestra conductor, or the like

portfolio (port FO lee oh) *n.*: a flat, portable case for carrying loose papers, drawings, and the like

poultice (POLE tiss) *n.*: a small moist bandage of cloth or herbs

precision (prih SIZH un) *n.*: being exact about every detail

predator (PREH duh tor) *n.*: an animal that hunts other animals for food

principal (PRIN sih pul) *adj.*: first in importance

propelled (pruh PELD) *v.*: moved; driven

proposal (pruh PO zul) *n.*: a suggested plan

pungent (PUN junt) *adj.*: sharp and strong (used only to describe a taste or smell)

Q

quibbled (KWIH buld) *v.*: argued about some small, unimportant detail

quivered (KWIV erd) *v.*: shook slightly

quivery (KWIH vuh ree) *adj.*: shaky

R

raja (RAH zha) *n.*: the title of a chieftain or prince in India and areas of southeast Asia

realign (REE uh LYN) *v.*: to return to their proper position

reef *n.*: a ridge of rocks or sand near the surface of the water

rehabilitation (REE huh BIH luh TAY shun) *n.*: a returning to good health

relinquish (rih LINK wish) *v.*: let go of

resentment (ree ZENT ment) *n.*: a feeling of displeasure with someone who, one believes, has caused injury or unhappiness

retreated (rih TREE ted) *v.*: moved back toward the place it had come from

S

sanctuaries (SANK chew AIR eez) *n.*: a portion of land set aside by the government, where wildlife can live in safety from hunters

sapling (SAP ling) *n.*: young tree

scavenging (SKAH vun jing) *v.*: taking or gathering something useable from among unwanted things

scoffed (SKOFT) *v.*: mocked; ridiculed

semicircular (SEM ee SUR kyuh lur) *adj.*: shaped like half of a circle

shaft *n.*: the long, straight stem of something

shanties (SHAN teez) *n.*: cabins or houses that are roughly built and in a state of disrepair

siege (SEEJ) *n.*: a serious attack, as in illness

singe (SINJ) *v.*: to burn slightly

snare *n.*: a trap

soar (SORE) *v.*: fly high into the air

sow (rhymes with now) *n.*: an adult, female pig

sprinted (SPRINT ed) *v.*: raced at full speed for a short distance

stealthily (STELL thih lee) *adv.*: softly and secretly

stifling (STYF ling) *adj.*: so hot and still as to make it difficult to breathe

stunned (STUND) *v.*: shocked

susceptible (suh SEP tih buhl) *adj.*: more likely to be affected by something

suspended (sus SPEND ed) *v.*: temporarily stopped

swig *n.*: a mouthful of liquid

sympathetic (SIM puh THET ik) *adj.*: understanding and supportive

T

technique (tek NEEK) *n.*: method

tenement (TEH nuh munt) *n.*: a run-down and often overcrowded apartment house

tepid (TEP id) *adj.*: lukewarm

thatched *adj.*: having a roof made of straw

thaw *v.*: melt

thicket (THIK it) *n.*: many bushes growing close together

thrashes *v.*: beats against

thrives *v.*: grows and improves

timid (TIH mid) *adj.*: shy and easily frightened

tooling (TOOL ing) *v.*: driving or riding in a vehicle

transport (trans PORT) *v.*: to move; to carry

treacherous (TRECH uh russ) *adj.*: very dangerous

trembling (TREMB ling) *v.*: shaking slightly from fear, cold, or excitement

trough (TROFF) *n.*: a long, boxlike container used to hold food or water for animals

trudged (TRUJD) *v.*: walked slowly and heavily

U

undulating (UN dyuh LAY ting) *v.*: moving with a wavelike motion

upheaval (up HEE vul) *n.*: a great disturbance

V

venture (VEN chur) *v.*: to go carefully into an unknown or dangerous place

vertical (VUR tih kul) *adj.*: going up and down, not from side to side

vicious (VISH uss) *adj.*: harsh and cruel

W

wallowed (WAH lode) *v.*: rolled about in a clumsy way

wan (WAHN) *adj.*: pale and weak

wedged (WEJD) *v.*: packed in tightly

whiff *n.*: a slight smell

acknowledgments

Illustrators

Lauren Chaikin: Heatwave!; Dancing Bees

Aviva Goldfarb: Leah's Pony; The Gift

Aviva Gross: Sato and the Elephants; The Garden of Happiness; The Bridge Dancers

Eva Martin: The Way; Purple Snake; Hurt No Living Thing; Today the Dolphins Came to Play

Lydia Martin: Amelia's Road; The Wright Brothers; Earthquake Terror; Toto; Underwater Rescue; Maria's House; Analysis of Baseball; If You Think You Are Beaten; Here She Is; Since Hanna Moved Away; Be Glad Your Nose Is On Your Face; The Inventor Thinks Up Helicopters; Michael Is Afraid of the Storm; In This Jungle; City I Love

Amelia's Road: *Amelia's Road* Text Copyright © 1993 by Linda Jacobs Altman. Permission arranged with LEE & LOW BOOKS INC., 95 Madison Avenue, New York, NY 10016.

Analysis of Baseball: Reprinted with permission of The Literary Estate of May Swenson.

And Now the Good News: From AND THEN THERE WAS ONE: THE MYSTERIES OF EXTINCTION by Margery Facklam. Copyright © 1990 by Margery Facklam (text); Copyright © 1990 by Pamela Johnson (illustrations). By permission of LITTLE BROWN & COMPANY.

Be Glad Your Nose Is On Your Face: TEXT COPYRIGHT (c) 1984 BY JACK PRELUTSKY. Used by permission of HarperCollins Publishers.

Birds' Square Dance: "Birds' Square Dance" first appeared in RANGER RICK, November, 1988. Reprinted by permission of the author.

Boss of the Plains: "Boss of the Plains: The Hat That Won the West" by Laurie Carlson, reprinted by permission of the author.

The Bridge Dancers: *The Bridge Dancers,* by Carol Saller, text © copyright 1991 by the author. Reprinted by permission of the author.

A Bugler Named Dougal MacDougal: Copyright © 1935 by Ogden Nash, renewed. Reprinted by permission of Curtis Brown, Ltd.

City I Love: From HOME TO ME: POEMS ACROSS AMERICA by Lee Bennett Hopkins. Copyright © 2002 by Lee Bennett Hopkins. Reprinted by permission of Orchard Books, an imprint of Scholastic Inc.

Dad, Jackie, and Me: First published in the United States under the title DAD, JACKIE, AND ME by Myron Uhlberg, illustrated by Colin Bootman. Text Copyright © 2005 by Myron Uhlberg. Illustrations Copyright © 2005 by Colin Bootman. Published by arrangement with Peachtree Publishers.

Dancing Bees: "Dancing Bees" from *Bees Dance and Whales Sing: The Mysteries of Animal Communication* by Margery Facklam. Text copyright © 1992 by Margery Facklam. Reprinted by permission of Peggy Thomas.

Dust of Snow: "Dust of Snow" by Robert Frost from the book THE POETRY OF ROBERT FROST edited by Edward Connery Lathem. Copyright © 1923, 1969 by Henry Holt and Company. Copyright © 1951 by Robert Frost. Reprinted by permission of Henry Holt and Company. All rights reserved.

Earthquake Terror: Excerpt(s) from EARTHQUAKE TERROR by Peg Kehret, copyright © 1996 by Peg Kehret. Used by permission of Dutton Children's Books, an imprint of Penguin Young Readers Group, a division of Penguin Random House LLC. All rights reserved.

Eddie, Incorporated: From **Eddie, Incorporated** by Phyllis Reynolds Naylor. Text copyright © 1980 by Phyllis Reynolds Naylor. Reprinted with the permission of Atheneum Books for Young Readers, an imprint of Simon & Schuster Children's Publishing Division. All rights reserved.

For You: Copyright © 1987 by Karla Kuskin. Reprinted by permission of S©ott Treimel New York.

The Garden of Happiness: THE GARDEN OF HAPPINESS by Erika Tamar. Text copyright © 1996 by Erika Tamar. Reprinted by permission of Houghton Mifflin Harcourt Publishing Company. All rights reserved.

The Gift: Excerpt(s) from THE GIFT by Helen Coutant, text copyright © 1983 by Helen Coutant. Used by permission of Alfred A. Knopf, an imprint of Random House Children's Books, a division of Penguin Random House LLC. All rights reserved.

Good Hotdogs: From MY WICKED WICKED WAYS. Copyright © 1987 by Sandra Cisneros. By special arrangement with Third Woman Press. Published by Vintage Books in paperback and ebook, in hardcover by Alfred A. Knopf, and originally by Third Woman Press. By permission of Susan Bergholz Literary Services, New York, NY and Lamy, NM. All rights reserved.

A Gullible Rancher Named Clyde: "A Gullible Rancher Named Clyde" by Graham Lester; reprinted by permission of the author.

The Hatmaker's Sign: *The Hatmaker's Sign* © 1998 by Candace Fleming. Text used with permission of the Author and BookStop Literary Agency. All rights reserved.

Heatwave!: Reprinted by permission of Walker & Company.

Homeward the Arrow's Flight: An excerpt from *Homeward the Arrow's Flight* by Marion Marsh Brown, copyright © 1980, 1995, by Marion Marsh Brown, reprinted by permission of Field Mouse Productions.

The Imperfect/Perfect Book Report: "The Imperfect/Perfect Book Report" from *Teacher's Pet* by Johanna Hurwitz. Text © 1988 by Johanna Hurwitz. Reprinted by permission of the author.

In This Jungle: From A CRAZY FLIGHT AND OTHER POEMS by Myra Cohn Livingston. Copyright c 1969 Myra Cohn Livingston. C Renewed 1997. All Rights Reserved. Used by permission of Marian Reiner.

The Inventor Thinks Up Helicopters: "The Inventor Thinks Up Helicopters" from THE TIGERS BROUGHT PINK LEMONADE by Patricia Hubbell. Copyright c 1988 Patricia Hubbell. Used by permission of Marian Reiner.

Jackrabbit: From **Desert Voices** by Byrd Baylor. Text copyright © 1981 by Byrd Baylor. Reprinted with the permission of Atheneum Books for Young Readers, an imprint of Simon & Schuster Children's Publishing Division. All rights reserved.

Johnny Appleseed: "Johnny Appleseed" by Stephen Vincent Benet. From A BOOK OF AMERICANS by Rosemary and Stephen Vincent Benet. Henry Holt & Company. Copyright © 1933 by Rosemary and Stephen Vincent Benet. Copyright renewed © 1961 Rosemary Carr Benet. Used by permission of Brandt & Hochman Literary Agents, Inc.

Justin Lebo: From IT'S OUR WORLD, TOO!: YOUNG PEOPLE WHO ARE MAKING A DIFFERENCE © 1993 by Phillip Hoose. Reprinted by permission of Farrar, Straus, Giroux Books for Young Readers. All rights reserved.

Leah's Pony: *Leah's Pony* by Elizabeth Friedrich, illustrated by Michael Garland. Copyright © 1996 by Elizabeth Friedrich and Michael Garland. Published by Boyds Mills Press. Reprinted by permission.

March Bear: "March Bear" from *Turtle in July* by Marilyn Singer. Text copyright © 1989 by Marilyn Singer. Reprinted by permission of the author.

Michael Is Afraid of the Storm: *Reprinted By Consent of Brooks Permissions.*

Mom's Best Friend: *Mom's Best Friend* Text Copyright © 1992 by Sally Hobart Alexander. Used with permission of the Author and BookStop Literary Agency. All rights reserved.

Name This American: "Name This American" © by Hanna Reinmuth is reprinted with the permission of the publisher *Plays, The Drama Magazine for Young People*/Sterling Partners, Inc. This play is for reading purposes only; for permission to produce and/or perform, write to *Plays*, 897 Washington Street #160, Newton, MA 02460.

A Native of Chalamazug: "A Native of Chalamazug" by Graham Lester; reprinted by permission of the author.

One Grain of Rice: From ONE GRAIN OF RICE by Demi Copyright © 1997 by Demi. Reprinted by permission of Scholastic Inc.

Owl Moon: Illustrations, by John Schoenherr, copyright © 1987 by John Schoenherr; and "Entire Text" from OWL MOON by Jane Yolen, text copyright © 1987 by Jane Yolen. Used by permission of Philomel, an imprint of Penguin Young Readers Group, a division of Penguin Random House LLC. All rights reserved.

Popsicle: "Popsicle" from SPLISH SPLASH by Joan Bransfield Graham. Text copyright © 1994 by Joan Bransfield Graham. Illustration copyright © 1994 by Steven Scott. Reprinted by permission of Houghton Mifflin Harcourt Publishing Company. All rights reserved.

Purple Snake: The poem "Purple Snake" from Confetti: Poems for Children Text copyright © 1996 by Pat Mora. Permission arranged with LEE & LOW BOOKS Inc., 95 Madison Avenue, New York, NY 10016.

Sato and the Elephants: *Sato and the Elephants* by Juanita Havill. Text copyright © 1993 by Juanita Havill. Reprinted by permission of the author.

Seasons Haiku: Copyright c 1978 Myra Cohn Livingston. All Rights Renewed and Reserved. Used by permission of Marian Reiner.

A Seeing Poem: "A Seeing Poem" Copyright © 1974 by Robert Froman. First published in *Seeing Things: A Book of Poems*, published by HarperCollins Publishers. Used by permission of Curtis Brown, Ltd.

The Seven Children: "The First Day" from IT'S KWANZAA TIME! by Clay and Linda Goss, text copyright © 1994, 1995 by Clay and Linda Goss. Used by permission of Philomel, an imprint of Penguin Young Readers Group, a division of Penguin Random House LLC. All rights reserved.

The Shark: "The Shark" from FAST AND SLOW by John Ciardi. Copyright © 1975 by John Ciardi. Reprinted by permission of Houghton Mifflin Harcourt Publishing Company. All rights reserved.

Since Hanna Moved Away: From **If I Were in Charge of the World and Other Worries** by Judith Viorst. Text copyright © 1981 by Judith Viorst. Reprinted with the permission of Atheneum Books for Young Readers, an imprint of Simon & Schuster Children's Publishing Division. All rights reserved.

Some Opposites: "Some Opposites" from OPPOSITES: Poems and Drawings by Richard Wilbur. Copyright © 1973 by Richard Wilbur. Reprinted by permission of Houghton Mifflin Harcourt Publishing Company. All rights reserved.

Stone Fox: TEXT COPYRIGHT (C) 1980 BY JOHN REYNOLDS GARDINER. Used by permission of HarperCollins Publishers.

Supergrandpa: *Super Grandpa*, book with audio CD, written and narrated by David M. Schwartz; illustrated by Bert Dodson. © Tortuga Press, 2005.

Thistles: Text of "Thistles" from THE ROSE ON MY CAKE. Copyright © 1964, renewed 1992 by Karla Kuskin. Used by permission of Scott Treimel NY.

The Tiger, the Persimmon, and the Rabbit's Tail: "The Tiger, the Persimmon and the Rabbit's Tail" from *Korean Folk & Fairy Tales* retold by Suzanne Crowder Han. Copyright © 1991 by Suzanne Crowder Han. Reprinted by permission of Hollym Corporation.

Tortillas Like Africa: "Tortillas Like Africa" from CANTO FAMILIAR by Gary Soto. Copyright © 1995 by Gary Soto. Reprinted by permission of Houghton Mifflin Harcourt Publishing Company. All rights reserved.

Toto: Copyright © 1971 by Marietta Moskin published by the Coward, McCann, and Geoghegan. Reprinted with permission of the Carol Mann Agency.

Two Big Bears: TEXT COPYRIGHT 1932, 1960 Little House Heritage Trust. Used by permission of HarperCollins Publishers.

Underwater Rescue: TEXT COPYRIGHT (c) 1990 BY WAYNE GROVER. Used by permission of HarperCollins Publishers.

The Way: ©1994 by Nancy Springer. Used by permission of Nancy Springer in care of the Jean V. Naggar Literary Agency, Inc. (permissions@jvnla.com)

Whirligig Beetles: TEXT COPYRIGHT (C) 1988 BY PAUL FLEISCHMAN. Used by permission of HarperCollins Publishers.

The Wright Brothers: Excerpt(s) from THE WRIGHT BROTHERS by Quentin Reynolds, text copyright © 1950 by Random House LLC and renewed 1978 by James R. Reynolds and Frederick H. Rohlfs, Esq. and Random House LLC. Used by permission of Random House Children's Books, a division of Penguin Random House LLC. All rights reserved.

You and I: From MY SONG IS BEAUTIFUL by MARY ANN HOBERMAN. Copyright © 1994 by Mary Ann Hoberman. By permission of LITTLE BROWN & COMPANY.

Note: We have expended much effort to contact all copyright holders to receive permission for their works. We will correct any omissions brought to our attention in future editions.

index of authors and titles